P9-DTG-638

THE
BIBLE

BOOK BY BOOK

STUDY
ANALYZE
UNDERSTAND

Edited by Richenda Milton-Daws

**CHARTWELL
BOOKS**

Inspiring | Educating | Creating | Entertaining

Brimming with creative inspiration, how-to projects, and useful information to enrich your everyday life, Quarto Knows is a favorite destination for those pursuing their interests and passions. Visit our site and dig deeper with our books into your area of interest: Quarto Creates, Quarto Cooks, Quarto Homes, Quarto Lives, Quarto Drives, Quarto Explores, Quarto Gifts, or Quarto Kids.

© 2018 Quarto Publishing Group USA Inc.

First published in 2018 by Chartwell Books,
an imprint of The Quarto Group,
142 West 36th Street, 4th Floor,
New York, NY 10018, USA
T (212) 779-4972 F (212) 779-6058
www.QuartoKnows.com

All rights reserved. No part of this book may be reproduced in any form without written permission of the copyright owners. All images in this book have been reproduced with the knowledge and prior consent of the artists concerned, and no responsibility is accepted by producer, publisher, or printer for any infringement of copyright or otherwise, arising from the contents of this publication. Every effort has been made to ensure that credits accurately comply with information supplied. We apologize for any inaccuracies that may have occurred and will resolve inaccurate or missing information in a subsequent reprinting of the book.

Chartwell Books titles are also available at discount for retail, wholesale, promotional, and bulk purchase. For details, contact the Special Sales Manager by email at specialsales@quarto.com or by mail at The Quarto Group, Attn: Special Sales Manager, 401 Second Avenue North, Suite 310, Minneapolis, MN 55401, USA.

10 9 8 7 6 5 4 3 2 1

ISBN: 978-0-7858-3538-7

Printed in the United States of America

SUSTAINABLE FORESTRY INITIATIVE

Certified Sourcing
www.sfiprogram.org
SFI-01681

Label applies to text stock

Contents

CONTENTS

CONTENTS

CONTENTS

The Old Testament

'And the dove came in to him in the evening; and, lo, in her mouth was an olive leaf pluckt off' [Gen. viii.,10]

GENESIS

**The Creation; the Fall and its consequences;
God chooses His People.**

THE ESSENTIAL STORY OF GENESIS

God, having in the beginning created the Heaven and the Earth, separated the light from the darkness on the first day.

On the second day, he created the firmament, and divided the waters which were under the firmament from those which were above it.

On the third day, he divided the land from the seas; he also commanded the Earth to bring forth grass, herbs, and trees.

On the fourth day, he created the sun, the moon, and the stars.

On the fifth day, he created fishes and birds.

On the sixth day, he created beasts and reptiles; formed man after his own image and likeness, and blessed all his creatures.

On the seventh day, God rested from all his work, and sanctified that day.

The first man, named Adam, was placed in a garden in Eden, with Eve, his wife. There they ate the fruit of the tree of the knowledge of good and evil, against the LORD's command; for which they were expelled from the garden, and became subject to diseases and death; but received promises of mercy through a Redeemer.

CAIN AND ABEL

A dam and Eve had two sons, Cain, a tiller of the land who grew crops, and Abel, a shepherd. Since, after being expelled from the Garden of Eden, Adam and Eve were unable to talk directly to God, they built an altar of stones and burned gifts to the LORD, praying for forgiveness of their sins. Cain offered the fruit of the ground; Abel the firstborn of his flock. But while God accepted Abel's sacrifice, he rejected Cain's.

Angry at this gross injustice, Cain killed his brother in a fit of fury, but this made things much worse for him. God cursed Cain henceforth to be a fugitive and a vagabond – and, in response to Cain's pleas that he would inevitably be killed, the LORD set a mark upon him and promised that whoever killed him would in turn suffer vengeance sevenfold. So Cain set out in despair to dwell in the land of Nod.

Adam and Eve had another child, Seth, among whose descendants was Enoch (the seventh generation from Adam and Eve), a good, pious man who spent his life in the fellowship of the LORD, "walking with God." Great-grandfather of Noah, he prophesied that God would bring all sinners to judgment, and, like Elijah, he did not die but was taken up to Heaven by God.

NOAH

W hen the generations of Man multiplied and began to fill the Earth, God saw such wickedness among humanity that he repented creating man and determined to destroy all living things. But Noah, a righteous man, found grace in the eyes of the LORD, and God instructed him to build an Ark, telling him that He was about to bring such a flood upon the Earth that all flesh would perish.

However, God made a covenant with Noah, telling him to bring into the Ark his family and a male and a female of every sort of living thing that is unclean; and sevenfold of clean creatures and fowl of the air. These were to survive the deluge and repopulate the Earth afresh, which would thus be cleansed of the wickedness that had arisen. Noah constructed the Ark according to God's directions and embarked his family and the animals God ordained to be saved.

Then came the flood, rain that lasted 40 days and 40 nights, until the waters covered the entire Earth and even the mountains. For 150 days Noah and the Ark were afloat before God caused the waters to recede. Noah sent out a raven and then a dove, but neither could find land; after another seven days, when Noah sent forth the dove, it returned with an olive leaf, demonstrating the existence of dry land. The face of the Earth had become dry, and the Ark came to rest upon Mount Ararat.

BABEL

From the location of the Ark, the descendants of Noah's sons moved and, as their numbers increased, began to spread out. Their migration took them toward the site of what would one day be Babylon, or Babel, and here they decided to build a great Tower, to establish their reputations before contact was lost between them, and to reach up to Heaven. Since they could find no suitable stone in the area, they made bricks, and instead of mortar used bitumen. The Tower grew but was never completed, for God saw what they were doing. This was a deviation from the way he had planned for man, so instead of simply throwing down their tower, he caused them to speak many different languages, so that they could not all understand one another. Work on the Tower was thrown into confusion and stopped. Meanwhile the different individuals who found that they spoke the same tongue formed groups and began to separate themselves from the rest. Thus mankind spread over the Earth.

ABRAHAM

In Ur of the Chaldees there dwelt a man called Abram, who was to become the first of the Patriarchs. God told him to move away from his kindred, promising that he would make a great nation from him. So Abram and his wife Sarai, with his nephew Lot and family, moved to Canaan. This land, God promised him, would belong to him and to his offspring. In a vision, God appeared to Abram and, indicating the stars above them, told him that his descendants were to number more than these. But, Abram asked God, how could this be so? He was childless, his wife barren. God reassured him that he would indeed have children and made a Covenant with him. He would have a son and a land in which to live; in return, Abram promised faithfully to serve the LORD. Henceforth, God told him, he would be named Abraham, "Father of Many Nations"; and his wife would be called Sarah; and all the males of God's chosen must be circumcised.

When, forced by famine, Abraham took Sarah to Egypt, he was fearful that her beauty would cause jealousy and result in his death; so he persuaded her to make out that she was his sister. Her beauty brought the attention of the Pharaoh, and they were treated well until the Pharaoh's household became ill, and the newcomers were blamed and sent away.

When they returned, Abraham's fortunes improved, and he became so wealthy, with much livestock, that the time came for Lot to part company with his flocks, moving down to the plain of Jordan, while Abram stayed in Canaan.

Lot eventually settled not far from Sodom, a city fast gaining a reputation for vice and sin. On one occasion he became caught up in war between the coastal cities and was taken prisoner; but his uncle rescued him.

Nearby were two cities, Sodom and Gomorrah, which were becoming dens of wickedness and vice. Seeing this, God determined to destroy them, but he set a test whereby they could be saved if only he could find fifty good men there. Abraham, realizing that his nephew Lot lived there and might be caught up in the destruction, appealed to God, who agreed to reduce his quota of virtuous men to ten. When God's angels entered Sodom Lot welcomed them, and, finding that he was the only good man there, they warned him that he must quickly leave the city, for it was about to be destroyed. But neither he nor his family must look back as they flee. So Lot, with his wife and daughters, departed in haste – but his wife did look back and was at once turned into a pillar of salt.

Lot and his family flee Sodom.

Abraham and Sarah had a servant called Hagar, and since Sarah was barren, it was agreed that Abraham should father a child with Hagar; this child was named Ishmael. But God assured Abraham that Sarah would indeed bear him a child, and his name was Isaac.

ISAAC

One day God visited Abraham and Sarah, and promised that, despite her advancing years, Sarah would give birth to a son by Abraham, and some years later, Isaac was born. Meanwhile relations between Sarah and Hagar had deteriorated – at one point, Hagar, with child by Abraham, had fled into the desert, only to be met at a spring and told by God to go back. After the birth of Isaac, Sarah persuaded Abraham to send the servant and her son away. Not least was Sarah's concern that only Isaac should be Abraham's heir. Again Hagar struggled through the desert with her small child, and when her water ran out she despaired. But God appeared and reassured her that they were not outcasts in his eyes, and that her son had an important future, and they were saved. They settled in the area of Paran, and Ishmael grew up to be an archer and ancestor of twelve tribes, called Ishmaelites or Midianites.

Some time later God devised a terrible test of Abraham's faith. He told him to take his son, Isaac, to a nearby mountain and there offer him as a burnt sacrifice to the LORD. With Isaac bound on top of the pyre, Abraham took his knife to kill his son – but God stopped his hand, for Abraham had passed the test and God had thus demonstrated that he did not need human sacrifice.

Meanwhile Isaac had grown into a man, and it was important for the Covenant with God that he be found a wife. So Abraham sent out one of his servants to search for such a woman in his old homeland. One day, at a well, he encountered a young woman whom he asked for a drink, which was gladly given. The girl was Rebekah, the granddaughter of Abraham's brother Nahor, beautiful and unbetrothed. This was seen as a sign from God, and her family readily agreed to the match.

JACOB

For some years, Isaac and Rebekah failed to conceive, and it was only after Isaac prayed to the LORD for help that Rebekah at last gave birth to twin sons – Esau and Jacob. While Esau was beloved of Isaac, Jacob was Rebekah's favorite. When they grew into manhood, there took place an incident that would change their futures. When Esau, firstborn of the twins, returned from the fields tired and hungry, Jacob offered him bread and pottage of lentils but demanded that Esau give up his birthright in return. Esau carelessly agreed.

Rebekah, observing this, conspired with Jacob to go further. Isaac was now old, with not long to live, and both his eyesight and hearing were poor. While Esau was out in the fields, Jacob went to Isaac, offering him his favorite food and asking for his father's blessing, which was really due to Esau. The old man, reaching out and touching hairy flesh, was deceived into thinking that this was the elder of the two, so he gave his blessing, which amounted to making Jacob his heir. But the smooth-skinned Jacob had clad himself in goatskin and his brother's clothes, which convinced Isaac.

Esau's return revealed the deception, but it was too late. Jacob fled his brother's wrath, moving to the land of Laban, Rebekah's brother, in Haran. There he worked for his uncle and fell in love with his daughter, Rachel. When he asked for her hand in marriage, it was happily given, for Jacob was seen to be favored by God. But now deception was practiced on Jacob, and by sleight of hand Laban married him to Leah, Rachel's elder sister. On realizing who was under the bridal veil, Jacob protested, but polygamy was customary at this time, and Laban promised that after a time he should marry Rachel too.

And so things turned out, and Leah bore Jacob children, six boys and a girl; only after some years did Rachel conceive and give birth to a son, Joseph, who was obviously very special to her and to Jacob.

As time passed, Jacob's relationship with Laban deteriorated, and he decided to move back to his homeland, leaving without telling Laban, who pursued him. When he caught up, there was an argument, but eventually they were reconciled and Jacob's party continued, only to encounter an angry Esau, with hundreds of followers. But again there was reconciliation.

Violence did break out later, after Leah's daughter, Dinah, was raped by a neighbor, Shechem. Following a feigned acceptance of this and agreement with Shechem and his family, the sons of Jacob fell on the Shechemites and slaughtered them.

God meanwhile appeared to Jacob and assured him that, as with Abraham and Isaac, his forebears, he would be father to a great nation; henceforth, he would be called Israel.

Rachel eventually gave birth to another son, whom Jacob called Benjamin; like his brother Joseph, he would play an important role in the story of Jacob's children. But Rachel died in childbirth.

JOSEPH

Of Jacob's children, those borne by Rachel were especially dear to their father, Joseph receiving such attentions that this engendered the jealousy of his brothers, made worse when Jacob presented him with a coat of many colors. At an early age, too, Joseph showed a talent for interpreting dreams, beginning with his own, which seemed to glorify the dreamer, further irritating his brethren. Indeed, his brothers disliked him and determined to get rid of him. Their opportunity came one day when Joseph went to join them in the fields, whereupon they seized him and sold him into slavery to a passing band of Ishmaelites. Taking his ornamented robe, they bloodied it and presented it to their father as evidence that Joseph had been attacked and devoured by a wild beast.

The merchants took Joseph to Egypt, where he was sold as a slave to Potiphar, Pharaoh's chamberlain. Joseph grew to be tall and handsome, attracting the attention of the chamberlain's wife, who clandestinely propositioned him but was repeatedly rejected. In rage at being thus humiliated by a mere slave, she denounced the young man to his master as having attempted to lie with her, and he was cast into prison.

There he encountered two of Pharaoh's staff, his Chief Butler (a man of high rank) and his Chief Baker, who had engendered the wrath of their LORD. Now Joseph's talent for explaining dreams came to the rescue of his fortunes: when they told him what they had dreamt, Joseph explained that they foretold the release of one of them, the Chief Butler, in three days' time, and the condemnation of the other. This proved true, and the Chief Butler was released.

Some time later the Pharaoh himself suffered a bout of disturbing dreams, which he could not understand. Remembering Joseph, still languishing in prison, the Chief Butler brought him before Pharaoh.

Joseph interpreted the dreams – there would be seven good years followed by seven years of famine. Pharaoh found this credible and saw it as a timely warning that the abundance of the good years should not be squandered but some stored for harder times. He appointed Joseph to take the necessary measures so that when famine came the land should not suffer.

Joseph proved himself an excellent servant to Pharaoh and rose in his LORD's esteem so that he became rich and powerful in Egypt, second in all the land: "And Pharaoh called Joseph's name Zaphnath-paaneah; and he gave him to wife Asenath the daughter of Potipherah priest of On". *(Genesis 41:45)*

His prudent actions in building up stores of grain in the granaries during the good years staved off the effects of the famine when it came; he also took all the land of Egypt into the royal ownership, then gave it back to the people on condition that they remit a fifth of their produce to Pharaoh.

In Canaan, meanwhile, the famine hit hard, and just as Abraham had done many years before, the sons of Jacob set out for Egypt to find help. There they were sent before Pharaoh's great servant but failed to recognize him as the brother they had sold into slavery. Nor did he reveal his identity to them, but sent them back to Jacob with food, keeping one of the brothers, Simeon, as hostage, and directing them to bring before him the youngest of the family.

When they returned with Benjamin to Egypt, Joseph organized a feast for them, and still they did not realize the identity of their host. Now Joseph planned a trick: when they set off back to Canaan, he planted a silver cup in Benjamin's sack, then sent men to bring the brothers back, accusing them of theft.

The silver cup was discovered, and Judah offered himself in Benjamin's place for punishment. Joseph, in effect, had his moral revenge; he now revealed his identity to his astonished brothers and sent them off to Canaan, telling them to bring their father to Egypt.

Jacob was reunited with his favorite son, and Pharaoh's minister settled the family in Egypt, in a place called Goshen. There, under his protection, they flourished, and when Jacob died he left Joseph's second son, Ephraim, as his heir. Jacob was taken to be buried in Hebron with his forebears, Abraham, Sarah, Isaac, and Rebekah.

COMMENTARY ON THE BOOK OF GENESIS

The book consists of two very unequal divisions. I. The early history of mankind, i.–xi.; II. The history of the Patriarchs, the Fathers or the .Jewish race, xii.–1. The main structure of the book rests on the principle of genealogies. The phrase "These are the generations" marking different sections occurs ten times (one of these however being a mere repetition xxxvi. 9), and in every instance except the first, which refers to the Creation of the world, is a heading to a genealogical tree or certain portions of family history. In ii. 4 it is doubtful whether the phrase "These are the generations of the heaven and the earth" closes the first account, of creation, or whether it opens the second. In v. 1, we have "This is the hook of the generations of Adam" Afterwards the phrase is, "These are the generations" of Noah in vi. 9, of the sons of Noah in x.1; of Shem in xi. 10; of Terah the father of Abram in xi. 27; of Ishmael in xxv. 12; of Isaac in xxv. 19; of Esau in xxxvi. 1, 9; of Jacob in xxxvii. 2. But these genealogical trees do not exactly correspond with the vital structure of the book, which is remarkable for its organic unity. The narrative groups itself round five principal personages, Adam, Noah, Abraham, Isaac and Jacob.

I. *Adam*. The creation of the world and the earliest history of mankind (i.–iii.). As yet no divergence of the families of man.

II. *Noah*. The history of Adam's descendants to the death of Noah (iv.–ix.). Here we have (1) the line of Cain branching off; while the history follows the fortunes of Seth, whose descendants are (2) traced in genealogical succession, and in an unbroken line as far as Noah; and (3) the history of Noah himself (vi.–ix.) continued to his death.

III. *Abraham*. Noah's posterity till the death of Abraham. (1) The peopling of the whole earth by the descendants of Noah's three sons (xi. 1 9). The history of two of these is then dropped and (2) the line of Shem only pursued (xi. 10–32) as far as Terah and Abraham, where the genealogical table breaks off; (3) Abraham is now the prominent figure (xii. 1–xxv. 18). But as Terah had two other sons, Nahor and Haran (xi. 27), some notices respecting their families are added. Lot's migration with Abraham into the land of Canaan is mentioned, as well as the fact that he was the father of Moab and Ammon (xix. 37, 38), nations whose later history was intimately connected with that of the posterity of Abraham. Nahor remained in Mesopotamia, but his family is briefly enumerated (xxii. 20-24), chiefly no doubt for Rebekah's sake who was afterwards the wife of Isaac. Of Abraham's own children there branches off first the line of Ishmael (xxi. 9 &c.) and next the children by Keturah; and the genealogical notices of these two branches of his posterity are frequently brought together (xxv. 1-6 and 12-18) in order that being here severally dismissed, the main stream of the narrative may flow in the channel of Isaac's fortunes.

IV *Isaac*. His life (xxv. 19—xxxv. 29) is in itself retiring and uneventful. But in his sons Jacob and Esau the final separation takes place, leaving the field clear for the great story of the chosen seed. Even when Nahor's family comes on the scene, as it does in ch. xxix., we hear only so much of it as is necessary to throw light on Jacob's history.

V *Jacob*. The history of Jacob and Joseph. Here after Isaac's death we have (*a*) the genealogy of Esau (xxxvi.), who then drops out of the narrative in order that (*b*) the history of the Patriarchs may be carried on without interruption to the death of Joseph (xxxvii.—l.). A specific plan is thus preserved throughout. The main purpose is never forgotten. God's relation to Israel holds the first place in the writer's mind. The introductory chapters are a history of the world only so far as that is a preparation for the history of the chosen seed.

The book then is evidently constructed on a plan. It coheres by an internal principle of unity. The whole structure presents a very clearly marked outline. There are however manifest traces in this as in the other books of the use and incorporation of earlier documents. There are two accounts of the Creation, ch. i. and ii. Gen. ii. 4—iii. 24 is as clearly a, distinct document as Gen. i.—ii. 3. Two accounts of the Flood have been worked up to form the existing narrative. Gen. xiv. is another document. For the most part considerable sections of Genesis are stamped, as has been said, by a different use of the Divine Names, but other signs of *a* different authorship have been noticed, *e.g.* the frequent use of certain words and phrases by which whole sections are characterized.

THE BOOK OF GENESIS: CHAPTER BY CHAPTER

The Creation.	1	Creation.
	2	Sabbath. Eden. Marriage.
	3	The Serpent. Eve. The Fall.
First Artificers.	4	Cain and Abel. First city, called Enoch. Lamech. First artificers: tents – Jabal; musical instruments – Jubal; metal working – Tubal-cain.
	5	Genealogy of patriarchs. Translation of Enoch.
Noah.	6	Wickedness of the world. The Ark constructed.
	7	Noah and his family. The Flood.
	8	The Ark on Ararat. Noah builds and altar.
	9	Respecting blood. Law against murder. The rainbow of the Covenant. Noah drunken.
	10	Generations of Noah.
Babel.	11	Babel built. Confusion of Tongues.
Abram.	12	Abram called. Canaan promised. Abram in Egypt.
	13	Lot and Sodom.
Melchizedek.	14	Battle of the nine kings. Melchizedek.
	15	Abram's heir promised. Canaan promised again. Vision of furnace and lamp.
	16	Sarai and Hagar. Ishmael born.

Abraham.	17	Circumcision. Abram named "Abraham". Sarai named "Sarah".
	18	Abraham entertains angels. Intercedes for Sodom
Lot.	19	Lot entertains angels. Sodom destroyed. Lot's wife. Origin of Moab and Ammon.
	20	Abraham at Gerar. Sarah and Abimelech.
Isaac.	21	Isaac born. Hagar and Ishmael. The well. Beersheba.
	22	Abraham offers Isaac.
	23	Death of Sarah.
	24	Abraham's faithful servant. Rebekah. Laban. Isaac marries Rebekah.
Esau and Jacob.	25	Abraham marries Keturah. Their sons. Ishmael and his sons. Death of Abraham. Esau and Jacob born. Esau sells his birthright.
Isaac and Rebekah.	26	Isaac at Gerar. Rebekah and Abimelech. Esau's wives. Isaac in old age.
	27	Jacob obtains his father's blessing.
Jacob's ladder.	28	Jacob goes to Padan-aram. Vision of Jacob's ladder. Stone of Bethel. Jacob's vow.
Jacob and his sons.	29	Laban. Jacob and Rachel. Leah. Reuben, Simeon, Levi and Judah born.
	30	Bilhah, Rachel's maid. Zilpah, Leah's maid. Dan, Naphtali, Gad, Asher, Issachar, and Zebulun born. Joseph born of Rachel.

	31	Jacob leaves Laban. Rachel steals Laban's images. Mizpah.
	32	Jacob's vision at Mahanaim. He wrestles with an ange.
	33	Meeting of Jacob and Esau. The altar at El-elohe-Israel.
	34	Dinah and Shechem. Cruelty of Simeon and Levi.
	35	Jacob goes to Bethel. The altar at El-beth-el. Deborah's death. Jacob is called "Israel." Benjamin's birth and Rachel's death. Isaac's death.
	36	Esau's wives and descendants.
Joseph.	37	Joseph and his brethren. His dreams. He is sold.
	38	Tamar and Judah. Pharez and Zarah born.
	39	Joseph in Potiphar's house. His mistress tempts him. Joseph in prison.
	40	Pharoah's butler and baker.
	41	Pharoah's dreams. Joseph raised to power. Joseph's sons Manasseh and Ephraim born. Years of plenty, and years of dearth. A general famine.
	42	Jacob's sons sent to Egypt for corn. Simeon detained. Judah takes Benjamin.
	43	Joseph entertains his brethren.
	44	Joseph's policy to detain his brethren. Judah's supplication.
	45	Joseph makes himself known. Jacob revived by the news that Joseph is still alive.
Jacob goes down to Egypt	46	Jacob journeys towards Egypt. He offers sacrifices at Beersheba.

	47	Jacob and five sons before Pharoah. Pharoah enriched by his storehouses. Jacob's approaching death.
	48	He blesses Ephraim and Manasseh.
	49	Jacob predicts the future of his sons; and dies.
Death of Jacob, and of Joseph.	50	Mourning for Jacob. Burial at Machpelan. Joseph requires an oath as to his bones (Heb. xi. 22). Death of Joseph.

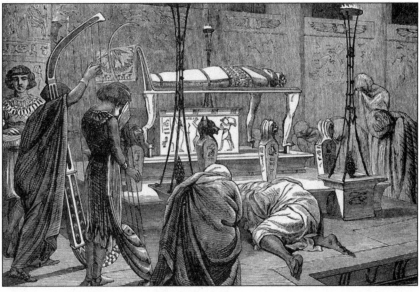

Joseph embalmed.

EXODUS

**God's rescue of the Hebrews from Egyptian slavery;
they become His People.**

THE ESSENTIAL STORY OF EXODUS

T he Hebrews, now living in Egypt, multiplied, but their high standing with Pharaoh declined over the centuries; Jacob and Joseph became distant memories, and the people gradually became forced labor, working on the vast building projects for the government. But their numbers grew such that the Pharaoh became concerned about the security of his kingdom with such an increasing "alien" population in the borderlands. So he sought a cruel solution: all male children of the Hebrews were to be put to death at birth, a measure the Hebrew midwives could frustrate only temporarily.

Among the victims of this drastic measure was a Levite couple, who, doubtless like many others, tried to hide their newborn son. When at last they saw they could no longer avoid the Egyptian murderers, they abandoned the baby in a floating basket in the rushes along the banks of the River Nile, hoping that the plight of the child would touch a sympathetic heart. And indeed it did, for the basket was discovered by Pharaoh's daughter, who, in defiance of her father's decree, adopted the baby, taking him back to the palace and naming him Moses.

The child thus grew up in a privileged world, educated and set apart from his fellow Hebrews. As he grew to manhood, his identity and loyalties must have troubled him, and this exploded in violence when he chanced upon the sight of a Hebrew being beaten by an Egyptian. In a fit of anger, Moses killed the Egyptian; then, realizing that he must in time be found out, despite his position, he fled into the Moabite desert, where he eluded the vengeance of Pharaoh. There he joined the family of Jethro, a priest, and married his daughter Zipporah.

Time passed, and those who sought his death died. Then one day as he was near Mount Horeb, tending to his father-in-law's flock of sheep, he beheld a bush that seemed afire yet was not consumed by the flames. Fascinated, he drew near and heard the voice of God.

The LORD told him that he had seen and lamented the miserable situation of his chosen people; now, however, he would release them from bondage and lead them to "a land flowing with milk and honey." And Moses would be his instrument.

In vain did Moses protest his inadequacy for such a huge task. He would not be believed by anybody: but God demonstrated three miracles that would persuade them. And, Moses objected, he was not eloquent; to which God, becoming impatient, replied that he should have the services of his elder brother, Aaron, as spokesman.

So Moses returned to Egypt to begin God's work. Having proved to the Hebrew elders, by means of the three miracles, that he was indeed the instrument of God, Moses went with Aaron to Pharaoh, and demanded that the Hebrews be free to leave Egypt. But Pharaoh was unyielding: why should he part with his workforce? Instead he increased the burden upon the slaves by making them gather their own straw for their brick-making instead of providing it as before. Life became harder for the Hebrews, who did not hesitate to complain to Moses for what he had brought about.

But God commanded Moses and Aaron to go back to Pharaoh and this time demonstrate the miracle of turning Aaron's staff into a serpent. This Pharaoh's magicians could also do; whereupon Aaron's staff ate all of theirs. And again, Pharaoh was intransigent. So God told Moses that he would bring down a series of plagues upon Egypt, which would eventually force the Egyptians to let the Hebrews leave. Confronting the king, Moses turned the river to blood, and then called up an infestation of frogs. Again the Egyptian magicians could match this.

'Aaron cast down his rod before Pharaoh, and before his servants, and it became a serpent.' [Ex. vii., 10]

However, the Egyptian magicians could not imitate the plagues that followed, and for each plague Pharaoh seemed to give way but then hardened his heart once more. The disease to livestock did not affect the Hebrews' herds and flocks; the boils did not affect them; and when hail, rain, and tempest thrashed down on Egypt, destroying crops and the harvest, no storm hit Goshen, where the Hebrews lived. The locusts destroyed what was left of the Egyptian harvest; and then God turned the land dark for three days – except in Goshen.

It was now time for God's final punishment of the Egyptians, the death of the firstborn in every household. At midnight, the Angel of the Lord would strike; but God instructed Moses that all his people should roast and eat lamb that night, with unleavened bread; and they should paint their door frames with the lamb's blood, as a sign. This became the feast of the Passover, to be commemorated each year, as it is among Jews today.

This was the final straw for Pharaoh, whose own son was among the dead. He bid Moses take his people away. Laden with gold and jewels donated as an encouragement to leave by the ordinary Egyptians, who just wanted an end to the plagues, the Hebrews set out to the east, guided by a great pillar of cloud, into the desert.

God, knowing that a direct approach to the Promised Land would bring conflict with the Philistines, and that the Hebrews might falter, led them instead towards the Red Sea. Meanwhile Pharaoh was regretting his decision to allow the Hebrews to leave, despite the suffering that had been caused to Egypt. With infantry, cavalry, and chariots he set out in pursuit of the children of Israel.

At the shores of the sea, the Hebrews paused, only to look back and see the Egyptian army closing fast. They seemed to be trapped. But the pillar of cloud moved between them and their pursuers, turning night into day for the Hebrews. That night Moses obeyed God's instructions to stretch his hand over the sea: and the waters divided, the Hebrews passing across the dry seabed with a wall of water to each side. Once they were safely across, Moses stretched out again and the waters closed upon the pursuing Egyptians, engulfing them. After more than four centuries, the Hebrews were finally out of Egypt.

The Red Sea behind them, the Israelites set out into the desert of Shur. Before long, however, grumbles reached Moses' ears about the lack of food and water. At Elim they found an oasis, but deeper into the desert of Sin the murmuring grew such that Moses appealed to God for help. God replied that he would provide: and that evening a great flock of quail settled about the camp. In the mornings, the dew dried to reveal a white flaky substance, which the Israelites could gather and make into bread. This they called manna: little did they realize that they would have to live on this for forty years.

At Rephidim they were attacked by the Amalekites and driven off with God's help. And at Rephidim too Moses received a visit from his father-in-law, Jethro, who brought Moses' wife and children. They feasted, and Jethro saw the strain put upon Moses by his great responsibilities, so he suggested he appoint officials, including judges, among the people to help him.

In the third month of their exodus, the Israelites came to the desert of Sinai and camped before Mount Sinai. Here, upon the mountain, God spoke to Moses, telling him that he would now give him the Laws of his Covenant.

God now confirmed the Covenant to Moses and set out the Laws, which Moses wrote into a book and read aloud to the assembled people. After building an altar and making sacrifices, Moses ascended the mountain with Aaron, his two sons and forty elders, where they met God and ate and drank with him to seal the Covenant. Then Moses went up alone again for forty

A quail.

days and nights and God put the Laws on tablets of stone.

So long was Moses on Mount Sinai that the Israelites lost patience and faith. They prevailed upon Aaron to make a new god for them to worship, so he gathered jewelry from among them and made of it a golden calf. This the Israelites began worshiping.

So when he at last came down from the mountain, it was a blasphemous scene that met Moses' eyes. God had warned him that this was happening, but it did not prevent Moses becoming angry and smashing down the tablets from God. Only Moses' intercession stopped God destroying all his chosen people. Moses now issued an ultimatum – the people must be for God or against him. At once the Levites pledged their loyalty, and to them Moses allotted the task of slaying the blasphemous ringleaders and destroying the golden calf.

God also commanded Moses to construct a place where God could dwell and be with the Israelites on their journey, and issued very specific details of its construction and layout, together with rules for the priesthood and worship. The Levites were put in charge of this and of transporting it as the Israelites marched on toward the Promised Land.

COMMENTARY ON THE BOOK OF EXODUS

Exodus is so called because its opening portion details the circumstances connected with the departure of the Israelites out of Egypt. The book, which is a continuation of the narrative in Genesis, consists of two principal divisions, I. Historical, i. 1–xviii. 27; and II. Legislative, xix. 1–xl. 38. The former of these may be subdivided into (1) the preparation for the deliverance of Israel from their bondage in Egypt; (2) the accomplishment of that deliverance.

I. The first section, i. 1–xii. 36, records the great increase of Jacob's posterity in Egypt and their oppression under a new dynasty which "knew not Joseph" (ch. i.); the birth, education and flight of Moses, and his marriage with a daughter of the priest of Midian; his call at the burning bush to be the deliverer of his people, encouraged by the revelation of the name of Jahveh, by miraculous signs, and by help from his brother Aaron (iii. 1–iv. 17); his return to Egypt in consequence (iv. 18–31); his first ineffectual attempt to prevail upon Pharaoh to let the Israelites go, which only resulted in an increase of their burdens (v.1–21; a further preparation of Moses and Aaron for their office, together with their genealogies (v.22–vii. 7); the successive signs and wonders, and especially the Ten Plagues, by means of which the deliverance of Israel is at length accomplished. This includes the institution of the Passover (vii. 8–xii. 36); the departure itself, together with instructions concerning the Passover and the sanctification of the firstborn (xii. 37– xiii. 16); the march to the Red Sea, the destruction of Pharaoh's army and Moses' song of victory (xiii. 17– xv. 21); events on the journey from the Red Sea to Sinai, the bitter waters of Marah, the giving of quails and manna, the observance of the sabbath, the miraculous supply of water from the rock at Rephidim and the battle there with the Amalekites (xv. 22– xvii. 16); the arrival of Jethro in the camp and his advice as to the civil government of the people (xviii.).

II. The solemn establishment of the Theocracy at Sinai. The people are set apart "as a kingdom of priests and an holy nation" (xix. 6); the Ten Commandments are given and are followed by the simplest and earliest code of laws intended to regulate the social life of the people (xx.–xxiii.); an Angel is promised as their

Guide to the Promised Land, and the covenant between God and Moses, Nadab and Abihu and the 70 elders is ratified (xxiii. 20–xxiv. 18); instructions are given respecting the Tabernacle, the Ark, the altar of burnt offering, the separation of Aaron and his sons, the vestments which they are to wear, the ceremonies to be observed at their consecration, the altar of incense, the lavers and the holy oil; the selection of Bezaleel and Aholiab for the construction of the Tabernacle, the observance of the sabbath and the delivery of the two tables of the testimony into the hands of Moses (xxv. 1–xxxi. 18); the sin of the people in the matter of the golden calf; their rejection in consequence and their restoration to God's favor at the intercession of Moses (xxxii. 1–xxxiv. 35); lastly, the construction of the Tabernacle and all pertaining to its service in accordance with the instructions previously given (xxxv. 1–xl. 38). "In this account of the actual construction everything is arranged from the outside of the Tabernacle to the innermost part of it; whereas in the instruction given to Moses on Mount Sinai the beginning is made at the centre with the Ark and so outwards, except the supplementary arrangements in ch. xxx." The statement in vi. 3 "I appeared unto Abraham, Isaac and Jacob as 'El Shaddai, but by my name Jahveh was I not

The utensils of the tabernacle.

known unto them" plainly shows that the earlier use of the name in Genesis is due to a different writer, and confirms the theory of different documents.

Exodus gives the early history of the nation in three clearly marked stages: first a nation enslaved, then a nation redeemed, lastly a nation set apart, and through the blending of its religious and political life consecrated to the service of God.

THE BOOK OF EXODUS: CHAPTER BY CHAPTER

The Israelites in Egypt.	1	The Israelites oppressed. The killing of the male infants ordered by Pharaoh.
Moses.	2	Moses born. He is preserved alive. He slays an Egyptian. He flees to Midian. He marries Zipporah.
The Bush.	3	Moses and Jethro (called also Reuel and Raguel). The burning bush.
	4	The rod of Moses. Zipporah and her son. Aaron meets Moses.
Pharaoh.	5	Moses and Aaron speak to Pharaoh. The Israelites' burdens increased.
	6	Genealogy of Reuben. Genealogy of Simeon. Genealogy of Levi.
Plagues of Egypt.	7	Miracle of the rod and serpent. Plague of rivers of blood.
	8	Plague of frogs. Plague of lice. Plague of flies.
	9	Plague of cattle. Plague of boils. Plague of hail.
	10	Plague of locusts. Plague of darkness.
	11	Israelites borrow of Egyptians. The last plague foretold.

Passover. **Last Plague.**	12	Sacred year begun. Passover instituted. Unleavened bread. Death of the firstborn. Israel quit Egypt and reach Succoth. Law of the Passover.
	13	First born sanctified. Firstlings of beasts set apart. Joseph's bones removed. March from Succoth to Etham. The pillar of cloud and the pillar of fire.
Red Sea.	14	Pharaoh pursues Israel. Passage of the Red Sea. The Egyptians drowned.
Wilderness. **Manna.**	15 16	Moses' song. Bitter waters of Marah. Elim, with wells and palm trees. March from Elim to Sin. Murmuring for bread. Quails sent. Manna sent.
	17	March from Sin to Rephidim. Amalek defeated. Altar – JEHOVAH-NISSI.
	18	Jethro's visit to Moses.
Sinai.	19	Arrival at Sinai.
	20	Ten commandments given.
Laws.	21	Political laws.
	22	Further laws.
	23	Laws concluded. Promise of the land.
	24	Moses in the mount.
Tabernacle.	25	Directions about offerings; Ark of the Covenant, and articles for the Tabernacle.
	26	Curtains for the Tabernacle.
	27	Altar of Burnt Offering. Outer court. Oil for lamp.

Priests.	28	Priests' dress
	29	Consecration of priests.
	30	Altar of Incense, etc. The atonement money.
	31	Bezaleel and Aholiab, skilful workmen. The Sabbath appointed.
Tables of the law.	32	Aaron and the golden calf. Tables of the law brought and broken.
	33	The LORD talks with Moses. Moses asks to see God's glory.
	34	The two tables renewed. Moses' face veiled.
Tabernacle.	35	The Sabbath sacred. Free gifts for the Tabernacle.
	36	Bezaleel and Aholiab work. The people's liberality restrained.
	37	The Ark; mercy-seat; table; candlestick.
	38	Altar of Burnt Offering. Laver (See Ex. xxx. 18.) Sum of offerings. The atonement money.
	39	Cloths of service and holy garments. "HOLINESS TO THE LORD."
	40	The Tabernacle reared. The Cloud covers it.

LEVITICUS

**The detailed description of the laws by which
devout people should live.**

THE ESSENTIAL SUMMARY OF LEVITICUS

The title of this book is taken from the Septuagint heading *"Leviticon"*, "the Levitical Book"; so-called because it contained the laws, rules, and regulations, of the various offerings, sacrifices, and ceremonies, appointed with the Levitical Priesthood. This Book is described as "The Law of the Priests."

This book may be divided as follows:

I. The laws touching sacrifices (chap. i.–vii.)
II. An historical section containing first, the consecration of Aaron and his sons (chap. viii.); next, his first offering for himself and his people (chap. ix.); and lastly, the destruction of Nadab and Abihu, for their presumptuous office (chap. x.)
III. The laws concerning purity and impurity, and the appropriate sacrifices and ordinances for putting away impurity (chap. xi.–xvi.)
IV. Laws chiefly intended to mark the separation between Israel and the heathen nations (chap. xvii.–xx.)
V. Laws concerning the priests (chap. xxi., xxii.); and certain holy days and festivals (chap. xxiii.–xxv.), together with an episode (chap. xxiv.)
VI. Promises and threats (chap. xxvi. 2–46).

VII. An appendix containing the laws concerning vows (chap. xxvii.)

COMMENTARY ON THE BOOK OF LEVITICUS

The book, which by its opening words is seen to be a continuation of Exodus, consists of the following sections:

I.   The sacrificial ordinances (i.—vii.). This may be subdivided into *(a)* the general law respecting sacrifice (i.—vi. 7), the burnt-offering i. 1—17, the meal-offering ii. 1—16, the peace-offering iii. 1—17, the sin-offering iv. 1—v. 13, the guilt-offering v. 14—vi. 7; and *(b)* supplementary instructions as to the various sacrifices for the priests, vi. 8—vii. 38.
II. The ritual observed in the consecration of the priests, viii. (exactly following Ex. xxix.) and ix., together with the historical statement of the death of Nadab and Abihu, because they offered strange fire, and other particulars connected with the consecration (x.).
III. Laws relating to ceremonial uncleanness xi.—xv.: *(a)* Animals which may not be eaten, and contact with which is forbidden, xi. 1—47; *(b)* uncleanness of childbirth xii.; *(c)* uncleanness of leprosy, six different forms of it enumerated and the separation of the leper enjoined; leprosy in a house, xiii.—xiv.; occasional states of the body causing uncleanness; these laws, a protection from death which is the penalty for defiling the tabernacle of Jahveh (xv.).
IV. The Day of Atonement and its ordinances, xvi.
V.   The Law of Holiness, xvii.—xxvi.

This was originally it would seem a distinct law-book; an older stratum of priestly legislation lying at the basis of it. The resemblances to the legislation in Ezekiel are close and striking, and various suggestions have been made to account for them. Some have conjectured (holding that the Priestly portions of the Pentateuch are post-exilic) that Ezekiel himself was the author of these chapters; others, that they are derived from his legislation; the traditional view being of course that Ezekiel borrowed from Leviticus. The subdivisions of this corpus are as follows: communion with Jahveh in sacrifice; the blood of all slain animals must be offered with the fat at the door of the tent of meeting so long as the Israelites live in the camp, xvii. 1–9; all eating of blood forbidden, or that which dies of itself or is torn of beasts (10–16). A series of enactments follows touching incestuous commerce, unnatural lusts, sacrifice of children to Molech, &c., with a warning of the consequences of transgression (xviii.). Then come a number of laws which are not arranged on any very intelligible principle, introduced by the solemn formula, "Ye shall be holy, for I Jahveh your God am holy" (xix. 1–2); reverence for parents, keeping the sabbath enjoined and idolatry forbidden, directions respecting the peace-offering (3–8); breaches of the law of love enumerated and the observance of the Second Great Commandment, "Thou shalt love thy neighbour as thyself," enjoined (9–18); forbidding of mixture of cattle, in sowing the field, and in garments (19); of uncleanness with a betrothed bondmaid; law concerning fruit-trees; superstitious observances, as eating blood (see xvii. 10 ff.), using enchantments, cutting of the hair and flesh, prostitution (observance of sabbaths and reverencing of the sanctuary interposed, 20–30) and having recourse to wizards forbidden; reverence for the aged, kindness to the stranger, just weights and balances enjoined (31–37). Chapter xx. is usually regarded as a kind of appendix to xviii. repeating its prohibitions and enumerating the punishments for transgression which are omitted there, but they are rather "two independent though substantially parallel Toroth on the same subject." Holiness in the priests, their marriages, their families, and their service at the altar (xxi.), and especially in the high-priest (10–15); further directions with regard to the ceremonial purity of the priests (xxii.). The Feasts which are holy convocations: the sabbath (xxiii. 1–4); the Passover (5–8) and the offering of firstfruits (9–14); the Feast of Weeks, seven sabbaths complete or 50 days (Pentecost), 15–22 with a repetition of the enactment about gleaning in xix. 9; the Feast of Trumpets (23–25); the Day of Atonement (26–32); the Feast of Tabernacles, of which there are apparently two accounts 33–36 and 39–43, for a distinct summing up follows each, 37, 38 and 44. Chapter xxiv. gives directions concerning the pure olive-oil for the lamp which is to burn continually before Jahveh (1–4, *cf.* Ex. xxvii. 20, 21); and the continual shewbread (5–9, *of* Ex. xxv. 30, xi. 23); tells the story of a half-breed who in a quarrel blasphemes the Name and is sentenced to death by stoning; and this is followed by certain civil laws which are to be the same for the stranger as for the Israelite (10–23). Chapter xxv. contains the Law of Jubilee directing the redemption of the land (which Jahveh claims as His own), houses and persons. Chapter xxvi. repeats the laws forbidding idolatry and enjoining the keeping of the sabbath and reverence of the sanctuary, and then pronounces the Blessing and the Curse as the Covenant is kept or broken. The code presents in this respect a certain analogy to Deuteronomy which closes with a similar peroration. It is marked by a peculiarity which distinguishes it from other portions of the Law, *viz,* the frequent recurrence at the close of each paragraph of the phrase: "I am Jahveh." Verse 46 summing up the whole legislation must have been the original termination of the book. Chapter xxvii. is supplementary, dealing with vows and the principles on which things that have been devoted may be redeemed. The book opens with the solemn formula "And Jahveh called unto Moses and spake to him out of the tent of meeting, saying, &c.," and each section of the code is prefaced by the formula "And Jahveh spake unto Moses saying" (iv. 1, vi. **1,** viii. 1, xii. 1, &c.). In xi. 1, xiii. **1, xv. 1,** it runs "unto Moses and Aaron." It closes with "These are the commandments which Jahveh commanded Moses for the children of Israel in Mount Sinai."

THE BOOK OF LEVITICUS: CHAPTER BY CHAPTER

Offerings.	1	Burnt offering.
	2	Meat offering.
	3	Peace offering.
	4	Sin offering.
Sins and Offerings.	5	Trespass offering. Sins of ignorance.
	6	Trespass offering. Sins of knowledge.

	7	Law of trespass offering. Priests' portion in trespass and peace offerings.
	8	Aaron and sons consecrated.
	9	First offerings of Aaron. Fire descends on the altar.
	10	Nabab and Abihu destroyed.
Levitical Laws.	11	Meats allowed or forbidden.
	12	Purification of women.
	13	Laws and tokens of leprosy.
	14	Cleansing the leper. Leprosy in a house.
	15	Uncleanness and cleansing of men; and women.
Scape-goat.	16	High priest entering the holy place. The scape-goat. Yearly feast of expiation.
	17	Slain beasts to be offered at the Tabernacle door.
	18	Unlawful marriages, &c.
	19	Laws on charity, honesty, &c.
	20	On idolatry, unclean practices and wizards.
	21	Of priests, mourning and blemishes.
	22	Who may eat of holy things.
Feasts.	23	Feasts of the LORD — Sabbath. Passover (unleavened bread). First fruits (the wave sheaf; Feast of the harvest xxiii. 16; xxxiv, 22). Pentecost (Feast of weeks; Feast of In-gathering – Ex. Xxiii, 16; the wave loaves —Lev. xxiii, 17. Trumpets (xxiii. 24–32; Num. x. 1–10). Tabernacles (xxiii. 34–36; 39–43).
	24	Oil for lamps. Shewbread. Law of blasphemy. Blasphemer stoned.
	25	Sabbath of seventh year. Jubilee of fiftieth year.
	26	Of idolatry. Promises and warnings.
	27	Estimation of vows.

NUMBERS

The Israelites are counted at the beginning of their wanderings, and again just before entering the Promised Land.

THE ESSENTIAL SUMMARY OF NUMBERS

The book takes its title from the *Numbering* of Israel, which is described in chapters i.–iii., and in chapter xxvi. It contains generally the history of the Israelites from the time of their leaving Sinai till their arrival at the borders of the Promised Land. It is divided as follows:

I.   The preparations for the departure from Sinai (chap. i.–x. 10).
II. The journey from Sinai to the borders of Canaan (chap. x. 11,–xiv. 45).
III. A brief notice of laws given, and events which happened during the thirty-seven years' wandering in the Wilderness (chap. xv.–xix. 22).
IV. The history of the last year, from the second arrival of the Israelites in Kadish till they reach "the plains of Moab by Jordan near Jericho" (chap. xx.–xxxvi., 13).

The book concludes with a recapitulation of the various encampments of the Israelites in the desert; the command to destroy the Canaanites; the boundaries of the Promised Land, and the men appointed to divide it; the appointment of the cities of the Levites and the cities of refuge; and further directions respecting heiresses.

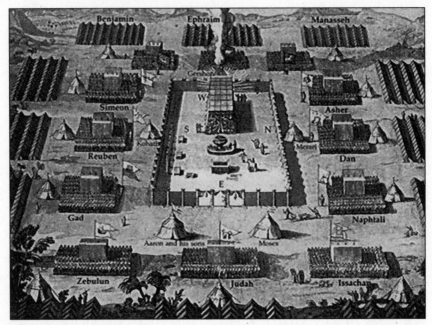

The camp in the wilderness.

COMMENTARY ON THE BOOK OF NUMBERS

Numbers is so called from the double *numbering* or census of the people; the first of which is given in chapters i.—iv., and the second in chapter xxvi. It contains notices of events in the wilderness, more especially in the second year after the Exodus and the close of the wandering, interspersed with legislation.

I. The first principal section (i. 1—x. 10) is the preparation for the departure from Sinai. In ch. i.–iv. we have the first census in the wilderness. Israel is about to occupy the Promised Land and must be organized as Jahveh's army for that purpose. Hence there is recorded (a) the numbering of the 12 tribes (i. 1–54); their position in the encampment (ii. 1–34); the charge of the Levites and their numbering by families (iii. 1–51); the charge of the Levites on the march (iv. 1–49), (b) certain laws apparently supplementary to the legislation of Leviticus; the removal of the unclean from the camp (v. 1–4); the law of restitution (v. 5–10); the trial of jealously (v. 11–31); the law of the Nazirites (vi. 1–21); the priestly blessing (vi. 22–27), *(c)* final arrangements before breaking up the encampment at Sinai; the offerings of the princes at the dedication of the Tabernacle (vii.); Aaron's charge to light the lamps (viii. 1–4); the consecration of the Levites (viii. 5–26); the second observance of the Passover (the first in the wilderness); certain provisions made to meet the case of those who by reason of defilement were unable to keep it (ix. 1–14); the pillar of cloud and the fire regulate the march and the encampment (ix. 15–23); two trumpets of silver to be used by the priests to give the signal for moving the camp and on other occasions (x. 1–10).

II. March from Sinai to the borders of Canaan (x. 11—xiv. 45). The first moving of the camp after the erection of the Tabernacle, and order of march (x. 11–28); Moses entreats Hobab to remain with him (x. 2932); departure from Sinai, led by the Ark (x. 33–36) an account of the several stations and events connected with them, as the murmuring, and the consuming fire at Taberah; the loathing of the manna and the lusting after flesh (xi. 4–9); the complaint of Moses that he cannot bear the burden thus put upon him, and the appointment of 70 elders to help him (xi. 10–29); the quails sent and the judgement following thereon which gave its name to the station Kibroth-hattaavah (the graves of lust); arrival at Hazeroth (xi. 30–35), where Aaron and Miriam oppose Moses because of his wife, and Miriam is smitten with leprosy, but healed at the intercession of Moses (xii. 1–16). The sending of the spies, their report, the refusal of the people to enter Canaan, notwithstanding the efforts of Joshua and Caleb; the anger of Jahveh kindled but partly averted at the intercession of Moses; the doom pronounced that the nation shall wander 40 years in the wilderness, and the rash attempt to invade the land which results in a disastrous defeat (xiii. 1—xiv. 45).

III. The section which follows is partly legislative, partly narrative, but without any note of time. We have laws touching the meal-offering, drink-offering, offering for sins of ignorance, &c. (xv. 1–31); the stoning of one who gathered sticks on the sabbath (32–36); the direction to put fringes on their garments as mementoes (37–41); the rebellion of Korah, Dathan and Abiram, and the murmuring and punishment of the people (xvi.); the budding of Aaron's rod as a witness that the tribe of Levi was chosen (xvii.); the direction given that Aaron and his sons should bear the iniquity of the people, and the duties of priests and Levites clearly defined (xviii.); the law of ceremonial defilement caused by death; the water of purification (xix.).

IV.   The history of the last year in the wilderness from the second arrival of the Israelites in Kadesh till they reach "the plains of Moab by Jordan near Jericho" (xx. 1–xxxvi. 13). Miriam dies (xx. 1); the people murmur for want of water and Moses and Aaron "speaking unadvisedly" are not permitted to enter the Promised Land (xx. 2–13); Edom refuses the people permission to pass through his country (14–21); the death of Aaron at Mount Hor (22–29); the Canaanite king of Arad attacks them but is defeated—a notice which seems out of place, as Arad is in the south

The men sent out to explore the land of Canaan return to Moses and Aaron bringing fruit (Numbers xiii: 25-29).

of Palestine, and the narrative continues " they journeyed from Mount Hor, &c." (xxi. 1–3); the people murmur again by reason of the roughness of the way, and are bitten by fiery serpents, but healed by looking at the Brazen Serpent (4–9); there is again a gap in the narrative. We are told nothing of the march along the eastern edge of Edom, but find ourselves suddenly transported to the borders of Moab. Here the Israelites successively encounter and defeat the kings of the Amorites and of Bashan, wresting from them their territory and permanently occupying it (xxi. 10–35); their successes alarm the king of Moab, who distrusting his superiority in the field sends for Balaam to curse his enemies, hence the episode of Balaam (xxii. 1.–xxiv. 25); the Israelites under the influence of the Moabitish women join in the worship of Baal-Peor, and are punished. The everlasting priesthood is promised to Phinehas because of his zeal for God in this matter (xxv.); a second numbering of the people takes place preparatory to their crossing the Jordan, none included in the first census was found in this except Caleb and Joshua (xxvi.); a question arises as to the inheritance of daughters, and a decision is given thereon (xxvii. 1–11); Moses is warned of his death and Joshua appointed to succeed him (12–23); a catalogue of the festival offerings of the community, "a later supplement to the Torah on the feasts in Lev. xxiii.," with details of sacrifice for *each day* of the Feast of Tabernacles (xx-viii., xxix.); the law of vows (xxx.); narrative of the vengeance taken on the Midianites and Balaam (xxxi.); the partition of the country east of the Jordan among the tribes of Reuben and Gad and the half tribe of Manasseh (xxxii.); a recapitulation, though with some difference, of the various encampments of the Israelites in the desert (xxxiii. 1–49); the command to destroy the Canaanites (50–56); the boundaries of the Promised Land, and the men who are to divide it (xxxiv.); the appointment of the Levitical cities and cities of refuge, together with laws concerning murder and manslaughter (xxxv.); further directions respecting heiresses with special reference to the case mentioned in xxvii. (xxxvi. 1–12) and summing up of the legislation given " in the land of Moab " (13), forming the conclusion of the book. The book is remarkable for the number of fragments of ancient poetry preserved in it. *Cf.* vi. 24–26, x. 35, 36, xxi. 14, 15, *ib.* 17, 18, *ib.* 27–30.

THE BOOK OF NUMBERS: CHAPTER BY CHAPTER

Tribes.	1	The tribes numbered.
	2	Order of the tribes encamping.
	3	Sons of Aaron. Levites numbered. Charges of Gershonites – Kohathites – Merarites. First-born redeemed by Levites and by money.
	4	Age and time of the Levites' service.
	5	The unclean to be removed from the camp. Law of restitution. Trial of jealousy.
	6	Nazarites. Priests' blessing.
	7	Princes offering at the Tabernacle.
	8	Consecration of Levites. The second Passover.
The cloud.	9	The cloud and the Tabernacle.
	10	The silver trumpets. March from Sinai to Paran. Order of march.
	11	The burning at Taberah. Flesh desired, and manna loathed. Seventy elders chosen. Quails sent.
	12	Miriam and Aaron murmur.
	13	Twelve spies sent to search the land.
Twelve spies.	14	People discouraged by ten of the spies. Forty years of wandering decreed. Israel discomforted.
	15	Meat offerings and drink offerings. Sabbath breaker stoned. Law of fringes.
	16	Rebellion of Korah, Dathan and Abiram. Aaron stays the plague.
Aaron's rod.	17	Aaron's rod buds and blossoms.
	18	Priests' portion. Levites' portion.
	19	Water of separation.

NUMBERS

	20	Miriam dies. Moses smites the rock at Meribah. Edom forbids the passage of Israel. Aaron dies.
Fiery serpents.	21	Fiery serpents. The brazen serpent. Sihon and Og overcome.
Balak and Balaam.	22	Balak sends for Balaam to curse Israel.
	23	Balak's sacrifice. Balaam's prophecy.
	24	Balaam further prophecies.
	25	Phinehas kills Zimri and Cozbi.
	26	Israelites numbered again.
	27	Zelophehad's daughters sue for their inheritance.
	28	Continual burnt offerings.
	29	Offerings at the feasts.
	30	Vows.
	31	Midianites spoiled and Balaam slain.
Reuben and Gad.	32	Reubenites and Gadites sue for their inheritance.
	33	The forty-two journeys of the Israelites.
	34	Limits of the land.
Levites' cities.	35	Levites' forty-eight cities and suburbs. Six of them cities of revenge. Laws as to murder.
	36	Zelophehad's daughters marry, as commanded, in their own tribe.

DEUTERONOMY

**A reiteration of God's Commandments; the death of Moses
before he can enter the Promised Land.**

THE ESSENTIAL SUMMARY OF DEUTERONOMY

The fifth Book of Moses is known as the Book of the Second Law – because it contains the second statement of the laws given to Moses, and by him to Israel. The Book consists chiefly of three discourses, delivered by Moses shortly before his death, and derives its name from the fact that it is a repetition of the Law. These discourses were spoken to all Israel, in the plains of Moab, on the eastern side of the Jordan, in the eleventh month of the last year of their wanderings, the fortieth year after their exodus from Egypt.

I. In The First Discourse Moses strives briefly, but very earnestly, to warn the people against the sins for which their fathers failed to enter the Promised Land, and to impress upon them the one simple lesson of obedience; that they might, in their turn, be ready to enter into the land. With this special object, he recapitulates the chief events of the last forty years in the wilderness.

II. The Second Discourse enters more fully into the actual precepts of the Law; in fact, it may be viewed as the body of the whole address, the former being an introduction.

III. The Third Discourse relates almost entirely to the solemn sanctions of the Law: the blessing and the curse. Moses now speaks in conjunction with the elders of the people, and with the priests and Levites, whose office it would be to carry out the ceremony, which was prescribed, in anticipation of the people's settlement in Palestine. The place selected for this ceremony was that sacred spot in the centre of the land, where Abraham and Jacob had first pitched their tents, under the oaks of Moreh, and where the first altar to God had been erected—the valley of Shechem, bounded on the north by Mount Ebal, and on the south by Mount Gerizim. As soon as they should have crossed over Jordan, the people were commanded to set up, on the summit of Ebal, great stones covered with plaster, and inscribed with the Law of God. They were also to build an altar; and this seems to have been distinct from the stones, though the point is somewhat doubtful. Then the twelve tribes were to be divided. between the two hills. Simeon, Levi, Judah, Issachar, Joseph, and Benjamin were to station themselves upon Gerizim, to recite the blessings which Jehovah promised them as the reward of their future fidelity to Him; while Reuben, Gad, Asher, Zebulun, Dan and Naphtali, standing on Ebal, were to denounce the curse of the LORD upon the people should they turn from Him. Moses then proceeds to amplify the blessing and the curse, but chiefly the latter, as the warning was more needed.

Having finished these discourses, Moses encouraged the people and Joshua their new leader to go over Jordan and take possession of the land. He then wrote "this Law", and delivered it to the Levites to be kept in the Ark of the Covenant, as a perpetual witness against the people; and he commanded them to read it to all Israel when assembled at the Feast of Tabernacles, every seventh year.

By the command of Jehovah, who appeared in the cloud to Moses and Joshua when they presented themselves at the door of the tabernacle, Moses added to the book of the Law a *Song*, which the children of Israel were enjoined to learn, as a witness for Jehovah against them. This "Song of Moses" recounts the blessings of God, the Rock — His perfect work, His righteous ways, and the corrupt requital of His people.

Moses now received the final summons for his departure. But first he uttered, not now as the legislator and teacher of his people, but as the prophet wrapt in the visions of the future, his blessing on the twelve tribes. The *Blessing of Moses* speaks only of the favors that God would shower on the tribes; and it describes

39

the happiness of the whole people who are mentioned here and in the preceding Song, by the symbolical name of JESHURUN, the beloved, which is only used again by Isaiah.

The book closes with an account of the farewell between Moses and the people, his ascent of Mount Nebo, and a statement of his death, and his burial in the mountain by Jehovah, in a secret place, the object of the LORD being, no doubt, to prevent the people from making the tomb of their great leader a place of idolatrous worship.

COMMENTARY ON THE BOOK OF DEUTERONOMY

The book contains an account of the last great discourses of Moses delivered in the plains of Moab just before his death. It is however in style quite unlike the earlier books, and expressions occur in it which seem to indicate that it was written in Palestine, *e.g.* the phrase "the other side Jordan," denoting that the writer was on the western side (i. 1, 5 &c., R.V.), and the historical statement in ii. 12 which refers to what took place after the occupation of Canaan.

More than any other book of the Pentateuch, it is a homogenous whole. It contains the following sections: I. chaps. i.—iv., the First Discourse, and statement of circumstances under which it was delivered; II. chaps. v.—xxvi., Second Discourse. This Discourse beginning at v. 1 is introduced by the superscription in iv. 45–49. " It is obvious," says Kuenen, "that v.—xi. is intended as an introduction to xii.—xxvi." There is complete agreement in style, language, details between the Introduction, v.—xi., and xii.—xxvi. which contains the legislative portion of the book. This is a single Book of Law, a repetition as the title (Deuteronomy) implies of the law, the unity of which is admitted on all hands.

(i)   It opens with an emphatic command to destroy all idolatrous objects of worship in the land of Canaan, only one central place for the worship of Jahveh is to be allowed, thither all sacrifices, tithes, freewill offerings, &c., are to be brought; animal food however may be partaken of at home, only blood must not be eaten; this is again and again forbidden;

a solemn warning against the abominations connected with heathen worship, and an urgent exhortation to obedience, conclude the first division of the Code (xii.). Then follow special instances of enticement to false worship: the prophet or dreamer of dreams, the near member of the family, the city which is gone after idols, all these are to be exterminated lest they become a snare (xiii.). Israel is to remember that he is holy unto Jahveh and to keep himself from superstitious observances and unclean food (xiv. 1–21); tithes of the fruits of the field and firstlings of the cattle are to be consecrated to Jahveh in the place which He appoints, &c., and the tithe of every third year is to be for the Levite, the stranger, the fatherless and the widow (22–29). Every seventh year is to be a year of release by creditors (only this is not to prevent the exercise of charity to the poor), and the slave is to be manumitted after seven years' service (xv. 1–18); precise directions as to the sanctifying and eating of firstlings, whether at the Sanctuary (19, 20) or at home (21, 23), are followed by the Kalendar of Festivals, Passover (xvi. 1–8), Feast of Weeks (9–12), Tabernacles (13–17).

(ii) The next group of laws deals chiefly with the orders of the state and the administration of justice; with the judges (xvi. 18–20), the supreme court at the central sanctuary (xvii. 8–13); the king (14–20); the priests (xviii. 1–8); the prophets (9–22); the cities of refuge (xix. 1–13); the removal of landmarks (14); the two witnesses necessary for a conviction (xix. 15); but these are broken somewhat abruptly by the prohibition of ashéras and maccébas (xvi. 21, 22), by the command to offer beasts without blemish to Jahveh (xvii. 1), and by a law on the stoning of idolaters (2–7), which however by its requirement of two witnesses is brought into connexion with the general precepts concerning the administration of justice (xix. 15–21). Then follow the laws for war (xx.), shorter laws concerning expiation of murder in the open field, marriage with females taken in war; rights of firstborn sons; punishment of rebellious sons; removal of bodies of malefactors from the gibbet before evening (xxi.); laws enforcing brotherly dealing, kindness to animals, protection to life; against mixing unlike sorts in sowing seed, in using beasts or making clothes;

41

tassels on the four corners of the garment; punishment of a man who slanders his bride, laws concerning adultery, rape, fornication before marriage; incest (xxii.); qualification for admission into the assembly, to secure the cleanness of the camp; against surrender of runaway slaves; prohibition of prostitution in the worship of Jahveh; laws concerning usury, vows, the use of a neighbor's cornfield (xxiii.);. divorce; newly married men exempted from public duty for a year; a millstone may not be taken in pledge; kidnapping forbidden; the law of leprosy to be strictly observed; of taking pledges; justice to the day-laborer; punishment to be inflicted only on the culprit himself; regulations in favor of foreigners, orphans and widows; scourging as a punishment; provision for the ox that treads the corn; marriage with a deceased brother's wife; observance of decencies where two men are at blows; unjust weights and measures forbidden (xxiv. 1—xxv. 16).

The corpus of laws closes with a return to the Covenant relationship between Jahveh and the people; Amalek is to be rooted out; the firstfruits are to be offered at the one sanctuary; the tithes are solemnly to be given up in the third year, and the people are to pledge themselves to observe the laws and ordinances and to keep the covenant of Jahveh, who on His side will bless and exalt Israel (xxvi.). This last chapter as Kuenen has remarked is the winding up of the whole legislation, and shows that in spite of the want of anything like sequence in many of the separate enactments, the whole section xii.—xxvi. constitutes "a single book of law."

The rest of the book contains: The command to write the words of the law on plastered stones; the blessings to be pronounced on Mount Gerizim, and the curses on Mount Ebal (xxvii.); the last exhortation of Moses announcing the blessings of obedience and the curses upon disobedience, the confirmation of the covenant, with the solemn appeal that he has set before them life and death and that the choice rests with themselves (xxviii.). The closing scenes of Moses' life. He writes this Law and delivers it to the Levitical priests and elders, it is to be kept by the side of the Ark and read at the Feast of Tabernacles every seventh year (xxix.—xxxi.); Moses' song (xxxii.); his Dying Blessing (xxxiii.); his death and burial by Jahveh (xxxiv.). There is much difference of opinion as to the authorship of these latter chapters, and the dates of the several portions.

The book, or at least the main portion of it, is assigned by modern critics to the age of Josiah, or at the earliest of Manasseh, this being the Law-book discovered in the Temple in the reign of Josiah, and chiefly on the ground that it insists so strongly on the centralization of the cultus which, though attempted by Hezekiah, was not accomplished till Josiah's Reformation. But there are serious difficulties in the way of this theory. In any case, the legislation is a repetition and an expansion in hortatory form the earliest code in Exod. xx.—xxiii., and in substance at least is Mosaic. The writer or redactor of the book distinctly asserts that Moses is the author of the legislation and that he provided for its custody (xxxi. 24–26) and transmission.

Moses receiving the commandments.

THE BOOK OF DEUTERONOMY: CHAPTER BY CHAPTER

Retrospect.	1	Moses' address on Israel's forty years in the wilderness.
	2	Prohibition against attacking Edom, Moab or Ammon.
Og.	3	Og, the giant, and his lands.
	4	Exhortation to obedience. Caution against idolatory. Bezer, Ramoth, Golan, cities of refuge.
	5	Covenant of Horeb, and the ten commandments recapitulated.
	6	Continued exhortations to obedience.
	7	Association with the Canaanites forbidden.
	8	Obedience enforced from God's gracious dealings.
	9	Israel reminded of past transgressions.
	10	God's dealings recounted.
	11	Various motives to love and obedience. Blessings and curse set before Israel.
Idolatry and idolaters.	12	Monuments of idolatry to be destroyed. God's service to be continued. Blood forbidden for food.
	13	Tempters to idolatry to be stoned. Idolatrous cities to be destroyed.
	14	Meats clean and unclean.
	15	Year of release.
	16	The three yearly feasts.
	17	Idolaters to be slain. Disputes to be settled by priests and judges. Election and duty of a king.
	18	Priests' and Levites' inheritance. Abominations of the heathen to be avoided. A prophet to appear – like unto Moses.
Cities of refuge.	19	Cities of refuge in Canaan.
	20	Laws for war.
	21	Murder when secret, to be expiated. The first-born to be heir. A stubborn son to be stoned.

	22	Humanity to man and inferior creatures. Adultery , &c.
The Congregation.	23	Who may not enter the congregation. The Ammonite and the Moabite. Concerning the Edomite and the Egyptian. Of fugitive slaves. On plucking a neighbor's grapes or corn.
Humane laws.	24	Various humane laws — Divorce. Pledges. Man-stealers. Hired persons. Gleaning.
Amalek.	25	Forty stripes. Muzzling the ox. The widow of a brother. Unjust weights. Amalek to be blotted out.
	26	Offerings and tithes. Covenant between God and the people.
Mount Ebal. Curses & Blessings.	27	Law to be written on stones, and set up in Mount Ebal. Curses to be pronounced.
	28	Blessings for obedience. Curses for disobedience.
	29	Motives for obedience. Israel presented before the LORD.
	30	Prophecies and promises of mercy. Immediate decision required.
	31	Moses encourages the people and Joshua. Moses delivers the law for septennial reading. Moses warned of death, and of Israel's apostasy.
	32	Moses' prophetic song.
	33	Moses' prophetic blessing on the tribes.
	34	Moses views the promised land. Moses dies and Joshua succeeds him. Eulogy on Moses.

JOSHUA

**Joshua leads the Israelites into the Promised Land.
The conquest of Canaan.**

THE ESSENTIAL STORY OF JOSHUA

Moses' successor as leader of the Israelites was Joshua, long his closest companion and one of the two spies sent into Canaan who reported positively. It was now Joshua's task to lead his people in the conquest of the Promised Land.

The first step was the crossing of the River Jordan, then in flood. Miraculously, however, as soon as the priests leading the crossing stepped into the water, the waters subsided, and the Israelites crossed safely. To commemorate this, Joshua decreed that a memorial be built in the middle of the river.

Those of military age who entered Canaan were uncircumcised, for the generations that had made the Exodus from Egypt were now dead. So at Gilgal the whole nation was circumcised, signalling a new beginning. The manna that had fed them for so long ceased, and the day after the celebration of the Passover they ate for the first time the produce of the land of milk and honey.

Jericho was the first city to fall and, as with all the conquest, God's hand was visible in the outcome: he instructed Joshua to march his troops around the impregnable-looking walls of the city for six days; on the seventh they were to do the same but the priests should blow their trumpets, and the walls would collapse. And so it happened, and Jericho fell to the Israelites.

The city of Ai followed, totally destroyed and all its people killed, according to God's instruction for total annihilation. Joshua then turned south, conquering the cities there, before advancing north as far as Sidon. Then Joshua set about allocating the newly conquered land to the twelve tribes.

By the time of his death, all Canaan had been taken. At Shechem, the Covenant was renewed, and Joshua was buried. And at Shechem they buried the bones of Joseph, which they had brought out of Egypt, at the plot of land Jacob had bought.

Commentary on the Book of Joshua

The book of Joshua, so called not because he is the author, but because he is the principal figure in it, opens with the entrance of Joshua into his office as Leader of the people in succession to Moses and closes with his and Eleazar's death and burial. It consists of two nearly equal parts: **I.** the conquest of Canaan under Joshua (i.–xii.); II. the allotment of the land among the tribes, with Joshua's final exhortations before his death (xiii.–xxiv.). The book is thus a complete whole in itself. The Jewish tradition as has been said separates it from the Five Books of the Law and places it in a different division of the Sacred Writings. It belongs however to the Five Books as containing (a) the fulfilment of the promises made in Genesis concerning the possession of Canaan; *(b)* the accomplishment of the commands given by Moses to Joshua *(cf. i. 1,* &c. with Num. xxvii. 15, &c., Deut. iii. 28, xxxi. 1–8; i. 12, &c. with Num. xxxii., Deut. iii. 18, &c.; viii. 30, &c. with Deut. xi. 29, &c., xxvii. 1–8, 11–14; xiii. with Num. xxxiv.; xiv. 6–15 with Num. xiv. 24, Deut. i. 36; xvii. 1–6 with Num. xxvii. 1–11, xxxvi. 1–12; xx. with Num. xxxv.); *(c)* the establishment of the theocracy for which the whole Pentateuch is a preparation; *(d)* as being of the same literary structure as the preceding books, the three or rather four main documents out of which the Pentateuch is composed reappearing here.

In section I. we have (i); from i. 1–v. 12, the preparations for the conquest of the land and the sending of the spies (ii.), the crossing of the Jordan which parts miraculously before the Ark (iii., iv.), the renewal of the Covenant by the circumcision of the people, the observance of the Passover, the ceasing of the manna (v. 2–12); (ii) the beginning of the holy war, the captain of Jahveh's host appears to Joshua and directs him how to compass Jericho; the miraculous fall of the city (v. 13–vi. 27); the war interrupted by the sin of Achan who takes of the spoil which had been devoted; Joshua fails in consequence to take Ai. Achan is discovered, his confession and punishment (vii.); a second attack on Ai successful, Bethel taken, the covenant confirmed at Mount Ebal (viii.: *cf.* Deut. xi. 29, 30, xxvii.); the southern confederacy against Israel; the Gibeonites by an artifice make peace with Joshua; five kings of the Amorites combine to punish them, but are defeated by Joshua in the battle of Beth-horon, when sun and moon stand still at the command of Joshua; the Amorite army destroyed, the five kings hanged; other successes of Joshua (ix., x.); the northern confederacy, Jabin king of Hazor uniting with other kings in the north of Canaan; Joshua defeats them and destroys their cities (xi. 1–15); result of the conquest, extent of territory covered by Joshua's campaigns (xi. 16–20); the war in the south renewed against the Anakim (xi. 21–23); the territory of the two kings east of Jordan whom Moses smote when he divided the two tribes and a half (xii. 1–6); thirty-one kings west of Jordan smitten by Joshua (xii. 7–24).

II. The allotment of the land (xiii.–xxi.); the command to allot the land, though much still remained to be conquered, having respect to what Moses had done and also to the rule that Levi was to have no share in it (xiii. 1–14); first, the inheritance given by Moses to Reuben (15–23); secondly, to Gad (24–28); thirdly, to half the tribe of Manasseh (29–31); summing up of this work by Moses (32, 33). The allotment of western Palestine; the provision to be made for nine tribes and a half by Joshua with Eleazar the high-priest and the heads of the fathers' houses (xiv. 1–5, *cf.* Num. xxxiv. 16–29); Caleb's claim to Hebron being acknowledged by Joshua (xiv. 6–15); the territorial division; first, Judah (xv. 1–12; Caleb's portion and conquest (13–19); the cities of Judah (20–62; Judah unable to take Jerusalem (63); next Joseph, *i.e.:* Ephraim and Manasseh (xvi. 1–4); Ephraim (5–9); cities within Manasseh being given to Ephraim (*cf. xvii.* 11) who fails to drive out the Canaanites from Gezer (10); Manasseh a firstborn of Joseph has a double portion (xvii. 1–11), but fails also to drive out the Canaanites (12, 13); the claim of the house of Joseph (xvii. 14–18). The Tabernacle set up at Shiloh. Joshua reproaches the seven remaining tribes for their slackness in occupying the land, orders a survey and casts lots for them (xviii. 1–10); territories and cities of Benjamin between Judah and Ephraim (11–28); Simeon, within the portion of Judah (xix. 1–9); Zebulun (10–16); Issachar (17–23); Asher (24–31); Naphtali (32–39); Dan (40–48); the gift of a city to Joshua and summing up of the section (49–51); appointment of the cities of refuge (xx., *cf.* Num. xxxv. and Dent. iv. 41–43); of the Levitical cities and distribution of Levitical families among the tribes (xxi. 1–42); summing up of the history of the conquest (43–45); closing scenes (xxii.–xxiv.); the return of the Eastern tribes to their own home (xxii. 1–8), their memorial altar on the west side of Jordan with the remonstrance of the other tribes and the explanation given and accepted (xxii. 9–34); a solemn warning addressed to the people by Joshua (xxiii.); his last words, &c.; renewal of the covenant at Shechem, which he writes "in the book of the law of God," setting up a great stone as a witness to the transaction " by the sanctuary of Jahveh" (xxiv. 1–28); the death of Joshua, and of Eleazar; their burial and the burial of Joseph's bones.

THE BOOK OF JOSHUA: CHAPTER BY CHAPTER

Joshua.	1	Joshua succeeds Moses. Preparation for passing the Jordan.
	2	Rahab and the two spies.
Jordan crossed.	3	Passage of the Jordan.
	4	Stones of memorial. Passage of the Jordan completed.
	5	The Canaanites afraid. Circumcision renewed. Passover kept at Gilgal. The manna ceases. The angel and Joshua.
Jericho.	6	Taking of Jericho.
	7	Defeat of Israelites at Ai.
Achan.		Achan's trespass.
	8	Taking of Ai.
The Gibeonites.	9	Crafty league of the Gibeonites.

Kings conquered.	10	Gibeon besieged by five kings. Joshua defeats the five kings. Sun and moon stand still. Joshua takes various cities.
	11	Joshua completes his conquests.
	12	List of conquered kings.
	13	Land not to be conquered. Levi not to share in the conquests.
	14	The land divided by lot among the tribes. Caleb obtains Hebron.
	15	Boundaries of Judah. Othniel's reward for taking Kirjath-sepher.
	16	Boundaries of Joseph and Ephraim.
	17	Manasseh's lot and boundaries. Zelophehad's daughters and portion. Canaanites to be bravely expelled.
Shiloh.	18	Tabernacle in Shiloh. Land surveyed and described. Boundary of Benjamin.
	19	Allotment of portions completed. Joshua's own portion.
Cities of Refuge.	20	Cities of refuge finally settled.
	21	Levites' cities.
	22	The two tribes and a half sent home. Building an altar of witness. Dangerous mistake respecting it rectified.
	23	Joshua's charge to Israel in prospect of death.
Joshua's death.	24	Joshua recapitulates God's dealings, and Israel renew the covenant. Joshua's death and burial. Joseph's bones buried in Shechem. Eleazar buried in Mount Ephraim.

JUDGES

**Israel's conquest of Canaan continues.
The people fight the neighboring tribes for survival.**

THE ESSENTIAL STORY OF JUDGES

Conquest does not necessarily bring peace. During the period following the death of Joshua, the Israelites lapsed into idolatry and gradually forgot their Covenant with God. The twelve tribes were also increasingly divided among themselves. As a result, they found themselves beset by enemies and often defeated, becoming subjects of other kings and states. This became a cycle, interrupted by God's appointment of a series of Judges, each of whom brought the people back to God and successfully defeated Israel's enemies.

Of those Judges, one was a woman named Deborah, whose practice it was to sit beneath a palm tree and there dispense advice to the people. She also had prophetic powers. When the depredations of the Canaanites became insupportable, she recruited a general, Barak. He was cautious, but Deborah directed him and told him that because of his vacillation the glory of the victory would not be wholly his; the enemy general would die by the hand of a woman. The battle duly won, the fleeing enemy general, Sisera, took refuge in the tent of Jael, wife of Heber, who offered him protection. When the exhausted Sisera lay down to sleep, Jael drove a tent peg through his temple.

This victory led to the destruction of the Canaanite king and peace for forty years; but then the Israelites turned their faces from the LORD again. And again God raised up a Judge, this time a man called Gideon, who, armed with faith, won a great victory over the Midianites against great odds. As a demonstration to the people that the victory was due to God rather than to numbers, God told Gideon to attack the Midianites with just 300 men. Dividing his force into three, he equipped them with trumpets and jars with torches inside. Approaching the enemy camp they set up such a noise that the Midianites fled.

Forty years of peace ensued before the death of Gideon, after which one of his sons, Abimelech, bribed and killed his way to power and made himself king for three years, before perishing during a siege when a woman threw down a millstone upon his head.

And Israel meanwhile relapsed, losing the favor of the LORD and leading to subjection and humiliation, only to be rescued each time by a Judge raised up by God.

SAMSON

One of the Judges of Israel was Samson, in whom the spirit of the LORD had manifested itself as great strength combined with great virtue, for he was dedicated to God at his birth, never to imbibe wine, touch anything dead or cut his hair. His wonderful feats of strength included wrestling with a lion, carrying off the gates of the Philistine city of Gaza and, armed with nothing more than the jawbone of an ass, killing a host of Philistines. Unwisely, he married a Philistine, named Delilah, whom her countrymen paid to discover the secret of his might. And eventually she found out that if his hair were cut this would constitute breaking his Covenant vow; so this she did while her husband slept.

Shorn of his hair and now deprived of his great strength, Samson was captured by the enemy, blinded and set to work at a grinding mill. But as his hair grew back, so returned his power. Then, one day the Philistines decided to show him off in their Temple of Dagon. Chained there, he prayed to God, who gave him back his mighty strength to push down the massive pillars of the temple, killing all 3,000 Philistines within.

Samson wrestles with a lion.

COMMENTARY ON THE BOOK OF JUDGES

The Book of Judges and the Book of Ruth contain all the Jewish history which has been preserved to us of the times between the death of Joshua and the birth of Samuel. The Book of Judges consists of three parts. (i) An introduction, extending from i. 1 to iii. 6. (ii) The history of various periods of transgression, and the oppressions and deliverances by which they were followed. This occupies from iii. 7 to xvi. 31. (iii) Two narratives, which show in a special manner the proneness of the people to idolatry and the lawlessness of the times that succeeded their partial occupation of Canaan (xvii.–xxi.).

The rulers whose exploits are narrated in this book are called 'judges,' but what is told of them relates far more to what they did as conquerors and deliverers of the people. When the enemy had been driven away we may assume that these conspicuous leaders regulated and consolidated the institutions of the country, but of such work the history is almost silent. We can see from Abimelech's conduct (ix. 2) that the office tended to become kingly, insomuch that he speaks as if there were a right of succession in the family of the judge. Such occurrences were likely to lead the people to thoughts of a kingdom before very long.

There is little to guide us as to the time when the book was compiled. But the allusion to the captivity of the ten tribes (xviii. 30) points to a date later than that event (B.C. 721). We know from Proverbs xxv. 1 that the reign of Hezekiah, who was then king of Judah, was a time of literary activity. It may very well be, therefore, that the Book of Judges was brought to its present form by some among the 'men of Hezekiah.' The disappearance of a large portion of the nation into captivity would give an impulse, to those who were able to do the work, to bring into connected form the early national history. And the style in some parts of the book bespeaks their early origin. Thus the song of Deborah and Barak, the parable of Jotham, and the riddle and other utterances of Samson are stamped with a very primitive character. The compiler states his purpose in the first words of the book. He means to compile a history of things which befell after Joshua was dead, but to connect his work with matter already existent he goes over in his introduction some things which happened in Joshua's lifetime, as is evident from a comparison of Jud. i. 10–15 with Joshua xiv. 1–15. Such passages as Judges ii. 6–10 and Joshua xxiv. 28–31 must have been drawn from the same source. But there is nothing in the compilation of the Book of Judges to lead us to believe that the compilers used their material otherwise than faithfully. And that the book was brought together from existing material at a date several centuries after the events which it records can in no wise diminish the trustworthiness of its lessons.

Among these lessons, however, chronology is clearly not one. For no attempt is made to give precision to the dates. Almost every record of time is made in round numbers, and can only be taken as an approximation, while we have nothing to help us to decide whether any of the judges were contemporary or over-lapped one another in the time when they were in power. The influence and power of some of them appear to have been rather tribal than national. Hence two of them might have been living at the same time. For example, we are told (x. 7), just before the rise of Jephthah, that God sold the people into the hands of the Philistines and into the hands of the children of Ammon. Now the exploits of Jephthah were all against the Ammonites. Some other leader, and there is nothing to indicate whether it was Shamgar (iii. 31) or Samson (xv. 5), must have been the agent to keep the Philistines in check on the west, while Jephthah's victories were gained over the eastern oppressors. Such an instance is sufficient to illustrate the entire neglect of chronology in the book, and the same thing is clear from the two appendices in chapters xvii.—xxi., which are quite out of their place in order of time. To attempt a chronological arrangement from the book itself is therefore out of the question. Nor are we helped by anything recorded in other parts of the Bible. A passage often referred to for this purpose is 1 Kings vi. 1. There we are told that the 4th year of Solomon's reign was the 480th after the Exodus. That no great stress can be laid on this number is clear, because the Septuagint says the 440th year, while Josephus makes it the 592nd. Now if we put together the numbers found in the Old Testament, we have 40 years between the Exodus and the death of Moses, 40 years' peace after Othniel, 80 after Ehud: Jabin's oppression lasted '20 years: there were 40 years' peace after Barak, 40 in Gideon's time: Tola was judge for 23 years, Jair for 22, Jephthah for 6, Ibzan for 7, Elon for 10, Abdon for 8. The servitude to the Philistines lasted 40 years, and Samson judged 20 years. After this we have as dates Eli 40 years, Samuel 20 (1 Sam. vii. 2) at least, David 40 and Solomon 4. These alone make 500 years, and we have allowed no time for the leadership of Joshua nor for the years between the death of Joshua and the judgeship of Othniel, nor yet again for the reign of Saul. Hence it is clear, if 480 be the correct number of years between the Exodus and Solomon, that some of these events in the Judges must have been contemporaneous. Again, the time from the capture of Gilead down to the days of Jephthah is stated (Jud. xi. 26) at 300 years. If to this sum we add the numbers recorded for the events between Jephthah and Solomon, we arrive at a total of 485 years without counting anything for the length of Saul's reign. Again, according to Acts xiii. 20, the time between the partition of the land under Joshua and the days of Samuel was 450 years; adding to this the other numbers down to Solomon and allowing, as St.

Paul did, 40 years for the reign of Saul we reach a total of 554 years. All these reckonings differ, and we have nothing left us whereby to confirm or contradict any of them.

A list of the judges, in their order and with the years assigned to them, will be found at the end of this section, but what has been said will show that these numbers are not recorded in such wise as to be available for a chronological arrangement of the history. The introduction (i. 1—ii. 5) narrates how Israel dealt with the Canaanites. Judah and Simeon fought together against the people, and their endeavours were largely successful, but though Jerusalem was smitten by them, Benjamin did not get possession of it (2 Sam. v. 6). The house of Joseph (i.e. Ephraim and Manasseh) had a certain measure of success, yet did not drive away all the heathen inhabitants, but were content with making them tributary 27-29). Zebulun pursued the same policy, while Asher and Naphtali were content to dwell among the Canaanites, even exacting tribute from very few of them (i. 30-33). The Danites found the work of conquering the Amorites more than they could effect, and had to seek another settlement (i. 34). For their remissness the people are rebuked by an angel (ii. 1-5), and at the time express their penitence. Then (ii. 6-iii. 6) follows an epitome of the subsequent histories. In the generation after Joshua the people forsook the LORD, and joined in the Canaanite idolatries. For this they were given into the hands of one spoiler after another, and when punishment had wrought temporary repentance, deliverers were raised up in various places to rescue them. This part of the introduction, which tells of Joshua's death, forms a close connexion between the books of Joshua and Judges, and concludes with a brief list of the Canaanitish people who were suffered to remain in the land (iii. 1-6).

The second portion of the book is four times broken by special mention of a gift of the Spirit of the LORD to the judge then in power. This help is spoken of in the case of Othniel (iii. 10), of Gideon (vi. 34), of Jephthah (xi. 29), and of Samson (xiii. 25), and makes them conspicuous above the rest. The sin which kindled God's anger was idolatry (iii. 7), the serving of 'the Baalim and the Asheroth' (R. V.). For this they were given into the power of Cushan-rishathaim, king of Mesopotamia. In answer to their cry the LORD raised up Othniel as a deliverer, after which was a time of rest for 40 years (iii. 8–11). For another transgression the people were given into the power of Eglon, king of Moab, for eighteen years, after which time they were delivered by a Benjamite named Ehud, who by stratagem slew Eglon, and roused Israel to slaughter their Moabite oppressors. A rest of fourscore years follows this deliverance (iii. 12–30). Next in order follows, but without details of time or circumstance, the deliverance from the Philistines by Shamgar (iii. 31).

Closely connected with the end of Ehud's life is the sin for which Israel was sold into the hand of Jabin, king of Canaan. From this oppressor deliverance was wrought by the murder of Sisera, his commander-in-chief (iv. 1—v. 31). Deborah, who was judge at this time, was also a prophetess. At her summons, Barak the son of Abinoam went with an army against Sisera, but because of his unwillingness at the first, the victory was given into the hands of Jael the wife of Heber the Kenite, into whose tent the retreating commander fled for rest and refuge. Joined with the prose narrative of these events is the song of Deborah and Barak, written in celebration of this deliverance, and manifestly a composition of very early date. The oppression for the relief of which Gideon was raised up (vii. viii. 32) was by the Midianites and had lasted seven years with such severity that the people hid from the enemy in dens and caves and the fastnesses of the mountains. Deliverance was promised by a prophet of the LORD, and Gideon was encouraged by an angelic messenger to undertake the rescue. As a first step, however, he was directed to overthrow the altar of Baal which his father had made, and to build an altar unto the LORD instead. This done, he gathered the men of Manasseh, Asher, Zebulun and Naphtali to fight against Midian. By signs given in answer to his entreaty he was assured of victory, and directed to reduce his large army of 32,000 to 300. A visit in the night to the camp of Midian made it clear how a dread of him was in the hearts of the enemy. Hence by a stratagem he startles the great army, who in their terror destroy each other, while the fugitives are slain by the Ephraimites as they attempt to cross the Jordan, the heads of two of their princes being brought in triumph to Gideon. The anger of the Ephraimites, because they had not been called with the other tribes, is prudently appeased, while the treachery of the men of Succoth and Fennel is promised, and soon receives, its due punishment. Two kings of Midian, Zebah and Zalmunna, are captured and slain, and the rescued Israelites would fain have made Gideon their king, but he refused, though he asked of them, as a present, the gold ornaments which each had taken from the prey. With these he made some sort of idol, called an ephod, and led the people into idolatry, which became grosser still after his death. Abimelech, the son of Gideon by a Shechemite concubine, slays all the other sons (70 in number) of his father, except one Jotham, and makes himself king when Gideon was dead. To this end he, secures the help of the men of Shechem, and Jotham by a striking parable predicts, and invokes, enmity between Abimelech and the Shechemites. This soon breaks out, and there is war in the land until Abimelech is killed by a piece of a millstone thrown over the wall of Thebez by a woman of that city (ix. 1–55). So came to its fulfilment the curse of Jotham. A deliverer was sorely needed after these miseries, and we are briefly told of two judges in succession, whose administration was uneventful. These were Tola of the tribe of Issachar, who was judge for 23 years (x. 1–2), and Jair, a Gileadite, for 22 years (x. 3–4). But again the people fell away, and the catalogue of their idols is now greatly increased. To the Baalim and the Ashtaroth there are added (x. 6) the gods of Syria, of Zidon, of Moab, of Ammon and of the Philistines; and the Ammonites are the enemy whom God now employs as His instruments of punishment. To these also are joined the Philistines (x. 7), though no relation of their attacks, or how they were repulsed, has been preserved to us. In their distress and in answer to their cry, Jephthah the Gileadite was raised up to deliver Israel (xi. 1–40). He had been banished from Gilead, but in their extremity the people recalled him. At first Jephthah tries the effect of negotiations with the Ammonite king, but these being unsuccessful, he prepares to fight with the enemy. Before the battle he vowed to offer, if successful, the first thing that came forth to meet him on his return. This rash vow cost the life of his only daughter, in whose memory there was kept a yearly lamentation. In consequence of the murmurings and threats of the Ephraimites because they had not been called to the battle, Jephthah attacks them and destroys 42,000 (xii. 1–7). To Jephthah succeeded Ibzan of Bethlehem for seven years (xii. 8–10); then Elon, a Zebulunite (xii. 11–12), was judge for ten years;

then Abdon, a Pirathonite, for eight years (xii. 13–15). Nothing but some particulars of their domestic life is told us of any of these.

The fourth oppression was by the Philistines and lasted 40 years. The judge who was appointed to deliver Israel from this enemy was Samson (xiii. 1—xvi. 31), whose birth was foretold to his parents by an angel, who at the same time directed that he should be a Nazirite all his life long. Samson belonged to the tribe of Dan, which had been driven from its first settlements by the Philistines. His life was of such a character, that we are not surprised when the record only states that 'he shall begin to deliver Israel' (xiii. 5). He was endued with immense strength, which was to continue with him while his Nazirite vow was observed and his hair unshorn. But at the beginning he sets his heart on taking a wife from among the Philistines, and on his way down to visit the woman he slew a lion which roared against him. At his second visit to keep the marriage feast a quarrel arose, which resulted in Samson slaying thirty men of the Philistine city of Ashkelon. The giving of his wife to another caused a final breach with the Philistines, whose standing corn Samson burnt, by sending into it foxes (or jackals) bearing lighted firebrands tied between them. Samson's own people, however, left him to resist their enemies alone, and rather sided with the Philistines. To this may perhaps be ascribed some of the great recklessness which he manifested in his future behaviour. His sin brought him into danger at Gaza, but his great strength saved him. Later on he betrayed to Delilah the secret of his strength, and she gave him up to the Philistines. Blinded and a prisoner he was mocked at by his enemies, but receiving his strength again from God, he slew more of the Philistines, in the ruin of their temple, than he had slain in all his life before.

The two narratives with which the Book of Judges concludes are contained in chapters xvii.–xviii. and in chapters xix.–xxi. respectively. They belong to an early part of the time covered by the book, for the events mentioned in the latter occurred while Phinehas, the grandson of Aaron, was high-priest (xx. 28), and in it Dan is spoken of as the northern limit of the land (xx. 1), so that the migration of the Danites spoken of in chapter xviii. must have already taken place. They are probably appended as illustrations of the evils prevalent throughout this period, and of the terrible consequences of the frequent transgressions. The first tells how Micah and his mother dwelling in the hill country of Ephraim fell away into the worship of idols, and how a Levite of Bethlehem was induced to become their priest. This took place at the time when some Danite spies were moving northward in search of additional land. These ask counsel of Micah's priest and are encouraged to go forward. They find a suitable place for their settlement at Laish. And having returned home they gather a force of six hundred men for the expedition. These on their northward journey rob Micah of his images and his priest, and after their conquest of Laish set up idolatrous worship in this new Dan. There is reason to suppose (see R. V. of xviii. 30) that the Levite who became Micah's priest was a grandson of Moses. This idolatrous worship continued till the ten tribes were carried captive. The second narrative makes evident the low moral condition of this time. A Levite of the Ephraimite hill country was fetching back his runaway concubine from Bethlehem. As they stayed for the night in Gibeah of Benjamin the woman was killed by the outrage of the men of Gibeah. To rouse the national indignation the man cut his concubine's body in pieces and sent a portion thereof to each tribe. The people came together to Mizpeh resolved to punish the men of Gibeah, who were defended by the other Benjamites. The Israelites were defeated in the two first engagements, but afterwards by a stratagem destroyed all the Ben-jamites except six hundred, and took an oath not to give wives to this remnant. The thought of blotting out one tribe from the twelve, however, moved them to be sorry for their oath. Hence they sent a force against Jabesh-gilead and carried off 400 maidens whom they gave to the Benjamites, and commanded the other men to seize wives for themselves at the time of a great feast in Shiloh. Thus their oath was unbroken, and the name of Benjamin was still preserved in the nation. The whole history finds a fit conclusion in the words, "In those days there was no king in Israel, every man did that which was right in his own eyes."

The subjoined table shows the different oppressions of the Israelites, and the several judges, in the order in which they are mentioned in the narrative.

THE BOOK OF JUDGES: CHAPTER BY CHAPTER

Adoni-bezek.	1	Judah makes conquests, aided by Simeon. King Adoni-bezek taken. Jerusalem's city taken and burnt. Othniel's exploit for Caleb's daughter. Cowardice and indolence of the tribes respecting the Canaanites.
	2	An angel rebukes the people at Bochim.
Othniel. **Ehud.** **Shamgar.**	3	Philistines and others move to prove Israel. Israel oppressed eight years by Mesopotamia. OTHNIEL, first judge, delivers from king of Mesopotamia. Israel oppressed eighteen years by Moab. EHUD, second judge, kills Eglon and delivers Israel. SHAMGAR, third judge.

Deborah and Barak.	4	Israel oppressed twenty years by king of Canaan. DEBORAH, fourth judge, with Barak, defeats Sisera and delivers Israel. Jael kills Sisera.
	5	Song of Deborah and Barak.
Gideon.	6	Israel oppressed by Midian seven years. GIDEON, fifth judge. An angel appears to him. Gideon's sacrifice consumed. The altar, Jehovah-shalom. Another altar built. Gideon's name changed to Jerubbaal. Gideon's fleece.
Pitchers broken.	7	Gideon's army reduced to 300 men that lapped. The Midianite's dream of the barley-cake. Breaking of the pitchers, and discomforting of the Midianites. The princes Oreb and Zeeb.
	8	The Ephraimites pacified. Zebah and Zalmunna, Kings of Midian. Succoth and Penuel destroyed. Gideon's seventy sons.
Abimelech, king.	9	ABIMELECH, Gideon's son, made king. Abimelech murders his brethren. Jotham's parable. Gaal's conspiracy told by Zebul. Abimelech destroys Shechem. Abimelech slain by a woman at Thebez.
Tola. **Jair.**	10	TOLA, sixth judge. JAIR, seventh judge. Thirty sons of Jair that rode on asses. Israel oppressed by the Philistines. The Amorites oppress Israel eighteen years.
Jephthah.	11	JEPHTHAH, eighth judge. Jephthah's victory. Jephthah's daughter.
Ibzan. **Elon.** **Abdon.**	12	Ephraimites quarrel with Jephthah. Ephraimites slain at the ford of Jordan, not pronouncing Shibboleth. IBZAN, ninth judge. Thirty sons and thirty daughters of Ibzan. ELON, tenth judge. ABDON, eleventh judge. Forty sons and thirty nephews of Abdon.

The Philistines. **Samson.**	13	Israel oppressed by the Philistines for forty years. Angel and Manoah's wife. Manoah's sacrifice. Samson born. SAMSON, twelfth judge.
	14	Samson chooses a wife of the Philistines. Samson kills a lion. Samson finds honey in the carcase. Samson makes a marriage-feast. Samson propounds a riddle. Samson spoils thirty Philistines. Samson is cheated of his wife.
Burning the corn.	15	Samson burns the Philistines' corn with foxes. The Philistines burn his wife's father's house. Samson smites the Philistines hip and thigh. Samson slays 1,000 men with a jawbone. The fountain En-hakkore in Lehi.
Gates of Gaza.	16	Samson carries off the gates of Gaza. Delilah allures and betrays Samson. The Philistines put out Samson's eyes. Samson's death and revenge.
Micah.	17	Micah and his images.
	18	The spies of Dan. Micah robbed of his priest and images. Laish taken. Dan built there and idolatry set up.
	19	Levite's concubine ill-used at Gibeah.
	20	The Benjamites nearly destroyed.
	21	Jabesh-gilead destroyed. Four hundred wives for the remaining Benjamites provided. Virgins dancing at Shiloh captured. Anarchy of Israel.

RUTH

How a Moabite woman became an ancestress of the Messiah.

THE ESSENTIAL STORY OF RUTH

This book is the history of the family of Elimelech, who in the days of the Judges because of a famine went away from Bethlehem to dwell in the land of Moab. There, the children, two sons, married Moabitish wives, and died, as did also their father. Naomi, the mother, returned to Bethlehem, and Ruth, one of her widowed daughters-in-law, came with her. Ruth, when gleaning in the field of Boaz, a kinsman of Elimelech, finds favour with him. Naomi wishes and plans that Boaz should marry Ruth, and he is ready to do so, if a nearer kinsman, to whom the right belongs according to the law in Deuteronomy xxv. 5–10, declines. He does decline, and so Ruth becomes the wife of Boaz. Her son was Obed, the father of Jesse, the father of David. The book appears to be intended to connect the history of David with the earlier times, and also to form a contrast, in its peaceful and pastoral simplicity, to the disorders of which we read so continually in the Book of Judges.

COMMENTARY ON THE BOOK OF RUTH

This pathetic record of a humble Hebrew family is written with striking simplicity. It originally formed the closing part of the Book of Judges and its authorship has been attributed to Samuel, Hezekiah and Ezra.

It would appear that the departure of Elimelech from Bethlehem and his settlement in Moab showed a lack of faith and trust in God. The outcome is painful and sad. The sons contract marriages with those who were not of Israel; and we have the early deaths of both Mahon and Chilion, following close upon the death of their father. Naomi turns towards her own country and her own people, a poverty-stricken, bereaved and desolate woman. But in the heart of her Moabitish daughter-in-law, Ruth, there was found "some good thing toward the LORD God of Israel"; and so, leaving her country and kindred, she elects to share the lowly lot of her sorrowing mother-in-law. It was an act of *faith* ("Thy God shall be my God"), and it met with unlooked for reward. Engrafted into the Jewish people, Ruth becomes the direct ancestress of David, and thus of the Messiah Himself (see Matt. i. 5, 6, 16; Luke iii. 23, 32).

THE BOOK OF RUTH: CHAPTER BY CHAPTER

To Moab.	1	Elimelech, Naomi, and two sons, emigrate from Bethlehem into Moab. Elimelech dies. Mahlon and Chilion die. Naomi part from Orpah, and returns home after ten years. Ruth goes with Naomi.
Naomi and Ruth.		
Boaz.	2	Ruth gleans in the field of Boaz. Boaz shows great kindness to Ruth.
	3	Boaz acknowledges the right of a kinsman.
	4	Boaz buys the inheritance and marries Ruth.

I SAMUEL

**The calling of Samuel; his anointing of the first two kings
of Israel; battles, jealousy and the death of King Saul.**

THE ESSENTIAL STORY OF I SAMUEL

The last of the Judges was the greatest, for Samuel would be
prophet and priest as well as Judge. His mother, Hannah,
despaired of having a child until God interceded, and in
thanks she dedicated the boy to God, his name meaning "Heard
by God."

Meanwhile the Judge and High Priest, Eli, had two sons, who
also became priests but whose abhorrent behavior aroused the
wrath of God, especially when Eli failed to restrain them. One
night, God spoke to the young Samuel, telling him that he would
punish these two worthless men.

This punishment was meted out when the Philistines captured
the Ark of the Covenant, a dreadful disaster for the Israelites.
During the battle, Eli's sons were killed, and on hearing the
shocking news, the old man fell off his chair, breaking his neck,
and died.

The Philistines took the ark back to Ashdod, and set it in the
Temple of their great god, Dagon, as a trophy. But within two
days the statue of the god had disintegrated, and the Philistines
began to suffer from the plague. In vain they moved the ark to
Gath, only to have the plague break out there. So they returned
the ark to the Israelites, who repented their foolishness and idolatry, putting away the idols of Baal and Ashtaroth they had been

worshipping, and listening instead to their new Judge, Samuel. And when the Philistines attacked the assembled Israelites at Mizpeh, God inflicted a great defeat upon them, and the Israelites recovered the lands they had previously lost to their enemy.

When he became old, Samuel appointed his sons as Judges, making the same mistake as Eli, for both were unworthy. The elders came to tell him so and demanded that the nation be ruled by a king. Samuel consulted God, who told him to listen to the people, and so set out to find a suitable candidate for the throne. God directed him to Saul, a tall, 30-year old Benjamite, who was acclaimed king.

Saul began his reign well, relieving the Ammonite siege of Jabesh, but in the next encounter with the Philistines his generalship, although successful in the end, was poor, and Samuel rebuked him. Saul continued campaigning on all sides, but there came a battle with the Amalekites at which he captured the enemy king, Agag. The Amalekite host had been destroyed, but Saul spared their ruler, and his men took the livestock of their foes as plunder. This was contrary to the instructions of God, however, who had specified total destruction. Samuel again remonstrated and had Agag put to death. And now God rejected Saul.

God now led Samuel to David, youngest son of Jesse, whom he had chosen to be king in Saul's place – but not yet. In the meantime, with God's favor withdrawn from Saul, an evil spirit tormented him. When David entered the royal court, the melancholy king found that the young man's harp-playing soothed him.

During another campaign against the Philistines, David visited the camp bringing provisions and heard the Philistine champion Goliath challenge the Israelites to single combat; hearing the challenge, he volunteered and faced the giant armor-clad champion with no more than a sling. With one stone he killed Goliath. David now attained high rank at court and led armies in the field against the Philistines with great success, but Saul increasingly saw the hand of the LORD – while he himself had been deserted, God's favor was all too clearly to be seen with David. In fits of depression, he twice nearly killed David, who fled, pursued into the hills by Saul with troops. Several attempts were made on

David's life, but he managed to escape, helped by his intimate friendship with Saul's son Jonathan.

On two occasions, David managed to infiltrate Saul's camp and took evidence that he had been in Saul's tent and could have killed the king but did not. Each time Saul repented outwardly, but he was increasingly alone. Samuel, who had turned away from him, had now died, but Saul consulted a witch at Endor, who raised Samuel's spirit, and Saul asked him for help. But Samuel had no words of comfort and predicted that his end was near.

These words came true very shortly afterwards: at the battle near Mount Gilboa, the Philistines were successful, Jonathan and Saul's other sons perishing in the battle. Saul, in despair at the defeat and his loss, fell upon his sword.

COMMENTARY ON THE FIRST BOOK OF SAMUEL

The two books of Samuel formed in the Hebrew only one, as did also the two books of Kings. In the Septuagint, they were each broken into two parts, and this division came to be recognized in the whole of Christian literature. The four books are very frequently called the four books of Kings. The books of Samuel take their name from the judge who plays so conspicuous a part at the commencement of them. The history in them opens with his birth and continues almost to the death of David.

The First Book of Samuel may be divided into three sections, of which the first, containing chapters i.–vii., is the history of Eli and Samuel as judges. It opens with the birth and dedication of Samuel, which stands in contrast to the evil-doing of Eli's sons. Their punishment is foretold, and they are slain in a war with the Philistines, in which the ark of God, sent for to the battlefield is captured by the enemy. They carry it away, but calamity and judgment fall on every place to which it is brought. At length they are advised to send it back and they do so, sending along with it various trespass-offerings. It first arrives at Beth-shemesh, where the inhabitants are punished for irreverently looking into it, and petition the men of Kirjath-jearim to come and fetch it away. In that city it remained for twenty years; in which period we are told of a time of penitence among the Israelites, and how Samuel gathered them at Mizpeh for a service of confession, after which the Philistines are conquered at Ebenezer, and peace is secured between Israel and the Amorites. The section concludes with a brief note about Samuel's administration, for the seats of which he selected three ancient holy places, and had also an altar in Ramah, where his home was.

The second section (chapters viii.–xiv.) tells how the people, because of the injustice of Samuel's sons, came to desire a king. The LORD was angry, but granted their request, and Samuel describes for them what they may expect from their future king. Saul, who came to Samuel to inquire about his father's asses, is secretly anointed as king, and certain signs are given him to assure him of God's choice. Later on follows a public appointment of Saul by lot at Mizpeh. The manner of the kingdom is written in a book by Samuel and laid up before the LORD. Saul is not accepted of all till he shows his fitness to be king by a victory over the Ammonites in defence of Jabesh-gilead. Samuel testifies of his own integrity and exhorts the people to the fear of the LORD, that they and their king may prosper.

Next we have a brief notice of Saul's army, and how war rose against the Philistines, during which Saul took upon him to offer sacrifice, and thus committed his first great sin. Samuel leaves him, and the Philistines are for a while victorious, till they are defeated by Jonathan. Saul's administration is for a time successful, but he is constantly exposed to the inroads of the Philistines.

In the third section (chapters xv.–xxxi.) we see the kingdom passing from Saul to David. By his disobedience in the Amalekite war, and by sparing Agag, Saul again offended God, and David is secretly anointed king by Samuel at the divine command. The Spirit of the LORD forsakes Saul, and he is troubled by an evil spirit. David. slaying Goliath, the Philistine champion, gains great favour with the people. Saul waxes jealous, and seeks both openly and by stratagem to slay David, whose popularity still increases. Saul tries to incite his servants to kill him, but he is saved, at one time, by Jonathan; at another, by Michal, the daughter of Saul, who was his wife. David now takes refuge with Samuel, leaving the court entirely, but keeping his covenant of friendship with Jonathan. He afterwards goes to Nob to the tabernacle, and obtains help from the high priest, which is noticed by Doeg, the Edomite, Saul's chief herdsman. On that information Saul subsequently slays the priests at Nob. After this David flees to Gath to king Achish, then is in hiding in the cave of Adullam. He takes his parents for safety into the land of Moab, himself coming back to his own country. But he is constantly in peril from treachery, as at Keilah and among the Ziphites. Saul pursues him relentlessly, and in the midst of these troubles Samuel dies. Then David retires to the southern wilderness, where he is churlishly treated by Nabal. He comes a second time into peril through the Ziphites, and though he has an opportunity of slaying Saul, yet spares him. Once more he goes to king Achish, who gives him the city of Ziklag, from which he makes raids on the tribes around, which Achish fancies are made on Israel, and hence invites David to go with him to war against his own people. Saul, in fear of the Philistines, consults the witch of Endor, who foretells his coming ruin. The Philistine princes will not have David with them in the war, so Achish lets him depart. In David's absence Ziklag had been plundered by the Amalekites, but pursuing he recovers the spoil and much beside. In the battle with the Philistines on mount Gilboa Saul and Jonathan are slain. The Philistines insult the dead bodies, but these are recovered and solemnly buried by the men of Jabesh-Gilead.

THE FIRST BOOK OF SAMUEL: CHAPTER BY CHAPTER

Eli. Samuel.	1	Elkanah and his wives Hannah and Peninnah. Hannah and Eli. Birth and dedication of Samuel.
Hannah's Song.	2	Hannah's song. Eli's wicked sons, Hophni and Phinehas. Samuel's ministry. Prophecy against Eli's house.
	3	Samuel and Eli.

The Ark.	4	The ark taken by Philistines. Hophni and Phinehas slain. Eli's sudden death. Ichabod born, and Phinheas' wife dies.
	5	The ark and Dagon. The ark at Gath and at Ekron.
	6	The ark sent back to Beth-she-mesh. The people smitten for looking into the ark.
	7	The ark at Kirjath-jearim, in Abinadab's house, during twenty years. Israel put away their gods. Philistines discomforted at Ebenezer. Israel's cities restored.
Samuel.		SAMUEL, the last judge.
	8	Joel and Abiah, Samuel's sons.
Saul.	9	Saul seeks his father's asses. Samuel communes with Saul.
	10	Samuel anoints Saul. Saul chosen king by lot.
	11	Jabesh-gilead besieged by Hahash. Saul delivers Jabesh-gilead.
	12	Samuel asserts his integrity. Samuel calls for thunder to reprove the people.
	13	Saul wars with the Philistines. The Philistines alarm the Israelites. Saul rashly sacrifices. The Philistines waste the land. "No smith in Israel."
Jonathan.	14	Jonathan attacks the Philistine garrison. Saul defeats the Philistines. Saul's rash vow. Saul's victories and family.
	15	Saul commissioned to destroy Amalek. Saul warns the Kenites. Saul's unfaithful performance of his duty. Saul rejected.
Agag.		Agag slain by Samuel.
	16	David anointed at Bethlehem. Saul soothed by David's harp.
Goliath.	17	Goliath challenges Israel. David slays Goliath.

Saul's javelin.	18	Jonathan's covenant with David. Saul attempts David's life. David marries Saul's daughter Michal.
	19	David's danger and Jonathan's intercession. Saul's jealousy and David's escape. Michal's artifice.
Jonathan and David	20	Jonathan and David renew their covenant of friendship. Signal of the arrows to save David.
Doeg.	21	David at Nob, with Ahimelech. He takes the hallowed bread and Goliath's sword. Doeg present and marks the transaction. David at Gath, and feigns madness.
Cave of Adullam.	22	David in the cave of Adullam. David sends his parents into Moab. David, admonished by God, flees into Judah. Doeg slays the priests. Abiathar escapes to David.
	23	David rescues Keilah from the Philistines. David escapes Saul.
	24	David cuts off Saul's skirt in the cave of Engedi.
Nabal.	25	Death of Samuel. Churlishness of Nabal. Wisdom of Abigail. Nabal's death. David marries Abigail.
	26	The Ziphites direct Saul to David. David takes Saul's spear and cruse. David obtains Saul's blessing.
David at Gath.	27	David again at Gath, and receives Ziklag for a residence. David smites the Geshurites and Gezirites.
Witch of Endor.	28	Achish's trust in David. Saul and the witch of Endor.
	29	David's help rejected by the Philistine Lords.
	30	Ziklag spoiled by the Amalekites. David pursueth. The battle at Gilboa.
	31	Saul and his sons slain.

II SAMUEL

David succeeds Saul as King. David's victories, popularity, sin and repentance.

THE ESSENTIAL STORY OF II SAMUEL

Upon the death of Saul, the king's fourth son, Ishbosheth (Esh-baal), was proclaimed king by the general of the army, Abner. David meanwhile moved from Ziklag to Hebron, where the elders of Judah anointed him king. The Israelites were thus split, and civil war became inevitable. After seven years of fighting, Abner (the power behind the throne of the feeble Ishbosheth) quarreled with his king over a former concubine of Saul, and Abner transferred his allegiance to David. They came to an agreement, part of which was that David's wife Michal (daughter of Saul) be restored to him. Abner did not long outlive the meeting at Hebron, however, slain by Joab, one of David's nephews, in pursuance of a long-standing feud. David was careful to distance himself from the act, did not punish the assassin, but instead laid a curse upon Joab's family.

Not long after this, Ishbosheth was himself assassinated, and the elders of the northern tribes came to Hebron to anoint David king at last of all the Jews.

The Philistines, realizing that a united kingdom would be more difficult to keep in check, attacked twice but were soundly defeated and repulsed. David could now set about consolidating his kingdom.

His first move was to attack and capture Jerusalem, the city of the Jebusites, which stood at the border between the previously warring kingdoms. A strong site, Jerusalem would become the city of David, both religious and administrative capital of his kingdom.

The Ark of the Covenant, captured by the Philistines many years earlier, then restored to the Israelites, had lain neglected at Kiriath-jearim for some half a century. Now, as part of David's plan to make Jerusalem the religious heart of his kingdom, it was brought to the city and installed in a new Tabernacle. Its arrival was a scene of much rejoicing, as David danced before the ark. But Michal condemned the king for unseemly behavior, only to be told that what she saw as vulgar was appropriate in the eyes of the LORD. And God responded by making the queen barren.

Military conquest beyond the borders of the kingdom now became David's primary concern. First he defeated the Philistines decisively, so that they were no longer a major power in the region (although he would later have to fight a campaign to prevent their resurgence). He attacked Moab, Syria, Edom, and the Ammonites, expanding his realm and creating a substantial empire which commanded trade routes north via Damascus and south via the Red Sea port of Ezion-Geber. Now equipped with a strong force of chariots, the kingdom of Israel had become the dominant power in the region.

The glory of David's reign was now to be tarnished by a grievous sin, however. While his main army was fighting the Ammonites, David happened to see a beautiful woman bathing, called her to his presence, and they lay together. This was Bathsheba, wife of Uriah, a Hittite in David's royal guard then active at the siege of Rabbah. The king then sent a message to Joab, in command of the siege, to place Uriah in the forefront of the fighting, but then to ensure he became isolated from his comrades and was killed. This Joab did. Uriah died; Bathsheba mourned; and after a time became wife to David and bearing him a son.

But God was displeased at this ruthless act and sent Nathan to the king. Nathan told David a parable analogous to the king's own wicked behavior, the listener unwittingly declaring that the perpetrator should die. Then Nathan revealed the message of the story and judgment – that David had himself sinned and would be punished by the LORD. David repented, but God caused his son by Bathsheba to die.

More tragedies were to follow, for a callous rape then set in motion a sequence of grave family troubles for the House of David. Amnon, his eldest son by Ahinoam, raped his half-sister, Tamar, who fled to her brother Absalom. David's anger at this was, fatally, not followed by action, allowing Absalom's resentment to fester until, two years later, his men murdered Amnon. Absalom fled the king's wrath to Geshur, where he remained in exile for three years. Meanwhile David grieved at this family tragedy and the loss of his beloved son – until persuaded to allow his return. Even then, it was another two years before father and son would meet face to face.

In time, Absalom became accepted again in Jerusalem and began to assume the position of heir-apparent, openly soliciting the goodwill of the people. Meanwhile he quietly built up his own personal following and set in plan a well-concealed conspiracy.

When the time seemed ripe, Absalom struck, staging a coup that took David completely by surprise. David fled with his household, and Absalom took control of Jerusalem.

Ahithophel, Bathsheba's grandfather, had been one of David's wisest advisors, but had disapproved of the king's treatment of his daughter. Now he stayed in Jerusalem to counsel Absalom and advised Absalom to sleep with those of David's concubines that had remained in the city, which he did, committing a deep public insult to his father that ensured there could be no reconciliation between them.

But David sent back spies, the leader of whom, Hushai, soon won the trust of the usurper king. His military advice prevailed: that Absalom should gather his strength before attacking David rather than follow Ahithophel's advice and send a flying column to capture him and thereby risk ambush and the bad impression that losses would cause. This gave David time to rally his forces so that when Absalom's army met his, in a great battle in the forest of Ephraim, the usurper's forces were defeated. Absalom's short-lived reign ended in an accident – riding through the forest, he was caught by a branch, where David's men found the dangling king and dispatched him.

David returned to his capital, but another ill effect of his son's rebellion was soon to show itself – a break between Judah and the northern tribes. David's main supporters in putting down the revolt were from Judah, and when he returned to Jerusalem these troops accompanied him, arousing jealousy among the northerners. One of them, a Benjamite named Sheba, incited a further mutiny but won scant support. Cornered in Abel Beth Maacah, he was beheaded by the unsympathetic inhabitants and his head thrown over the walls to the royal troops preparing to besiege the place.

A famine struck the kingdom and lasted three years before David appealed to God, to be told that this was punishment upon the people for Saul's sin, committed many years earlier, against the Gibeonites, a number of whom Saul had treacherously slain. The sin must be expiated, so David had the representatives of the Gibeonites brought to his court in order to offer amends. They specified that seven male descendants of Saul be given up for execution and then their bodies exposed at Gibeon.

When David took a census of the fighting men in his realm, God was displeased and gave him a choice of three punishments: three years of famine; three months of fleeing his enemies; or three days of plague. The latter ensued until God directed David to the threshing-floor of Araunah, which he purchased and there built an altar for burnt sacrifice. The plague stopped.

COMMENTARY ON THE SECOND BOOK OF SAMUEL

The Second Book of Samuel. In chapters i.–iv., we have the history of David's reign in Hebron. He puts to death the Amalekite who professes to have slain Saul; and he laments bitterly over the death of Saul and Jonathan. Going up to Hebron he is anointed king a second time. Abner proclaims Ishbosheth, Saul's son, king in Mahanaim, and a civil war begins in which David gains the advantage. An account is given of his wives and children, then of Abner's quarrel with Ishbosheth, through which he offers to help David to gain the whole kingdom. In the course of these arrangements Abner is killed by Joab and Abishai, and soon after Ishbosheth is murdered by two of his captains, and thus the way is opened for David to become king of all Israel.

The next four chapters (v.–viii.) describe his rule and its glories. He is anointed for the third time. He conquers Jerusalem, the Jebusite city, and a palace is built for him there by Hiram, king of Tyre. The Philistines, invading the land, are defeated at Baal-perazim. David brings the ark from Kirjath-jearim, but leaves it, because of Uzzah's death, in the house of Obed-edom. After three months he takes it into Jerusalem, and proposes to build a temple for Jehovah. Nathan at first approves, but by a vision is directed to forbid David's purpose. His son shall build the house. David thanks God and is resigned. Heathen enemies attack him, but are all overcome. Next follows an account of the king's officers.

Chapter ix. contains a notice of David's friendship to Mephibosheth, the son of Jonathan.

In chapters x.–xx. is the narrative of David's great sin and its consequences. David's ambassadors were insulted by the king of the Ammonites. Hence war arose, the Ammonites being helped by the Syrians. These latter are defeated, and the war is concentrated on Rabbah, the capital of the Ammonites. While this siege is in progress David commits adultery with Bathsheba, and causes her husband Uriah to be slain in the battlefield. The king marries Bathsheba, but is rebuked for his sin by the parable of Nathan, and the child of Uriah's wife dies. David's repentance is accepted, and her second son Solomon is born, and is beloved of the LORD. But the punishment is not removed. Amnon's conduct towards his half-sister Tamar leads Absalom to kill him, for which he has to flee, but through Joab's management is recalled. Soon Absalom revolts against his father, and David goes away beyond Jordan. Hushai is sent back to Jerusalem to defeat the treacherous counsel of Ahithophel. Absalom takes possession of Jerusalem, and is advised by Ahithophel to pursue and slay his father. Hushai gives different advice, which is followed. David escapes, and Ahithophel hangs himself. David comes to Mahanaim in Gilead, where he receives much kindness and help from Barzillai and others, and whither he is pursued by Absalom. In a battle victory declares for David, and Absalom fleeing is caught by his head in a tree, and is killed by Joab. News of his death is brought to David, who grieves exceedingly for his son. Joab forces him to refrain himself, and both Israel and Judah are anxious to bring the king back to Jerusalem. On his way back

Shimei, who had cursed David when he went in flight, comes to meet him and to ask forgiveness. David settles the differences between Ziba and Mephibosheth about the land which Ziba had procured wrongly from David's grant. Barzillai accompanies the king to the river Jordan, but will not, for age, go further, yet sends his son Chimham on to Jerusalem. There arises jealousy between Judah and the other tribes about the haste of Judah in bringing back the king. Sheba, a Benjamite, stirs up the tribes to revolt, but he is pursued and killed at Abel-beth-maachah. A short list of David's officers concludes this portion.

In the remaining chapters (xxi.–xxiv.) are several unconnected matters. First how the Gibeonites sought and obtained vengeance on Saul's family for the slaughter of their kinsmen by him. Then follow notices of Philistine giants from whom David and his mighty men were in peril. Next is a psalm of thanksgiving, differing very slightly from Psalm xviii.: after which follows another psalm, the last words of David. This is followed by a list of David's warriors and their exploits, and the book closes with David's census of the people, by which God's anger is provoked. Gad, David's seer, is sent to offer the king a choice of punishments. He chooses pestilence, and when 70,000 of the people have died, David humbles himself. He is commanded to purchase the threshing-floor of Araunah, where he builds an altar, and offers sacrifices, and the plague ceases.

THE SECOND BOOK OF SAMUEL: CHAPTER BY CHAPTER

	1	Amalekite slain, who said he had killed Saul. David's lamentation for Saul and Jonathan.
Ishbosheth. **Joab.**	2	David, KING OF JUDAH. Ishbosheth, king of Israel. Abner, Ishbosheth's general. Joab, David's general. Mortal combat, twelve on a side battle. Asahel, Joab's brother, pursues Abner, who slays him. Joab stays the pursuit of Israel.

Abner.	3	David's wives and sons. Abner, and Rizpah, the concubine. Abner reproved, revolts to David. Micah, Saul's daughter, restored to David. Joab slays Abner. David mourns for him.
	4	Ishbosheth murderd by two of his captains. David executes Ishbosheth's murderers.

David, king.
 	
Hiram.
	5	David, KING OF ALL ISRAEL.
		David takes the citadel of Jerusalem from the
		    Jebusites.
		Intercourse with Hiram, king of Tyre.
		Sons born to David in Jerusalem.
		Philistines smitten at Baal-perazim.
		Philistines smitten again in the valley of
		    Raphaim.

	6	David attempts to remove the ark to Jerusalem. Uzzah smitten for touching the ark. The ark in Obed-edom's house. David removes the ark to Zion; dancing before it. Michal ridicules David and is punished.
	7	David purposes to build the temple. Divine promises to David's seed. David's prayer and thanksgiving.
	8	David's conquests and spoils.
Mephibosheth.	9	David's kindness to Mephibosheth, Jonathan's son. Ziba is to serve him.
	10	David's ambassadors insulted by Hanun, king of the Ammonites. The Ammonites and Syrians defeated.
Uriah.	11	David's adultery with Bathsheba. David causes the death of Uriah.
	12	Nathan's parable of the ewe-lamb. David's repentance. Death of Bathsheba's child. Solomon's birth. Joab takes Rabbah.
	13	Amnon's base treatment of his sister Tamar. Absalom's revengeful murder of Amnon. Absalom flees to Geshur.
	14	Joab procures the woman of Tekoah to get Absalom restored. David recalls Absalom.

Absalom.	15	Absalom's rebellion. David's flight. Fidelity of Ittai, the Gittite. Zadok and Abiathar sent back with the ark of God. Hushai sent back to defeat Ahithophel's counsel.
Shimei.	16	Ziba falsely accuses his master, Mephibosheth. Shimei curses David. Ahithophel's counsel.
	17	Hushai defeats the counsel of Ahithophel. Escape of Jonathan and Ahimaaz, messengers to David. David retreats over Jordan. Ahithophel hangs himself. Shobi, Machir and Barzillae, show kindness to David.
	18	David's army and victory. Absalom slain. David's grief.
	19	David roused from his mourning. Shimei pardoned. Mephibosheth justifies himself. Barzillae and David.
Sheba.	20	Insurrection of Sheba, to draw off the ten tribes. Amasa appointed to collect an army. Joab, jealous of Amasa, kills him. Sheba decapitated at Abel. David's chief officers.
Seven of Saul's sons executed.	21	Judgment of famine, for Saul's cruelty to the Gibeonites. Execution of seven of Saul's sons in atonement. Rizpah's care over her sons' bodies. David gathers and buries the bones of Saul and his family. More wars with the Philistines and their giants.
	22	Psalm xviii. varied.
	23	David's last words. David's mighty men.
	24	David numbers the people. God offers David famine, war or pestilence. Altar reared in the threshing-floor of Araunah (Ornan), the Jebusite.

I KINGS

Death of David; Solomon chosen as King. His wisdom, and falling away to idolatry. The kingdom divided. Elijah the Prophet.

THE ESSENTIAL STORY OF I KINGS

David was now very old and close to death. Influenced by Bathsheba, David chose as his successor Solomon, her eldest surviving son. He inherited a realm that was strong, prosperous, and at peace. Solomon's reign was a golden age of Israel, fed by bountiful trade, and famous for its dazzling wealth.

Solomon's first actions were to secure his throne, which included the execution of his half-brother Adonijah, the rightful heir to the throne in terms of simple primogeniture, who had insolently asked for the hand of the old king's concubine, Abishag. Solomon doubtless saw him as a threat to his throne.

At Gibeon, God appeared to Solomon, and the new king asked for guidance and a discerning heart to govern God's people and to distinguish between right and wrong, which pleased the LORD. And indeed, wisdom, quite apart from wealth, was the quality that impressed visitors – not only sound judgment in all things, but a knowledge and erudition on all manner of subjects.

The crowning centerpiece of Solomon's reign was the construction of the great Temple. Building began in the fourth year of his reign and took seven years. The Bible provides a very detailed description of its dimensions, decoration, and furnishings. Built of both stone and wood, it featured prominently the famed

Trading ships bringing treasures.

cedars of Lebanon, provided by Solomon's friend and ally, Hiram of Tyre. The general plan followed that of the Tabernacle, which had traveled through the Wilderness with Moses from Egypt to the Promised Land. In the inner sanctum was installed the Ark of the Covenant, which David had brought up to Zion. Solomon dedicated the Temple in a fourteen-day festival, during which he is recorded as having sacrificed 22,000 cattle and 120,000 sheep and goats.

For the second time, God appeared to Solomon, accepting his Temple, but issuing a stern warning against non-observance of his commands and decrees.

Solomon also built a great royal palace, similarly ornamented and fitted out in sumptuous style, and he made use of the expertise of Hiram's people to build a fleet of trading ships on the Red Sea coast. These vessels plied their trade in three-yearly voyages, returning with gold, silver, ivory, and even apes and baboons.

The brilliance of the realm and its ruler attracted the attention of surrounding nations, and Solomon's distinguished guests included the daughter of Pharaoh of Egypt, and the Queen of Sheba, who came from her country far to the south. She arrived with a huge caravan laden with spices, gold, and precious stones, and was afforded a spectacular welcome.

But in the end, for all his wisdom and wealth, Solomon did not live up to God's expectations of him. Significantly he failed to observe God's commandments forbidding intermarriage with foreigners, and the Bible tells us that he proceeded to take 700 wives of royal birth and 300 concubines. Worse, these women brought their own religions, which Solomon accommodated, so that he gradually ceased to be fully devoted to God. This angered God: Solomon and the Israelites had been warned repeatedly; God promised that upon Solomon's death he would tear the kingdom in two.

Upon the death of Solomon, Rehoboam became king, but, as God had told Solomon, there was to be punishment for Solomon's breaking of the Covenant and God's commands. Internal strife in the kingdom, provoked by the king's heavy handed imposition of taxes and promises of a stern rule, led to a rebellion of the ten northern tribes, who broke away, Jeroboam setting himself up as king of Israel, with his capital city at Samaria. This was to become a permanent division, despite efforts by several kings to reunite the Jews.

Jeroboam was fearful of the effect of the pilgrimages his subjects would make to Jerusalem and to the Temple there, so he took measures to create a new priesthood and bull-calf idols, which he set up at Bethel and Dan, thus subverting the people from their religion. He proceeded with this heedless of the warnings given him by the blind prophet Ahijah of Shiloh: his actions condemned him in the eyes of God, and his dynasty was doomed.

Elijah was one of the most forceful prophets, strong in his determination to champion the Hebrew God (his name literally meant "Yahweh is my God") and to turn the Israelites back from the worship of idols – for Ahab, king of Israel, listened to the entreaties of his Tyrian wife, Jezebel, and introduced the worship of Melkart, the Phoenician version of Baal. Elijah warned him that God's punishment would be a drought. When this came about, Elijah went into in the wilderness, reassured by God that he would find water from a stream and would be fed by bread and flesh brought him by ravens. Many in Israel perished, but at Zarephath Elijah came upon a widow and her child who were on the verge of starving to death; miraculously, her flour, oil, and water did not run out, and Elijah saved the life of the child.

On returning to the king, Elijah challenged him to a contest of faith: two sacrificial altars were to be built, one to Baal, the other to the Hebrew God. This took place on Mount Carmel. The priests of Baal (the Bible accounts them as 450 prophets of Baal) set a bullock upon their altar, but despite a day of entreaties to their god could not provide divine fire to kindle the wood. Elijah's demonstration was made more demanding by thoroughly wetting the sacrifice, the wood and stones, and even by filling a trench around the altar with water. But when Elijah prayed, fire fell upon victim, wood, stone and even consumed the water. The people loudly acclaimed the victory of the Hebrew God; the priests of Baal were taken away and slaughtered.

Now came an end to the drought; heavy rain was about to fall, and Elijah warned the king. But he would not heed, and went off to eat and drink. When the rain fell, very heavily, the power of the LORD came upon Elijah and he ran faster than the king's chariot.

Seething with rage, meanwhile, Jezebel planned her revenge upon the prophet. But before her soldiers could seize him, Elijah fled into the southern wilderness of Judah. Despite the triumph of the two altars, Elijah felt desolate and hopeless and even asked God for death. But God sent an angel to minister to him, and eventually Elijah found refuge in a cave on Mount Horeb. Here a great wind, earthquake, and fire erupted all around before God revealed himself to the prophet in a "still small voice," reassuring him and revealing that Hazael would become king of Syria, Jehu king of Israel, and that Elisha would be Elijah's successor.

Despite the lesson of the two altars, King Ahab continued his wicked ways. A man called Naboth owned a particularly good vineyard in the region of Jezreel, and Ahab attempted to force him into selling it to the king. He refused, so Jezebel brought trumped-up charges against the poor man, accusing him of cursing the king and God. False witnesses acquired his committal and he was duly stoned to death. When Elijah heard about this, he confronted Ahab and his wife and assured them that they would pay for their sins; which, in time, they did. Upon Ahab's demise, Ahaziah proved as unworthy a successor as could be expected from this dynasty.

COMMENTARY ON THE FIRST BOOK OF KINGS

The **First Book of Kings** is separated from 2 Kings in the midst of the reign of Ahab's family over Israel without anything in the narrative which makes a proper break.

In chapters i.—xi. is given the history of the undivided kingdom. (i) On account of David's feebleness Adonijah tries to secure the kingdom, and this action leads to the anointing and coronation of Solomon. Adonijah is pardoned, and (ii) David before his death gives a charge to Solomon with special reference to Joab and Shimei. On his accession Solomon executes his father's injunctions, and also deprives Abiathar of the high-priesthood. (iii) He marries Pharaoh's daughter. God, in a vision at Gibeon, offers him a choice, and he chooses wisdom. His wisdom is made widely known by his decision in the case of a child claimed by two mothers. (iv) He parcels out the land under governors, and arranges how his own table shall be supplied by them. He prospers, and his dominion is wide. Wise people from other lands gather to him. (v) Hiram, king of Tyre, sends congratulations to Solomon, and undertakes to supply wood and workmen for the proposed temple. An account follows of the preparations for the building. (vi) Then a description of the building itself, which occupied seven years and a half. (vii) Thirteen years are spent in building Solomon's own house. Hiram does much of the work for the furniture of the temple and its court. (viii) Solomon brings the ark from the city of David to its place in the temple. The glory of the LORD fills the house. Solomon blesses the congregation, and with solemn prayer dedicates the temple. He offers many sacrifices, and the feast of tabernacles is kept for twice its usual length. (ix) The LORD answers Solomon in a vision, as at Gibeon. After this follows an account of the cities which Solomon built, and the levies needed for this work: of his navy, on the

Red Sea, and (x) of the visit of the Queen of Sheba: of Solomon's revenue, riches and fame: (xi) of his wives, and how by them he was drawn into idolatry. By this God's anger was provoked, and adversaries were raised up against Solomon; and to Jeroboam it was promised, by Ahijah the prophet, that ten of the twelve tribes should be rent away from the hand of Solomon. Solomon dies, and is succeeded by his son Rehoboam.

From chapter xii. to 2 Kings, chapter viii., the history is occupied with the two rival kingdoms until the overthrow of the house of Ahab. (xii) Rehoboam's refusal to relieve the burdens of the people causes ten tribes to revolt. He prepares to fight against Jeroboam, the king chosen by the revolted tribes, but is forbidden to do so. The calves are set up in Dan and Bethel, the priesthood thrown open to all the people, and a change made in the time of the feast of tabernacles. (xiii) A man of God is sent to Bethel to prophesy against the altar there. He is deceived by another prophet, and killed by a lion for his disobedience. (xiv) Sickness and death of Jeroboam's son. Jeroboam is succeeded by his son Nadab. Evil doings of Judah under Rehoboam, for which they are chastised by an invasion of Shishak, king of Egypt. (xv) Abijam, the son of Rehoboam, follows his father's bad example, but his son Asa attempts to suppress idolatry. He makes a league with Benhadad, king of Syria, against Baasha king of Israel. Baasha had murdered Nadab, and was a wicked king. (xvi) A prophecy against him by Jehu, the son of Hanani. Elah, son of Baasha, succeeds his father, and is murdered by Zimri, who after a seven days' reign takes his own life. A short civil war in Israel follows, after which Omri reigns and builds Samaria, and surpasses all former kings in wickedness, but is surpassed in evil by Ahab his son, who, having married Jezebel the daughter of the king of Zidon, introduces Baal-worship into the land. (xvii) Now we have an account of Elijah's struggle for the pure worship. He prophesies against Ahab, and, in consequence, must hide himself. He is fed by ravens at the brook Cherith. Thence he is sent to Zarephath, to a widow, where he and she are miraculously sustained. (xviii) From Zarephath he comes to meet Ahab, and in a contest with the priests of Baal puts them to shame, and they are subsequently slain by the people. (xix) Elijah is threatened by Jezebel and flees to Horeb, where he is divinely commissioned to anoint Hazael king over Syria, Jehu king over Israel, and Elisha to be prophet in his room, which latter order alone he fulfils. (xx) Benhadad besieges Samaria. The Syrians are overcome, but Ahab lets Benhadad go, for which God's anger and judgment against him are proclaimed by a prophet. (xxi) Ahab covets Naboth's vineyard, and Jezebel contrives that Naboth shall be put to death. Elijah pronounces God's judgment on both king and queen. (xxii) Ahab obtains the help of Jehoshaphat king of Judah, son of Asa, in a war with Syria. The false prophets encourage him, but Micaiah foretells his defeat. Jehoshaphat is in much danger and Ahab is killed, and the dogs lick his blood. Jehoshaphat reigns well in Judah, but Ahaziah, the son of Ahab, follows his father's evil ways, as well as those of Jeroboam.

At this point, an arbitrary break is made, and the First Book of Kings ends.

THE FIRST BOOK OF KINGS: CHAPTER BY CHAPTER

Nathan. **Solomon.**	1	Abishag cherishes David. Adonijah's rebellion. Zadock, Benaiah, Nathan, &c., adhere to David. Nathan speaks to Bathsheba. Bathsheba speaks to David. Nathan meets Bathsheba and David. David commands Solomon to be proclaimed. Adonijah breaks up a feast. He flees to the horns of the altar.
Adonijah. **Abiathar.**	2	David's charge to Solomon. David dies. Adonijah aspires to marry Abishag. Solomon executes Adonijah. Abiathar deprived of his priesthood. Joab executed. Benaiah succeeds to Joab, and Zadok to Abiathar. Shimei executed.
	3	Solomon marries Pharoah's daughter. He sacrifices at Gibeon, and God appears to him. Solomon asks for an understanding heart. Solomon's wise decision between two women.
	4	Solomon's officers. Solomon's wisdom.

Hiram.	5	Hiram grants timber to Solomon. Solomon's workmen.
Temple.	6	Building of Solomon's temple.
	7	Building of Solomon's house. Building of house for Pharoah's daughter. Pillars, vessels &c. made for temple.
	8	Feast of dedication of temple. Solomon's prayer. Solomon blesses the people. He offers sacrifice and holds a feast.
	9	God's covenant with Solomon. Solomon and Hiram exchange presents. Solomon's Gentile bondsmen. Solomon's three-yearly sacrifices. Solomon's navy fetches gold.
Queen of Sheba.	10	The Queen of Sheba and Solomon. Solomon's gold. His ivory throne. His chariots and horses. His tribute.
Solomon & wives.	11	Solomon's wives and concubines. Solomon seduced to idolatry. Hadad the Edomite, Solomon's adversary. Rezon, King of Syria, Solomon's adversary. Jeroboam, Solomon's adversary. Prophet Ahijah rends Jeroboam's garment. Predicts the rending of the tribes, and making Jeroboam king. 40.*–Solomon dies.
REHOBOAM. **Revolt of the ten tribes.** *Jeroboam.*	12	REHOBOAM made king of Judah. His foolish conduct. Ten tribes revolt. Adoram killed. Rehoboam forbidden to attack the ten tribes. *Jeroboam* made king of Israel. Sets up two golden calves in Bethel and Dan.
	13	Jeroboam's profane offering. Prediction of Josiah's birth (fulfilled 275 years later). Jeroboam's hand withers. The old prophet in Bethel. The man of God slain by a lion.

Shishak.	14	Sickness of Jeroboam's son Abijah. His wife inquires about it of Ahijah. Denunciation against Jeroboam, "who made Israel to sin". **22.–** Jeroboam dies. Idolatry of Judah. Invaded by Shishak Treasures of Jerusalem carried away. **17.–** Rehoboam dies.
ABIJAM. ASA.	15	ABIJAM succeeds his father Rehoboam as King of Judah. His bad character. Wars with Israel. **3.–** Abijam dies. ASA succeeds Abijam over Judah. His good character. Deposes his mother, the queen regent, for idolatry. Wars with Israel.
JEHOSAPHAT. *Nadab.* *Baasha.*	15	Makes a league with Benhadad, king of Syria. **41.–** Asa dies of diseased feet. JEHOSAPHAT succeeds Asa. **2.–** *Nadab,* son of Jeroboam succeeds him. *Baasha* slays Nadab, and usurps the throne. He reigns in Tirzah. He destroys the house of Jeroboam. His own bad character.
Elah. *Zimri.* *Omri.* *Ahab.* Jezebel.	16	Jehu's prophecy against Baasha. **24.–** Baasha's death and burial in Tirzah. *Elah,* his son succeeds him. **2.–** Elah killed in Tirzah, when drunk, by Zimri a captain. **7 days.–** *Zimri* reigns and slays Baasha's house. *Omri* made king by the army. Zimri burns himself in his palace. The people divide for Tibni, how falls. Omri builds Samaria, a new capital. His wicked character. **11.–** Dies and is buried in Samaria. *Ahab,* his son succeeds him. Marries Jezebel, an idolatress. Jericho rebuilt by Hiel, the Bethelite.
Elijah. Ravens feed Elijah.	17	Elijah predicts famine, on account of Ahab. Ravens feed him at the brook Cherith. The prophet multiplies the oil and meal of the widow of Zarephath. Raises her dead son.

	18	Famine for Samaria. Good Obadiah meets Elijah. His kindness to the prophets. Meeting between Ahab and Elijah. Elijah challenges Baal's priests. The sacrifice on Mount Carmel. A great rain.
Elijah at Horeb.	19	Jezebel threatens Elijah. Elijah in the wilderness. An angel feeds him. Fasts forty days and forty nights. At Horeb, the mount of God. God appears to Elijah in a cave. Elijah commanded to anoint Hazael, and Jehu, and Elisha. Elisha leaves the plough and follows Elijah.
Benhadad. **Syrians defeated.**	20	Benhadad besieges Samaria. The Syrians defeated. They renew their armies and return. The Syrians again defeated. Benhadad's humiliation and covenant. The smitten prophet predicts the consequences of sparing Benhadad.
Naboth.	21	Ahab wants Naboth's vineyard. Jezebel plans Naboth's destruction. Ahab takes the vineyard. He is threatened and repents.
Ahaziah.	22	Jehoshaphat aids Ahab to recover Ramoth-Gilead. Zedekiah, and other false prophets, encourage Ahab. Micaiah predicts his death, and is imprisoned. Jehoshaphat's narrow escape. Ahab shot between joints of the harness. Dogs lick up his blood and he is buried. **21.**–Length of Ahab's reign. *Ahaziah,* his son, succeeds Ahab. His ships sent to Ophir. Account of Jehoshaphat's reign. **25.**– Jehoshaphat dies, and is buried in the city of David. Ahaziah serves Baal.

Notes:
So that the reader may easily distinguish, the names of the kings of Judah are printed in CAPITALS, and the names of the kings of Israel are printed in *italics.*

*The figures placed preceding the death of any king mark the length of his reign.

II KINGS

**Bad kings. Elijah's mantle passed to Elisha.
Israel taken into captivity in Babylon.**

THE ESSENTIAL STORY OF II KINGS

One day a serious accident befell Ahaziah, the idolatrous king of Israel, and he sent to the priests for assurance of his recovery – not to the priests of God, but to those of Baal-zebub, the fly god. Elijah intercepted the messengers and sent back to Ahaziah the unwelcome message from God that he would assuredly die, so the king sent soldiers to seize him. Elijah called down fire upon two detachments of these troops; the third approached the prophet meekly, and he accompanied them back to court, where he stood, unafraid, and repeated the message of doom.

The end of Elijah's prophetic ministry was as dramatic as the rest of his life. In company with Elisha, whom he knew to be his successor, he traveled from Bethel to Jericho and on across the Jordan, parting the waters in style by striking them with his cloak. Then a chariot of fire, pulled by fiery horses, descended and Elijah was taken up to Heaven in a whirlwind, leaving Elisha to take on the burden of his work.

Elisha's ministry as a prophet was characterized by gentle acts of mercy. People and kings came to him for help and intercession with God, and, after praying to God each time, he was able to perform miracles. For example, when a delegation asked him to cure the unhealthy water of their town, not far from Jericho, he asked for a bowl of salt and threw this into the spring in question, and the water immediately became wholesome.

Another miracle concerning water took place when the kings of Judah, Israel, and Edom took the field with armies to crush a revolt of the Moabites and found themselves in a critical situation with water running out. Elisha was called for, and he instructed the kings to dig trenches; next morning, these were filled with water.

The River Jordan too was the location of one of his miracles, when his companions persuaded him that they should build new dwellings by the river. As construction proceeded, one of them dropped an axe – which they had borrowed – into the river. Elisha threw his stick into the water, whereupon the axehead surfaced and they hooked it out.

A Shunammite woman longing for a child asked Elisha to intercede with God, and she bore a son, who grew but then died. Elisha made haste to the woman's house, lay spreadeagled upon the body, and the child was miraculously brought back to life.

One day a widow appealed to Elisha to help with her late husband's debts. He told her to ask her neighbors if she could borrow empty jars and instructed her to pour oil into them. Miraculously, she kept pouring but the oil did not run out, so she was able to sell many jars of oil to pay off the debts. In a similar miracle, Elisha once fed a hundred people with but twenty loaves of bread.

Naaman, an officer in the army of the king of Aram, suffered from a bad skin disease, and his girl servant, who was a captive Israelite, suggested consulting the prophet. Elisha told the man to bathe seven times in the Jordan, which the officer did, with disappointing results, for he had expected instant relief. His servants rebuked him for his attitude and he went again to the Jordan and was cured. This story ends with the deceitful action of Elisha's servant, Gehazi. When the officer offered Elisha a reward for his cure, the prophet would have none of it. But later the servant returned to the officer, said Elisha had changed his mind, and received money. However, Gehazi could not hide his sin from Elisha: in punishment, his hand became leprous.

During a period of conflict between the Aramaeans and the kingdom of Israel, the Aramaeans became frustrated when they discovered that Elisha was able to warn the Jews of their enemy's deployments. So the king of Aram sent troops to seize the prophet, surrounding him at Doham. Elisha prayed to God, and the enemy were made blind, and he led them captive to the king of Israel, whose instinct was, of course, to kill them all. But Elisha stopped him, counseling him to feast and entertain them, which he reluctantly did. Then the Aramaeans were sent on their way and promised to stop their raids.

Even a prophet can run out of patience, however. One day Elisha was out walking when a gang of youths jeered at him; by now he had lost his hair, and they called him "thou bald head." Perhaps in slight over-reaction, Elisha called forth two bears, which proceeded to chase and maul the insulting youths.

When Elisha was on his death-bed, he received a visit from King Joash, who lamented the passing of the prophet (which was rich indeed, considering the nature of this king's reign). The old prophet told him to shoot an arrow through the east window (in the direction of Damascus), and told him that this was the arrow of victory he would win over Aram at Aphek. Then he told the king to strike the ground with his arrows, which he did, three times. Elisha told him those three blows symbolized three victories; but that he should have struck five times, and would then have won a complete victory.

Kings 2 is also concerned with the horrible death of the wicked queen Jezebel, and battles between the kings of Judah and the kings of Israel. Jehu was the king of Israel who led the destruction of Ahab's line. As well as killing Jehoram, King of Judah, in battle and fatally wounding Jehoram's son Ahaziah, Jehu had seventy of Ahab's sons executed, along with a further forty-two of the dynasty. Unfortunately, the throne of Judah was then seized by Athaliah, the mother of Ahaziah. By God's mercy, the child-heir Joash was saved from Athaliah's cruelty and after her death he became king and ended the idolatry which the nation had embraced. He was murded by his own servants and the subsequent kings returned to wickedness and idolatry. Eventually, part of Israel is conquered and taken into captivity by Tiglath-pileser, king of Assyria.

After the captivity of Israel, Hezekiah succeeded to the throne of Judah, and tried to rid the nation of idolatry. The nation was still under severe threat from the Assyrians, now led by King Sennacherib, however. The prophet Isaiah proved a support to Hezekiah, but foretold the captivity of the people of Judah and the exile to Babylon after the death of the reforming king. Hezekiah was followed by two bad kings, Manasseh and Amon, and a good king, Josiah on the throne. Huldah the prophetess foretold the destruction of Jerusalem, but not in Josiah's lifetime. Eventually, the nation was invaded and after the final siege of Jerusalem the king Zedekiah was blinded and taken away to Babylon. Jerusalem was overthrown, and the Temple sacked.

The book finishes with a supplemental notice of the liberation of King Jehoiachin from his prison at Babylon, twenty-six years later, and a still further extension to Jehoiachin's death, the time of which is not known, but which was probably not long after his liberation.

The death of Jezebel.

COMMENTARY ON THE SECOND BOOK OF KINGS

The Second Book of Kings commences with (i) a short notice of the rebellion of Moab against Israel. Ahaziah, king of Israel, injured by an accident, sends to consult Baal-zebub, god of Ekron. Elijah meets the messengers and sends them back to tell Ahaziah he shall not recover. The prophet calls down fire on those who would have seized him. Ahaziah dies. (ii) Elijah is carried to heaven by a whirlwind. A double portion of his spirit descends on Elisha. He divides the Jordan, heals the water at Jericho, and is mocked at Bethel, and the lads who mocked him are torn by bears. (iii) Jehoram, brother of Ahaziah, is king over Israel: puts away the image of Baal. He goes against Moab and is helped by Jehoshaphat and by the king of Edom. The king of Moab makes a desperate resistance. (iv) Elisha multiplies the widow's oil; raises to life the son of the hospitable Shunammite woman; heals the deadly pottage at Gilgal, and satisfies one hundred men with twenty loaves. (v) He heals the leprosy of Naaman the Syrian, with which disease Gehazi is smitten. (vi) He gives leave to the sons of the prophets to enlarge their dwelling, and causes an axehead to swim: he discloses the plans of the king of Syria, who sends men to seize him. Samaria is besieged, and there is a terrible famine. (vii) Elisha foretells plenty on the morrow. Flight of the Syrians, leaving their stores of provisions to the Israelites. (viii) The Shunammite lady has her lands restored for Elisha's sake. Hazael is told by Elisha that he shall be king of Syria. He departs and murders his master. Wicked reigns of Jehoram and Ahaziah in Judah. Ahaziah goes with Joram, king of Israel, to war at Ramoth-gilead, and visits that king at Jezreel when he is, wounded.

From chapters ix. to xvii., we have the history of the fall of the house of Ahab, and the events which occurred before the captivity of the ten tribes. (ix) Jehu is anointed king of Israel, to destroy the house of Ahab. He slays Joram in the field of Naboth, and wounds to the death Ahaziah, king of Judah, who was with him in Jezreel. Jezebel's dead body is eaten by the dogs. (x) Jehu has seventy of Ahab's sons beheaded, and destroys Ahab's line, and forty-two brethren of Ahaziah. He gains the support of Jehonadab the son of Rechab, and puts down the worship of Baal.

Israel begins to be cut off, Hazael smiting it on the east side. (xi) Athaliah, mother of Ahaziah, usurps the throne of Judah, and kills all the seed royal except the youthful Joash. By the plans of Jehoiada, Athaliah is slain, and an end is made of Baal-worship in Judah. (xii) Joash at first reigns well in Judah. He gives orders for the repair of the house of God, and sees it carried out. He procures the withdrawal of Hazael from Jerusalem. At last he is slain by his own servants. (xiii) Jehoahaz reigns wickedly in Israel, and Jehoash as wickedly after him. That king came to Elisha on his death-bed, and was promised a partial victory over the Syrians. A dead man is raised to life by touching Elisha's bones. (xiv) The good reign of Amaziah in Judah. He punishes the murderers of his father, and conquers the Edomites, but having provoked Jehoash, king of Israel, he is defeated by him and disgraced. Amaziah is murdered by a conspiracy, and is succeeded by his son Azariah (Uzziah), who recovers for Judah the port of Elath on the Red Sea. The success of Jeroboam the second. He restores the boundaries of Israel as the prophet Jonah had foretold. (xv) Azariah reigns well in Judah, but is struck with leprosy. Zechariah, the last of the line of Jehu, reigns ill in Israel and is murdered by Shallum, who after a month's rule is slain by Menahem, who is a very cruel king. He buys the help of the Assyrians. He is succeeded by a wicked son, Pekahiah, whom Pekah slays, but reigns as wickedly. Pekah is murdered, and the northern tribes are carried into captivity by Tiglath-pileser, king of Assyria. Jotham king of Judah. Rezin king of Syria, and Pekah king of Israel, sent by the LORD against Judah. (xvi) Ahaz reigns wickedly. He obtains help against Syria and Israel from Tiglath-pileser. Sets up a new altar, in the temple court at Jerusalem, after the fashion of one he had seen in Damascus. The house of the LORD much injured. (xvii) Hoshea, who had murdered Pekah, is king over Israel, but after a time is put down by the king of Assyria, who found him treacherous, and the rest of the ten tribes are now carried away. The reason of their downfall was their forgetfulness of Jehovah. Heathen nations are brought to occupy the land of Israel, and seeking to know something of the God of the land, there results a mixed religion.

In the succeeding chapters (xviii.—xxv.) we read the history of Judah after the captivity of Israel. (xviii) Hezekiah comes after

Aliaz, and institutes many reforms. Sennacherib, king of Assyria, invading Judah, is bought off at first by tribute, but sends afterwards his embassy to induce the people to revolt; (xix) Hezekiah is comforted by Isaiah. Sennacherib sends a blasphemous letter. Isaiah foretells his overthrow, which is wrought by a divinely sent plague, that destroys a great part of his army. He returns to Assyria, and is murdered by his two sons. (xx) Hezekiah receives from the LORD a message of death, but, in answer to his prayer, fifteen years more of life are granted him. Berodach-baladan, king of Babylon, sends an embassy to Hezekiah, who boastfully shews them his treasures. Isaiah foretells the Babylonian captivity. Hezekiah meekly accepts the message. An account is given of his works and his death. (xxi) His son Manasseh succeeds him, and sins by idolatry and cruelty. Amon follows, who is also wicked, and is murdered, but the populace punish the murderers, and put his son Josiah on the throne. (xxii) Josiah's good reign. He repairs the house of the LORD. The book of the law is found, and inquiry is made of Huldah the prophetess. She foretells the destruction of Jerusalem, but not in Josiah's lifetime. (xxiii) The king assembles the people and reads them the law. He destroys all traces of idolatry, both in Judaea and in Samaria. He holds a memorable Passover feast, and is praised above all kings, yet the sins of Manasseh could not go unpunished. Going against Pharaohnecoh, king of Egypt, Josiah is slain in battle. His son Jehoahaz has a short but evil reign, and is deposed by Pharaoh-necoh, who puts his brother Eliakim (Jehoiakim) on the throne, who also reigns wickedly. (xxiv) Being subdued by Nebuchadnezzar, king of Babylon, he rebels, and brings upon the land an invasion of Chaldeans and others. At his death, he is followed in the kingdom, and in his wickedness, by his son Jehoiachin, who, with all but the poorest people, is carried to Babylon. The king of Babylon makes Zedekiah king, who soon rebelled against him. (xxv) Then came the final siege of Jerusalem; Zedekiah is blinded and taken away to Babylon. Jerusalem is overthrown, and all its treasures carried away. Gedaliah was set over the few people left in the land, but he is slain, and the people make their way into Egypt. King Jehoiachin, in his captivity, finds favor with Evilmerodach, king of Babylon.

Zedekiah, blinded, is taken captive to Babylon.

THE SECOND BOOK OF KINGS: CHAPTER BY CHAPTER

Elijah and captains. *Jehoram.*	1	Ahaziah falls through a lattice. Inquires of Baal-zebub respecting his recovery. Warned by Elijah of his death. Twice sends captains to take him. Fire from heaven consumes them. Elijah tells the king he shall surely die; and he dies. Jehoram, his brother, succeeds him.
Elijah's ascent. **Elisha and bears.**	2	Elijah divides Jordan. Ascends to heaven. Drops his mantle, taken up by Elisha. Elisha divides Jordan. He heals the waters of Jericho. Bears kill his mockers.
Elisha and Moabites.	3	Jeroram's evil reign. Mesha, king of Moab, rebels. Jehosaphat aids Jehoram against Mesha. Miraculous supply of water. Moabites' singular defeat owing to the red water. King of Moab sacrifices his eldest son.

Widow's oil.	4	Elisha multiplies the widow's oil. Elisha promises the Shunamite at son. Elisha restores her dead son to life. Elisha rectifies the deadly pottage at Gilgal. Elisha feeds 100 men with twenty loaves.
Naaman's leprosy.	5	Naaman cured of his leprosy. Elisha's servant, Gehazi, smitten with it.
Elisha and Syrians. **Samaria besieged.**	6	Elisha restores the lost axe. Discloses the king of Syria's counsel. Blindness of the Syrians at Dothan. Siege of Samaria. Woman boils her son. Jehoram threatens the life of Elisha.
Seige raised.	7	Elisha predicts plenty in Samaria. The four lepers at the gate. Flight of the Syrians. The unbelieving LORD trodden to death.
   Hazael. **JEHORAM.** **AHAZIAH.**	8	The Shunamite's land restored. Benhadad sick. Elisha predicts his death. Hazael stifles Benhadad and usurps the throne of Syria. JEHORAM succeeds his father, Jehosaphat, in Judah (or reigns with him). He marries Ahab's daughter (grandaughter of Omri), and does evil. Edom and Libnah revolt from Judah. 8.*–Joram (or Jehoram) dies. AHAZIAH succeeds his father, Joram. Jehoram of Israel wounded by the Syrians at Ramoth-gilead. Ahaziah visits him at Jezreel.
  Jehu.	9	Elisha sends a young prophet to anoint Jehu at Ramoth-gilead. Jehu made king of Israel. He kills Jehoram in his chariot. Ahaziah wounded and dies. Jezebel's awful death.
    The prophets of Baal. **Jehoahaz.**	10	Ahab's seventy sons slain. Forty-two of his kindred slain. Jonadab, the son of Rechab, joins Jehu. The prophets of Baal slain and his temple destroyed. Jehu worships the golden calves. 28.–he dies and is buried in Samaria. Jehoahaz succeeds his father Jehu.

JOASH.	11	ATHALIAH, the mother of Ahaziah, usurps the throne of Judah. She murders the seed royal. Ahaziah's sister, Jehosheba, hides his son Joash. JOASH, in six years, crowned king, be Jehoidah. Athaliah slain.
	12	JOASH (also called JEHOASH) repairs the temple. Presents the hallowed treasures to Hazael. 39.–Murdered by his servants. Succeeded by his son, Amaziah.
Jehoahaz.	13	Jehoahaz, the son of Jehu, is king of Israel. Saved, by prayer, from Hazael. Israel still idolatrous. 17.–Jehoahaz dies and is buried in Samaria.
Jehoash.	13	Jehoash, his son, reigns. Weeps over Elisha when dying. Commanded to shoot and to strike with arrows, as signs of smiting Syria. Moabite bands invade the land. Elisha's bones raise a dead man. Hazael succeeded by Benhadad in Syria. Jehoash recovers the cities of Israel from the Syrians.
AMAZIAH. **AZARIAH.** *Jeroboam.* *Zachariah.*	14	AMAZIAH executes this father's murderers. His victory over Edom. Wars with Jehoash, king of Israel. Jehoash's parable of the thistle and cedar. Amaziah defeated and captured by Jehoash. Jehoash carries away the treasures of the temple. 16.– Jehoash dies, and his son Jeroboam succeeds him. 29.– Amaziah murderd at Lachish, and buried at Jerusalem. Succeeded by his son AZARIAH (also called UZZIAH). Jeroboam, son of Jehoash, reigns in Samaria. Recovers Damascus and Hamath. 41.– Dies, and is succeeded by his son Zachariah.

Shallum.	15	Azariah a leper. 52.– Dies, and is succeeded by his son Jotham. 6 months.– Zachariah murdered by Shallum. Shallum, an usurper over Israel. Prophecy concerning Jehu's family fulfilled. 1 month.– Shallum murdered by Menahem.
Menahem.		Menahem, the cruel king of Israel. His barbarities at Tiphsah. Bribes Pul, king of Syria, who invades him. 10.–Menahem dies, and is succeeded by his son
Pekahiah.		Pekahiah. 2.– Pekahiah murdered by Pekah.
Pekah. **Captivity begun.**		Pekah usurps the throne. Tilgath-pileser, king of Assyria, begins the captivity of the ten tribes. 20.– Pekah murdered by Hoshea.
JOTHAM.		JOTHAM reigns over Judah. Rezin, king of Syria, and Pekah, king of Israel, assail Judah. 15.– Jotham dies, and his Ahaz succeeds him.
AHAZ.	16	AHAZ, a cruel idolater. Gives the sacred and royal treasures to Tilgath-pileser, to aid him against Rezin and Pekah. Rezin slain, and Damascus taken by the King of Assyria. Ahaz commands Urijah, the priest, to set up a heathen altar, like one at Damascus.
HEZEKIAH.		16.– Ahaz dies, and HEZEKIAH, his son, reigns.
Hoshea.	17	9.– Hoshea, the son of Elah, reigns, having slain Pekah (xv. 30).
Shalmaneser.		Succumbs to Shalmaneser, king of Assyria. Conspires against him with So, king of Egypt. Shalmaneser imprisons Hoshea. He besieges Samaria three years. Israel carried captive and dispersed over Assyria. Shalmaneser colonizes Samaria with strangers. They are troubled by lions. An Israelitish priest placed in Bethel. The Samaritans make a mixture of religions.
	18	Hezekiah, king of Judah. Destroys the brazen serpent and every image used for idolatry.
Sennacherib.		Sennacherib takes his fenced cities. Hezekiah gives him the sacred treasure to depart.
Rabshakeh.		Rabshakeh's blasphemous speech.

Hezekiah's prayer.	19	Hezekiah sends to Isaiah, the prophet. Isaiah predicts the enemy's ruin. Sennacherib encounters Tirhakah, king of Ethiopia. Sends messengers, threatening Hezekiah. Hezekiah lays his profane letter before the LORD. Hezekiah's prayer. Isaiah's prophecy. 185,000 Assyrians perish. Sennacherib murdered by his sons – succeeded by Esar-haddon.
Hezekiah sick.	20	Hezekiah sick. His prayer in his sickness. His life lengthened fifteen years. Miraculous signs of sun going backwards ten degrees. Berodach-baladan, king of Babylon, courts Hezekiah. Hezekiah shows all his treasures. 29.– Hezekiah dies, and his son Manasseh reigns.
AMON.	21	MANASSEH, a gross and cruel idolater. 55.– He dies, and is buried in the garden. AMON, his idolatrous son reigns. 2.–His servants slay him. His son, Josiah, reigns.
JOSIAH.	22	JOSIAH reigns eight years of age. Repairs the temple. Hilkiah, the high priest, finds a copy of the law. Huldah, the prophetess, prophecies Jerusalem's destruction.
JEHOAHAZ.	23	Josiah publicly reads the book of the covenant. Destroys idolatry. Demolishes, as predicted, the altar at Bethel. Restores the Passover. 31.–Falls at Megiddo, in battle with Pharoah-nechoh, king of Egypt. JEHOAHAZ, his son, succeeds him. He does evil. Pharoah-nechoh dethrones him. Makes the brother of the dethroned a tributary king. 3 months.– Jehoahaz dies in Egypt. Eliakim, the new king, named by Pharoah, Jehoiakim.

JEHOIAKIM.	24	JEHOIAKIM tributary three years to Nebuchadnezzar of Babylon.
		Jehoiakim annoyed by bands of marauders.
JEHOIACHIN.		11.– Jehoiakim dies, and his son, JEHOIACHIN reigns.
		7.–Babylonish captivity commences and he is dethroned.
		His uncle Mattaniah, made king by the king of Babylon.
ZEDEKIAH.		His name changed to ZEDEKIAH.
		Rebels against the king of Babylon.
Nebuchadnezzar.	25	Nebuchadnezzar besieges Jerusalem.
		The people are starved out.
		Zedekiah's sons slain – his eyes put out – his is carried to Babylon.
		7.–Is king for only seven years.
Jerusalem burnt.		Jerusalem plundered and burnt.
Captivity.		The chief priest and principal men slain.
		The remnant, except some poor, carried captive.
Gedaliah.		Gedaliah made ruler of the few that remained.
		Ishmael slays Gedaliah.
		The people of the land flee into Egypt.
		Jehoiachin released from prison by Evil-merodach, after 36 years captivity.

Notes:
So that the reader may easily distinguish, the names of the kings of Judah are printed in CAPITALS, and the names of the kings of Israel are printed in italics.

*The figures placed preceding the death of any king mark the length of his reign.

I CHRONICLES

Genealogy of the Tribes; defeat of Saul; David becomes king; the Temple planned; Solomon chosen as king; death of David.

THE ESSENTIAL SUMMARY OF I CHRONICLES

The First Book of Chronicles is to a large extent a repetition of portions of the First and Second Books of Samuel. Together the two Books of Chronicles summarize the events of 3468 years.

The two books get their name from being the record made by the appointed historiographers in the kingdoms of Israel and Judah. The constant tradition of the Jews, in which they have been followed by the great mass of Christian commentators, is that these books were for the most part compiled by Ezra. One of the greatest difficulties connected with the captivity and the return must have been the maintenance of the genealogical distribution of the lands, which yet was a vital point of the Jewish economy. Another difficulty, intimately connected with the former, was the maintenance of the Temple services at Jerusalem. This could only be effected by the residence of the priests and Levites in Jerusalem in the order of their courses; and this residence was only practicable in case of the payment of the appointed tithes, first-fruits and other offerings. But then again, the registers of the Levitical genealogies were necessary, in order that it might be known who were entitled to such and such allowances, as porters, as singers, as priests, and so on. This was because all these offices went by families; and again, the payment of the tithes, first-fruits, &c., was dependent upon the different families of Israel being established, each in its inheritance. Therefore, one of the most pressing wants of the Jewish community, after their return from Babylon, would be trusty genealogical records. As regards the kingdom of Israel or Samaria, seeing it had utterly and hopelessly passed away, and that the existing inhabitants were among the bitterest "adversaries of Judah and Benjamin", it would naturally engage very little of the compiler's attention. These considerations explain exactly the plan and scope of that historical work which consists of the two books of Chronicles and the book of Ezra. For, having in the first eight chapters given the genealogical divisions and settlements of the various tribes, the compiler marks distinctly his own age and his own purpose, by informing us in chap. ix, 1 of the disturbance of those settlements by the Babylonian captivity, and, in the following verses, of the partial restoration of them at the return from Babylon (chap. ix. 2–34); and that this list refers to the families who had returned from Babylon is clear, not only from the context, but from its reinsertion, Neh. xi. 3–22 (compare also 1 Chron. ix. 19, with Ezra ii. 42, Neh. Vii. 45) with additional matter evidently extracted from the public archives, and relating to times subsequent to the return from Babylon, extending to Neh. xii. 27. Having thus shown the re-establishment of the returned families, each in their own inheritance to the houses of their fathers, the compiler proceeds to the other part of his plan, which is to give a continuous history of the kingdom of Judah from David to his own times, introduced by the closing scene of Saul's life (chap. x.), which introduction is itself prefaced by a genealogy of the house of Saul (chap. ix. 35–44).

As regards the *materials* used by Ezra, they are not difficult to discover. The genealogies are obviously transcribed from some register in which were preserved the genealogies of the tribes and families drawn up at different times; while the history is mainly drawn from the same documents as those used in the books of Kings.

COMMENTARY ON THE FIRST BOOK OF CHRONICLES

The two Books of **Chronicles** are counted as one in the Hebrew canon, and have the name 'Words of the days,' *i.e.* Annals. They are called in the Septuagint by a name which signifies 'things left out,' and were looked upon by the Greek translators as supplementary to the other historical books of the Old Testament.

In I. Chronicles, the chapters i.—ix. deal with genealogies. The lines of descent from Adam to Jacob are given in chapter i., then follow the genealogies of the sons of Jacob in the following order: Judah, in which the descendants of David are carried down to the grandchildren of Zerubbabel, who brought back some of the exiles from Babylon: Simeon, Reuben, Gad and Manasseh, some mention of the last-named tribe being found also in a later chapter. Then follow the descendants of Levi, dwelt on specially because of the priesthood, and because from this tribe came the great leaders of the Temple music: Heman, Asaph and Ethan (Jeduthun). Next we have the lines of Issachar, Benjamin, Naphtali, a second notice of Manasseh, because one part of the tribe was on the other side of Jordan: Ephraim, Asher, and a second notice of Benjamin, forming an introduction to the account of the ancient dwellers in Jerusalem, and to the genealogy of the house of Saul. These lists bring us to the end of chapter ix.

The remainder of the first book deals with the history of David, but treats it mainly in its relation to the establishment of the worship of the Temple. Little mention is made of any part of David's actions which might cast discredit on the king who gives his name to so many of the Psalms. Chapters x.—xiv. recount portions of the history which already have appeared in the books of Samuel: xv. and xvi. are occupied by the story of the bringing of the ark to Jerusalem and the arrangements for services which were consequent thereon. Chapters xvii.—xx. are again a repetition of previously recorded history; but in xxi. and xxii. David's sin in numbering the people is dwelt on, and the temptation thereto ascribed to Satan, but this recital is made to show how the king was brought to know that the place of the altar which he erected after the plague was to be the site of the future Temple, and to introduce an account of the preparation for its building. In xxiii., we are told of Solomon's acceptance as king during David's lifetime. Next comes an account of the courses of the Levites and their work; of the priests, the sons of Aaron, and then of the ordinary Levites under their twenty-four heads. Next follow notices of the singers, the doorkeepers, the Levites who kept the temple treasures, the officers, judges, military captains, and civil heads of tribes, a notice of the men who had charge of king David's substance, and those who were his chief officers and advisers. The last two chapters (xxviii., xxix.) tell how David gathered all his chief men together, and describe the great work of temple-building which is to be left to Solomon. The aged king by words and gifts stimulates the liberality of all the people, his joy at which is recorded in a solemn thanksgiving, which is followed by the anointing of Solomon amid great rejoicings and religious observances. The book closes with the king's death.

The First Book of Chronicles: Chapter by Chapter

Genealogies.	1	Genealogy of the Patriarchs, from Adam to Jacob.
	2	Genealogy from Jacob to David, and of others.
	3	Genealogy from David through thirty generations.
	4	Other genealogies from Judah.
	5	Genealogies from Reuben. Exploits of Reubenites, Gadites and half-tribe of Manasseh. Their captivity in Assyria.
	6	Genealogy from Levi to David's reign. Cities of priests and Levites.
	7	Genealogy of six other tribes.
	8	Genealogy of Benjamin to Saul.
	9	First inhabitants after the captivity in Babylon. Officers about the Temple.
Saul.	10	SAUL's overthrow and death.
David.	11	DAVID anointed at Hebron. His mighty men.
	12	Men that came to David at Ziklag and Hebron.

	13	The ark brought from Kirjath-jearim. Uzza or Uzzah. Obed-edom.
	14	King of Tyre and David. David's victories over the Philistines.
	15	Ark brought from Obed-edom's house.
	16	David's psalm composed on bringing up the ark.
	17	David purposes to build a house for God.
	18	David's victories over the Philistines and the Moabites.
Hanun.	19	Hanun, king of Ammon, insults David's ambassadors. The Ammonites and the Syrians fight against Israel.
	20	David defeats the Ammonites and Philistines
	21	David's sin in numbering the people. The plague – it is stayed.
	22	David prepares for building the temple.
Solomon.	23	SOLOMON made king. The Levites, their number and office.
	24	Twenty-four courses of priests, &c.
	25	Twenty-four courses of singers.
	26	Porters for the temple: officers and judges.
	27	Captains of the army. Chiefs of tribes. Domestic officers of David.
	28	David's last exhortations.
	29	Offerings for a temple. David's thanksgiving. David's death in a good old age.

II CHRONICLES

**The reign of Solomon; the building of the Temple;
bad kings; the Exile to Babylon.**

THE ESSENTIAL SUMMARY OF II CHRONICLES

While the background and source material for the two books of Chronicles are the same, this Second book treats almost exclusively of the Kings of Judah, scarcely any notice being taken of the Ten Tribes. The narratives in the two books of Chronicles either correspond with, or are supplementary to, the records in the Books of Samuel and Kings.

COMMENTARY ON THE SECOND BOOK OF CHRONICLES

The chapters i.–ix. of **Chronicles II** give an account of the reign of Solomon, repeating what is given in 1 Kings, only, as in the case of David, omitting everything which might detract from the praise of the house of David. From x.–xx. treats of the early history of the kingdom of Judah, giving no notices of the northern kingdom which are not absolutely unavoidable. Chapters xxi.–xxviii. describe the time from the death of Jehoshaphat to the death of Ahaz, and show the gradual falling away of the people from the true worship of Jehovah, while in the rest of the book (xxix.–xxxvi.) we are told of the efforts after reform in the reigns of Hezekiah, and later on of Josiah, at which two periods the religious history is much enlarged on. But the evil had gone too far for reform, and the captivity brings their national life to a close. The book ends with the proclamation of Cyrus for the rebuilding of the Temple, exactly as in the opening verses of the book of Ezra.

Some interesting light is thrown by the Chronicles on the sources from which the compilers of the Historical books drew their materials. For Solomon's reign the writer of the Kings refers (1 Kings xi. 41) only to 'the Book of the Acts of Solomon.' The chronicler, whose language is almost the exact counterpart of Kings, enumerates (2 Chron. ix. 29) three documents as his authorities, 'the book of Nathan the prophet, the prophecy of Ahijah the Shilonite, and the visions of Iddo the seer.' For the other reigns we are referred in Kings simply to 'the Book of the Chronicles of the Kings of Judah' and 'the Book of the Chronicles of the Kings of Israel.' Here again the chronicler breaks up these general titles, by referring to separate and special documents. Thus he cites for the reign of Rehoboam 'the Book of Shemaiah the prophet and Iddo the seer' (2 Chron. xii. 15): for Abijam's reign he refers (2 Chron. xiii. 22) to 'the story of the prophet Iddo': for Jehoshaphat's history his authority (2 Chron. xx. 34) is 'the Book of Jehu the son of Hanani,' which, he tells us, 'is inserted in the Book of the Kings of Israel.' Further, we read (2 Chron. xxvi. 22) that Isaiah the prophet wrote the history of Azariah (Uzziah) and also (2 Chron. xxxii. 32) the acts and good deeds of Hezekiah, and it is added that 'the vision of Isaiah' is included in 'the Book of the Kings of Judah and Israel.' The account of Manasseh's reign we read (2 Chron. xxxiii. 18) is to be found partly in 'the Book of the Kings of Israel,' and other things concerning him are among 'the sayings of the seers' (R.V. 'in the history of Hozai').

These instances make it clear that from the earliest times of the kingdom, if not before, writers living amid the events described, and generally of the prophetic order, recorded the history of their own times, and that from these are constructed the history of the nation as it has come down to us; the compilers, whether before or after the Captivity, selecting from contemporary records such portions as suited the purpose of their composition.

THE SECOND BOOK OF CHRONICLES: CHAPTER BY CHAPTER

Solomon.	1	Solomon sacrifices at Gibeon. God appears to Solomon in a dream. Grants his request for wisdom. Solomon's strength and riches.
	2	Solomon's labourers for building the temple. Huram (or Hiram), king of Tyre, assists him.
The Temple.	3	The building of the temple.
	4	The brazen altar, the brazen sea, the lavers, the golden candlesticks, &c.
	5	Dedication of the temple.
	6	Solomon's prayer.
	7	Feast of dedication.
	8	Solomon's buildings. His ships go to Ophir for gold.
Queen of Sheba.	9	Queen of Sheba and Solomon. Solomon's wealth.
Rehoboam.	10	REHOBOAM king: and revolt of the ten tribes.
	11	Rehoboam's conduct, and his marriages.
Shishak.	12	Shishak, king of Egypt, despoils the temple and takes the fenced cities. Rehoboam dies.
Abijah.	13	ABIJAH succeeds Rehoboam as king of Judah. Jeroboam attacks Abijah and is defeated. Abijah's wives and children.
Asa.	14	Abijah's death. ASA reigns. His powerful army. Attacked by Zerah, with his Ethiopian army of a million men. The LORD defeats the Ethiopians.
	15	Azariah promises good to Asa. Asa deposes his idolatrous mother Maachah.

	16	Asa forms an alliance with Benhadad, king of Syria, against Baasha of Israel. Hanani, the seer, reproves him; and is imprisoned. Asa dies of disease in the feet.
Jehosaphat.	17	JEHOSHAPHAT reigns. Demolishes the high places and groves. He employs Levites to teach the people. Becomes great and prosperous.
	18	Jehoshaphat joins Ahab, king of Israel, to go to battle against Ramoth-gilead. Micaiah predicts evil, and Zedekiah good. Micaiah imprisoned by Ahab. Ahab shot between the joints of the harness.
	19	Jehu, the seer, reproves Jehoshaphat for joining with Ahab. Jehoshaphat instructs the judges in their duty.
	20	Jehoshaphat threatened by Ammon, Moab and Edom. He proclaims a fast. The prayer he offered up. Jahaziel, the Levite, encourages him. The allies quarrel and destroy each other; and Jehoshaphat gathers the spoil.
Jehoram.	21	JEHORAM succeeds Jehoshaphat. He murders his brethren. Edom revolts. Jehoram's awful death, as predicted in a letter of Elijah.
Ahaziah. **Athaliah.**	22	AHAZIAH reigns. Aids Jehoram (or Joram), king of Israel, against the Syrians. He is slain by Jehu, the son of Nimshi. Queen ATHALIAH slays the seed royal, and reigns. Joash is saved by stealth.
Joash.	23	JOASH made king. Athaliah slain. Jehoiada, the chief priest, restores the worship of God.
	24	Joash reigns well while Jehoiada is alive. He afterwards sanctions idolatry. He slays Zechariah, the son of Jehoiada. Joash slain by his servants Zabad and Jehozabad.

Amaziah.	25	AMAZIAH reigns. Executes his father's murders. Hires an Israelitish army. Forfeits a hundred talents. Overthrows the Edomites. Commits idolatry with the gods of Edom. Amaziah challenges Israel, and is defeated. Is slain in a conspiracy at Lachish, his place of refuge.

Uzziah.	26	UZZIAH next reigns.
		He builds towers, and forms a large army.
		He encourages the invention of war
		    engines, &c.
		He invades the priests' office, and is smitten
		    with leprosy.

Jotham.	27	JOTHAM reigns. Jotham defeats Ammon, and brings the Ammonites under tribute.

Ahaz.
 	
Tilgath-pileser.
 	
Hezekiah.
	28	AHAZ reigns.
		His idolatry.
		His defeat by the Syrians.
		Pekah, king of Israel, defeats him, with the
		    loss of 120,000 men and 200,000 captives.
		The captives are restored by direction of the
		    prophet Obed.
		Ahaz, troubled by Edom and Philistia,
		    seeks aid from Assyria.
		Tilgath-pilnaser (or Tiglath-pileser)
		    disappoints and plunders Ahaz.
		Ahaz shuts up the temple and builds
		    idol-altars.
		He dies and HEZEKIAH succeeds him.

	29	Hezekiah restores the worship of God. He exhorts the priests and Levites. They sanctify themselves, and purge the temple. Sacrifices restored.
	30	Hezekiah proclaims a Passover. Idolatrous altars destroyed.
	31	Hezekiah re-establishes the priesthood.
Sennacherib.	32	Sennacherib's impious message and letters. His miraculous defeat. He is murdered. Hezekiah's sickness, recovery and death.

Manasseh. **Amon.**	33	MANASSEH reigns. His cruel idolatry. He is carried captive to Babylon. He humbles himself and is restored. He restores God's worship. He dies: and AMON succeeds him. Amon's idolatry. He is slain in a conspiracy.
Josiah. **Josiah seeks God.** **Hilkiah the priest.**	34	JOSIAH reigns. Josiah seeks God when but eight years old. He destroys idolatry. In his eighteenth year, he restores the temple. Hilkiah the priest finds the book of the law. He reads the law to the people.
	35	Josiah keeps a Passover. Opposes Necho, king of Egypt, on his way to the Euphrates; and is slain. Great lamentation for Josiah.

Jehoahaz.
 	
Eliakim.
 	
Jehoiakim captive.
	36	JEHOAHAZ succeeds his father, and is
		    enthroned by the Pharoah Necho in three
		    months.
		ELIAKIM his brother made king, and his
		    name changed to Jehoiakim.
		After eleven years, he is sent in fetters to
		    Babylon by Nebuchadnezzar.
		Nebuchadnezzar carries off the vessels of
		    the temple.

Jehoiachin.
 	
Zedekiah.
 	
Jerusalem laid
waste. Seventy
years captivity.
	36	JEHOIACHIN, son of Jehoiakim, reigns
		    three months.
		He also carried off prisoner to Babylon.
		ZEDEKIAH succeeds his relative Jehoiachin
		    and reigns eleven years.
		He revolts against Nebuchadnezzar and is
		    made a captive.
		Jerusalem laid waste and the seventy years'
		    captivity begun.

EZRA

**The Proclamation of Cyrus, and the return of the
Israelites to Jerusalem.**

THE ESSENTIAL STORY OF EZRA

The demise of the Babylonian Empire brought great changes
to the way the imperial administration functioned. More
autonomy was afforded the subject nations (it was cheaper
and more efficient), and they were allowed to resume worshipping their own gods. Cyrus, King of Persia, began sending
back the idols and effigies that had been taken to Babylon by
the previous conquerors. This applied also to the Jews, and the
exiles were now offered the freedom to return to their homeland. Fewer chose to return than those who stayed in Babylonia;
but in 538 a large party set off for Jerusalem led by Zerubbabel,
a grandson of King Joiachim, who was appointed Governor of
the region. He was also encouraged to rebuild the city and the
Temple, and Cyrus even gave back the sacred objects plundered
from the Temple by Nebuchadnezzar. At Zerubbabel's side went
Jeshua (Joshua), the High Priest.

During the period of exile, the Jews had inevitably built up
a memory of an idealized city: the Jerusalem they found was
disheartening in the extreme – a ruined wasteland (just as the
prophet Ezekiel had foretold) and unoccupied for half a century.
But they made a start, setting up an altar on the site of the original
and making sacrifice, and within two years the Temple foundations had been laid.

But now a conflict became apparent between "the children of the captivity" and "the people of the land," those left behind, who had intermarried with other peoples and included the Samaritans. The Jews refused them any part in the reconstruction. Resentments and distrust of the people from Babylon who presumed to take over the area led the Samaritans and others to make representations to the Persian court for the reconstruction work to be stopped. At first they succeeded, until court records in the imperial capital showed that the reconstruction had indeed been permitted. But these delays, added to a certain indifference and apathy among some of the returnees, slowed progress to a halt.

Among the first to return was Haggai, whose role it was to preach encouragement to the Jews. Born in Babylon, he longed, like the others, to see the Temple rebuilt. Zechariah was Haggai's companion prophet, also with with a message of hope and recovery. Past guilt could be atoned for; Zerubbabel and Jeshua would indeed complete the Temple and the kingdom be restored. In 515 the Temple was at last finished and dedicated, but much remained to be done in the still very empty city.

In 458 another band of Jews arrived, this time led by Ezra, who was to play a vital part in steering the restoration in the right spiritual direction. Of priestly Zadokite descent, he was an austere and commanding character, who came intent on infusing the community with new zeal and accelerating progress toward making Jerusalem once again the spiritual capital of the Jews.

Arrival in Jerusalem revealed clearly why so many Jews preferred to remain in Mesopotamia. It was a century and a half since their ancestors had been carried off, and they were established there. Many now owned property; some had risen to positions of seniority and authority within the imperial bureaucracy. In contrast, Ezra found the inhabitants of Judaea in poverty, struggling to cope and with Jerusalem far from rebuilt.

More important to Ezra, however, was the poor moral and spiritual state of affairs. Over the years, the Jews had mingled freely with the other races, including the colonists sent by the Babylonians, and intermarrying, which was expressly forbidden by the Mosaic Law. This was an impurity that needed to be cleansed, so Ezra set up a special divorce court (over which he himself presided) and Jews began setting aside their foreign wives.

COMMENTARY ON THE BOOK OF EZRA

Ezra and **Nehemiah** were counted by the Jews as one book and the former appears to be a continuation of 2 Chronicles, while Nehemiah's journal relates to a time not long after the return of the second body of exiles who came back under Ezra. Together they embrace a period of more than 100 years. Ezra commences with the proclamation of Cyrus, with which 2 Chronicles concludes, and proceeds to notice the restoration of the sacred vessels which Nebuchadnezzar had carried from Jerusalem. Sheshbazzar is the Babylonian name for Zerubbabel (see ii. 2), who is mentioned in Haggai and Zechariah. In chapter ii. we have a notice of the numbers of the returning exiles, with their means and their offerings. In iii. commences the notice of the setting up of the altar and the rebuilding of the Temple. Then (iv.) the adversaries offer to join them in their work, but being refused, malign the people at the court of Persia. The Ahasuerus of verse 6 in this chapter, and the Artaxerxes of 7, 8, 23, are by some thought to be Cambyses the son of Cyrus and the pseudo-Smerdis who reigned next for only seven months; others, who look upon verses 6–23 as a long parenthesis, introduced to show that the hindrances went on longer than the reign of Darius, take Ahasuerus to be the Ahasuerus of the book of Esther, who is most likely the Xerxes of classical history, and Artaxerxes to be his successor Artaxerxes Longimanus, who is the king intended in Ezra vii. and Neh. ii. In chapter v. the people are incited by Haggai and Zechariah to resume their building. The governor of the land and his companions at first are minded to stop them, but on writing to king Darius there is found (vi) among the royal records the decree of Cyrus, and Darius makes a similar decree, upon which the governor becomes friendly to the work of Zerubbabel and his people, and the Temple is finished and dedicated and a joyous passover is kept. The rest of the book, which is Ezra's own work, tells of the return of a second band of exiles over whom he had charge. This event would be about 80 years after Zerubbabel's coming to Jerusalem, and about 13 years before Nehemiah's mission. Ezra had his commission from Artaxerxes (Longimanus). Ezra takes steps for procuring some Levites to go with the returning band, and for the security of the treasure that was carried up. They reach Jerusalem, and there Ezra learns that many marriages have taken place between the returned Jews and strangers. He exhorts them to put their wives away, and they consent. The book concludes with a list of those who had thus offended. The Book of Ezra contains two passages, iv. 8–vi. 18 and vii. 12–26, which are not in Hebrew but in Aramaic.

THE BOOK OF EZRA: CHAPTER BY CHAPTER

Cyrus.	1	Cyrus' proclamation for rebuilding the Temple. The sacred vessels restored.
	2	The numbers that returned to Jerusalem.
Foundation of the Temple.	3	Altar set up and offerings. Foundations of the Temple laid.
Artaxerxes, or Smerdis.	4	Jews accused to Ahauserus. Letter against the Jews to Artaxerxes. Artaxerxes [Smerdis] stops the building.
Darius.	5	Haggai and Zechariah incite to renew the building. Zerubbabel and Jeshua continue work. Tatnai, the governor, and Sethar-boznai oppose. Their letter to Darius [called Hystaspes.]
The search.	6	Darius searches the rolls, finds Cyrus' decree, and orders the building to proceed. The Temple finished. Feast of dedication and Passover.
Artaxerxes, or Longimanus. Ezra's return.	7	Second return of the Jews in the reign of Artaxerxes [Longimanus]. Letter of Artaxerxes, warranting Ezra's return with his people, and with every aid.
	8	Ezra's companions in return. Safe journey, with much wealth.
Ezra's prayer.	9	Ezra mourns over the unholy marriages of the Jews. His prayer to God.
	10	The "strange" marriages reformed.

118

NEHEMIAH

**Nehemiah visits Jerusalem; he supervises the building
of the city wall, and continues Ezra's reforms.**

THE ESSENTIAL STORY OF NEHEMIAH

Nehemiah was cupbearer to the king Artaxerxes
[Longimanus]. Having heard of the misery in Jerusalem,
he became very downcast. The king observed this and
gave him a commission to go to Jerusalem. He arrived, and
arranged for the building of the walls of the city, in spite of the
mockery and opposition of the enemies. By prayer and watchfulness amid their labors, and by arming all the people while the
work was in progress, it was possible to carry it on. The people
complained to Nehemiah of their debt, mortgages and bondage.
He took measures for a remedy, and set an example of great self-
denial. The enemies now tried the effect of pretended friendship,
and after that of troublesome rumors, but in the end the wall was
completed, though there were even among the nobles of Judah
some who sympathized and communicated with the adversaries.

The rest of the book (chapters vii.—xiii.) treats of certain reforms
which Nehemiah inaugurated. First he prepared to take a census
of the people, and finds the list, the same which is given in Ezra
ii., of those who came up at the first. He promoted a revival of
religion, by regular reading of the Law, and by teaching the
people. They celebrated the feast of tabernacles with great joy.
Next is recorded a solemn fast, and after confession they bind
themselves to a covenant, which, was sealed by the chief men

on behalf of the rest. They pledge themselves to walk before the LORD, not to intermarry with strangers, to observe the sabbath, to contribute regularly to the services of the sanctuary, and to give duly their first-fruits and their tithes. Next there is given a list of the names of those who were dwelling in Jerusalem, and a description of the way in which the Nethinim, the Levites and the people generally were distributed throughout Judah and Benjamin. Next follow lists of the heads of the priestly courses, the line of the high priests, and various lists of the Levites. After the recital of these arrangements, we are told how the newly-finished wall was dedicated; how the arrangements of David and Solomon for the service of the priests and Levites, and for their maintenance, were restored. Then the mixed multitude is separated from Israel, as commanded in the law of Moses. Next we read how, in an absence of Nehemiah for about twelve years, Eliashib the priest had been unfaithful in his trust, and had prepared for Tobiah a chamber in the LORD's house. This abuse was corrected by Nehemiah on his return; Nehemiah expelled Tobiah and all his belongings, took means to prevent the profanation of the sabbath, and checked the marriages with heathen women, even expelling a grandson of Eliashib, who by such a marriage had defiled the priesthood.

COMMENTARY ON THE BOOK OF NEHEMIAH

This book is called 'the words of Nehemiah the son of Hachaliah.' The name **Nehemiah** means Comforted of Jehovah. There appear to have been at least three persons bearing this name at the time of the return from the Babylonish Captivity. One is mentioned as going up under the leading of Zerubbabel (Ezra ii. 2): a period of about ninety years intervenes between the going up of this Nehemiah and that of the writer of this Book. And the other is "Nehemiah, the son of Azbuk, the ruler of half of Beth-zur" (Neh. iii. 16); a man evidently under the control of Nehemiah, the son of Hachaliah. The latter leaves a position of honor and dignity ("I was the king's cup-bearer") and, like Moses, chooses rather to identify himself with the people of God. His object was "to seek the welfare of the children of Israel."

Nehemiah was the kings' cupbearer.

Armed with the powers embodied in the "letters" of Artaxerxes Longimanus, he rebuilds the wall of Jerusalem, albeit in troubled times. He arouses the people to spiritual revival (viii., ix., x.). He compiles or completes the national registers. After governing for twelve years, he returns to the court of Babylon according to the agreement in ii. 6. But feeling that his presence was needed in Judea, he a second time obtains permission to return to the land and city of his fathers; and again sets himself to rectify the evils which existed. There the narrative breaks off. And thus terminates the last of the historical books of the Old Testament.

The book is full of interest because of the direct appeals which Nehemiah so frequently makes to the LORD to bear in mind the labors which he has borne.

The Book of Nehemiah: Chapter by Chapter

Nehemiah's prayer.	1	Nehemiah in the palace of Shushan. His mourning and prayer for Jerusalem. His office was king's cupbearer.
	2	Nehemiah commissioned by Artaxerxes [Longimanus] to visit Jerusalem. He invites the Jews to build in despite of Sanballat and Tobiah.
	3	Names and orders of the builders.
	4	The builders work armed.
	5	The practice of usury reformed.
Sanballat.	6	Sanballat's subtle attempts to stop the work. The wall finished.
	7	Hanani and Hananiah take charge of Jerusalem. Register of those that came from Babylon. Oblations for the work.
Reading the law.	8	Ezra reads and expounds the law. The feast of Tabernacles kept.
	9	A solemn fast. The Levites' confession.
	10	Names of those who sealed the solemn covenant. The nature of the covenant sealed.
	11	Volunteers, and every tenth man, appointed to people Jerusalem. The residue scattered over the other parts of the land.
Priests and Levites.	12	Priests and Levites which went up with Zerubbabel. Processions meet each other right and left at the dedication of the walls. Priests and Levites' appointment in the Temple.
	13	Nehemiah reforms various abuses of the Temple – sabbath – and marriage.

ESTHER

**Esther is chosen queen in Babylon and saves her people.
Her courage is remembered in the Jewish festival of Purim.**

The Essential Story of Esther

The story of Esther is a great romance of the captivity. Esther was a beautiful Benjamite girl among the exiles in Babylonia, an orphan raised by her cousin Mordecai, who was a minor official at the king's palace. When King Artaxerxes' queen, Vashti, was deemed to have disgraced herself by disobeying her husband, she was put aside; Esther was brought to the attention of the king at his winter palace of Susa, and he made her his new queen.

Trouble began when Mordecai offended the court favorite, Haman, who, upon discovering that Mordecai was a Jew, determined upon an evil plan. He would take revenge upon the insulting Jew by petitioning the king to sign a decree for the slaughter of all the Jews in Babylon, whom he accused of plotting rebellion – with the added incentive of seizing their money and property. This he achieved – but there was a constitutional delay before the edict would be put into effect, which gave time for Mordecai to learn what was in store.

He spoke with Esther, who determined on a scheme to thwart Haman. She invited both the king and her enemy to two banquets on successive nights. After the first banquet, the king asked to see the royal records and discovered that Mordecai had rendered conspicuous service to the throne – he had prevented an assassination attempt upon the king. But he had never been rewarded for this, so Artaxerxes consulted his court favorite. But the conceited and egotistical Haman quite misunderstood the king, thinking he meant himself, so he recommended high honors.

At the banquet the following day Esther courageously spoke to the king, revealing that she was herself of Jewish origin and telling Artaxerxes about Haman's ill intent toward Mordecai and the falsehoods behind his petition. Revealing that she was a Jew was dangerous in itself; but the king at once understood. The edict could not be stopped – once an edict bore the seal of the king's ring it could not be revoked. Instead he issued a second decree permitting the Jews to fight back. Meanwhile Haman was arraigned before the king and sentenced to death, together with his ten sons, while Esther was granted his lands and property, and the honors and promotion Haman had recommended to the king for himself were heaped upon Mordecai. The Jewish exiles, prepared for the onslaught, destroyed Haman's attackers, saved by the cunning and courage of Queen Esther. The celebration of this event gave rise to the feast of Purim.

COMMENTARY ON THE BOOK OF ESTHER

The Book of Esther contains the history which led to the institution of the Jewish feast, Purim. Ahasuerus, king of Persia, most probably Xerxes, gives orders to his queen Vashti to chew her beauty to the people and the princes. Because of her refusal, the king is advised to divorce her. A new queen is to be chosen from the fairest maidens, and the choice falls on Esther, the adopted daughter of Mordecai the Jew. She does not disclose her kindred. Mordecai had aforetime saved the king's life from a plot. The chief man at the court of Ahasuerus was Haman the Agagite, and to him Mordecai did not pay due reverence. For this reason Haman, having cast lots to find a suitable day for his petition, obtains a decree to put the Jews to death, and to take their goods as spoil. There is great grief among the Jews, and Esther is charged by Mordecai to interpose by going before the king. This she does in spite of the peril of such a course, and

Mordecai ... Esther 3.2.

invites the king and Haman to a banquet, and repeats the invitation for the next day. Haman, thus high in favor, as it seems, with the queen as well as the king, yet repines at Mordecai's neglect of him, and prepares a gallows on which, when the time comes, Mordecai shall be hanged. Meanwhile in the intervening night the king, reading in the Chronicles of Mordecai's former service, finds it has been unrewarded. Haman comes to ask permission to hang Mordecai, and is made the agent to do him great honor: whereupon his friends tell him that he is doomed to fall before this Jew. At her second banquet, Esther makes her petition to the king for her own life and that of her people, and discloses Haman's plots. The king orders Haman to be hanged on the gallows he had prepared, and bestows his office on Mordecai. Then Esther procures letters to be sent throughout the land to hinder the effect of the decree which Haman had procured. The joy of the Jews is great at Mordecai's honor. But in spite of the favor of the king the enemies of the Jews try to carry out Haman's intentions. The Jews defend themselves, and a second day is granted them in Shushan to take vengeance on their foes. The bodies of Haman's sons are hanged. The day following is kept as a great feast-day. And two days of feasting are appointed to be observed for all time, by command of Mordecai and Esther, in feasting and gladness and hospitality and liberality to those in need. They are called Purim, because of the lot (Pur) which Haman had cast for the destruction of the Jews. The book closes with a brief notice of the power of king Ahasuerus, and the advancement of Mordecai, who sought the welfare of his people and spoke peace to all his seed.

The book of Esther contains no mention of God, and its spirit of revenge is somewhat alien to the better ages of Judaism. The historical character of the book, though it is probably incorrect in details, is vouched for by the observance of the Purim-feast in memory of the deliverance.

THE BOOK OF ESTHER: CHAPTER BY CHAPTER

Ahasuerus' feast.	1	Six months' feast given by Ahasuerus in Shushan to the princes of Media and Persia. The people feast seven days. Queen Vashti deprived of her dignity.
Esther.	2	Esther preferred. Conspiracy against the king by two chamberlains. Revealed by Mordecai to Esther, and by her to the king.

Haman. **Mordecai.**	3	Haman the Agagite (or Amalekite) raised to eminence. Mordecai refuses to pay homage to Haman. Haman, in revenge, procures a decree to destroy all the Jews.
	4	Great mourning of Mordecai and the Jews. Mordecai persuades Esther to intercede with the king. She desires the Jews to fast.
Ester received at court.	5	Esther touches the king's golden sceptre, and is received at court. She invites the king and Haman to a banquet. The king accedes, and Haman rejoices.
	6	Restless sleep of Ahasuerus , and discovery in his records that Mordecai had never been rewarded for his fidelity. Haman waits to enter and obtain the king's consent to execute Mordecai. The king orders Haman to do honour to Mordecai. Mordecai led through Shushan on horseback in royal state by Haman.
Esther's banquet. **Haman hanged.**	7	Esther's banquet, and denunciation of Haman. The King's wrath against Haman. Haman is hanged on the gallows prepared for Mordecai.
Mordecai advanced.	8	Mordecai advanced in Haman's stead. Esther pleads with the king on behalf of her nation. The royal decrees are not reversible; but the king issues one permitting the Jews to resist their enemies.
	9	The Jews slay 500 men in Shushan, and 300; and kill and hang Haman' ten sons. The Jews slay 75,000 men in the provinces. The feast of Purim ordered to be kept in memory of this event; because Haman had cast *Pur*, the lot, to fix a day to massacre the Jews.
	10	Ahasuerus' greatness. Mordecai's prosperity.

JOB

**The sufferings of Job; he argues with his friends and talks
with God. Eventually, his prosperity is restored.**

THE ESSENTIAL SUMMARY OF JOB

The Book of Job is the first of five poetical books, and takes its name from the central character. It ponders the age-old question, Why do righteous people suffer? Job is a God-fearing and prosperous man living in the Land of Uz. Satan asks God's permission to test Job, first with great losses (of his wealth, then of his sons and daughters), and then with painful physical ailments. In his sufferings Job is given cold comfort by three 'friends', Eliphaz, Bildad and Zophar. Despite his sufferings, Job will not speak against God. Later, a fourth 'comforter' joins the debate – a younger man called Elihu. Elihu warns Job against speaking critically of God. Finally, God Himself speaks and leaves Job in awe of the wonders of His creation. God brings Job's sufferings to an end and blesses him with more children, renewed prosperity, and a long life.

COMMENTARY ON THE BOOK OF JOB

This very ancient book narrates the afflictions which befell the righteous patriarch Job, by divine permission, and discusses the moral problem which they represent. It consists of a Prologue (ch. i.–ii.) and an Epilogue (ch. xlii. 7–17) written in prose; with a series of argumentative discourses (ch. iii.–xlii. 6) unsurpassed for poetry of thought and diction. The opening verses describe Job as a man "perfect and upright," and blessed in family and substance. The scene then changes to Heaven; where the "sons of God" come to present themselves before Jehovah, and the adversary Satan comes also among them. On his cynically asking, "doth Job fear God for nought?", he is allowed to try him by successive losses of possessions and of his sons and daughters; and afterwards to smite him in person with a sore disease, elephantiasis, yet so as to spare his life. His wife tempts him to curse God and die; but he is resigned alike in losses and bodily afflictions. "In all this did not Job sin with his lips" (ch. ii. 10). The delivery of Job into the hand of Satan may be compared with St. Luke xxii. 31, where the adversary again has his request, that he may have power over the disciples to sift them as wheat.

When Job's three friends, Eliphaz, Bildad, and Zophar, heard of the evil that had befallen him they came to condole with him, and they sat with him in silence seven days and nights, "for they saw that his grief was very great." Then Job opened his mouth and cursed the day of his birth (ch. iii.).

Ch. iv.–xxxi., xxxviii.–xlii.: In the Prologue the end is seen from the beginning, but all is obscure in the arena of the lower world. There Job and his friends strive hotly with one another as to the cause and the significance of his afflictions in the three cycles of speeches, ch. iv.–xiv., ch. xv.–xxi. and ch. xxii.–xxxi. respectively. Each cycle should contain attacks by Eliphaz, Bildad and Zophar, with Job's reply to each, six speeches in all; but Zophar's third speech is missing, and Job, having replied to Bildad in ch. xxvi., "continued his parable" to the end of ch. xxxi., where it is said, "The words of Job are ended." It has been argued very plausibly that the apparently lost speech has been merged in the words of Job by the accidental omission of the statement, that "Zophar the Naamathite answered and said," just before ch. xxvii. 13, "This is the portion of a wicked man with God, &c.," which is a repetition of Zophar's concluding words in ch. xx. 29 and is inconsistent with Job's complaint of the prosperity of the wicked in ch. xxi. But explanations of the seeming contradiction have been offered, and it has been held that, "where the regular mechanism of the several parts leads us to expect a third speech likewise from Zophar," he fails to come forward only because he has nothing more to say, and that his silence and the meagreness of Bildad's indictment in ch. xxv. and the fulness of Job's defence (ch. xxvi. —xxxi.) are meant for indications that the attack of the three friends has been repelled. Eliphaz speaks always first of the three, and with the authority of an ancient seer to whom the LORD reveals Himself (ch. iv. 12 -16). Accordingly it is to him that the LORD speaks in ch. xlii. 7, "My wrath is kindled against thee, and against thy two friends: for ye have not spoken of me the thing that is right, as my servant Job hath." Bildad is the master of traditions, who takes his stand upon the wisdom of the past: "For inquire, I pray thee, of the former age, ... For we are but of yesterday, and know nothing" (ch. viii. 8, 9). Zophar, if their inferior in spiritual endowments and erudition, does not yield to them at all in self-confidence (ch. xi., xx.). To what end are rhetoric and abstruse speculation? "Should a man full of talk be justified?" "Canst thou by searching find out God?" He makes haste to reply out of the spirit of his understanding, and is troubled with no doubt of the uniform working of his law: "This is the portion of a wicked man from God." Throughout the discussion the good and evil that befall men are assumed to come as rewards and punishments from the hand of God, without the intervention of second causes. One "stricken, smitten of God, and afflicted" (Isaiah liii. 4), as Job was, must have been a sinner. His friends ring the changes on this thesis. He maintains his innocence, and the question necessarily arises, "Is God unrighteous?" (Rom. iii. 5). The thought wrings from him words without knowledge (ch. xxxviii. 2), which he eventually retracts (ch. xlii. 3); yet he is declared to have spoken the thing that is right of the divine government (ch. xlii. 7), as having refuted their superficial arguments, and shown that there was a mystery in the incidence of suffering which only a fresh revelation could solve. The two answers of Jehovah out of the whirlwind (ch. xxxviii.—xl. 2; ch. xl. 6—xli.) give no solution of this to the understanding, but they set forth the glory of God in creation by typical instances, and put the unanswerable questions, "Shall he that contendeth with the Almighty instruct Him ?" "Wilt thou condemn Me, that thou mayest be righteous?" Job's craving for light is satisfied by the vision of God, at length vouchsafed in answer to his appeals. "I have heard of Thee by the hearing of the ear: but now mine eye seeth Thee."

Ch. xxxii.–xxxvii. The Three having ceased to answer Job because he was righteous in his own eyes, a fresh interlocutor, Elihu, is introduced with some verses in prose in continuation of the Prologue. He had waited for them to speak, as being much older than himself, but on their failure to confute Job he himself could not but take up his parable. He accepts their view of Job's sinfulness, and charges him with adding rebellion to his sin (ch. xxxiv. 37) by his defiant attitude toward God, whom he regards as having afflicted him wrongfully. Elihu's main thesis is that the Almighty will "not pervert judgement," and he is shocked at the impiety of one who can think this possible. His disapprobation is expressed in the strongest terms. "Job hath said, I am righteous: and God hath taken away my judgement ... What man is like Job, who drinketh up scorning like water?" (ch. xxxiv. 5, 7). Afflictions may have been sent with a gracious purpose, although sinners by their contumacy turn them to their destruction (ch. xxxvi. 8–13). God is the righteous governor of all sorts and conditions of men, of nations as of individuals (ch. xxxiv. 29). To this Job makes no reply. Elihu had thrown down the challenge, "If thou hast anything to say, answer me: speak, for I desire to justify thee" (ch. xxxiii. 32); and we may suppose that Job does not take it up because he cannot justify his attitude of mind toward God. These chapters are thought by many to be an addition to the original book of Job for the following reasons: (1) They break the connexion between the "words of Job" (ch. xxxi.) and the answer to them in ch. xxxviii., "Then Jehovah answered Job out of the whirlwind, &c." But it may be said that the storm of ch. xxxvii. 2–5 leads up to the "whirlwind" out of which the LORD answers, and that not until after the reproofs of Elihu, which he accepts in silence, was Job in a fit frame of mind to receive the answer "of the Almighty. (2) There is no mention of Elihu, no praise or dispraise of his contribution to the discussion, in the Epilogue. This is, no doubt, a difficulty. But the writer may have thought that he had commended him sufficiently by making Job fail to find an answer to him. Moreover the statement that the LORD answered "Job" points to the intervention of another speaker after his last words. (3) Elihu's standpoint, it is said, does not differ materially from that of the Three, and he brings the problem no nearer to its solution. But this was not the opinion of the writer, whether of the whole book or of the Elihu-chapters, if Job's failure to answer means anything. (4) The chapters have so many references (ch. xxxiii. 8, 9, 15, xxxiv. 3, 5, 6, xxxv. 2, 3, 7, &c.) to other parts of the book that the composer of them must have had the rest of the book before him. It does not follow that he was not himself the writer of it. (5) The style of the episode shows it to have been by a different author. To this it is answered that it is intended to be characteristic of the fresh speaker. If the main part of the book was written in character, being, as some say, full of archaic touches due to the poetic art of the writer, where shall we draw the line and say, Thus far extends his creative faculty and no further?

It has been thought on the one hand that the Book of Job is literal history in every part, and on the other that it is a "parable," and Job never existed. The latter opinion is no new one, but is put forward by an eminent rabbi in the course of a discussion in the Babylonian Talmud (*Baba Bathra 15a*). The truth must be somewhere between these extremes. Few will see in ch. xxxviii.—xli. a verbatim report of words of the Almighty, nor have the speeches of Job and the Three the character of an extempore dialogue. The mention of Job with Noah and Daniel in Ezekiel xiv. 14, 20 requires only that there should have been a tradition about him, which the book embodies, and the literary form of the discussion in the book may be due in great measure to the imagination of the writer. The date of the book may be widely different from the date of Job. It has been held that Moses wrote it, compiling the dialogue from more ancient sources: it is now held by many that it cannot have been written before the Babylonian Captivity. Granted that the scene of the dialogue is laid in the patriarchal age, it is said that the numerous and consistent marks of extreme antiquity which pervade the book are due to consummate art in the author, who however allows occasional allusions to his latter-day surroundings to escape him. Generally, for instance, the speakers, who are not of Israel, use the names of God proper to their supposed age and place, but at times they show a knowledge of the Tetragrammaton (ch. i. 21, xii. 9). The reference to the worship of the host of heaven in ch. xxxi. 26 is said to imply a knowledge of Deut. iv. 19. Space does not admit of more than a passing word on this topic, but the matter is one which will repay careful study. The chief positive argument for a late date of the book is its religious standpoint. On this too a word must suffice: compare Prov. xiii. 9, "the lamp of the wicked shall be put out," with Job's sceptical question, "How often is the lamp of the wicked put out?" (ch. xxi. 17), and we see that the time has come when the primitive law of temporal retribution has been found not to work uniformly. A later stage of thought had been reached than by the Solomonic age, to which however some great scholars have assigned the book. A later date is suggested by ch. xii. 17–19, "He leadeth counsellers away spoiled, &c.," which may be thought to describe the deportation of the Ten Tribes or of Judah, if the reference be to any event in Biblical history.

The theory that Job is "a parable" is true in the sense that he is a typical character. He does not speak merely as an individual when he says, "Wherefore are we counted as beasts, and reputed vile in your sight?" (ch. xviii. 3. cf. Psalm xliv. 11). God's perfect and upright servant Job (ch. ii. 3) has traits in common with the servant of the LORD described by Isaiah. The two portraitures should be carefully compared. In order of thought, if not in date, the Book of Job precedes the latter part of the Book of Isaiah, not rising to the height of the Evangelical Prophet's representation of the Suffering Saviour. But it contributes negatively, and to some extent positively, to larger views than prevailed in earlier times of the divine government of the world. One afflicted by God's permission, it is now seen, may be innocent, and yet it must be somehow demonstrable that God is not unrighteous. The hope of a vision of God after this life is confidently expressed (ch. xix. 25–27) in a sense and words which no one can exactly explain. But the complete solution of the problem of the book is set above human reason alike in the Prologue, which shows the purpose of the Almighty, and in His answers to Job. In its true place in history the book is a landmark in the course of a progressive Revelation, and it "opens the ear to instruction" which the people of God were to receive in the fulness of time. In the Septuagint of ch. ii. 11 the friends of Job are styled Kings. In the New Testament ch. v. 13 is quoted in 1 Cor. iii. 19, and "the patience of Job" is referred to by St. James.

THE BOOK OF JOB: CHAPTER BY CHAPTER

Job's prosperity.	1	Job's prosperity. Satan's malignity. Job's losses. "The LORD gave, and the LORD hath taken away."
	2	Job's increased trials. His patience. His wife tempts him to self-destruction. His three friends, Eliphaz, Bildad, Zophar.
Job speaks.	3	Job's passionate expressions of grief.
Eliphaz speaks.	4	Eliphaz charges Job with wickedness, because he is afflicted. He relates a vision.
	5	The end of the wicked. The sanctified afflictions of the righteous.
	6	Job complains of his severe afflictions. And of the reproaches of his friends.
	7	Job declares the shortness and miseries of life.
Bildad speaks.	8	Bildad charges Job with hypocrisy.
Job.	9	Job owns God's justice, and vindicates his own character.
	10	Job complains to God.
Zophar speaks.	11	Zophar reproves Job for justifying himself.
Job.	12	Job answers by satire; and then describes God's dominion and omnipotence.
	13	Job reproves his friends for partiality. Job appeals to God.
	14	Job reflects on man's mortality.
Eliphaz.	15	Eliphaz charges Job with impiety.
Job.	16	Job charges his friends with being unmerciful. He maintains his innocence.
	17	Job expresses his belief that he is near death.
Bildad.	18	Bildad charges Job with impatience. He shows the calamaties of the wicked.
Job.	19	Job declares his belief in the resurrection.

Zophar.	20	Zophar describes the disappointment and portion of the wicked.
Job.	21	Job argues that characters are not to be determined by their outward state.
Eliphaz.	22	Eliphaz exhorts Job to repentance.
Job.	23	Job appeals to God and longs to appear before him.
	24	He describes the oppressions of the wicked.
Bildad.	25	Bildad shows that man cannot be justified before God.
Job.	26	Job shows that God's ways are inscrutable.
	7	Job declares his own sincerity.
	28	Man fathoms many mysteries in nature; but God's ways in providence are unsearchable.
	29	Reminiscences of service to God; and of His blessing.
	30	Mournful change of circumstance.
	31	Protestations of integrity.
Elihu.	32	Elihu interposes between Job and his friends.
	33	He reproves Job for his complaints.
	34	He accuses Job of charging God with injustice.
	35	He exalts the ways of God.
	36	He vindicates the character and providence of God.
	37	He shows the greatness of God's power and wisdom.
God speaks.	38	God speaks from the whirlwind.
	39	He contrasts His power with man's weakness; and points to the wonders of the animal creation.
Job's confession.	40	Job's humble confession of vileness. God describes His own power.
	41	God still reasons with Job.
	42	Job humbles himself. He intercedes for his erring friends. Job is restored to prosperity. He lives 140 years longer.

PSALMS

A collection of 150 hymns or prayers, reflecting every human emotion and a deep relationship with God.

THE ESSENTIAL SUMMARY OF PSALMS

The Psalms are doubtless the work of several hands: among the chief may be reckoned David, Moses, Solomon and Asaph. The Book of Psalms contains 150 separate Psalms, which may be parted into five great divisions or books, which were formed at different periods.

The Psalms in most instances reveal the outpourings of the soul to God, and manifest the inner life. Those who know what it is to have communion with God realize in this Book that three thousand years ago the true worshippers had the same experiences as are passed through today; and that then, as now, God was found to be a "refuge and a strength; a very present help in trouble." In the Hebrew the Psalms ix., x., xxv., xxxiv., xxxvii., cxi., cxii., cxix., and cxlv., are acrostic in their construction.

Ps. cli is not generally found in the book, but like many others it is thought to have been written by David. This psalm is reproduced in full at the end of this section, with a short explanatory note.

COMMENTARY ON THE BOOK OF PSALMS

The Psalms collectively are called in Hebrew *Tehillim* or "Praises," but the word *mizmor* (Sept. *psalnzos*), which denotes a composition set to music, is found in the titles of many of them, and *Tehillah* in that of Ps. cxlv. only. The book is the first in order of the "Scriptures" (*Kethubim*) or Hagiographa, which with the Law and the Prophets make up the Hebrew Old Testament. The same three divisions are referred to in St. Luke xxiv. 44 as "the law of Moses, the prophets and the psalms," where the Psalms stand for the whole Hagiographa because they stand first in it, as the Book of Genesis is named in Hebrew from its first word *"In the beginning."* The Davidic writings formed part of Nehemiah's "library" (2 Macc. ii. 13). The Psalms from ix. to cxlvii. are numbered differently in the Hebrew and the Septuagint, two Hebrew psalms being reckoned as one, or one as two, in the Greek in the four cases:

Heb. ix. and x.	....	Sept. ix.
Heb. cxiv. and cxv.	....	Sept. cxiii.
Heb. cxvi.	....	Sept. cxiv. and cxv.
Heb. cxlvii.	....	Sept. cxlvi. and cxlvii.

Ps. ii. follows Ps. i. without a break in some Hebrew manuscripts, and it is cited under the head of Ps. i. in Acts xiii. 33 according to the Codex Bezoe and some other authorities.

The Hebrew Psalter is divided into five books, ending with Pss. xli., lxxii., lxxxix., cvi., cl. respectively, each terminal psalm concluding with or being of the nature of a doxology. As Moses gave Israel the five books of the Law, so (says the Midrash) David gave them the Psalms in five books. The Psalms, like the sections of the Pentateuch, may be classed as Jehovistic or Elohistic, whatever may be the real significance of that distinction. The following table shows the total number of psalms and the number that are anonymous in each book, and then specifies those ascribed in one sense or other to David, Solomon, Moses, the sons of Korah, Asaph, Ethan, Heman and Jeduthun, the rest being anonymous. After Book II. is written, "The prayers of David the son of Jesse are ended," but many later psalms are ascribed to David. The

Heman psalm is ascribed also to the sons of Korah, and the Jeduthun psalms two of them to David, and the third to Asaph.

Book	No.	Anon.	David	Solomon	Moses	Sons of Korah	Asaph	Ethan	Heman	Jeduthun
I	41	4	Except i, ii, x, xxxiii							xxxix
II	31	4	li–lxv, lxviii–lxx	lxxii		xlii, xliv–xlix	l			lxi
III	17	0	xxxvi			lxxxiv, lxxxv, lxxxvii, lxxxviii	lxxiii–lxxxiii	lxxxix	lxxxviii	lxxvii
IV	17	14	ci, ciii		xc					
V	44	28	cviii–cx, cxxii, cxxiv, cxxxi, cxxxiii, cxxxviii–cxlv	cxxvii						

DAVID. Seventy-three of the psalms, including nearly all in the first book, being thus ascribed to David, it was natural that the whole collection should be referred to as his, and that this convenient way of speaking should give rise in time to the popular belief that "the sweet psalmist of Israel" himself wrote all the so-called Psalms of David. Sacred psalmody is ascribed to him in general terms in 1 and 2 Chron., the accompanying instruments also being called "instruments of David," as in Neh. xii. 36 and Am. vi. 5. Jewish and Christian writers have explained away anachronisms such as that of attributing the anonymous captivity psalm, "By the rivers of Babylon" (Ps. cxxxvii.), to David (Sept.) by saying that he wrote it as a prophecy. Compare Ps. xcvi., "O sing unto the LORD a new song, &c.," which is often ascribed to David and to the occasion of the building of the house of the LORD *after the captivity*. In some cases in which a psalm is ascribed to David in the Hebrew also it seems that he could not have written it, and it has been concluded that the Hebrew titles are inaccurate and valueless. Before saying this we should be sure what meaning they were intended to convey. A prayer "of" (Hebrew, *to* or *for*) a person may be a prayer which he has himself composed and uttered (Hab. iii. 1), but a prayer "of " Moses (Ps. xc.), or of " David (Pss. xvii., lxxxvi.), or "of" (marg. *for*) an afflicted one (Ps. cii.), may none the less be a composition of some later "psalmist of Israel" befitting the character and circumstances of the person to whom it is ascribed. A psalm said to be "of" David may have been written generally in the character of David or with allusion to some particular occasion, as Ps. iii. (Absalom), vii. (Cush), xxx. (Dedication), xxxiv. (Abimelech), li. (Bathsheba), lii. (Doeg), liv. (Ziphim), lvi. (Gath), lvii. and cxlii. (the cave), lix. (when Saul sent), &c. The same preposition is used in assigning a psalm to the chief Musician or Precentor for performance and to David or Solomon or the sabbath day (Pss. iv.—vi., viii., ix., xi.—xiv., lxxii., xcii., &c.). In what sense and with what latitude it is to be taken must be determined in each case. While we have the best authority for regarding David as a psalmist and the chief of psalmists, not a few of the "Psalms of David" are certainly by other authors, and some have been assigned with more or less confidence to so late an age as that of the Maccabees. In special cases, as below, we have external testimony to the authorship and parallel texts of the whole or portions of a psalm.

Ps. xviii., "To the chief Musician, to the servant of the Lord, to David, &c." This psalm is found also in 2 Sam. xxii., where it is attributed to David as author. The two texts differing in places, the question arises, which is the more primitive? Possible clerical errors apart, the priority on the whole seems to rest with the text in Samuel, the psalm in the Psalter having been apparently altered for liturgical use. This result might have been anticipated. Many Christian hymns in Hymnals have been so altered from their original form. The differences between the two texts may be thought to testify to the fact that at a very early period the Jewish scribes were less scrupulously accurate in copying the Holy Scriptures than we know them to have been later; but we must not make too much of this present instance, for it is one thing to transcribe a psalm with variations for concurrent use in the Psalter and quite another to alter it in its original context. In any case, the differences in the two forms of it are not such as to affect the spirit and tenor of the psalm. Another instance of parallel texts is afforded by 1 Chron. xvi. 8–36, which comprises Ps. cv. 1–15, xcvi., cvii. 1, cvi. 47–8. The occasion is the bringing of the Ark of God to its resting-place, when David charges Asaph and his brethren to praise the LORD. Opinions differ as to the relation of the two texts.

SOLOMON. Ps. lxxii. is entitled "A Psalm *for* (marg. *of*) Solomon," and Ps. cxxvii. "A Song of degrees for (marg. *of*) Solomon." According to the Syriac the latter was spoken by David concerning Haggai [cf. i. 4] and Zechariah, who urged the building of the Temple. There is no conclusive reason to think either psalm Solomon's.

MOSES. Ps. xc. is called a prayer " of Moses." The title, as we have shown, being ambiguous, it is for the commentators to decide on other grounds whether the psalm is Mosaic.

KORAH. According to one view the ascription of certain psalms to the sons of Korah signifies that they wrote them. Another view is that they are designated not as authors but performers, like the "chief Musician." Korahites are mentioned as choristers in 2 Chron. xx. 19; and Heman, a descendant of Korah (Numb. xxvi. 11; 1 Chron. yi. 33), had fourteen sons and three daughters, all of whom "were under the hands of their father for song, &c." (1 Chron. xxv. 1–6). The titles of the Korah psalms leave it an open question to what generation of the "sons of Korah" they are assigned. Ps. lxxxviii. is "for the sons of Korah, to the chief Musician, Maschil of Heman the Ezrahite."

ASAPH. The Asaph psalms may have been thought to be written by Asaph, since Hezekiah and the princes gave commandment to praise the LORD "with the words of David and of Asaph the seer" (2 Chron. xxix. 30). But since Asaph was not only a writer of psalms but one of David's chief musicians, some of his sons also being musicians (1 Chron. xv. 19, xxv. 1), it has been argued that "to Asaph" may mean "to the Asaph family," as musicians.

HEMAN. ETHAN. JEDUTHUN. Solomon was wiser than "Ethan the Ezrahite, and Heman, &c." (1 Kings iv. 31). Jeduthun has been identified with Ethan. The title of Ps. xxxix. might denote that he was "chief Musician." But *on* Jeduthun" in Ps. lxii. and Ps. lxxvii. may mean *"after the manner of* Jeduthun," or on an instrument so called, or set to the time of a song so named or commencing.

THE SEPTUAGINT. This ascribes several of the anonymous psalms to David. In some manuscripts of it, most of the Pss.

xlii.–xlix. are ascribed both to him and to the sons of Korah. It varies or adds to the titles in other cases, as lxvi. (*anastaseos*), lxxi. (sons of Jonadab, &c.), lxxvi. and lxxx. (the Assyrian), xcvi. (rebuilding of temple), cxliv. (Goliath), cxlvi., &c. (Haggai and Zach.). It adds Ps. cli. as spoken by David of his duel with Goliath. Generally it testifies to the titles as we have them in the Hebrew, but fails to explain their difficulties. Some of its readings in them show critical appreciation of the place of the psalms in history.

The key to the meaning of the Psalter is a right conception of the personality of the psalmist, who at times assumes a character above the level of humanity, and speaks not as the historical Israelite but as the ideal Israel, the blameless or wrongfully suffering Servant of the LORD. Salient events in sacred history and the inspired writer's own surroundings serve as the vehicle of aspirations to be realized only in the Messiah and Messianic times. If he prays for or predicts disaster to his enemies it is because his enemies are the wicked (Ps. xxvii. 2), they and he being transfigured into embodiments of evil and good. His utterances must be interpreted with due allowance for their poetical and spiritual elements, and not with a prosaic literalism. Notice the opinion that the curses of Ps. cix. 6–20 are spoken not by David but by his enemies. This requires that we should read in verse 5, "And they have rewarded me ... saying," the word saying (not in the Hebrew) being supplied as in Ps. xxii. 7 and elsewhere.

No book of the Old Testament is more Christian in its inner sense or more fully attested as such by the use made of it than the Psalms. Out of a total of 283 direct citations from the Old Testament in the New, 116 have been counted from that one book. The Church by its preference for the Psalms reverses the sentence of the Synagogue, which judged the psalmists' inspiration inferior to that of the prophets, and set Moses on high above them all, so that no prophet might teach any new thing but only what was implicitly contained in the Law. This is not the place to discuss whether the New Testament by its citations determines the meaning or authorship of this or that psalm. The student should first of all endeavor to ascertain the original sense and setting of each as part of the Old Testament, and afterwards coordinate his results with what other data seem to require. The ascription of words to a typical per-sonage like David does not always and necessarily imply that they were spoken by the king "of flesh and blood" of that name, and an argument which seems to rest upon that assumption may prove valid if the words are ideally true as spoken in the character of David.

Titles are added to some of the Psalms, but it is open to question whether these are as old as the words to which they are attached. They mainly refer to the manner in which the words were to be sung or accompanied. Some Psalms were to be accompanied by stringed instruments (*Neginah, Neginoth* Pss. iv., liv., lv., lxi., lxvii., lxxvi. and Hab. 19), others by wind instruments (*Nehiloth* Ps. v.); while such titles as 'Set to *Alamoth*' (Ps. xlvi.) = maidens, 'Set to the *Sheminith*' (Pss. vi., xii.) – the octave, seem to imply that there was singing in parts. Some of the titles appear to be intended to indicate the character of the Psalm, as *Maschil* = giving instruction (Pss. xxxii., xlii., xliv., xlv,, lii.–lv., lxxiv., lxxviii., lxxxviii., lxxxix. and cxlii.), *Michtam*, rendered by some *Golden Psalm* (Pss. xvi., lvi.–lx.); while *Shiggaion* (Ps. vii.) with *Shigionoth* (Hab. iii. 1) may refer to the irregular erratic style of the compositions, *Gittith*= belonging to Gath (Pss. lxxvi., lxxxiv) may relate either to the melody or to the instrument used in the performance. The other titles are all most probably names of tunes, well known at the time, to which the Psalms were appointed to be sung. These are:

Aijeleth shahar (R. V. A. hash-shahar) 'The hind of the morning,' Ps. xxii.

Al-taschith (R.V. Al-tashheth) 'Destroy not,' Pss. lvii.–lix., lxxv.

Jonath-elem-rechokim (R. V. J. e. rehokim) 'The silent dove of them that are afar off,' Ps. lvi.

Mahalath, Ps. liii.

Mahalath Leannoth, Ps. lxxxviii.

Muth-labben, Ps. ix.

Shoshannim 'Lilies,' Pss. xlv., lxix. *Shoshannim Eduth* 'Lilies. A testimony,' Ps. lxxx.

Shushan-eduth 'The lily of testimony,' Ps. lx.

THE BOOK OF PSALMS: PSALM BY PSALM

First line	Ps.	Subject	Reputed Author
Blessed is the man.	i	The happiness of the godly. The miserableness wicked.	Ezra.
Why do the heathen?	ii	Triumphs of Christ's kingdom.	David.
LORD, how are they increased!	iii	Security of God's protection.	David.
Hear me when I call.	iv	God's favor is man's happiness.	David.
Give ear to my words.	v	A morning prayer.	David.
O LORD, rebuke me not in Thine anger.	vi	Pleading under chastening.	David.
O LORD, my God, in Thee do I put my trust.	vii	Imploring protection from enemies.	David.
O LORD, our LORD, how excellent is thy name.	viii	An evening hymn.	David.
I will praise Thee, O LORD.	ix	Thanksgiving for victory.*	David.
Why standest though afar off, O LORD?	x	Prayer for deliverance.*	Unknown.
In the LORD put I my trust.	xi	Confidence in God.	David.
Help, LORD: for the godly man ceaseth.	xii	Degeneracy lamented.	David.
How long wilt Thou forget me?	xiii	Entreating divine aid.	David.
The fool has said in his heart.	xiv	Infidelity deplored.	David.
LORD, who shall abide in Thy tabernacle?	xv	The faithful and upright.	David.
Preserve me, O God.	xvi	Messiah's confidence in God. His sufferings, death and resurrection.	David.

First line	Ps.	Subject	Reputed Author
Hear the right, O LORD.	xvii	Prayer against enemies.	David.
I will love Thee, O LORD, my strength.	xviii	Review of past deliverances.	David.
The heavens declare the glory of God.	xix	On the works and the Word of God.	David.
The LORD hear thee in the day of trouble.	xx	Prayer for safety and success.	David.
The king shall joy in Thy strength.	xxi	Thanksgiving for many blessings.	David.
My God, my God, why has Thou forsaken?	xxii	Messiah's prayer in His sufferings.	David.
The LORD is my Shepherd.	xxiii	A pastoral hymn, on God's providential care.	David.
The earth is the LORD's.	xxiv	Messiah's ascension.	David.
Unto Thee, O LORD, do I lift up my soul.	xxv	Prayer for pardon and preservation.*	David.
Judge me, O LORD.	xxvi	Pleading integrity.	David.
The LORD is my light.	xxvii	Review of dangers and deliverance.	David.
Unto Thee will I cry, O LORD, my rock.	xxviii	A Prayer of confidence.	David.
Give unto the LORD, O ye mighty &c.	xxix	The thunderstorm.	David.
I will extol thee, O LORD,	xxx	Deliverance from sickness.	David.
In Thee, O LORD, do I put my trust.	xxxi	Confidence and praise.	David.
Blessed is he whose transgression is forgiven.	xxxii	Blessedness of forgiveness.	David.
Rejoice in the LORD, all ye righteous.	xxxiii	Rejoicing in the LORD.	Unknown.
I will bless the LORD at all times.	xxxiv	Thanksgiving for deliverance.*	David.

First line	Ps.	Subject	Reputed Author
Plead my cause, O LORD.	xxxv	Prayer against enemies and persecutors.	David.
The transgression of the wicked.	xxxvi	Wickedness of men. Goodness of God.	David.
Fret not thyself because of evildoers.	xxxvii	The course and end of the wicked and the righteous contrasted.*	David.
O LORD, rebuke me not in thy wrath!	xxxviii	Humiliation under God's chastisement.	David.
I said I will take heed in my ways.	xxxix	The shortness and vanity of life [a funeral psalm].	David.
I waited patiently for the LORD.	xl	Experience of God's mercy. Prediction of the incarnation, obedience and ministry of Messiah.	David.
Blessed his he that considereth the poor.	xli	The blessedness of compassion.	David.
As the hart panteth.	xlii	Longing for communion with God.	David.
Judge me, O God.	xliii	A check to despondency.	David.
We have heard with our ears, O God.	xliv	Former mercies and present evils contrasted.	Unknown.
My heart is inditing a good matter.	xlv	A song of loves – Messiah's beauty and glory.	Unknown.
God is our refuge.	xlvi	God our refuge.	Unknown.
O, clap your hands.	xlvii	Joy and rejoicing – the ark on Zion the supposed subject.	Unknown.
Great is the LORD!	xlviii	Zion's beauty and security.	Unknown.
Hear this, all ye people.	xlix	Vanity of wealth and greatness.	Unknown.
The mighty God, even the LORD hath spoken.	l	God's majesty as judge. Hypocrisy reproved.	Asaph.
Have mercy on me, O God.	li	The penitent's psalm.	David.

First line	Ps.	Subject	Reputed Author
Why boastest thou thyself?	lii	Doeg the Edomite.	David.
The fool hath said.	liii	14th Psalm repeated.	David.
Save me O God! By thy name!	liv	Prayer and praise, when the Ziphim would have betrayed David.	David.
Give ear to my prayer, O God.	lv	Prayer against treacherous enemies.	David.
Be merciful to me, O God; for man &c.	lvi	Confidence in God amidst enemies.	David.
Be merciful to me, O God; be merciful.	lvii	Imploring divine protection.	David.
Do you indeed speak righteousness?	lviii	Wicked judges and counsellors reproved.	David.
Deliver me from mine enemies.	lix	David prays against Saul's spies sent to kill him.	David.
O God, thou hast cast us off.	lx	Prospect of victory over Edom.	David.
Hear my cry, O God!	lxi	God, a rock, shelter and tower.	David.
Truly my soul waiteth upon God.	lxii	God, the rock of salvation.	David.
O God, Thou art my God.	lxiii	Longing for the sanctuary.	David.
Hear my voice, O God!	lxiv	Treachery of, and triumph over, enemies.	David.
Praise waiteth for thee, O God, in Sion.	lxv	Praise for spiritual and temporal mercies.	David.
Make a joyful noise unto God.	lxvi	Exhortation to all the earth to praise.	David.
God be merciful to us!	lxvii	Prayer for conversion of the world.	Unknown.
Let God arise!	lxviii	Triumphal song. [A psalm of Christ's ascension.]	David.
Save me, O God!	lxix	The psalmist complains of his afflictions.	David.

First line	Ps.	Subject	Reputed Author
Make haste, O God!	lxx	Closing verses of Psalm xl.	David.
In Thee, O Lord, do I put my trust.	lxxi	Confidence in God in old age.	David.
Give the King Thy judgments!	lxxii	Solomon's prosperous reign as a type of Messiah's.	David.
Truly God is good to Israel.	lxxiii	Dangers of worldly prosperity.	
O God, why hast Thou cast us off?	lxxiv	The desolation of the Temple is lamented.	Jeremiah.
Unto thee, O God, do we give thanks.	lxxv	God is a just judge.	Asaph.
In Judah God is known.	lxxvi	God known by His people.	
I cried unto God with my voice.	lxxvii	In trouble, the godly remember former deliverances.	
Give ear, O my people!	lxxviii	Review of Israel's history.	
O God, the heathen are come.	lxxix	On Nebuchadnezzar's destruction of Jerusalem.	Jeremiah.
Give ear, O Shepherd.	lxxx	Israel God's vineyard.	
Sing aloud unto God.	lxxxi	Ode for the feast of trumpets.	
God standeth in the congregation.	lxxxii	The magistrate's Psalm.	
Keep not Thou silence, O God.	lxxxiii	Prayer against the enemies of Israel.	
How amiable are thy tabernacles!	lxxxiv	God's presence realized in His sanctuary.	Unknown.
Lord, Thou hast been favourable unto Thy land.	lxxxv	The return from the captivity rejoiced in.	Unknown.
Bow down Thine ear!	lxxxvi	A prayer for audience and aid against enemies.	David.
His foundation is in the holy mountains.	lxxxvii	Zion praised.	Unknown.

First line	Ps.	Subject	Reputed Author
O LORD God of my salvation.	lxxxviii	Prayer for deliverance n prospect of death.	Heman.
I will sing of the mercies of the LORD.	lxxxix	God's covenant with David and his seed.	Ethan.
LORD, Thou hast been our dwelling place.	xc	The brevity of life.	Moses.
He that dwelleth in the secret place of the Most High.	xci	Divine protection.	Moses or David.
It is a good thing to give thanks.	xcii	Psalm for the Sabbath day.	Unknown.
The LORD reigneth; He is clothed with majesty.	xciii	God the universal Sovereign.	Unknown.
O LORD God, to whom vengeance belongeth.	xciv	Appeal to God against oppressors. The blessedness of affliction.	David.
Oh come, let us sing unto the LORD!	xcv	Invitation to praise and worship.	David.
Oh, sing unto the LORD a new song!	xcvi	Praise to God, the Creator and the Judge.	David.
The LORD reigneth: let the earth rejoice!	xcvii	God's mysterious, wise and just government.	David.
Oh, sing unto the LORD a new song!	xcviii	A psalm of victory.	David.
The LORD reigneth: let the people tremble.	xcix	God to be exalted.	David.
Make a joyful noise unto the LORD.	c	God the creator and shepherd of his people.	Unknown.
I will sing of mercy and judgment.	ci	Resolutions to follow on to holiness.	David.
Hear my prayer, O LORD!	cii	Prayer for deliverance under heavy affliction. (Also Messianic.)	Unknown.

First line	Ps.	Subject	Reputed Author
Bless the Lord, O my soul; and all that is within me!	ciii	Thanksgiving for blessings and mercies of a life.	David
Bless the Lord, O my soul. O Lord my God, &c.	civ	The power and goodness of God.	David.
Oh, give thanks unto the Lord; call upon His name.	cv	Recapitulation of God's goodness.	David.
Praise ye the Lord. Oh, give thanks!	cvi	Israel's ingratitude and rebellion.	Unknown.
Oh, give thanks unto the Lord, for He is good!	cvii	Thanksgiving for the providential mercies, especially to travellers, sick persons, prisoners and mariners.	Unknown.
O God, my heart is fixed.	cviii	The 57th and 60th psalms included in one.	David.
Hold not Thy peace.	cix	Prayer against the wicked, predicting fate of Judas.	David.
The Lord said unto my Lord.	cx	The kingdom, priesthood, and triumphs of Messiah.	David.
Praise ye the Lord. I will praise the Lord.	cxi	General thanksgiving.*	Unknown.
Praise ye the Lord. Blessed is the man.	cxii	The happiness of the God-fearing man.*	Unknown.
Praise ye the Lord. Praise, O ye servants.	cxiii	God's condescension.	Unknown.
When Israel went out of Egypt.	cxiv	Miracles at the Red Sea.	Unknown.
Not unto us, O Lord.	cxv	Vanity of idols. A triumphal song.	Unknown.
I love the Lord.	cxvi	Recovery from illness.	David, or Hezekiah.
Oh, praise the Lord, all ye nations.	cxvii	All nations called to praise God for His kindness and truth.	Unknown.
Oh, give thanks unto the Lord.	cxviii	Praising God for victory.	David.

First line	Ps.	Subject	Reputed Author
Blessed are the undefiled in the way.	cxix	The Meditation, Prayer, and Soul-communing of an earnest man of God.*	Ezra, or Daniel.
In my distress, I cried unto the LORD.	cxx	A complaint of calumny and detraction. [The first of fifteen "songs of degrees" or songs of the steps, relating to the progress of the worshippers going up to Jerusalem to worship, on which occasion they were sung consecutively.]	Unknown.
I will lift up mine eyes.	cxxi	Confidence in God as the protector.	Unknown.
I was glad when they said unto me, &c.	cxxii	Delight in the worship of the sanctuary.	David
Unto Thee I lift up mine eyes.	cxxiii	Crying to God under contempt and insult.	Unknown.
If it had not been the LORD who was on our side.	cxxiv	Signal deliverance from enemies.	David
They that trust in the LORD.	cxxv	Security of those who make God their trust.	Unknown.
When the LORD turned again the captivity.	cxxvi	Deliverance from the captivity.	Perhaps Ezra.
Except the LORD build the house.	cxxvii	Success dependent on God's blessings.	Solomon.
Blessed is every one that feareth the LORD.	cxxviii	Family blessings.	Unknown.
Many a time have they afflicted me.	cxxix	Deliverance from persecution.	Unknown.
Out of the depths.	cxxx	Prayer for pardon.	Unknown.
LORD, my heart is not haughty.	cxxxi	Humility of soul.	David.
LORD, remember David.	cxxxii	Anxiety about the ark.	Unknown.
Behold, how good and how pleasant.	cxxxiii	Brotherly love, or the unity of Israel.	David.

First line	Ps.	Subject	Reputed Author
Behold, bless ye the LORD.	cxxxiv	Priests and Levites called to praise the LORD.	Unknown.
Praise ye the LORD! Praise ye the name.	cxxxv	A song of thanksgiving.	Unknown.
O give thanks.	cxxxvi	God's mercies perpetual. [This is the Jews' great Hallel, or Psalm of Praise.]	David or Solomon.
By the rivers of Babylon.	cxxxvii	Israel's tears by Babylon's waters.	Unknown.
I will praise Thee with my whole heart.	cxxxviii	Reliance upon God.	David.
O LORD, Thou has searched me.	cxxxix	God's omniscience.	David.
Deliver me, O LORD.	cxl	Prayer for deliverance from enemies.	David.
LORD, I cry unto Thee.	cxli	Prayer against temptation.	David.
I cried unto the LORD with my voice.	cxlii	Prayer for the soul's release in trouble.	David.
Hear my prayer, O LORD.	cxliii	Prayer for pardon and grace.	David.
Blessed be the LORD my strength.	cxliv	Gratitude, humility, praise and prayer.	David.
I will extol thee, my God, O King.	cxlv	God's greatness and goodness.*	David.
Praise ye the LORD! Praise the LORD, O my soul!	cxlvi	God the only safe help in need.	Haggai or Zechariah.
Praise ye the LORD, for it is good.	cxlvii	Praise to the God of nature, providence and grace.	Haggai or Zechariah.
Praise ye the LORD! Praise ye the LORD from the heavens.	cxlviii	All creatures invited to praise.	Haggai or Zechariah.
Praise ye the LORD. Sing unto the LORD a new song.	cxlix	Praise for Israel's victories.	Perhaps Nehemiah.
Praise ye the LORD! Praise God in His sanctuary!	cl	Praise, praise.	Perhaps Ezra.

*These Psalms are *acrostic* in their construction.

PSALM 151*

This psalm is ascribed to David as his own composition (though it is not listed with the others, and usually appears only in the Apocrypha). It is thought to have been written after he had fought in single combat with Goliath.

1   I was small among my brothers,
    and youngest in my father's house;
    I tended my father's sheep.

2   My hands made a harp,
    my fingers fashioned a lyre.

3   And who will declare it to my LORD?
    The LORD himself; it is he who hears.

4   It was he who sent his messenger
    and took me from my father's sheep,
    and anointed me with his anointing oil.

5   My brothers were handsome and tall,
    but the LORD was not pleased with them.

6   I went out to meet the Philistine,
    and he cursed me by his idols.

7   But I drew his own sword;
    I beheaded him, and removed reproach from the people
    of Israel.

*Not available in the Authorized Version. This translation is from the Revised Standard Version (RSV).

PROVERBS

A collection of wise and pithy sayings,
largely attributed to King Solomon.

THE ESSENTIAL SUMMARY OF PROVERBS

T he Proverbs are almost universally ascribed to Solomon, who "spake three thousand proverbs" (1 Kings iv. 32). These compressed, sententious, pithy sayings well embody the opinions of one to whom wisdom had originally been a special and Divine bestowment; and who had, so to speak, traded with this talent until the report of his intelligence had travelled into distant lands and "the wisdom of Solomon" had itself become a proverbial expression.

The Book of Proverbs opens with a clear statement that these are "the Proverbs of Solomon". Chapters xxv.–xxix. appear to constitute a supplementary collection. Chapter xxx. Consists of the "words of Agur, the son of Jakeh"; and the last chapter contains "the words of King Lemuel," and embody the teachings of a wise and sagacious mother. It has been held that the Book of Proverbs is but the essence of worldly wisdom, the experience of intelligent selfishness. But the constant references to "the LORD" indicate the spiritual basis on which the fabric of the book rests; and the frequent references in the New Testament to this Book prove its close connection in the apostolic mind with the entire system of gospel truth.

COMMENTARY ON THE BOOK OF PROVERBS

The Book of Proverbs (Sept. *paroimiai*) is called in Hebrew from its first word. It was also called Wisdom (ch. i. 2, 20) by early Christian writers, in accordance (as it seems) with Jewish tradition. The epithet all-virtuous (Gr. panaretos) was commonly added. The same title was used of the apocryphal books Wisdom and Ecclesiasticus. The Hebrew word rendered proverb is *mashal*, a similitude or parable, but the book contains many maxims and sayings not properly so called. In the Midrash the formula "*mashat*, to what is the matter like?" was used in introducing a parable, with which may be compared the way of speaking in St. Matt. xiii. 24, 31, 33. In St. Luke iv. 23, "Ye will surely say unto me this parable (A.V. proverb), Physician, heal thyself," there is a comparison to a physician and his work. The proverb is essentially figurative and its typical form parallelistic, as ch. xi. 22, "A jewel of gold in a swine's snout: a fair woman which is without discretion." But the figure is sometimes given without its interpretation, as "Stolen waters are sweet, and bread eaten in secret is pleasant" (ch. ix. 17), or "The fathers have eaten sour grapes, and the children's teeth are set on edge" (Ezek. xviii. 2). The transition is easy from the normal form of proverb, "As the whirlwind passeth, so is the wicked no more: but the righteous is an everlasting foundation" (ch. x. 25), to the figurative diction of ch. xii. 3, "the root of the righteous shall not be moved," and thence to the bare statement, "There shall no evil happen to the just: but the wicked shall be filled with mischief" (ver. 21), which is no proverb, but a simple "word of understanding" (ch. i. 2). The addresses of Wisdom consist of proverbs within a proverb, for it is "in a figure" (Heb. xi. 19) that she speaks in the character of the virtuous woman, not to mention that she is also "a tree of life to them that lay hold upon her" (ch. iii. 18). Solomon's wisdom is described in 1 Kings iv. 29–34: "He spake three thousand proverbs; and his songs were a thousand and five." It is not said that he wrote down any of his proverbs; and if all in the Book of Proverbs were his, the great majority of the three thousand would still have been lost. The book, like Ecclesiastes, was criticised, according to the Babylonian Talmud (Shabbath 30 b), where we read that it was sought to make it apocryphal on account of its contradictions, as "Answer not a fool according to his folly ... Answer a fool according to his folly" (ch. xxvi. 4, 5). Elsewhere some more serious objections were made to it, for there is much in it which does not rise above the plane of worldly wisdom. But it contains also thoughts which are the germ of the philosophy of revealed religion, Christian and Jewish, and it presupposes everywhere that "The fear of the LORD is the beginning of wisdom" (ch. i. 7, ix. 10). Its use of the most holy name Jehovah would have given it a certain sanctity in Jewish eyes. The least spiritual of the Proverbs are yet invaluable (it has been said) as reminding us that the voice of Divine Inspiration does not disdain to utter homely truths. They teach us that goodness is also wisdom, and wickedness folly. In Hebrew manuscripts the Hagiographa begins with Psalms, Proverbs, Job, or with Psalms, Job, Proverbs; but St. Jerome testifies to the order, Job, David, and then Solomon with his trilogy as in the A.V. The Book of Proverbs itself tells us that it was not put together by Solomon, part of it claiming to have been added by the scribes of King Hezekiah. It subdivides itself as follows. Chap. i.—ix. Title and contents (ch. i. 1–6) with prologue on Wisdom and Folly. Solomon is named as author of the Proverbs generally, but perhaps not specially of this section. Other parcemiasts are recognised in ch. i. 6: "To understand a proverb the words of the wise, and their dark sayings." The prologue is, in a word, the book of Wisdom, the offspring and agent of God and the teacher of men. "Wisdoms crieth without" (ch. i. 20), the plural denoting all-wisdom. She is Achamoth in the gnostic angelology. There is wisdom and wisdom: a wisdom of the craftsman, " and all manner of cunning (lit. wise) men, &c." (1 Chron. xxii. 15), and a wisdom whose "seat is the bosom of God, her voice the harmony of the world" (ch. viii. 30). Wisdom in Greek also ranges from technical skill to a "divine philosophy." The lower serves as the vehicle of a higher sense in St. Paul's "wise masterbuilder" (1 Cor. iii. 10) and again in Wisd. vii. 22, "For wisdom, which is the worker of all things, taught me." The entire collection down to its most homely counsels is a book of "wisdoms." Some have made this part of Proverbs earlier and some later than the body of the work. Some date it before the verses on wisdom in Job xxviii. and some after. The strange woman's "peace offerings" (ch. vii. 14) point to early times as of the monarchy. With Solomon's choice of wisdom carrying with it riches and honor (2 Chron. i. 12) compare Prov. iii. 16, "Length of days is in her right hand; and in her left hand riches and honor." Ch. x.–xxii. 16. Proverbs of Solomon. This is the main part of the book, and probably its earliest part on the whole. It consists of an anthology of proverbs and sentences which must be studied in detail. Like the Wisdom section (ch. iii. 18) it allegorizes the tree of life (ch. xi. 30, xiii. 12, xv. 4), and it has sayings, as on the talebearer (ch. xviii. 8) and the brawling woman (ch. xxi. 9), which link it to the Hezekian collection. Compare ch. xv. 11, "Sheol and Abaddon are before the LORD," with Job xxvi. 6. Ch. xxii. 17–xxiv. 22 and xxiv. 23–34. Words of the Wise. These sections commence without a break in our Bibles, one with, "Incline thine ear, and hear the words of the wise," and the other with, "These also are of the wise." The ascription of the Proverbs to Solomon in 1 can only be taken generally. Notice the Deuteronomic precept, "Remove not the ancient landmark" (ch. xxii. 28, xxiii. 10), and compare ch. xxiv. 23 with Levit. xix. 15. Ch. xxv.–xxix. "These are also proverbs of Solomon, which the men of Hezekiah king of Judah copied out." The greater part of the work is older than this appendix by the "men of Hezekiah." Ch. xxx. The burden of Agur. Compare the mysterious saying in ver. 4, "Who hath ascended up into heaven, &c.," with St. John iii. 13 and Eph. iv. 10. If the fourth thing that is "comely in going" is a king "when his army is with him," the word rendered "no rising up" (ver. 31) must be the Arabic word *qaum* preceded by the article *at* (or *el*). Compare the name Almodad in Gen. x. 26 and the "stones of elgabhish" in Ezekiel xiii. 11 and xxxviii. 22; and for the sense compare the processional "goings" in the sanctuary (Ps. lxviii. 24). Ch. xxxi. The burden of Lemuel. The description of the virtuous woman may be of different authorship, but the chapter as it stands is a continuous whole. King Lemuel's mother teaches him "Give not thy strength unto women," and the contrasted picture of the ideal wife follows naturally. It is in twenty-two verses, beginning severally with the letters of the alphabet in their present order. As the Jews have an alphabet of confession for the Day of Atonement, Aslamnu, Bagadnu, Gazalnu, &c., and as the all-holy is he who fulfils the law "from Aleph to Tau," so this woman's virtues exhaust the alphabet, and the book fitly closes with an incarnation of the Wisdom that is graced with every virtue and of price above "rubies" (ch. viii. 11, xxxi. 10. Cf. Job xxviii.). The virtuous woman is the one among a thousand whom the Preacher failed to find (ver. 10; Eccl. vii. 28). Psalms cxi., cxii., cxix., &c. and Lam. i.—iv. are alphabetic. Granted that the acrostic style is not primitive, it does not help us to fix a close limit of date. The Septuagint version of Proverbs abounds in glosses and additions, of which but a few instances must suffice. Ch. iii. 9, "just labors." Ch. iv. 26, 27, of. Heb. xii. 13. Ch. vi. 8, the bee. Ch. xxvi. 11, cf. 2 Pet. ii. 22. Ch. xxvii. 16 in this version styles Boreas euphemistically epidexios. In the New Testament the book is quoted some twenty times by St. Paul and in the Catholic Epistles, and again in Heb. xii. and Rev. mostly according to the Septuagint, the citation in Rom. xii. 20, "If thine enemy hunger, &c.," the two citations of Prov. x. 12, and the predominant use of ch. iii., being especially noteworthy. Nothing is cited as Solomon's, but we read in the Gospel of his glory and his wisdom. According as Wisdom is to be regarded as a "master workman" or a "nursling" in Prov. viii. 30, we may see an embodiment of the thought in St. John i. 3 or 18. Pray. viii. 22 was much contested in the Arian controversy.

THE BOOK OF PROVERBS: CHAPTER BY CHAPTER

Wisdom.	1	Wisdom.
	2	The advantages of wisdom.
	3	Wisdom the chief good.
	4	Cautions and counsels.
Wisdom's warnings on Chastity, &c.	5	Wisdom's warnings against female seducers.
	6	Cautions against suretyship, idleness and vice.
	7	Arts and the destructiveness of the adulteress.
	8	Wisdom personified.
	9	Feast of wisdom.

Virtues and vices.	10	Proverbs begin: Wisdom; industry; hatred; &c.
	11	Honesty; pride; tale-bearing; mercy; liberality; &c.
	12	The virtuous woman; the wise man; wrath; deceit; lying; sloth.
	13	Prudence; diligence.
	14	Lessons of prudence; marks of folly.
The tongue.	15	How to use the tongue.
	16	Government of the heart and conduct.
	17	Strife produces misery. Kindness hides faults. Friendship is shown in adversity. Prudent silence commended.
	18	Tale-bearing; idleness; poor and rich.
	19	Knowledge; benevolence; piety; and their opposites.
	20	Wine; divers weights; bargaining.
	21	The king's heart; the brawling woman; the false witness.
	22	The good name; the rich and poor; the prudent man. Training a child; sowing iniquity; robbing the poor. Friendship with the angry; sureties for debts; removing land-marks.
Morals.	23	Temperance and chastity.
	24	On envy and fretfulness. The field of the slothful.
Hezekiah's collection.	25	Proverbs collected by Hezekiah's scribes. Duties of kings; conduct towards neighbors; confidence in an unfaithful man; kind treatment of an enemy.
	26	How to answer fools; character of the slothful; dangers of strife; deceit and hatred.
	27	Presuming on time; wrath; faithful reproof; friendship; prudence and foresight.
	28	Oppressing the poor. Obedience to law. Evil rulers. Hastening to be rich.

	29	Hardihood in sin. Correcting children. Pride has its fall.
Agur's prayer.	30	Argur's words. His confession. His prayer.
Four generations.		*Four generations:* Cursing. Pure in their own eyes. Lofty-eyed. Sharp-teethed.
Four things unsatisfied.		*Three things, yea four, never satisfied:* The yawning grave. The barren womb. The thirsty earth. The devouring fire.
Four things wonderful.		*Three things, yea four, wonderful, or difficult to trace:* The eagle's flight. The serpent's track on the rock. The ship's course. Human organism.
Four disquieting things.		*Three things, yea four, disquiet the earth:* The slave in power. The pampered glutton. The ill-tempered wife. The maid-servant mistress.
Four wise things.	30	*Four things, patterns of wisdom:* The ants. The conies. The locusts. The spiders.
Four that go well.		*Four things remarkable for strength and dignity:* The lion. The greyhound. The he-goat. The king.
Words of Lemuel.	31	Advice to a young prince: against wantonness and wine; whom to choose for a queen. *(Verses 10–31 are acrostic.)*

159

ECCLESIASTES

All life is brief; seek wisdom and do God's will.

THE ESSENTIAL SUMMARY OF ECCLESIASTES

This book has been called the greatest collection of pessimism in literature. It includes declarations on the value of wisdom interspersed with reflections on the vanity of human ambition and folly. All men will return to dust like the beasts of the field. They should therefore live well, seeking wisdom and fearing God.

COMMENTARY ON THE BOOK OF ECCLESIASTES

Ecclesiastes (Sept.) is in Hebrew Koheleth (Aq. *koleth*), a title of somewhat doubtful meaning, although clearly akin to a word meaning assembly. Wyclif explains it as "talker to the puple or togidere clepere." Our rendering Preacher (Luth. Prediger) comes through St. Jerome's *Concionator*. The word being of the feminine form, some think that it denotes Wisdom personified, who harangues the assembled people (Prov. i. 20, viii. 1): but compare the masculine *Sophereth* in Neh. vii. 57 and Ezra ii. 55. The Midrash explains that Solomon was called Koheleth because "his words were spoken in the assembly" (1 Kings viii. 1, 2). A Jewish commentator of unknown name and date is said by Aben Ezra (1092–1167 AD) to have resolved the Preacher into an "assembly" of the disciples of Solomon, who spake "each according to his opinion." Ecclesiastes, like Job, has a Prologue and an Epilogue, the body of the work being made up of reflections on the primary problems of life as they present themselves to the critical observer. These are all attributed to one and the same "Preacher," whose varying moods have led some to postulate a diversity of thinkers.

Ch. i. 1–11. The Prologue. "The words of the Preacher, the son of David, king in Jerusalem. Vanity of vanities, saith the Preacher ... all is vanity ... there is no new thing under the sun" (ver. 1, 2, 9). He reflects upon the eternal routine of Nature and the transitoriness of men.

Ch. i. 12—xii. 8. "I the Preacher was king over Israel in Jerusalem" (i. 12). He claims to have had greater wisdom and magnificence than all that were before him in Jerusalem (i. 16, ii. 9). He resolves to compare wisdom with "madness and folly," and finds only that "in much wisdom is much grief" (i. 17, 18). Wisdom may excel folly, but the wise and the fool come to the same end: this also is vanity (ii. 13–17). The doctrine of opportuneness in ch. iii. is a salient feature of the book. "To everything there is a season." God saw His work and pronounced it very good: the Preacher saw that He had made everything "beautiful *in its season*," and had set "the world" in men's heart without their being able to understand His work in its entirety. Their large capacity of enjoyment in their limited sphere is the gift of God (iii. 13, v. 18). Failures of justice "under the sun" raise the hope of a judgment to come in its season. Yet "who knoweth the spirit of man?" (iii. 21). Does it go upward or is it like the spirit of the beasts that perish? This verse is much disputed, but it shows at least that the question of a future life was in the thought of the writer. Perhaps after all the fool who "foldeth his hands" is wiser in his generation than the most successful toiler (iv. 4–8). But there is unwisdom in hasty pronouncements, "for God is in heaven, and thou upon earth" (v. 2), and what is amiss may be the necessary outcome (as we should say) of "second causes," the supreme power not dealing directly with the individual subject (v. 8). In the latter part of the book, while the old threads are taken up from time to time, there is less of sustained speculation and more of simple proverbial philosophy, as ch. vii. 1, "Good is a name [Prov. xxii. 1] more than good oil"—with a play on *shem, shemen*; ch. viii. 4, of a king, "who may say unto him, What doest thou?" (Job ix. 12); ch. ix. 4, "A living dog is better than a dead lion"; ch. x. 1, "Dead flies cause the ointment of the apothecary to send forth a stinking savor"; ch. xi. 1, "Cast thy bread upon the waters: for thou shalt find it after many days." The section ch. xii. 1–7 teaches, "Remember thy Creator in the days of thy youth"; and it describes the closing scene of life in a highly poetical passage, which seems to convey a sense by the mere music of its words, although its interpreters are as little in harmony as the expounders of the Song of Songs. The majority, resting upon a Rabbinic tradition, find in the whole a more or less complete anatomy of the human frame. But the recurrent "or ever" (ver. 1, 2, 6) divides it into three subsections, the first literal, the second and third partly figurative: the third, ver. 6, 7, consists of figures and their interpretation, and the parallelism suggests that the second should be divided in like manner, namely, at ver. 3, "In the day when." The same formula marks the transition from a like figure to its interpretation in Isaiah xxx. 26. With the bird, the millstone and other details of this subsection compare Rev. xviii. 2, 22, &c. "Vanity of vanities, saith the Preacher, all is vanity" (ver. 8).

Ch. xii. 9–14. The Epilogue. The Preacher "set in order many proverbs." The conclusion of the whole matter is, "Fear God, and keep his commandments." God will bring everything into judgment, "whether it be good, or whether it be evil." Notwithstanding that the epilogue is uniform in style with the rest of the work, it is sometimes assumed to be by a later writer, either to save the Solomonic authorship, or because it consists of "words of Torah," which do not harmonize with the supposed final conclusion, that "all is vanity." Would the book have been ascribed to its traditional author if this had been its last word?

Although Koheleth has all the features of the historical Solomon—king, man of pleasure, wisest of men, poet and paroemiast, it may be doubted whether the book really claims him as its author. We must agree with Rashbam (1085–1155 AD) that the epilogue, which sums up in editorial style, was written of and not by him; and we may think that the Preacher's own announcement that he had been "king over Israel in Jerusalem " (ch. i. 12) bewrays one who looked back after the division of the kingdom to the son of David's reign in the southern metropolis " over all

Israel " (1 Kings xi. 42). There are also in the book sayings on the powers that be which would come more naturally from one of the misgoverned than from a ruler; and some things, as his fair trial of "madness and folly" (ch. i. 17), which make it doubtful whether the speaker is intended to be any real person at all. The Babylonian Talmud (*Baba Bathra* 15 *a*) says that " Hezekiah and his company [Prov. xxv. 1] wrote Isaiah, Proverbs, Song of Songs, Koheleth."

Ecclesiastes has been assigned to various periods, from Solomon to Herod the Great. The apocryphal Wisdom of Solomon, which has been called Anti-Ecclesiastes, seems to be providing an antidote to its teaching in several places. Compare Eccl. iv. 2, "I praised the dead, &c.": Wisd. i. 12, "Seek not death in the error of your life." Wisd. ii. 1, 2, "For they said, reasoning with themselves, but not aright, &c.": Eccl. iii. 19, "the sons of men are a chance, &c." The son of Sirach, on the contrary, apparently copies and imitates it, and we may infer that he included it in "the rest of the books" (Prologue to Ecclus.), or Hagiographa. Thus it falls somewhere between Ecclesiasticus and Proverbs, to which it probably alludes in ch. xii. 9. In style and language it approximates in some respects to the later Hebrew.

The wise would have made Koheleth an apocryphal book on account of its contradictions, chap. vii. 3 (marg.), 9, &c., but that "its beginning is words of Torah and its end words of Torah" (T. B. *Shabbath* 30 *b*). The prologue and the epilogue are the inspired writer's orthodox setting of the negative results of the philosophy of his day, and the thought which crowns the whole is that the fear of God is the end, as Solomon had said that it was the beginning (Prov. i. 7, ix. 10), of wisdom.

The Book of Ecclesiastes: Chapter by Chapter

Vanity.	1	The vanity of earthly things.
	2	The vanity of carnal pleasures.
	3	A time for all things.
	4	Vanity: in oppression; in labor; in solitude; even in royalty.
	5	Vanity: in formal worship; in increasing riches.
	6	Vanity of unenjoyed riches.
	7	A good name. The house of mourning. Wisdom praised.
On kings.	8	Kings to be respected. Difference between the righteous and the wicked.
	9	Worldly condition no test of character. The little city.
	10	On wisdom and folly. The dead fly. The riding servant. The prating fool.
	11	Benevolence. Responsibility.
	12	Youthful piety. Vanity of age. Judgment.

SONG OF SOLOMON

A song of the love between Christ and His Church.

THE ESSENTIAL SUMMARY OF THE SONG OF SOLOMON

This book is a love poem, or a collection of fragments of love poems, which has been interpreted as an allegory of the love between God and the people of Israel or, among Christians, of the love between Christ and the Church.

COMMENTARY ON THE SONG OF SOLOMON

The Song of Solomon or **Canticles** is called in Hebrew the **Song of Songs**. This title is a superlative, like Heaven of Heavens and Holy of Holies, and denotes a song of supreme excellence, and not a song made up of songs as the Bible of books. The work is indeed a mosaic of poetical speeches in which all eyes do not see the same pattern, but the correspondence of its parts points to unity of design, although the book may now be (as has been said) like a lock whose key has been lost. In what consists its excellence? The answer depends upon the interpretation of the Song. Some make it a parable of singular depth and subtlety, and an apocalypse of the future of the Church to the end of the world. Some see in it only a romance in glorification of true love: a shepherdess loves a shepherd, and is wooed by King Solomon, and withstands the temptation to be faithless to her swain. Rabbi Akiba in the Mishnah (*Yadaim* iii. 5) defends and commends the Song in hyperbolical language, and he lays down, with a play upon the form of its title, that all the Scriptures are Holy (lit. holiness), but the Song of Songs is Holy of Holies. The ascription "to Solomon" seems to mean that he is the real or reputed author rather than the subject of the Song. Its abundance of names of plants and animals is in the manner of the royal poet who "spake of trees" from the cedar to the hyssop and "spake also of beasts" (1 Kings iv. 33); and it refers to royalty and its paraphernalia in terms which befit the peaceful and prosperous state of Solomon. Some who deny his authorship date the book a bare half century later than his times, while a few bring it down to the third century B.C. These lay stress on some of its peculiarities of diction, which on the other side are explained as provincialisms appropriate to the scene of action. It is disputed whether there are two or three principal characters in the Song, in addition to the chorus of "daughters of Jerusalem" and some occasional interlocutors. According to the following analysis, which (with variations) many adopt, there are three chief speakers, the Shulamite, the shepherd and the king, and the drama is in five acts, three of which end with the adjuration, that "ye stir not up nor awaken love until it please" (ch. ii. 7, iii. 5, viii. 4).

Ch. 7. A Shulamite maiden is brought to the royal residence and put in charge of the "daughters of Jerusalem" or court ladies. She longs for her shepherd lover and repels the advances of the king. She adjures the court ladies not to tempt her to love another.

Ch. ii. 5. She describes a past visit from the shepherd in her home; and a recent dream that she had sought and found him. She adjures the court ladies as before.

Ch. iii. 6—v. 1. Solomon in all his glory seeks to win the heart of the Shulamite. The shepherd's real or imagined offer to rescue his betrothed from her extreme peril: "Come with me from Lebanon, my spouse ... from the lions' dens, from the mountains of the leopards." He praises her charms and her constancy.

Ch. v. 2–viii. 4. Dream of the Shulamite, in which she seeks but fails to find her vanished lover. She describes the person of her beloved. The king flatters her, but all her desire is for the shepherd, whom she calls upon to return with her to their native place. She adjures the court ladies as before.

Ch. viii. 5–14. The return home. The divine flame of love. The reward of constancy.

To all this it has been objected that "Solomon" would not have celebrated his discomfiture by a rustic rival in a "song of songs," and that some words in the Song, the call "from Lebanon" for instance, are more naturally ascribed to the king, himself the accepted suitor, and called by a figure of speech a shepherd, than, as above, to a shepherd distinct from him. Dividing the fourth "act" at ch. vi. 10, we may say that the Song consists of a first part, of 62 verses, with subsections commencing at ch. i. 1, ii. 8, iii. 6, and a second part, of 55 verses, with subsections commencing at ch. v. 2, vi. 10, viii. 5. The first part describes the arrival of Solomon as the bridegroom in his nuptial crown (ch. iii. 11). With the king's call to the Shulamite in this part, "With me from Lebanon [to Jerusalem], &c." (ch. iv. 8), compare hers to him in the second part, "Come, my beloved, let us go forth into the field, &c." (ch. vii. 11, viii. 2). His love would raise her to a higher life, "Forget thy people and thy father's house " (Ps. xlv. 10): she would have him condescend to her low estate. There are many other such correspondences between the two parts which the reader will note for himself or find pointed out in commentaries. If the resemblance of "Shulammith" (Shulamite) to "Shelomith," the feminine of Solomon, was designed, this favors the latter view of the plot; but neither way of distributing the parts is without its difficulties. Some, taking the Song to be an epithalamium on the marriage of Solomon with Pharaoh's daughter (ch. vii. 1, Sept. Aminadab), divide it into seven parts, corresponding to the supposed seven days of the festivities. Some see in it the three characters, Solomon, the Shulamite, and Pharaoh's daughter.

Much of the obscurity of the book is owing to the impossibility of deciding absolutely to what speakers some things in it are to be assigned. Thus in ch. vi. 13 is it Solomon that says, "Return, return, O Shulamite," or the chorus? According to one opinion, they call her back: she asks what they want to see in her: they say, "A dance of Mahanaim": she dances, and they (not Solomon) describe her from foot to head, ending with "a king is bound in thy tresses" (ch. vii. 5). Then the king speaks down to v. 9a, and the bride breaks in at the words "best wine": she confesses herself his absolutely—notice the climax ii. 16, vi. 3, vii. 10, and invites him to her home, Come, my beloved, &c." (ch. vii. 11).

The Song culminates in her apotheosis of love in ch. viii. 6, 7, "the flashes thereof are flashes of fire, a very flame of the LORD if a man would give all the substance of his house for love, it would be utterly contemned." Compare St. John's "Love is of God ... God is love." A man may give his all and not have love (1 Cor. xiii. 3).

The Church is thought of in Eph. v. 25–27 as the destined bride, "not having spot, or wrinkle, or any such thing." The realism of the picture is remarkable and of a piece with descriptions in the Song, from ch. iv. 7 of which the Apostle may have borrowed his phrase "not having spot." Ch. vii. 11, "Come, my beloved," may be referred to in Rev. xxii. 17, a curious reading of which is mentioned in the Speaker's Commentary on the Song, "Sponsus [ch. iv. 8] et Sponsa [vii. 11] dicunt, Veni."

The numerous interpretations of the Song fall into two classes, according as the love described is regarded as simply human or as a symbol of the love of Jehovah and the congregation of Israel, which in the New Testament becomes the love of Christ and the Church. This theory may of course be held without the extravagances with which so many commentators have invested it. Of literal interpreters some have stigmatized the Song as unworthy of a place among canonical books, while many pronounce its theme a most fit one for the pen of a sacred writer. But, whatever it may have meant to its author, it does not appear that it was eventually enrolled among the books of Holy Scripture on the ground of its literal sense. If those who explained away the objections to it (Aboth de R. N., cap. i) were of one mind with Rabbi Akiba, they must have seen more in it than a secular "Song of loves" (Ps. Xlv. 1). A history of its interpretations in the Synagogue is given by Salfield in the Magazin für die Wiss. Des Judenthums, Jahrg. v. and vi. (1878–79.

THE SONG OF SOLOMON: CHAPTER BY CHAPTER

1	Mutual love of Christ and His Church.
2	Spiritual intercourse between Christ and His Church.
3	The Church seeking Christ.
4	The graces of the Church.
5	The beauty of Christ.
6	Mutual commendations of Christ and His Church.
7	The Church's beauty.
8	The Church's love to Christ. Christ's love to the Gentiles.

ISAIAH

The longest and the most influential of the prophetical books.

THE ESSENTIAL STORY OF ISAIAH

It was during the year that Uzziah, leper king of Judah, died that the prophet Isaiah received his calling from God. One of the greatest of the prophets, Isaiah was active for more than forty years, during the turbulent reigns of Uzziah, Jotham, Ahaz, Hezekiah, and Manasseh in Judah.

The most political of the prophets, he was probably of high birth and thus with access to the court, so that King Hezekiah in particular relied on his counsel. In addition to being a prophet, Isaiah was a statesman, reformer, teacher of kings, and a theologian. The theme of his ministry was set by God at the moment of his calling: that retribution was to come for the impieties and sins of the Jews – but that after suffering a new beginning would come.

Much of Isaiah's message had been foreshadowed by Amos (see The Old Testament Thirtieth Book). Like Amos, he was concerned with the social injustice of the times and the complacent, mechanical worship in the Temple, which had become the center of a fetishistic cult and a meaningless end in itself, adulterated by the importation of foreign practices and gods – and the sheer ingratitude of the people to God. But Isaiah had a more direct influence than Amos or Micah (his contemporary), largely because of his connections in high places, and he also gathered a group of disciples to perpetuate his teaching.

170

During Isaiah's time, the kingdom of Israel was defeated, reduced, and eventually destroyed by the Assyrians. In addition to paying tribute to Assyria – which meant repeated raids on the Temple treasury – King Ahaz of Judah attempted to appease the Assyrians by allowing the introduction of other religions, including those concerned with the sun, moon, and stars, while an Assyrian-style altar replaced the original in the Temple courtyard. In vain did Isaiah tell Ahaz that he was in error. Alliances and political maneuvers would not work: the Jews must place their trust in the hands of God alone.

As the situation of Israel went from bad to worse, Judah watched fearfully under the direction of a new king. Hezekiah enjoyed a good relationship with Isaiah, and for more than a dozen years followed his wise counsel. He instituted a religious reformation of the kingdom, a root and branch destruction of the alien cults that had so corrupted Judah. Idols of alien gods were destroyed, altars pulled down, and even the brazen serpent melted down. This, dating from the time of Moses, had become, perversely, a religious symbol in its own right — the priests burned incense to it. For Hezekiah and Isaiah it was idolatry, a mere piece of bronze.

Hezekiah also celebrated the Passover, which seems again to have been neglected for a long time, and he encouraged the inhabitants of what remained of the northern kingdom to participate in the feast at Jerusalem. He also took measures to improve the defenses of Jerusalem, which had been badly damaged by an incursion by King Pekah of Israel some years before. And construction work was also undertaken to improve and secure the supply of water to the city, vital if it were to survive a long siege.

It was during the reign of Hezekiah that Judah witnessed the end of their fellow kingdom. Already reduced to little more than the city state of Samaria, the Israelites revolted against Assyria, bringing down the full weight of the mighty empire and their own destruction. The Assyrian king, Shalmaneser V, razed the city and deported the people, never to be heard of again. In their place the land was colonized from the east. These newcomers brought their own gods and cults, but they also intermarried with some of those Jews who remained, and a hybrid form of worship that included the Hebrew God evolved. These people became known as the Samaritans – but the lack of purity in their religion made them anathema to the Jews of Judah (which explains the force of Christ's parable some seven centuries later). Meanwhile a precious few of the northern Jews came as refugees to Judah, increasing its population and strengthening it.

Judah was now a very small, isolated country between the mighty, ambitious and menacing powers of Assyria and Egypt (the power of Babylon being yet to make itself felt). There was always an Egyptian presence in the court of Jerusalem, and eventually it succeeded in seducing Hezekiah into alliance – contrary to the vociferous advice of Isaiah. The result was an expedition by the Assyrian King Sennacherib, which deprived Judah of many of its cities and towns, including Lachish. Hezekiah paid out a substantial tribute to induce the Assyrians to retire; but it was not long before they were back, demanding the unconditional surrender of Jerusalem. Isaiah reassured Hezekiah, for God would come to their aid. The Assyrians departed to campaign elsewhere but were soon back in strength, encamped about the city, which was now under siege. As Isaiah had warned, the promises of help from Egypt did not prove forthcoming.

In this crisis, Hezekiah and Isaiah prayed for help. And God responded, sending an angel of death into the enemy camp. Miraculously rescued, Jerusalem watched the ruins of the Assyrian army depart. For a while, the city was saved; in Nineveh, a palace coup ended the reign of Sennacherib, and the threat from Assyria abated. But Isaiah's message, unheard in the celebration of the miracle, remaiwned the same. Destruction and suffering were inescapable in the longer term. Babylon was no answer, for in time it would prove an even sterner tyrant than Assyria – princes of the throne of David, Isaiah predicted, would one day be mere palace slaves in Babylon.

But yet there was hope. After all the destruction and suffering, a remnant would rebuild God's city — a new Jerusalem would arise, righteous and faithful to the true God.

COMMENTARY ON THE BOOK OF ISAIAH

Isaiah, son of Amos, a prophet of Judah, of whom personally little is known beyond the fact that he lived in the capital, was married (viii. 3) and the father of several children (vii. 3; viii. 1–4;, cf. v. 18), prophesied from the last year of Uzziah (vi. 1) at least till the invasion of Sennacherib, a period of 40 years (cir. 740–701), living possibly into the reign of Manasseh (2 Chr. xxvi, 22.; xxxii. 32), by whom according to a tradition (in Justin and apocryphal "Ascension of Isaiah") he was "sawn asunder" (cf. Heb. xi. 37). He rose to great influence at the court of Hezekiah (xxxvii. 1 *seq.*), was the fear of the political parties of his day (xxix. 15; xxx. 1, 2), and, though eschewing all means of influence beyond the word of prophecy, was the most commanding figure in Jewish politics for nearly half a century.

The book has two divisions: ch. i.—xxxix prophecies belonging to a great variety of occasions, and ch. xl.—lxvi., a book in the main homogeneous. The chronological arrangement in i.—xxxix. has been disturbed by throwing the prophecies against foreign nations (xv.—xxiii.) together, as in Jer. and Ezek., with which an oracle against Babylon (xiii., xiv.; of. xxi. 1–10) and a great prophecy of the general judgment on the world (xxiv.—xxvii.) have been connected, though probably due to later prophets. I. Ch. vi., inaugural vision. 1, vision of the LORD, the King, God alone, surrounded by servants who serve Him (1—4). 2, reaction of vision on the prophet's mind; his feeling of uncleanness and fear of death; his sin purged. (5—7). 3, lifted thus into sympathy with the great King and those around Him, he is sent on a mission to Israel, to announce impending judgments till the people be reduced to a "remnant," which shall become the root of a new nation (8—13). This passage, containing the thought of what Jehovah is, what the people are, and what must be the issue, expresses all the prophet's great conceptions. II. Ch. ii.—iv., v., prophecies between his call and the outbreak of Syro-Ephraimitic war (739—735), containing allusions to early reign of Ahaz (iii. 12). 1, ii. 1—4, a former prophet has said that Zion shall be the religious center of the world, and Jehovah God of all men. 2, ch. ii. 5—iv. 1, ere then purifying judgments must fall on Israel, because of their idolatry (ii. 8), pride (ii. 11; iii. 16), and oppressions (iii. 14, 15). The "day of the LORD" shall be on all that is proud and lofty, and the LORD alone shall be exalted in that day (ii. 11, 17). 3, iv. 2—6, when these judgments are overpast they that remain in Zion shall be holy. Ch. v. may be somewhat later. III. Ch. vii.—ix. 7, ch. xvii., prophecies during the Syro-Ephesian war, and first operations of the Assyrians, called in by Ahaz. Ch. vii.—ix. 7 contain references to deportation of northern tribes by Tiglath Pileser in 734 (ix. 1, 2), while xvii. is anterior to the fall of Damascus (732). Ch. vi. appears as preface to this group, which contains the great Messianic prophecies of Immanuel and the "Son given," the Prince of Peace (with viii. 9, 10 comp. xvii. 12 vii.—ix. 14). IV. Prophecies of the second Assyrian period (Shalmaneser 727—722, Sargon 722—705), ix. 8—x. 4 after the northern deportation; xxviii. before the fall of Samaria (722); x. 5—xii. and probably xiv. 24—27 after its destruction; xx. when Sargon's army was before Ashdod (711). To this group belongs the Messianic prophecy of the "rod out of the stem of Jesse" (xi.). V. Prophecies of the third Assyrian period, invasion of Sennacherib (704—701); xiv. 28—32 on death of Sargon; xxix.—xxxii. during earlier operations of Senn.; i. ? xxii. xxxiii. xxxvii. somewhat later. To this period probably belong the prophecies against the nations: xv., xvi. revival of an older prophecy against Moab; xviii. Ethiopia; xix. Egypt; xxi. 11—17 Edom and Arab tribes; xxiii. Tyre. These also contain lofty Messianic hopes (xviii. 7; xix. 18—25; xxiii. 15—18). To the book thus composed have been added an oracle against Edom (xxxiv., xxxv.), probably of the Exile period, and the historical appendix on the invasion of Sennacherib (xxxvi.—xxxix. = 2 K. xviii. 13 *seq*.).

The prophecies of Isaiah form the most powerful and splendid literature in the Bible, particularly xxviii.—xxxiii., which are unequalled for grandeur, music, and the softness of idyllic peace. Some aspects of his teaching: — 1, the God of Israel is Jehovah the King, the holy universal sovereign (vi. 5), the revelation of whose majesty will shake terribly the earth 19, 21). 2, consequently sin is pride of heart, rebellion that "provokes the eyes of His glory" (iii. 8). He has "a day" against all that is proud, and it shall be brought low (ii. 12–iii. 9; v. 15, 16; cf. iii. 16, the haughty women; ix. 9, Samaria; x. 12, 13, heart of king of Assyria). Idolatry and spiritual deadness are insensibility to His holy majesty (vi. 9, 10;

xxix. 9, 12). 3, therefore also true religion is faith in the great and holy King ("if ye will not believe, ye shall not be established," vii. 9; "the Egyptians are men, not God," xxxi. 1—3; *cf.* viii. 9, 10, 13, 17; x. 20, 21; xvii. 7; xxx. 15). 4, the holy King is a fire which must consume (iv. 4; xxxiii. 13-16); yet the Holy One has become "Holy One of Israel," He dwells in Zion (viii. 18), has founded Zion (xiv. 32), and laid in it a stone (xxviii. 16, symbol of the eternal stability of His kingdom and rule among men), and His judgments will leave a "remnant" which will grow into a new people (iv. 3; vi. 13; viii. 18; x. 21; xxx. 18 *seq.*; xxxii. 15 *seq.*; xxxiii. 20 *seq.*). 5, secure in this faith in the "King," the prophet looks across the raging floods of the nations with serenity (viii. 7—10; x. 16-19, 33, 34; xvii. 12—14; xviii. 3—6; xxix. 5—8; xxx. 27—33), and sees the Kingdom of the LORD rising behind, ruled by the "Prince of Peace," "God with us " (ch. vii.; viii. 21—ix. 7; xxxiii. 20 *seq.*).

Ch. xl.—lxvi. are now usually ascribed to an unknown prophet of the Exile, on the ground that the scene of the prophecies and the great figures of which the prophet speaks, as Cyrus, the Chaldeans, &c., are those of this period (xl. 2; xliii. 14; xlv. 1, 13; xlvi.—xlvii.; xliii. 5—7; xlviii. 20; xlix. 14 *seq.*; li. 3; lxii. 4; lxiv. 9—12). The prophecies are in the main from the pen of one author, contemporary with Cyrus (550—538). The great conception of the prophet is that the Kingdom of the LORD — Israel's restoration and the evangelizing of the world — is at hand. The external event with which this conception is connected is the restoration from exile by Cyrus, but this event is but a nucleus around which vast religious anticipations cluster, and it becomes idealized into a restoration of Israel, which is: 1, universal (xliii. 5—7; xlviii. 20—22; xlix. 17 *seq.*; lii. 1 *seq.*; lv. 12, &c.); and 2, final and the inauguration of Israel's eternal glory (xl. 10, 11; xliv. 3; xlv. 17; ch. lx.); and 3, which is the immediate means to the evangelizing of all nations (xl. 5; xlii. 9—12; xliv. 1—5; lx.). It is in truth the LORD Himself who brings in His kingdom, which is but the revelation of His glory, His sole Godhead, to all flesh (xl. 5; xlii. 8), and the guarantee of its coming is just His being God alone, a true God and a Savior (xlv. 5, 6, 18, 21—23), but He uses agents: 1, Cyrus, whose operations facilitate the rise of the kingdom externally, first by destroying Babylon, the idolatrous world, and forever discrediting the idols (xliii. 14; xliv. 21—xlv. 9, 16);

and secondly, by freeing captive Israel and building Jerusalem and the Temple (xliv. 28; xlv. 13). And 2, the Servant of the LORD, who brings in the kingdom on its spiritual side, first, by having borne the sins of the people (xl. 2; ch. liii.), one condition of their restoration; secondly, by awakening the faith and spiritual life in the scattered tribes, which is another condition (xlii. 5—8; xlix. 8—12; I. 5—10; lxi. 1—6); and thirdly, in being through Israel, thus restored, the light of the nations (xlii. 1—6; xlix. 1—6; ch. lx.). I. Ch. xl.—xlviii., first sketch of the inbringing of the kingdom, more on its external side: the great agents, Jehovah, God alone (xl. 12—31; xli. 1—7, 21—29; xliii. 8—13, &c.); the Servant (xlii.); Cyrus (xlv.); the downfall of Babylon (xlvi.; xlvii.); the redemption of Israel (xlviii. 20—22) the forgiveness of the people's sin (xliii. 25; xliv. 22), and the joy of creation (xlii. 10—12; xliv. 23). II. Ch. xlix.—lxii., a duplicate of xl.—xlviii., describing the same thing more on its internal side; the atoning of the people's sin (liii.), the exaltation of the Servant and restoration of Zion (xlix.) and Zion's final glory (liv.—lx.). III. Ch. lxiii.—lxvi., prophecies more miscellaneous. Opinions differ as to the "Servant," but all are at one in believing that the prophet's conceptions of the Servant's mind and work found fulfilment in Jesus Christ.

THE BOOK OF ISAIAH: CHAPTER BY CHAPTER

Time of Prophesying.		
Reign of Uzziah.	1	Judah's ingratitude and general depravity. Folly of mere outward forms. Call to repentance. Destruction of transgressors.
	2	The gospel dispensation. "The idols He shall utterly abolish." *The first four verses are almost identical with Micah iv. 1–4.*
	3	Calamities approaching luxurious Jerusalem, especially her vain females.
	4	Seven women – one man. The "escaped" of Israel.
	5	God's vineyard. "Woes" upon the wicked.
Reign of Jotham.	6	Isaiah's vision of God's glory.

Reign of Ahaz.	7	Judah invaded by Syria and Israel. Deliverance promised to Ahaz. Prediction of the birth of Immanuel.
	8	Roll to be inscribed, Ma-her-shalal-hash-baz. Child to be so named. The name so given as a sign of the destruction of the two confederate kings of Israel and Syria.
	9	Promises of the true light, and the Wonderful, Counsellor, &c.
	10	Judgments on the impenitent. The "remnant". Deliverance from Assyria.
	11	The rod and branch out of Jesse. The restoration of Israel.
	12	A song of praise for deliverance.
	13	Judgments against Babylon.
Reign of Hezekiah.	14	Song of exaltation against fallen Babylon.
	15	The burden [oracle, sentence] of Moab.
	16	Moab exhorted to submission.
	17	The burden [oracle, sentence] of Damascus. Transition to Sennacherib's invasion and overthrow.
	18	"Woe to the land shadowing with wings," or Egypt, whither the Jews turned for protection.
	19	The burden [oracle, sentence] of Egypt.
	20	Predictions against Egypt and Ethiopia.
	21	Predictions against Babylon, Edom, and Arabia.
	22	The burden [oracle, sentence] of the valley of vision – (Jerusalem so described, surrounded with hills.) Description of the confusion of Jerusalem on the approach of the Assyrians.
	23	The burden [oracle, sentence] of Tyre. Her destruction by the Chaldeans.
	24	Divine judgments on the land of Israel.

	25	Thanksgiving for deliverance, and prediction of gospel times.
	26	Song on Judah's protector.
God's vineyard.	27	Leviathan (Babylon, or the enemies of God's people) punished. Song of the protected vineyard. Israel to be restored.
	28	Judgment and mercy for Judah and Israel.
	29	"Woe to Ariel!" [the altar of God, or Judah,] announcing invasion (by Sennacherib.)
	30	The Jews' vain confidence in Egypt. Mercies for Judah and Jerusalem. Wrath upon Assyria.
	31	Vain confidence in Egypt. Overthrow of Assyria.
	32	Prophecy concerning Messiah's kingdom.
	33	The spoiler [Sennacherib] threatened.
	34	God's people avenged.
	35	The desert blossoming, or Messiah's kingdom flourishing.
Rabshakeh's message.	36	Rabshakeh's haughty message to Hezekiah.
	37	Hezekiah sends for Isaiah. Hezekiah's prayer. Isaiah's prediction of Sennacherib's destruction.
Hezekiah sick.	38	Hezekiah sick. His life prolonged. His song of thanksgiving.
	39	Hezekiah shows his treasure to the Babylonian ambassadors. The Babylonian captivity foretold.
	40	Comfort for God's people. Prediction of the coming of John the Baptist. The majesty of God. The vanity of idols.
	41	Israel encouraged to trust and confidence.
	42	Prediction respecting Messiah ["My Servant".]

	43	Promises of salvation and restoration to Israel.
	44	Promises of the Spirit. Folly of idolatry. Cyrus the deliverer.
	45	Predictions respecting Cyrus.
Cyrus predicted.	46	Babylon's idols.
	47	Prediction of Babylon's degradation and ruin.
	48	Israel reproved for neglect of God's warnings.
Christ the light.	49	Christ sent as "a light to lighten the Gentiles." God's love to His people.
	50	The Jews accused of divorcing themselves from God.
	51	Consolations and promises for God's people.
	52	Zion called to arouse from her humiliation, and contemplate her deliverance. Transition to the person, life and work of the Messiah.
Messiah's sufferings.	53	Rejection, sufferings and death of Messiah ["My Servant".]
	54	Jew and Gentile brought under the dominion of Christ. The "covenant" of God with Israel.
	55	Universal Gospel invitations.
	56	Strangers and foreigners to be admitted to the privileges of the restored Israel. The "blind watchmen."
	57	The removal of the righteous in mercy. Idolaters sternly reproved.
	58	Hypocrisy reproved. The fast that God chooses.
	59	Condemnation of iniquities. Promises of Messiah.
	60	Prediction of the glory of restored Israel.
Messiah's anointing.	61	Messiah's anointing to His ministry. Israel's final glory.

	62	The prophet's prayer for Zion. The duty of her watchmen.
	63	The coming of the Divine Conqueror. Prayer for Divine restoration.
	64	Prayer for a manifestation of God's power. Confession of sin and supplication for mercy.
	65	The Gentiles called. The iniquities of the Jews condemned. The saved remnant. God's "holy mountain."
	66	God's regard to the humble. Mere ceremonies vain. Israel and the Gentiles. The Lord's controversy with evil-doers. All nations shall be gathered in.

Isaiah.

JEREMIAH

The writings of another great prophet of the Exile.

THE ESSENTIAL STORY OF JEREMIAH

During the reign of Josiah, Jeremiah was called by God to speak His word. Jeremiah, the son of Hilkiah from a family of priests, was very young at this time, and felt sure he could not be ready for such a task. He protested that he would not know what to say. But the LORD reached out and touched his lips, and gave him the words. He told Jeremiah to rebuke the people of Israel and Judah for their faithlessness and idolatry. When the people ignored Jeremiah, or mocked him, God sent them a warning of approaching judgment and devastation.

Jeremiah watched a potter working with clay on his wheel. When one of the pots turned out to be misshapen, the potter crushed the clay in his hands to remake it. God explained to Jeremiah that He is like a potter. He is the creator of His people, the one who brings them into being. But if they turn away from God and worship idols, God will crush them like clay and start again.'

Judea was stricken with drought and famine. Rather than repenting, the people blamed Jeremiah and ill-treated him. So much so that he regretted his vocation. Meanwhile, the people and their kings continued in their cruel and selfish ways.

By the time Jeremiah was old, Zedekiah was on the throne of Judah. Jeremiah tried to persuade Zedekiah to lead the Israelites back to God again, but he didn't listen. Jeremiah tried to warn

Jeremiah predicts the capture of Jerusalem [32: vv. 26–35.]

him that God was angry with his people, and that there would be more destruction if they continued in their wickedness. Zedekiah continued to ignore him.

Nebuchadnezzar's Babylonian army marched on Jerusalem, setting up camp around the city's walls and laying seige. The people of Jerusalem began to starve. One night, Zedekiah and many of his soldiers managed to escape, but Nebuchadnezzar's army hunted them down, killing some and capturing others. Zedekiah was blinded and thrown into prison. The Babylonians burned and looted Jerusalem Anything of any value they either destroyed or took away with them. They took all the people who could be useful to them back to Babylon as slaves.

Jeremiah's heart ached for Zedekiah and his people, now prisoners of Nebuchadnezzar. He urged them to work hard and to pray for those who oppress them, to marry and have children so that they should increase in number. He prophesied that all nations would be horrified by the fate of those left behind in Jerusalem. However, he also sounded a note of optimism, in time the people would turn their hearts again to God, and He would answer their prayers. They would return to their land and the nation would be restored.

COMMENTARY ON THE BOOK OF JEREMIAH

Jeremiah, born of a priestly family in Anathoth, now Anata, a small place a little North of Jerusalem, from ancient times a priestly domain (1 K. ii. 26), and where his family owned land (ch. xxxvi. 8), prophesied from the 13th year of Josiah (i. 2) till after the Exile (xxxix.—xliv.), a period of more than 40 years (B.C. 626–586). Called young (i. 6), his reputation rose slowly; though already 5 years in office at the finding of the Book of the Law (2 K. xxii. 8), and the Reform of Josiah (621), he seems to have had no hand in these transactions (ch. xi. is not earlier than Jehoiakim), with regard to which he appears to have cherished no illusions. But from the death of Josiah (608) till his own in Egypt, though wielding only the word of prophecy, he was a prominent figure in all the history of that tragic period. Though not without the occasional sympathy of the Elders (xxvi. 17) and the lower classes (xxxviii. 7), he had to stem almost alone the tide of idolatry and immorality, of self-deception founded on superficial reforms (iii. 4, 5; vii. 8–10), and of fanatical confidence in Jehovah's protection, in which all classes were carried away. His life was a continual struggle with the ruling orders and the people, in which he was subjected to cruel and bitter insults by the temple priests (xx. 2) and other officials (xxxvii. 13), and was often in danger of his life from the mob (xxvi. 8, 9), his townsmen and kindred at Anathoth (xi. 19), the frivolous and cruel (xxii. 13; xxxvi. 23; xxvi. 20 King Jehoiakim (xxxvi. 19), and the military of the day (xxxviii. 4). The strife, so alien to his nature, wearied him: he longed for a lodge in the wilderness (ix. 2), mourned the perpetual conflict in which his life was passed (xv. 10), cursed the day of his birth (xx. 14), bitterly lamented that he had allowed himself to be enticed to become a prophet (xx. 7; cf. i. 4–10), and resolved to have done with the "Word of the LORD"—but in vain, His "word" was in his heart like a fire shut up in his bones, and he must declare it (xx. 9). Though he crossed every inclination and resisted every project of the princes and people, their secret conscience was often on his side (xxvi. 19); Zedekiah was disposed to listen to him (xxi.; xxxviii. 14–28), and did what he could to mitigate his sufferings (xxxvii. 16–21; xxxviii. 10), but was too conscious of being in the hands of stronger men to act according to his own impulse (xxxviii. 5); and the wretched exiles, though they rejected his counsels under the pretext that they were the suggestions of Baruch (xliii. 1-3), insisted on dragging him with them as a kind of fetish to Egypt (xliii. 6), where according to tradition (of little worth however) they ended by stoning him to death.

According to ch. xxxvi., Jeremiah unable to speak in public (possibly owing to the incidents ch. xix., xx.) dictated to Baruch in 4th year of Jehoiakim (604) the substance of the prophetic discourses of the past 22 years, with directions to read the roll in the hearing of the people. This being done next year, the roll was brought to the king, who after hearing it, cut it in pieces and threw it into the fire. Whereupon Jeremiah dictated it anew to Baruch, enlarging it with great additions (xxxvi. 32). This 2nd ed. formed the nucleus of our present book, and contained probably ch. i.--xx. in the main, xxv. with parts of xlvi.—xlix., perhaps xlv., and the historical sections relating to reign of Jehoiakim, xxvi., xxxvi., if these were written so early. To this were added afterwards prophecies of the reign of Zedekiah, and historical sections relating to the capture of the city and succeeding events.

The order of the book is in the main chronological, though this order is disturbed in two ways: some historical sections being disjoined from the discourses to which they refer (xxvi.; xxxvi.), possibly because written later; and some passages, having a common subject, though of different dates, being thrown together (e.g. xxii.; xxiii. relating to rulers). I. Prophecies of reign of Josiah (626–608 BC), ch. i.—vi. II. Prophecies under Jehoiakim (608–597), ch. vii.—xx., though perhaps some parts may be of brief reign of Jehoiachin (597), e.g. xiii. 18 *seq.* To vii., the historical commentary is xxvi., and xxxvi should probably be read after xix., xx. Ch. xxxv. narrates an incident probably of the last days of Jehoiakim. III. Prophecies under Zedekiah (597–586), ch. xxi.—xxxviii., divisible into several groups. *(a)* ch. xxi.—xxiii., on pastors or rulers of the people, with promise of the king Messiah (xxiii. 1–6); ch. xxiv., on exiles carried away with Jehoiachin. *(b)* ch. xxvi.—xxix., on the false prophets (*cf.* xxiii. 9 *seq.*), containing the prophet's letter to the exiles in Babylon, warning against the prophets there (xxix.). *(c)* ch. xxx.—xxxiii., prophecies of the Restoration of Israel and the New Covenant (xxxi. 31), containing story of the prophet's buying a field, showing the firmness of his faith in the people's restitution (xxxii.). *(d)* ch. xxxiv.—xxxviii., narratives of the treatment of the prophet and other events during the last times of the siege. IV. Ch. xxxix.—xliv., the prophet's history and other events after the fall of the city. V. Ch. xlvi.—li., prophecies against foreign nations; and finally historical conclusion of the book, ch. lii. (= 2 K. xxiv. 18—xxv. 30). The present place of xlvi.—li. is hardly original; if the book took shape under the hands of Baruch ch. xlv. would naturally close it. Ch. l., li. in their present form at least are later than Jeremiah, and other chapters of the group seem to have been amplified; and probably ch. xlvi.—li. formed a distinct collection or roll whose place in the book fluctuated (in LXX. it stands after ch. xxv. 13).

A chief thought of the prophet is the purely ethical nature of Jehovah, and consequently the *inwardness* of His relation to the mind of His servants. Illustrations of this are these points: 1, his condemnation of the whole past religious history of the nation; it has been no service of Jehovah (ii.; iii.; vi.). 2, futility of external service, and material symbols, sacrifices, ark, temple (vii. 21–28; vii. 9–11; iii. 16–18). 3, inadequacy of the superficial reforms on which the people prided themselves (ii. 23; iii. 4, 5, 10; vii. 8–11); not reform, but regeneration, is required ("sow not among thorns" iv. 3; *cf.* references to the "heart," iv. 4, 14; v. 23; xi. 20; xvii. 9; xxxi. 33, &c.). 4, consequent elevation of the individual as the subject of Jehovah's fellowship, and demand for morality (v. 1, 7, 26–28; ix. 1–6; ch. xviii.). 5, hence his conception of prophecy as a "standing in the counsel of the Lord," a relation of mind to mind, and his scorn of the "dreams" of the false prophets (xviii. 21–32). The verification of prophecy lies in the consciousness of the true prophet, and in the stringent moral nature of the prophecy; it is only prophecies of "peace" that require justification by the event (xxviii. 7–9). 6, hence, finally, the calmness with which Jeremiah contemplates the ruin of the state, buys a field on the eve of the city's fall (xxxii.), and counsels submission to Babylon (xxi. 9; xxix. 1–7; xxxviii. 17). Though the state falls, Jehovah remains, and religion remains in the life of the individual. And so his view of the nature of the New Covenant: the Lord writes it on the heart of the individual, and prophetic teaching ceases in that new age (xxxi. 33).

THE BOOK OF JEREMIAH: CHAPTER BY CHAPTER

Reign of Josiah.	1	Jeremiah's call to the prophetic office.
	2	God's kindness to Israel, and Israel's ingratitude to God.
	3	The sin of Israel and of Judah.
Call to repentance.	4	A call to both Israel and Judah to repent. Warnings of approaching judgment. A lamentation for Judah.
	5	Scarcity of the righteous.
	6	Judah in danger from the Chaldeans.
	7	Crimes charged against the Jews.
	8	Judgments against impenitent Judah and Jerusalem.
Call to mourning.	9	The prophet's lamentation. Judgments upon Gentiles, and upon Israel. A call to mourning.
	10	The true God and idols contrasted. Jehovah's lament over His people's transgression.
	11	Israel violates God's covenant. Plot against Jeremiah's life by the men of Anathoth.
Reign of Jehoiakim.	12	God righteous in His judgments. Those judgments approaching [by the Chaldeans].
	13	Linen girdle marred at the Euphrates, a type of the decay of Judah. Parables of filled bottles of wine, foreshadowing destruction. Exhortation to repentance.
	14	Grievous droughts and famine. Jeremiah's prayer and pleading.
	15	Rejection of the Jews.
	16	Judgment declared, yet restoration promised.
	17	Judah's idolatry and violation of the Sabbath.
	18	The clay and the potter.
	19	Tophet, the place of idolatry, to be the place of slaughter; indicted by the sign of the prophet in breaking a potter's vessel in there.

Pashur.	20	Pashur, the governor of the temple, smites Jeremiah, and puts him in stocks. Jeremiah changes Pashur's name to Magor-missabib [terror all around] He pronounces his captivity and doom. Jeremiah regrets being a prophet.
Reign of Zedekiah.	21	Zedekiah applies to Jeremiah to inquire if he could not escape from Nebuchadnezzar. Jeremiah predicts Zedekiah's downfall. *[From the next chapter, it would seem that this one is misplaced; probably it should follow chap. 28.]*
	22	The prophet exhorts to repentance. Judgment of Shallum – Jehoiakim – Coniah.
	23	A woe against wicked pastors. THE RIGHTEOUS BRANCH – "THE LORD OUR RIGHTEOUSNESS."
	24	The type of two baskets of figs. The seventy years' captivity foretold.
	25	Judgments pronounced against various nations.
Reign of Jehoiakim.	26	Jeremiah exhorts to repentance. Jeremiah denounced by the priests and the people. Jeremiah tried and vindicated by the princes and the elders. Urijah the prophet put to death by Jehoiakim.
	27	Jeremiah sends bonds and yokes to various kings, as types of their subjection to Babylon.
Reign of Zedekiah.	28	Hananiah's false prophecy, and breaking of Jeremiah's yoke. Jeremiah predicts Hananiah's perishing by early death.
	29	Jeremiah's letter to the captives in Babylon urging submission. Jeremiah predicts the fearful end of the lying prophets in Babylon, Ahab and Zedekiah. Shemaiah's letters and doom.
Promises.	30	Promises of Israel's return. "Ye – my people: I – your God."
	31	More promises. The new covenant predicted. (See Heb. Viii. 10–12,)

Jeremiah buys a field.	32	Jeremiah imprisoned by Zedekiah. Jeremiah buys a field, in the assurance of a restoration. Jeremiah's prayer for Israel. Jeremiah receives the Divine assurance of Israel's restoration.
The Branch.	33	Further Divine assurances of restoration. Reign of THE BRANCH OF RIGHTEOUSNESS predicted.
	34	Zedekiah's captivity plainly foretold. The re-enslavement of those who had been manumitted.
Rechabites. Reign of Jehoiakim.	35	The Rechabites. Their example a reproof to the Jews for disobedience.
Jehoiakim burns the roll.	36	Jeremiah's roll of his prophecies, written by Baruch. Baruch reads the roll in the court of the temple. Jehoiakim burns the roll. Jeremiah dictates the words of another, with additions; which Baruch writes.
Reign of Zedekiah.	37	Jeremiah imprisoned in the house of Jonathan the scribe. Zedekiah removes Jeremiah from the dungeon to the court of the prison.
Jeremiah in the dungeon.	38	*The princes cast Jeremiah into a miry dungeon. Ebed-melech, the Ethiopian eunuch, obtains permission to draw Jeremiah up from the dungeon. Jeremiah advises Zedekiah to surrender to the king of Babylon.
Zedekiah's eyes put out. Jerusalem burned.	39	Jerusalem taken. Zedekiah's flight. Zedekiah taken to Riblah, and his sons slain in his presence. The nobles slain. Zedekiah's eyes put out; and he is carried to Babylon. Jerusalem burned. The poor left to till the land. Jeremiah kindly treated. God's promise to Ebed-melech.
Gedaliah the governor.	40	Jeremiah has the choice of staying with Gedaliah. Conspiracy against Gedaliah.

Ishmael.	41	Ishmael, of the seed royal, slays Gedaliah in Mizpah, and all the people about him. He entraps eighty national mourners, by hypocrisy, and slays them. Ishmael carries off the residue of the people, towards the land of the Ammonites. Johanan overtakes and overcomes Ishmael, who escapes with eight men.
	42	Jeremiah predicts the ruin of the Jews who go into Egypt.
	43	The Jews go into Egypt, taking also Jeremiah and Baruch. Jeremiah prophesies by type, Nebuchadnezzar's conquest of Egypt.
	44	Jeremiah reproves the Jews in Egypt for their idolatry. The captivity of Pharaoh-hophra, king of Egypt, foretold.
	45	Baruch encouraged against danger.
Doom of Egypt,	46	Prophecies against— Egypt;
Of Philistines.	47	The Philistines;
Moab.	48	Moab;
Doom of Ammon, Edom, Syria, Kedar, Persia,	49	The Ammonites; Edom; Damascus [Syria]; Kedar; Elam [Persia];
Babylon.	50	Babylon;
	51	Babylon.
Judah taken capture.	52	Account of Zedekiah's rebellion against the king of Babylon. Articles of the Temple carried to Babylon Babylon. Jehoiachin released from prison, and kindly and honourably treated.

LAMENTATIONS

Also known as The Lamentations of Jeremiah.

THE ESSENTIAL SUMMARY OF LAMENTATIONS

This book, which some scholars believe is also by Jeremiah, was written after the captivity of Zedekiah and the Jewish nation by Nebuchadnezzar and his Babylonian army. It is a great lament for a fallen city and a suffering people.

COMMENTARY ON THE BOOK OF LAMENTATIONS

The Book of Lamentations or Dirges over the fall of Jerusalem and the nation is one of the 5 Megilloth (rolls) used for special anniversaries, being read on the 9th of Ab, the day of the destruction of the Temple. The poems are acrostic, ch. i., ii., iv. having each 22 verses beginning with the successive letters of the alphabet; ch. iii. 66 short verses, every three beginning each with one letter; while ch. v., though not alphabetical, has also 22 verses. The dirge measure is a line divided unequally by cesura, the latter or shorter half having an elegiac cadence—

How doth the city sit solitary—that was full of people!
She is become like a widow—that was great among the nations!
The princess among the countries—is made tributary.

Ch. i., general description of desolation and exile. The poet speaks, vv. 1–11. The once-joyous city sits solitary, weeping all the night, with none to comfort her, for her lovers (allied nations) have turned against her (1, 2); her people have sought refuge among the nations, but find no rest; her enemies are become the head, because of her sin; they have seen her filthiness and despise her; the nations have entered her holy sanctuaries (3–11). In 12–22 Zion herself appeals to mankind whether any sorrow be like her sorrow which the LORD has brought on her (12–17). He is just; yet her afflictions are unparalleled (18–22). Ch. ii., more particular enumeration of the successive strokes inflicted by the LORD: the ruin of city and temple, and all the habitations of Jacob (1, 2), the fenced cities, the army (3–5), even the place of His own abode, where He has made assembly and sabbath to be forgotten; there is no more prophetic vision (6–10). 2, the poet is overcome when he recalls the terrible days of the siege, when the famished children died in their mothers' bosoms (11, 12); Zion's fate is without a parallel, and due to the unfaithfulness of her prophets (13, 14); she is become a mockery among the nations (15–17). 3, let her present without ceasing before the LORD the unexampled strokes He has inflicted: have women anywhere eaten their own fruit? Has the blood of priests been shed in the very sanctuary of the LORD? (18–22). Ch. iii. has greater literary art. The speaker is "the man who has seen affliction by the rod of the LORD's wrath." 1, he narrates the severe divine dealing with him, greatly after the manner of Job (1–19). 2, he falls into a strain of reflective meditation and weighing of considerations, marked by sense of sin and inextinguishable hope in the LORD's mercy, which has hardly a parallel in Scripture, towards the end of which he identifies himself with the people (20–51). 3, he returns to his afflictions, figuratively called "waters" and a "pit," and calls for the requital of his adversaries (52–66). The "man" is no individual person, but the personification either of the people of the LORD, or of the godly among them. Ch. iv., the most graphic and circumstantial of all, is occupied with the last days of the siege. 1, the terrible sufferings of the children and cruel insensibility of parents under the famine (1–6); the blackened, shrivelled forms of the hunger-stricken nobles (7–10)—surely a judgment more awful than that of Sodom. 2, it would have seemed incredible to the

191

nations, but is due to the sins of prophets and priests (11, 12); the scenes of blood and horror enacted by them in the streets of the city (13–16). 3, last days: vain expectation of help from Egypt (17); the enemy's engines command the streets (18); flight and capture of the king (19, 20). Reflection that Zion's sin is expiated; the cup shall pass to Edom (21, 22). Ch. v., condition of the people after the fall of the city; ending with the cry, Will the LORD forget us for ever?

This beautiful little book is very instructive, e.g. in regard to the scenes in the city during the siege and the feelings of the people (ch. iv.); the profound impression made by the destruction of the city and temple, Jehovah's own place of abode, by His own hand, and His withdrawal of all revelation (i. 21; ii. 1–11; iii. 42–44; iv. 12); the feeling of sin awakened by it (i. 8–10, 14, 18; ii. 14; iii. 42; iv. 13); and the deep sense of national humiliation (i. 21; ii. 15–17 iii. 46), reappearing often in Job and Is. xl.–lxvi. The date must be some years after the fall of the city (of which the author was an eyewitness) though anterior to any movements of the nations against Babylon. Little can be urged against the belief that the whole is from one pen: unlike i. ii. iv. ch. iii. does not begin with *How!*, and the speaker is not Zion as elsewhere. Ch. v. is not alphabetical, has less poetical power, and might be later, though "for ever" (v. 20) cannot be much urged for this (Ps. xiii. 1), nor the ascription of present calamities to the sins of a former generation (v. 7; *cf.* Ezek. xviii. 2).

The tradition of Jeremiah's authorship arose probably from taking "pit" (iii. 53) literally, then assuming him to be the speaker in ch. iii., and finally ascribing the whole to him. Against his authorship is: 1, ref. to failure of prophecy (ii. 9); 2, the term "breath of our nostrils" applied to Zedekiah, and the hope of living under him in exile (iv. 20)—altogether unlike his attitude (xxi. 9; xxxviii. 17); 3, the hope of help from Egypt (iv. 17) – contrary to his conviction (xxxvii. 7–10); 4, the condition of ch. V. does not reflect the treatment of Jeremiah by the Chaldeans (xl. 4). 5, the language is unique and quite different from that of Jeremiah.

THE BOOK OF LAMENTATIONS: CHAPTER BY CHAPTER

Jerusalem solitary.	1	Jerusalem sitteth solitary. She justifies God's dealings. Implores Him to avenge her on her enemies.
	2	The prophet laments the desolation of Jerusalem.
Calls for succour.	3	The prophet, as typical of the nation, bewails the calamities. Claims the LORD as his portion. And calls upon God for succour.
	4	Zion's changed condition lamented. "The pitiful women have sodden their own children." Final restoration promised. Edom threatened.
	5	Prayer, confessing sin, and imploring deliverance.

A lament for Jerusalem: "All her people sigh, they seek bread …" [1: v.11.]

EZEKIEL

The prophet-visionary Ezekiel rebukes sin, but comforts the Exiles.

THE ESSENTIAL STORY OF EZEKIEL

E zekiel was a younger contemporary of Jeremiah and was in training for the priesthood before he was carried off among the first group of deportees from Jerusalem to Babylon. He was to become God's messenger to the Exiles, forecasting the destruction of Jerusalem (which was yet to come at that time), and later a hope of a new beginning.

His calling to be a prophet was dramatic indeed, the first of a series of visions or revelations. He saw what appeared to be a great storm coming up from the north, a huge cloud lit suddenly by flashes of lightning, brilliant light and deafening noise. In the midst of this was a vast four-wheeled chariot, drawn by four cherubim and moving in all directions. Above there appeared a gigantic figure in the shape of a man, which he described as the glory of God – he was glimpsing the Almighty. God spoke. Addressing Ezekiel as the "Son of Man," he told him that he was to be God's messenger to the Exiles.

The early visions were of God's judgment on his people, which Ezekiel had to relay to his fellow Exiles partly by a sort of play-acting, symbolizing the end of Jerusalem, its siege and fall. He was also given a vision of the Temple, transported there to see how it was being violated by the worship of idols and alien gods. Horrified by the abominations he witnessed, Ezekiel then saw a great chariot-throne ascend and head eastward above the Mount of Olives. God's departure from the Temple and from Jerusalem was thus symbolized, a message to the Exiles that he had come with them.

God also sent messages in the form of parables. One such told of a great forest fire to the south, indicating the destruction of the southern kingdom of Judah, just as the northern kingdom had perished before. Another concerned two adulterous sisters. Oholah, symbolizing Samaria, prostituted herself to Egyptians and Assyrians, but God handed her to the Assyrians for punishment. Her sister, Ohalibah, standing for Jerusalem, was no better and imitated her sister, but God meted out her punishment too.

After the fall of Jerusalem, and the further mass deportations, Ezekiel's visions took on a different tone, looking to a better future, which was in tune with the longings of the Exiles. He saw a valley of dry bones into which God breathed life; and later a great vision of a city on a hill, centered upon a new Temple, which was described in considerable detail, particular attention being given to the priesthood. Only the descendants of Zadok, the High Priest of Solomon, would be allowed to enter the inner sanctum and perform the liturgy. The Levites, heretofore the keepers of the Temple (as they had been of the Tabernacle in Moses' time) were effectively demoted on account of their sin in tolerating and condoning idolatry in the Temple for so long; henceforth their role would be restricted to the more menial tasks. From the Temple flowed a life-giving river, its banks lined with fruit-bearing trees that never lost their leaves. The vision depicted God's return to a new Temple, to dwell among his people again in an earthly paradise.

COMMENTARY ON THE BOOK OF EZEKIEL

Ezekiel, son of Buzi, a priest of the family of Zadok, was one of the captives carried away by Nebuchadnezzar along with Jehoiachin (597). With his compatriots he was settled at Tel Abib on the Chebar, probably some confluent of the Euphrates in Babylonia, not the Chabor at Circesium. Here he had a house (viii. 1), and was possibly married (xxiv. 18). He prophesied from the 5th (i. 2) at least to the 27th year of Jehoiachin's captivity (xxix.

17), a period of 22 years (592–570), though few details of his life are furnished.

The book has three great divisions: first, ch. i.–xxiv., prophecies of judgment against Jerusalem and the nation, foreshowing their inevitable ruin; second, ch. xxv.–xxxix., prophecies of restoration, in two parts: ch. xxv.–xxxii., against the nations, Israel's enemies, and ch. xxxiii.–xxxix., special prophecies of the people's restitution; third, ch. xl.–xlviii., an appendix, virtually falling under second division, being visions of the reconstruction of the Temple, the worship and the nation. Ch. i.—xxxix. are similar in manner and contents to other prophetic literature; ch. xl.—xlviii. are unique in prophecy.

First part, ch. i.—xxiv. I. Ch. i.—iii., the prophet's call. 1, vision of his God who sends him (i.). 2, his mission to Israel as a prophet (ii. 1–7); act of eating a book, symbol of his inspiration (ii. 8–iii. 9); he goes to the Exiles, receiving a clearer view of his mission, *viz.* to be a watchman to warn every individual soul (iii. 10–21). 3, command to abstain for a time (*cf.* xxiv. 27; xxxiii. 22) from public preaching (iii. 22–27). II. Ch. iv.–vii., symbols of destruction of city and nation. 1, ch. iv., symbols of siege, famine, and bearing of iniquity in exile (for 390 days, v. 5, LXX. reads 190). 2, ch. v., against the inhabitants. 3, ch. vi., against the whole idolatrous land. 4, ch. vii., dirge over the nation's downfall. III. Ch. viii.—xi., more precise predictions and symbols of the destruction of the city at the LORD's hand, because of the idolatrous pollution of His house. 1, ch. viii., the multiplied idolatries in the temple. 2, ch. ix., divine agents slay the inhabitants. 3, ch. x., fire from God falls upon the city. 4, ch. xi., the LORD's withdrawal from the place of His abode. IV. Ch. xii.—xix., the same theme of the nation's ruin, partly in the form of answers to objections that unbelief might raise. 1, ch. xii. 1–20, symbol of the king's secret flight and capture. 2, ch. xii. 21–28, the popular delusion that prophecies failed or referred to the distant future shall receive a speedy and terrible refutation. 3, ch. xiii., xiv., those vain hopes are fostered by the false prophets, who shall perish along with those whom they deceive. 4, ch. xv., shall the LORD destroy the nation of Israel? Israel among the nations is like the vine-branch among the trees; what is it good for? Above all, what is it good for now when half-burnt in the fire? Only to be flung into the fire and utterly consumed. 5, oh. xvi., the LORD's unchanging grace, and Jerusalem's persistent ingratitude and unfaithfulness. 6, ch. xvii., Zedekiah's perfidy against the king of Babylon shall be punished. 7, ch. xviii., not for the sins of the fathers, but for their own shall the people perish; the righteous shall live in his righteousness, and the sinner die in his sin; let each soul repent and live. 8, ch. xix., dirge over Judah and her royal house. V. Ch. xx.—xxiv. 1, ch. xx., not for Israel's sake, but for His name's sake, that He might be known by the nations to be God, has the LORD spared Israel all through her history. 2, ch. xxi., the sword of the LORD whetted against Jerusalem. 3, ch. xxii., Jerusalem's aggravated sins. 4, ch. xxiii., the life-history of the two adulterous women, Oholah and Oholibah (Samaria and Jerusalem). 5, ch. xxiv., a rusted caldron set on the coals—final symbol of Jerusalem's destruction and purification.

Second part, ch. xxv.—xxxix., prophecies of restitution. I. Ch. xxv.—xxxii., against the nations, Israel's adversaries. 1, the small nations around Israel, who have helped and rejoiced in her destruction (xxv.). 2, Tyre and Sidon, which shall no more be a thorn (xxvi.—xxviii.); 3, Egypt, which shall no longer be a delusive stay (xxix.—xxxii.). II. Ch. xxxiii.—xxxix., strict prophecies of restoration. 1, the prophet's place in the restoration: he is a watchman to warn each soul, that by repentance and righteousness it may live, and thus a new nation arise (xxxiii.). 2, a new ruler, "my servant David" (Messiah), shall take the place of the former evil shepherds, and feed the flock for ever (xxxiv.). 3, the land, rescued from the grasp of Edom and the nations who have usurped it, shall be Israel's for ever; it shall be luxuriant in fertility and teem with people (xxxv.—xxxvi.). 4, the people, scattered among all nations and dead, like dry bones in the valley, shall be reawakened into life and restored; Ephraim and Judah, no more divided, shall have one King for ever (xxxvii.). 5, it shall be inviolable: final attack of the distant nations, Gog and his followers, upon the restored community; their destruction by the LORD, who shall be recognised by the world to be God alone (xxxviii.—xxxix.).

Third part, ch. xl.—xlviii., visions (seen in the year 572) of the reconstructed Temple (xl.—xlii.); the return of the LORD to His house (xliii. 1-12); the altar (v. 13-27). The prince, priests and

Levites, with their revenues and duties (xliv.–xlvi.); the boundaries of the land and settlement of the tribes (xlvii., xlviii.). Some have concluded from the differences between Ezekiel and the Levitical legislation that the latter is more recent. The distinction between priests and Levites, and the limitation of the latter to subordinate services, receive a historical explanation—the Levites are the former priests of the high-places degraded for their idolatries (xliv. 9–14).

The orderly plan of the book suggests that it was finally put together at a late period, though reposing on oral discourses delivered from time to time (viii. 1; xi. 25; xiv. 1), the tone of i.–xxiv., in which Israel is a "rebellious house," differing from that in xxv. *seq.*, in which the LORD speaks of Israel as "my people," "my flock." The prevailing symbolism of the book is of two kinds: ideal symbols, always gigantic and often beautiful, as Tyre under the figure of a gallant ship; Egypt as the crocodile; Babylon as a great speckled eagle; Judah and her royal dynasty as a mother lioness with whelps; Samaria and Jerusalem as unfaithful women doting on lovers; and secondly, symbolical actions (iv.; v. xii., &c.). Many of the latter can hardly have been actually performed (iv. 4; v. 1; xxi. 19; *cf.* xx. 49; xxiv. 3); and the ecstasies and visions to which Ezekiel was subject have received much amplification and literary adornment (i.; xl. *seq.*). Ezekiel adopts and expands many of the thoughts of Jeremiah, as was natural in one who had heard the latter prophet from a child. 1, he differs from Jeremiah and older prophets (Jer. ii. 2, 3; Hos. ix. 10; Is. i. 21) in pushing Israel's idolatries back into the wilderness, and even into Egypt (xx. 7, 8; xxiii. 3, 8). 2, he amplifies Jeremiah's doctrine of the individual's responsibility and freedom, in answer to a feeling of the people that they suffered for the sins of their fathers, and were under a ban which no repentance or righteousness of their own could break (xviii. 2; 10). (1) the individual soul in relation to God is not involved in the sins of the fathers or others; nor (2) is it under a destiny forged by its own past; it possesses a freedom which can morally break with the past (xviii.; xxxiii.). 3, his conception of the consciousness of Jehovah, God alone, and yet, historically and in the eyes of the nations, God of Israel, suggests to him a remarkable philosophy of history (ch. xx.; xvi.; xxiii.; xxxviii.; xxxix.).

The Book of Ezekiel: Chapter by Chapter

5th year of Jehoiachin's captivity.	1	Ezekiel's vision of four cherubim; – four wheels; God's glory, which he saw when among the captives by the river Chebar.
	2	Ezekiel's commission and instruction. Ezekiel's roll.
	3	Ezekiel eats the roll. Ezekiel's charge as a watchman of Israel.
Ruin of Jerusalem.	4	Types of Jerusalem's ruin, in vision: – • To portray Jerusalem on a tile. • To set up an iron pan, or plate, as a fortification. • To lie on his side before it for 390 days, to show the years of Israel's defection. • To make bread of various farinaceous articles, and show, by signs, the scanty food from the siege.
A sign.	5	The prophet's hair and beard shaved, then burnt, cut, and scattered; significant of the fate of Israel, by pestilence, famine, sword, and dispersion.
	6	Ezekiel prophesies to the mountains of Israel, threatening judgments for idolatry.
	7	Final desolation of Israel. The sanctuary defiled.
Image of jealousy.	8	Vision of the image of jealousy [provoking Gods' jealousy]. Chambers of imagery, &c. The wrath of God.
Angels of judgment.	9	Vision of the angels of judgment destroying Jerusalem. The man with the ink-horn marks the faithful few.
Cherubim.	10	Coals of fire scattered over the city. The Cherubim and the Divine glory forsake the Temple.
The glory departs.	11	Presumption of the princes of Israel. God's glory leaves the city.
	12	Ezekiel removes his dwelling as a sign of Judah's removal into captivity. He gives a second sign by taking his food with fear and trembling.

	13	The false prophets compared to buildings with untempered mortar. False prophetesses seducing the people to ease compared to sewing pillows under the armpits.
	14	Ezekiel's reply to the inquiry of the elders. Though Noah, Daniel and Job should be in Judah, God would spare only them.
	15	Judah a fruitless vine.
	16	Judah and Samaria compared to harlots, on account of their great idolatries.
Two great eagles.	17	Parable of two great eagles.
	18	Judah reproved for applying the proverb of the sour grapes. God's ways equal.
Lioness and cubs.	19	Parable of the lioness and her cubs applied to the princes of Israel. Similitude of the transplanted vine.
	20	The inquiring elders reproved for their idolatrous inclinations.
	21	A prophecy against Jerusalem and Israel. The type of sighing enjoined on the prophet. The sharpened sword. Divination of the king of Babylon.
	22	Catalogue of Jerusalem's sins. God's approaching judgments compared to a smelter's furnace.
Aholah and Aholibah.	23	Aholah and Aholibah, types of idolatrous Israel and Judah. Their dreadful punishment.
The boiling pot.	24	Parable of a boiling pot. Type of Ezekiel's not mourning for his dead wife.
Against Ammon, &c.	25	Prophecies against the: • Ammonites; • Moabites; • Edomites; • Philistines.
Against Tyre and her merchants.	26	Prophecies against Tyre.
	27	Further prophecies against Tyre, enumerating the extent of her trade and number of her merchants.

Against Egypt.	28	Prophetic announcement to the proud princes of Tyre. Zidon addressed.
	29	Prophecies against Egypt.
	30	Further prophecies against Egypt.
	31	Egypt warned by the downfall of proud Assyria, compared to the tall cedar.
	32	Egypt to fall among the mighty slain, Asshur, Elam, Mesech, Tubal, Edom, and Zidon.
	33	Ezekiel, Israel's watchman.
	34	Wicked shepherds warned. Promises of the good Shepherd.
Against Edom.	35	Prophecies renewed against Mount Seir, or Edom.
	36	Promises of a restoration to Israel, with a new heart and new spirit.
	37	Vision of resurrection of the dry bones. Type of the two sticks, foretelling the reunion of Judah and Israel.
God and Magog.	38	Prophecies against God and Magog.
	39	The same, renewed. Israel's restoration.
New Temple.	40	Vision of the new Temple.
	41	Its measure, chambers and ornaments.
	42	Same continued. Priests' chambers &c.
The glory returns.	43	Vision of God's glory entering the Temple. Measures and ordinances of the altars. The east gate for the Prince.
	44	Laws respecting the priests and Levites. The sons of Zadok.
	45	Division of the land.
The Prince.	46	Laws of the offerings. The Prince.
	47	Vision of the flowing waters. The mystic trees. Borders of the land.
	48	Names of the tribes. Plan and dimensions of the new city.

DANIEL

Daniel, a man without blemish, lives and prophesies in the
Babylonian court

THE ESSENTIAL STORY OF DANIEL

The name DANIEL means *God is my Judge* or *God the Judge*
– an appropriate name for one who always made Jehovah
the arbiter of his life. Daniel was carried captive to
Babylon when he was young, in the third year of the reign of
King Jehoiakim, King of Judah. Being a youth of considerable
promise, he was selected, along with a few others, to be taught the
language and sciences of Chaldea. Daniel was faithful to his God
and in the heathen and idolatrous court of the greatest monarch
on earth he held fast to his profession without wavering. He
was prepared, like Moses, to "suffer affliction with the people of
God rather than enjoy the pleasures of sin for a season." Daniel's
character presents no flaws. Most of the good men of the Bible
had some defect, some shortcoming, but Daniel's life seems to
have been without blemish. Even his enemies despaired of being
able to bring able to bring an accusation against him – fidelity
to Jehovah was his only crime. Thrice he is, in divine messages,
designated as "greatly beloved" (Daniel ix. 23; x. 11, 19). For a
period of over sixty years he lived in the corrupt Babylonian
court, a stainless man. He was not there, it must be remembered,
by his own will or wish; he was there in the direct providence
of God.

Like Joseph, son of Jacob, Daniel was an interpreter of dreams, turning to God for help. One night the mighty king, Nebuchadnezzar, experienced a dream that puzzled and disturbed him, but none of his court magicians, astrologers, or other such luminaries could shed light on the king's dream. The angry monarch ordered them all to be slaughtered, but fortunately someone mentioned this to Daniel, who interceded with the king. If he could interpret the dream, would the king rescind his command? That night Daniel consulted his three friends and prayed to God for help. By morning he had his answer, which he set before the king.

The dream had been of a vast statue, with a head of gold, chest and arms of silver, belly and thighs of bronze, legs of iron, and feet a mixture of iron and clay. Nebuchadnezzar had seen a rock, hewn not by human hands, smash the feet of the statue, whereupon the whole collapsed into tiny fragments and was blown away on the wind, while the rock grew to fill the world.

Daniel explained that, while no man could interpret this dream, God could. It was a vision of the future. The head was Nebuchadnezzar's own glorious empire, for he was the King of Kings; each of the other elements represented successor empires which would rise and fall, the last, that or iron and clay, being divided, with the strength of iron but the weakness of clay. The rock represented God's eternal kingdom, which would outlast them all. Nebuchadnezzar was deeply impressed. Daniel and his companions were richly rewarded, and the soothsayers spared.

Some while later, Nebuchadnezzar decided to set up a new idol for worship, a statue of gold of great height, which he set in the plain of Dura. The people were to fall down and worship this upon summons by music played on a variety of instruments, and it was dedicated in a splendid ceremony. Failure to worship, the king ordained, would be met with death by fire in a blazing furnace. The people did as they were bid; but not so the Jews. When this was noted, Shadrach, Meshach, and Abed-nego were singled out as examples of disobedience and brought before the king. Intransigent, they were duly sentenced, and the fiery furnace was heated especially high. Tightly bound, they were cast into the flames, where they were joined by an angel. But the fire did not consume them, and they emerged without even having their clothes singed. King Nebuchadnezzar, astounded, decreed that any person speaking ill of the Exiles' God would be cut into little pieces.

Another dream subsequently troubled Nebuchadnezzar's nights. It was of a great beautiful tree, so high it reached to the heavens, its branches laden with fruit, with the beasts of the Earth dwelling in its shade and birds nesting above. Then he heard a message from Heaven commanding that the tree be cut down, so that all that was left would be the stump and roots. The king would live with the mind of an animal, eating grass like cattle.

Daniel once more consulted God to interpret the dream. The tree represented the king, strong, with dominion over far and wide; but he would be driven from his people to live with the animals, eating grass, and feeling the dew on his back, until after an allotted time he acknowledged that God is the sovereign over the kingdom of men. Only then would he be restored to his high position. He must renounce his sins, embrace the LORD and show compassion for all men.

A year later it happened – Nebuchadnezzar went mad. And at the end of the specified time, his sanity was restored, he praised God and returned to his throne.

Some time after the death of Nebuchadnezzar, there sat on the throne of Babylon a king called Nabonidus, who made his son Belshazzar co-ruler and retired to the country. By now the Babylonian monarchs had forgotten the lessons that Nebuchadnezzar had learned and gave themselves over to debauchery and impiety. One night Belshazzar threw a particularly lavish feast, and used the gold goblets looted from the Temple in Jerusalem for the wine. As they were eating and drinking, there suddenly appeared a hand, mysteriously writing on the wall. This apparition terrified the king, who called upon his magicians and soothsayers to explain what it meant. They could not, but the queen remembered Daniel's interpretation of Nebuchadnezzar's dreams, and he was called for.

Now an old man, Daniel examined the writing and explained its meaning. The words were about numbers, essentially "number," "weigh," and "divide." They meant that the king's days were numbered – he had ignored the lessons of his ancestor, had not honored God and had desecrated the sacred objects from the

Temple. And that very night the Persian Cyrus captured Babylon with great slaughter.

Daniel survived the end of the Babylonian Empire. Indeed, the Persian conquerors evidently saw in Daniel a man of competence, and he rose further in the administration. But this provoked sharp jealousy among his Chaldean colleagues and rivals, who sought charges to bring against him. They could find nothing of corruption or negligence: so they chose instead a religious device to bring him down. A royal edict was promulgated forbidding worship of any god except the king for thirty days. Daniel ignored this, was reported and brought to trial. The penalty was to be confined in a den of lions. But no harm came to him, for God protected his servant. Next morning the king was astonished and penitent: the false accusers were rounded up, with their wives and children, and consigned to the lions' den, where they were appropriately consumed by the hungry beasts. The king meanwhile issued a new edict that the God of Daniel should receive his due reverence.

During the remainder of his days, Daniel received a number of visions, most forecasting what was to come, the struggle for power in the world and the eventual triumph of God.

COMMENTARY ON THE BOOK OF DANIEL

D aniel, carried captive by Nebuchadnezzar in 3rd year of Jehoiakim (*cf.* 2 Chr. xxxvi. 6, 10), rose to eminence among the wise men of Chaldea (i.; ii.), was made governor of Babylon (ii. 48), and flourished at the court of the Chaldean and Persian kings till 3rd year of Cyrus (x. 1; 605—535). Ezekiel commemorates between Noah and Job a Daniel renowned for piety (xiv. 14) and wisdom (xxviii. 3), and among the exiles who returned under Ezra a Daniel is named. (Ezra viii. 2).

The book has two divisions: ch. i.—vi., narratives regarding Daniel and his three companions; and ch. vii.—xii., prophetic visions, seen by Daniel and reported in his own name. Ch. 28 is written in Aramaic, and the rest in Hebrew. Opinions differ as to the nature of the book. 1, the traditional view is that it is historical, and that Daniel of the time of the captivity is the author.

2, others consider it to be of the Maccabean age (after B.C. 170), and to have a practical religious aim, the narratives and visions being free literary forms adopted in order the better to convey the instruction (as Job, Eccles.); 3, while others, though referring its present form to the Maccabean age (ch. xi.), suppose it to rest on earlier documents. The book evidently owes its origin to a time when heathenism was pressing hard on Israel, not only by fiery trials, but also by the seductions of its life and thought; and, generally, the book may be said to be a reflection of the mind of pious Israel in its reaction against the heathen world. 1, as to the present—the God of Israel is the true and only wise God, who enlightens and elevates His servants above all men (i.; ii.; iv.; v.); who has all power, and both can and will protect those who cleave to Him against nations and kings, even the most powerful (iii.; v.; vi.). And 2, as to the future—the advent of His kingdom is assured; preceded by a brief time of great tribulation, it will rise on the ruins of the kingdoms of the world and be universal, all things under the whole heavens being given to the people of the saints of the Most High (ii.; vii.—xii.).

The lessons of i.–vi. are the same, whether they be strict history or free literary creations, as for example, the merit and blessing of keeping oneself pure from the seductive delights of heathenism (i.); the greatness of the God of Israel, God only wise, who gives wisdom to His servants, and whose wonders the heathen have only to know to acknowledge Him (ii. 47); the duty of being true to the God of the fathers at all cost, His power to deliver and the assurance that He will, and the susceptibility of the heathen mind to the impression of the greatness of the God of Israel, to whom homage will be done when His redemption of His servants is seen (iii.), &c. Such lessons, though fitting the Exile, are equally suitable to the trying times of Antiochus Epiphanes (comp. the acts of that tyrant, vii. 20; viii. 9–12, 23–25; ix. 26, 27; xi. 21, 31–33, 36 seq.). The tone of friendliness adopted by the author towards the Chaldean and Persian monarchies (in contrast to the Seleucids) is remarkable (ch. iv.; vi. 13, 18–23).

The prophetic visions, vii.—xii. with ch. ii. These all present under different forms the same idea of a succession of world-monarchies (four in all), of which the last towards its end will severely persecute the saints (i.e. Israel), but shall be brought to an end by the Judgment of God and the advent of His kingdom. Ch. viii., though incomplete, is simplest, and gives the key to the rest. 1, vv. 1–4, a ram with two horns (Medo-Persian dynasty, v. 20), the greater horn coming up last (Cyrus). 2, vv. 5–8, a he-goat with a great horn (Alexander, v. 21), eventually broken and replaced by four others (his four generals, v. 22). 3, vv. 9–12, out of one of them (Syro-Greek, or, Seleucid dynasty) arose a "little horn," which persecuted the saints, abolished sacrifice and profaned the sanctuary (Antiochus Epiphanes). Here the Medo-Persian is one kingdom, the "little horn" is Antiochus, and the tribulation caused by him marks "the time of the end" (viii. 19). Ch. vii. presents the same succession under the symbolism of wild beasts, but completes it at the beginning by naming the first kingdom (Nebuchadnezzar, v. 4), and shows how at the end the world-kingdoms give place to the kingdom of God (vv. 9–14). The judgment was set and one like a son of man was brought to the Ancient of days, and a dominion universal and eternal was given to Him. The "son of man" here may be a symbol for the people of the saints in contrast to the brute world-kingdoms (v. 22, 26, 27), it was certainly afterwards interpreted of the personal Messiah. In ch. ii. the colossal man with head of gold, but deteriorating into silver, brass and iron towards the extremities (a brilliant conception, well ascribed to the great mind of Nebuchadnezzar), represents the same fourfold succession. The colossus is smitten and scattered as dust to the winds by a stone cut out without hands (the kingdom of God), which becomes a great mountain and fills the earth. Ch. x.–xii. pursue the same line of thought; the tribulation caused by Antiochus (xi. 21–45) is brought to an end by the salvation of God, accompanied by the Resurrection of the dead (xii. 1–4). In all the visions the perfect kingdom of God rises close behind the great tribulation of Antiochus (as in Is. vii.–ix., xi. the Messiah appears just on the back of the Assyrian devastations), and it is probable that the difficult ch. ix. has the same terminus. The 70 years of Jeremiah (Jer. xxv. 11, 12) are regarded as 70 weeks of years (490 years), divisible into 7, 62 and 1. The second half of the 1 or last 7 (the 3½ years, "time, times and half a time") is the period of tribulation, which immediately precedes the bringing in of "everlasting righteousness." The point from which the computation starts is uncertain, and perhaps strict chronological accuracy is hardly to be sought, as the prophet may operate partly with round numbers.—The book is full of beauty and power, and fitted to console and confirm the people of God under trial, whether from the persecutions or the blandishments of the world.

THE BOOK OF DANIEL: CHAPTER BY CHAPTER

In Babylon.	1	Jehoiakim's captivity (2 Chron. 36, 6). Nebuchadnezzar's command to educate Daniel, Hananiah, Mishael and Azariah iin the Chaldean learning, during three years. Their names changed to Belteshazzar, Shadrach, Meshach and Abed-nego. Daniel begs not to feed on the king's meat, and is fed on pulse. The four excel in wisdom, and obtain royal favor.
Nebuchadnezzar's dream.	2	Nebuchadnezzar dreams; forgets his dream and threatens the wise men with death if they do not unfold it. The king's dream revealed to Daniel in a night vision. He tells the dream of the great image to Nebuchadnezzar and interprets it. Daniel made ruler over the province of Babylon, and chief of the wise men. Daniel's companions promoted.
Nebuchadnezzar's charge.	3	Nebuchadnezzar's golden image, and proclamation to worship it. Shadrach, Meshach and Abed-nego accused of contempt. They are thrown into the fiery furnace. Their miraculous deliverance.
The dream of a great tree. **His madness.**	4	Nebuchadnezzar's record of his dream of a great tree cut down to its stump. Daniel's interpretation of it. Nebuchadnezzar's extraordinary madness, and recovery.

Belshazzar's feast. **Darius.**	5	Belshazzar's feast and profanation of the vessels of the temple. The handwriting on the wall. Daniel's interpretation of the writing. Slaughter of the king, and conquest of his kingdom. Darius the Median reigns.
Daniel and the lions.	6	Daniel made first president of the kingdom. Conspiracy against Daniel. Daniel's fidelity to God. He is cast into the den of lions. The king's regret and anxiety. Daniel's miraculous preservation. Destruction of his enemies.
Vision of the four beasts.	7	Daniel's vision of the four beasts. The "Ancient of Days" in judgment. The kingdom of Messiah.
Ram and he-goat.	8	Daniel's visions of the ram and he-goat. The 2300 days. Vision interpreted.
Seventy weeks.	9	Daniel's prayer and confession. Gabriel's visit to Daniel. Prophecy of the seventy weeks.
Vision of Messiah.	10	Daniel's vision of Messiah. Michael helps Daniel.
	11	Overthrow of Persia by Greece. Contests between the kings of the north and the south. Other predictions.
	12	Michael, the prince, stands up for Israel. The 1290 days. The 1335 days. "Blessed is he that waiteth."

HOSEA

The faithlessness of the prophet's wife mirrors Israel's faithlessness to God.

THE ESSENTIAL STORY OF HOSEA

Hosea (or Hoshea) was a native of the northern kingdom, who began prophesying a little after Amos (see Book Thirty) began his ministry. His message was that the people had forsaken their God and that retribution would surely come. Hosea's message was colored by his own personal experience, so that his life was in a sense a metaphor for Israel.

God had directed him to marry a woman called Gomer, and she proved unfaithful to him. God, it seems, knew that this would be so, and her cheating led Hosea to the gradual realization that the children of their marriage were not in fact his children. Here the Book of Hosea uses metaphors: the children were named Jezreel (standing for bloodshed, this area having been fought over many times); Lo-Ruhamah ("unpitied"); and Lo-ammi ("not my people" or "not my kin"). Although Hosea realized her unfaithfulness, and at some stage she left and ended as a slave to another man, Hosea rescued her and brought her back "on probation." God had told him to keep loving her, just as he still loved his people. The people needed bringing back to loyalty to their God.

So Hosea's marriage was like the relationship between God and his people – Hosea pleaded with his unfaithful wife just as God addressed his faithless people. While the priests had failed to make God's Laws known and had enriched themselves at the public expense, a generation had grown to adulthood without knowing their true God. Israel, prophesied Hosea, would become a slave-nation to Assyria. The people would be sent dispossessed, wandering among the nations – a prediction that came to be the dominating aspect of Jewish history. But Hosea's contemporaries took no notice of him.

COMMENTARY ON THE BOOK OF HOSEA

Hosea, son of Beeri, is the only prophet of the Northern Kingdom who has left written prophecies. Though of unknown birthplace he was certainly a native of the north, from his language ("our king," vii. 5), his familiarity with the country (iv. 15; v. 1; vi. 8; xii. 11), his acquaintance with the morals of the people (ch. ii.; iv. 2; vii. 1; xii. 7), the state of parties (vii. 6; viii. 9; xii. 11), and from the more distant allusions to Judah (iv. 15; v. 5; vi. 11). Part of his prophetic career preceded the death of Jeroboam II. (i. 4), and part fell amidst the revolutionary struggles following his death (749). He probably did not live beyond the accession of Pekah (736), as he makes no allusion to the Syro-Ephraimitic war, nor to the deportation of the northern tribes by Tiglath Pileser two years later. Gilead and Mizpah beyond the Jordan are still integral parts of the kingdom (v. 1; vi. 8; xii. 11). Shaman (x. 14), if a king of Assyria, may be Shalmaneser III.; the title "Jareb" given to the king of Assyria is still obscure (v. 13; x. 6).

The book has two parts, ch. i.–iii., and iv.–xiv. Ch. i., iii., with the exposition ch. ii., sketch by means of symbols the future destiny of Israel. Hosea, bidden to take a wife of whoredoms, took Gomer, who bare a son, to be named Jezreel. The name merely recalls the bloody act of Jehu (2 K. x.), and sounds the knell of his house (i. 2–5). Then a daughter was born, Lo-Ruhamah, " Unpitied," meaning that the LORD's mind was alienated from His people (i. 6, 7); and finally a son, Lo-ammi, "not my people," intimating the exile of Israel, and their ceasing for a time to be the people of the LORD (i. 8, 9). This last with the restoration (i. 10–ii. 1) is more fully thrown into symbol, ch. iii. Hosea is bidden "again go love a woman, beloved of a paramour and an adulteress." The woman

211

is the same Gomer, to whom he returns in love, though not for a time in union. The LORD's love shall return to His people, whom He shall keep in long restraint and discipline in exile, to be again redeemed and His people forever. Ch. ii. is the exposition of this symbolical history: Israel's whoredoms with the Baals (the calf images, no gods, viii. 6), ii. 2–5; her perplexities when "unpitied," 6–13; her exile and discipline in the wilderness, 14–18; the new espousals and obtaining of mercy forever, 19–23.

Ch. iv.–xiv., though belonging to different periods, cannot be dated in particulars. They contain complaints of: 1. The immorality and violence everywhere prevailing: adultery and excess in wine (iv. 2; vii. 4, 5), treachery and robbery, in which even the priests engaged (vii. 6; vi. 8), a secular spirit and moral shallowness on which no impression could be made (xii. 7; vii. 2; vi. 1–4). 2. The debased religious conceptions and worship, called "whoredom" and service of Baal, i.e. worship of the calves, with Canaanite rites and conceptions of Jehovah more befitting a nature-god like Baal (ii. 2, 5, 7–13; iv. 13; v. 3). Gross immoralities accompanied this service, in which even the young women took part (iv. 14). The conception of Deity was wholly false, there was no "knowledge of God" in the land (iv. 1); the service was mere sacrifice of flesh and heathenish merry-making (viii. 13; ix. 1); Jehovah desired "goodness" not sacrifices (vi. 6). 3. The foolish political alliances of the day, called also "hiring loves," rival parties dragging the country alternately to Egypt and Assyria (v. 13; vii. 11, 12; viii. 9, 10). The rise of the Northern Kingdom itself was a fatal error (viii. 4; xiii. 10), bringing with it the false worship (viii. 4, 5); an error that shall be retrieved in the latter day, when the people shall seek Jehovah their God and David their king (i. 11; iii. 5).

Hosea's fundamental idea is the "love" of the LORD to the community. In love He redeemed them from Egypt (xi. 1); their history has been but an illustration of His love (xi. 4, ch. even the greatest of His chastisements, casting the people out into the wilderness, is inflicted in love (ii. 14; ch. iii.); and their restoration shall be: due to His love (ii. 19; .xiv. 4). Over against this moral Being, who is love, the prophet creates another moral person, the Community of Israel, with a personal identity, all through her history, but characterized always by want of affection, treachery, infidelity. Her idolatries, alliances abroad, the political schism at home, are but revelations of a state of mind, always unsatisfied and untrue. This idealism of Israel as a moral Person affects the prophet's view of the future. No distinction is drawn between classes, as in Amos. Israel's calamities reveal to her the meaning of her conduct and her history, and she returns to her first husband (ii. 7); the whole people, the ideal Person, is converted and restored (ii. 19). With this conception is connected the question of the prophet's marriage (ch. i., iii.). It has been held: 1, that he literally married a woman already known as a sinner—which is repulsive and contrary to the idea of Israel's early purity (ix. 10; xi. 1; Jer. ii. 2); 2, that the whole is an allegory; 3, that there is a basis of reality in the story, though it is embellished in order the better to exhibit the truth. Gomer became unfaithful, and he saw in his relations with her the relation of Jehovah to His people, and thus received his great prophetic conception (i. 2). That conception is, that the love of the LORD to His people is unquenchable; that love is stronger than custom or law or even than moral repugnance (ch. iii.; Jer. iii. 1).

The profound thought and pathos of this prophet of the north have deeply influenced succeeding writers (Jer.; Ez. xvi., xxxiii.; Is. xl.—lxvi.). The new betrothal of Israel to the LORD (ii. 19) anticipates Jeremiah's new covenant (xxxi. 31).

THE BOOK OF HOSEA: CHAPTER BY CHAPTER

Reigns of Uzziah, Jotham, Ahaz and Hezekiah, kings of Judah.	1	The prophet marries Gomer. Her children – Jezreel, a son; Lo-Ruhamah, a daughter, and Lo-ammi, a son.
	2	Israel's way hedged up. Her idolatries reproved.
	3	The adulteress purchased. Israel's days without a king, prince, sacrifice, image, ephod, teraphim.
	4	Idolatries of Israel. Judah warned.

	5	Judgment denounced against priests, people, and princes for their sins. *[In this and in subsequent chapters, the name Ephraim is used for Israel.]*
Call to repentance.	6	A call to repentance. A complaint of Ephraim's inconstancy.
	7	The sinful state of Israel.
	8	Destruction threatened for their wickedness.
Israel's distress.	9	Distress and captivity of Israel for iniquity.
	10	Israel and empty vine. Exhorted to repentance.
	11	Ephraim's ingratitude and disobedience.
Vain hopes.	12	Ephraim's vain hopes. Judah threatened.
	13	Ephraim's aggravated sins. Promises of mercy.
	14	Israel exhorted to repent. God promises healing.

JOEL

**An obscure prophet tells of The Day of the Lord,
of judgment and destruction.**

The Essential Story of Joel

L ittle is known of this prophet. It is not even known for certain whether he lived during the reign of Uzziah, Manasseh or Josiah – and there is a difference of a century and three-quarters between the first and the last of these kings.

The first chapter and ten verses of the second chapter are taken up with a very striking description of the destructive progress of a swarm of locusts. The invasion by these tiny spoilers was quite probably literal, but it was also emblematic of the devastation that would be caused by the invading hosts of the Chaldeans.

Joel calls this plague of locusts "The Day of the Lord", and calls upon the people to repent. But then he prophecies another greater and more terrible day of destruction which will be heralded by signs and portents. God will gather the people of all nations and bring them down into the Valley of Jehoshaphat, where they will be judged.

Commentary on the Book of Joel

J oel, the son of Pethuel, was a prophet of Judah, familiar with Jerusalem and the temple service, hence by some supposed to have been a priest. The prophecy, occasioned apparently by lengthened visitations of drought and locusts—plagues so severe that they seemed the heralds of the great "day of the LORD"—falls into two parts; ch. i. 1—ii. 17, and ch. ii. 18—iii. 21 (iv. 21 in Heb.). The first part consists of two prophetic discourses (ch. i. and ii. 1-17), each of which, beginning with a graphic description of a plague (ch. i. drought and locusts; ii. 1-17, the army of locusts), leads up to an exhortation to repentance (i. 15 seq.; ii. 12-17). The second part contains promises from Jehovah: 1, promise of temporal blessings, removal of the plagues, abundance of rain, and plenty for man and beast (ii. 18-27); 2, promise that afterwards the Spirit shall be poured out on all flesh, and the knowledge of the LORD be universal; and then shall come the terrible day of the LORD. They that call on the name of the LORD shall be saved, and in mount Zion shall be those that escape (ii. 28-32; iii. 1-5 in Heb.). Though embraced in the Day of the LORD, a separate picture is given of the fate of the heathen world. The "nations" are gathered together into the valley of Jehoshaphat ("Jehovah judges") to be judged. The scene is a great conflict, the mowing of a harvest, the treading of a winepress; the issue reveals the heathen world a "desolation," but Judah shall dwell forever (ch. iii.; iv. in Heb.).

Three modes of interpretation have been followed: the literal, the allegorical, and the apocalyptic. The first considers the "locusts" real; the second as figures for enemies of God's people, the four successive swarms pointing to repeated invasions, as by the four world-monarchies of Daniel; and the third regards them as supernatural agencies or beings belonging to the manifestations of the time of the end (Rev. ix.). Such passages as ii. 4, 7, where the locusts are compared to horsemen, are against the allegorical view; and such as ii. 21-25 decidedly in favor of the literal interpretation, although so severe was the calamity that the prophet saw in it tokens of the nearness of God's judgment and His great day. The age of the prophecy is also uncertain. There is no reference to Assyria or Babylon, and it might be anterior to these empires; no king is mentioned, power being in the hands of the "priests" (i. 14; ii. 15), and hence it has been placed in the minority of Joash (before 850). On the other hand, the great monarchies might have passed away, and the prophecy be of the time of the return from exile, when the priests were the actual rulers of the community. Several things rather favor a late date: 1, no allusion is made to Northern Israel, the people of God is Judah (ii. 1, 32; iii. 1, 12, 17, 20). 2, no allusion is made to the conflict with idolatry, which fills the pages of the earlier prophets; false worship appears overcome. 3, the devotion of the prophet to the ritual (i. 9; ii. 14) has no parallel before Ezekiel. 4, the antithesis between Judah and "all nations" might be the generalization of a later time, earlier prophets usually referring to some one nation as the foe of Israel.—Religious truths prominent in the prophecy are: the Day of the LORD (Is. ii. 12; xiii. 6; Zeph. i. 14; Am. v. 18); the escaped "remnant" (ii. 32; Is. vi. 13; x. 21); the saving faith which "calls" on the LORD, and on the other side the LORD's "call" (ii. 32). The prophecy of the "Spirit," the characteristic of the new dispensation (Acts ii. 17), is fuller than elsewhere (Is. xxxii. 15; Jer. xxxi. 33; Zech. xii. 10). The imagery has greatly influenced later scripture: the locusts (ii. with Rev. ix.), the Day of the LORD (i. 15; ii. 11, 31; Matt. xxiv. 29; Rev. vi. 12), the harvest of judgment (iii. 13; Rev. xiv. 15), and the fountain (iii. 18; Rev. xxii. 1; *cf.* Ezek. xlvii. 1).

THE BOOK OF JOEL: CHAPTER BY CHAPTER

The locusts.	1	Famine by locusts and caterpillars; God's "great army".
	2	The trumpet of alarm sounded. Promises of mercy and grace.
Valley of Jehoshaphat.	3	The valley of Jehoshaphat; and judgments there on the enemies of Judah.

AMOS

**God does not leave Himself without a witness.
Amos prophesies to the Northern Kingdom.**

THE ESSENTIAL STORY OF AMOS

The prophet Amos, who was active during the reigns of Kings Uzziah and Jeroboam II, was a herdsman and tree-grower (a "pincher of sycamores") living a few miles south of Bethlehem when he was called by God to bear witness. Although a native of Judah, his main work was in the northern kingdom, beginning at Bethel, where he went for business and attended a religious feast.

He spoke out at a time of prosperity and relative peace against the way in which material concerns had blurred morality. Religious practices were still carried on, but the outward observance masked a divorce from morality. Bribery and corruption was widespread; the rich got richer, the poor poorer; justice was debased, and immorality was open and shameless. The people had forgotten God: but God, he said, sees all, even the greed, venality, and sharp practice, which would all be punished.

At Bethel, the High Priest, Amaziah, rudely told him to go back to Judah; Amos's response was that he was a simple man called by God. He wanted nothing from the "hireling prophets," whose words were dictated by political interest.

He experienced five visions that embodied the message:

- Devouring locusts sent by God; but upon Amos's pleading, God relented.
- Judgment by fire: again he interceded and God relented.
- God stands with a plumb-line to judge how Israel had diverged from the upright path.
- A basket of ripe fruit: God told him that as the fruit was ripe, so was Israel for judgment.
- Finally, he saw God standing by the altar, and the LORD spoke to him about the coming total destruction he would bring.

Amos's visions.

For Amos, the sin lay less in the idolatry than the moral and social decline in the absence of righteousness. The greatest perils to nations came not by poverty but by prosperity. And God was not just the God of the Hebrews but God of the whole earth. Jews who thought that the Day of Judgment would bring justice in their favor and would strike other nations were misleading themselves: God would mete out justice upon them.

COMMENTARY ON THE BOOK OF AMOS

Amos prophesied in the days of Uzziah king of Judah and Jeroboam, the son of Joash, king of Israel, two years before the earthquake (i. 1; cf. Zech. xiv. 5). Jeroboam probably died about 750, and Uzziah about 740. The prophet's mission, apparently not of long duration, belongs to the first half of the eighth century.

Amos was a native of Tekoa, 12 miles south of Jerusalem, the ruins of which still remain. Here he was a shepherd (i. 1; vii. 14). He disclaims being one of the "sons of the prophets" (vii. 14), though with no disparagement of these societies, much less of the prophetic office (ii. 11). Nothing is known of the causes, if there were any secondary causes, which led to his prophesying against the Northern Kingdom, nor anything of his subsequent history.

The book contains these sections: I. Ch. i.—ii., a view of the sins of all the nations, with threats of the universal judgment of Jehovah. The cloud of judgment laden with disaster trails round the whole horizon, discharging itself upon the nations in succession, Judah included, till it settles at last over Israel. They that have the Law are judged by the Law, and those without law by the law of the human mind common to all men, which the nations have transgressed in their inhuman treatment of one another. II. Ch. iii.—iv. 3, threats of judgment upon the people of Israel because of their injustice to one another and the oppression of the poor by the privileged classes. III. Ch. iv. 4—v., threats of judgment because of the false worship of the people and their vain conceptions of the nature of Jehovah. Their ritual service was only sinning, for the conception of the God to whom they offered it in no way corresponded to Jehovah (iv. 4); He bids them seek *Him* and not seek to Beth-el (v. 4–6). IV. Ch. vi., a threat of judgment because of the luxury of the ruling classes, their national pride and religious indifference and blindness to the operations of Jehovah. V. Ch. vii.—ix. contain the same idea of the destruction of the nation, but expressed in symbols and visions, e.g. the application of the plumb-line (ch. vii.), the ripe summer fruit (viii.), and the smiting of the temple at Beth-el, that it fall on the heads of the worshippers (ix.). The prophet's great religious conception is that of the purely moral character of Jehovah, the righteous ruler of all nations and men. This universalism is expressed by the name "God of hosts," "God of Israel" being avoided; while false gods are not referred to except in the obscure passage, v. 25–27. Sin alone displeases Jehovah, His service is a righteous life, sacrifices of flesh have no meaning to Him (v. 21 *seq.*), hence the sinful nation must inevitably perish (ix. 8). The people's hopes that they could appease Him with offerings, that being their God He would save them, were a delusion; it was because He was their God that He would visit their iniquity upon them (iii. 2; ix. 7); the "Day of the LORD" which they longed for would be darkness, and not light, as if a man fled from a lion and a bear met him (v. 18, 19). Yet Israel cannot be utterly destroyed (ix. 8); sifted among all nations not a true grain will fall to the ground (ix. 9). The sinners of the people shall be destroyed, but the LORD will raise up again the tabernacle of David. The kingdom shall return to its ancient glory when undivided, and the world (as the prophet conceived it) shall be subject to it (ix. 11 *seq.*).

THE BOOK OF AMOS: CHAPTER BY CHAPTER

Reigns of Uzziah of Judah. And Jeroboam II, of Israel.	1	Predictions of judgments on: Syria; Philistines; Tyre; Edom; Ammonites.
	2	Predictions of judgments on: Moab; Judah; Israel.
	3	God's judgments against Israel who had enjoyed special favors. Predicted ruin, under the similitude of the devoured sheep, leaving but the legs or the ear in the mouth of the lion.
	4	Israel in luxury compared to the kine of Bashan.
	5	Rejection and captivity of Israel.
At ease in Zion.	6	Woe to them that are at ease in Zion!
	7	Plague of grasshoppers. God contends by fire. The answered prayers of Amos. The plumb-line applied to Israel. Amaziah, priest of Bethel, instigates Jeroboam against Amos. His attempts to dissuade Amos from prophesying.
	8	Type of the basket of summer fruit, indicating Israel's ripeness for punishment.
	9	Type of smiting the lintel of the Temple. Promises of future separation, under the figure of rebuilding a tabernacle.

OBADIAH

"The kingdom shall be the LORD's".

THE ESSENTIAL SUMMARY OF OBADIAH

The brief prophecy of Obadiah is concerned with the fate of Edom. In the days of Jehoram, Edom appears to have been actively hostile to Judah, and moreover its people set themselves against God. So most of the later prophets have stern words for Edom. It should be noticed though that most of the prophets finish with the anticipation of final and permanent blessedness for Israel, and Obadiah is no exception.

COMMENTARY ON THE BOOK OF OBADIAH

Obadiah prophesied against Edom: 1, Edom though building high in the rock shall be brought down to the ground by Jehovah and his treasures rifled, v. 1–9; 2, this because of his violence to Judah, his malicious joy over its calamity, and his participation with its destroyers in holding riot on God's holy mountain, 10–16; 3, but in Zion shall be the remnant, which shall be holy. Israel restored shall possess its ancient heritages and absorb all its foes, Edom, the Philistines and Phenicia, and the kingdom shall be the LORD's, 17–21.—Nothing is known of the prophet. The terms in which he describes the "calamity" of Jerusalem (10–16) can hardly refer to anything but its capture by the Chaldeans (586). For the part Edom took in this against his brother (v. 10) he incurred the abiding hatred of Israel (Jer. xlix.; Ezek. xxv. 12; xxxv. 4; Lam. iv. 21; Ps. cxxxvii. 7). The relations of Edom to Israel were changeful. Subdued by David it shook off the yoke under Jehoram (2 K. viii. 20). Reconquered by Amaziah and Uzziah (2 K. xiv. 7, 22) it rebelled under Ahaz (2 K. xvi. 6; 2 Chr. xxviii. 17); but in the narratives of these events no mention is made of any part taken by Edom in a capture of Jerusalem. On the other hand, when Obadiah 1–6, 8 is compared with Jeremiah xlix. 14–16, 9, 10, 7 (in this order) they appear dependent on one another. The prophecies of Jeremiah against the nations are pre-exilic and dependent on earlier writings. Hence some have referred Obadiah to the time of Jehoram's defeat by the Arabians (2 Chr. xxi. 16), in which it is assumed Edom took part; while others have supposed both Obadiah and Jeremiah dependent on an earlier prophecy. The problems connected with the prophecies of Jeremiah against the nations are still unsolved, while the reference of Obadiah to the fall of Jerusalem seems clear. Obadiah has many affinities with Joel.

THE BOOK OF OBADIAH: CHAPTER BY CHAPTER

Edom.	Edom's destruction announced for pride; vain confidence; and violence to sons of Jacob.
Day of the LORD.	The "Day of the LORD upon the heathen. Upon Mount Zion deliverance.

JONAH

An unwilling prophet is sent by God to the sinful city of Nineveh.

THE ESSENTIAL STORY OF JONAH

Jonah was a prophet who came probably from the area of Galilee. He was commanded by God to go to Nineveh, capital of the mighty Assyrian Empire, and announce God's impending judgment upon their wickedness.

But Jonah did not go. Not only did he believe that God would bring salvation only for the Jews; he feared that if the Assyrians did indeed repent, God would spare them. Jonah preferred that they should all meet the doom he believed they so richly deserved.

So instead of heading for Nineveh, he boarded a Phoenician ship bound for the other end of the Mediterranean, Tarshish (or Tartessus, modern Cadiz). En route, God called up a great storm, and, despite the best efforts of the mariners, the vessel could make no progress toward the safety of land. Then the crew began to realize that one of the people on board must have offended a god, and eventually Jonah admitted that he must be the guilty one. Reluctantly, and after further efforts to make landfall, the sailors followed Jonah's selfless advice to cast him overboard. At once the storm abated, and the ship made a safe course, the ship's crew acknowledging the power of the Hebrew God.

But this was not the end of Jonah, for he was swallowed by a great fish, and languished, contrite, in its belly for three days and nights, praying to God for forgiveness. At the end of that time, the fish vomited him onto the shore, and he received God's command again: to go to Nineveh and warn them.

At Nineveh, Jonah found a receptive audience and the signs of repentance. But this did not please the prophet, and he sat gloomily outside the city walls. There God taught him another lesson. To shade him from the intense heat, a castor-oil plant miraculously shot up; but then it was devoured by a worm, and Jonah despaired, wilting in the dry torment of the sun. Then God told him his lesson: if Jonah could care for the wellbeing of a plant, which he had not planted or nourished himself, how much more must God care for the great city, with its people, children, and animals? God had love for all: Gentiles would repent if they were taught; and salvation was not only for the Jews.

COMMENTARY ON THE BOOK OF JONAH

Jonah, son of Amittai, of Gath-hepher in Zebulon, lived under Jeroboam II., whose success in restoring the ancient boundaries of Israel he predicted (2 K. xiv. 25). This prophecy was probably never written, the opinion of some authors that it is to be identified with Isaiah xv., xvi. resting on no solid foundation. The present Book of Jonah does not assume to be from the hand of the prophet, but has the form of a narrative by a later writer of an episode in his life. It is disputed how far the narrative reposes on actual historical events, and also whether the tradition may not have assumed some shape orally before the present writer adopted it, or whether the details be the free creation of his own mind. At all events the historical elements, if they existed, have been amplified and embellished by the author so as to make them more graphically convey the moral lessons which it is his object to teach. In this respect the book presents a parallel to the Book of Job.

The key to the book is probably to be found in ch. iii. 10—iv. 1 seq., the reasons the prophet gives for his flight and unwillingness to preach to Nineveh. It is a repudiation of a narrow-hearted particularism which would confine to Israel a salvation of which the very nature of God and the susceptibilities of the human conscience everywhere prophesy the universality. 1. Jehovah is God alone, over all, the sea and the dry land (i. 9). The winds obey

Him, and the monsters of the deep. The men of Nineveh as well as Israel are the work of His hand, and His compassions are over all His works (iv. 2, 10, 11). 2. Everywhere the mind of men, even the heathen world, is susceptible to the sense of sin and the Godhead of Jehovah (i. 16; iii. 7 *seq.*; Ezek. iii. 6, and often in Dan., e.g. ii. 47; iii. 28; iv. 37; vi. 26). Jehovah's operations have only to be known for all men to believe in Him. 3. The conclusion, which the prophet sought to evade, hardly needs to be drawn. Israel's mission and the destiny of mankind are both plain. The book is a beautiful poem, whether it paints the humanity of the heathen sailors, or the mourning of the prophet over the decay of the grass of the field, or more particularly the divine tenderness in ministering to the diseased mind of the prophet with his imperfect conceptions, or in pitying the little children of Nineveh. It is not necessary to suppose that the book, which is late, was written with the view of counteracting a tendency of any particular time. Its teaching is a spontaneous outcome of the religion of Israel, the corollary, often drawn before, from the doctrine of Jehovah, God alone. What is new in it is not this, but the author's love of mankind, his kindly appreciation of that which is good and beautiful in men everywhere. This is the support from another side of his teaching. Men and God are both transfigured. Would that men knew the LORD, as they shall do!

THE BOOK OF JONAH: CHAPTER BY CHAPTER

Reign of Jeroboam II of Israel.	1	Jonah sent to Nineveh. Attempts to flee to Tarshish. A tempest arises. Lots cast for the guilty cause of tempest. Lot falls on Jonah, He is cast into the sea and swallowed up.
Jonah's prayer.	2	Jonah's prayer, and deliverance.
	3	Jonah's second commission. Nineveh repents.
	4	Jonah's anger. His gourd withers. God's mercy to Nineveh.

MICAH

Predictions about invasions, exile, God's love of justice and mercy, and the birth of the Messiah in Bethlehem.

THE ESSENTIAL STORY OF MICAH

Micah made his prophecies a little later than Amos and Hosea but was a contemporary of Isaiah. From small landowning stock, he addressed the lower orders of society, upbraiding the ruling classes and leaders, including wealthy landowners, always squeezing out smaller farmers, and judges and officials. The priests, he claimed, had misunderstood God: while practicing injustice, they yet relied on God or their own safety. In particular, he singled out the two capital cities of Jerusalem and Samaria for damnation.

His message was in the form of judgment, but then comfort and salvation. Man's moral sins offended God, and judgment would come. All was darkness, but yet there would be light with God. He prophesied that Jerusalem would one day become the religious center of the world; and he also made a prophecy that would resonate in the New Testament. From Bethlehem, he predicted, would come a Messiah, the ultimate deliverer.

COMMENTARY ON THE BOOK OF MICAH

Micah, a native of Moresheth Gath in the plain country of Judah (i. 1, 14), prophesied under Hezekiah (iii. 12; Jer. xxvi. 18), partly at least before the fall of Samaria in 722 6). The book has three divisions: I. Ch. i.—iii. prophecies of judgment and ruin on the State. II. Ch. iv., v. prophecies of restoration, with brilliant Messianic promises. III. Ch. vi., vii. prophecies of a mixed character, breathing a different spirit and belonging probably to a later period. First part: 1, a theophany of the Lord in judgement (i. 1-4), which lights first on Samaria, which shall become heaps (5-7), and then moves southward towards the "gate of my people, even Jerusalem";—graphic picture of the panic and flight of the inhabitants before the Assyrian (8-16). 2, the cause of this judgment is the idolatry at the high places (i. 5-7), but also the oppressions of the upper classes (ii. 1, 2). Micah, a native of the country, had ample opportunities of seeing how the poorer cultivators were dispossessed, "flayed and chopped in pieces" by the more powerful owners and creditors, their wives and children driven out and stripped naked (ii. 8-10; iii. 1-4). Added to this cruelty was the usual sensuality (ii. 11) and indifference to religion or even active opposition to the prophets who censured them (ii. 6). 3, therefore judgment shall be on the false prophets who encouraged such evils (iii. 5-8) and on the people—Zion shall be ploughed like a field. (iii. 9-12). Second part: 1, ch. iv., prediction of the restoration of the former kingdom to Jerusalem, introduced by the beautiful prophecy of the time when Zion shall be the religious centre of the world (found also Is. ii.). 2, ch. v., prophecy of the birth of the new king of the house of David (2-4), and the universal peace of his reign (5, 10-15). Third part: 1, a remonstrance of the Lord with His people, in which He recounts His past goodness to them (vi. 1-5). The touched conscience of the community seeks to know how He would be served? The answer is that He desires justice, goodness, and humility before God—an answer which sums up Amos, Hosea and Isaiah in three words (6-8). Because the opposite of these things prevails desolating judgment must be looked for (9-16). 2, new and terrible picture of the treacherous and anarchic state of society (vii. 1-7). 3, finally, the judgment seems to have fallen, and Zion sitting in darkness comforts herself with the hope that she shall yet see light, for who is God like unto Jehovah who pardoneth iniquity? (7–20). The connexion is obscure in several parts of the book. Ch. ii. 12, 13 cannot be meant as a specimen of the false prophets' style; it seems however to disturb the connexion. Ch. iv. 9, 10 suggest a different situation from iv. 11 *seq.;* while vii. 7–20 breathes the spirit and situation of Lamentations iii. 25 *seq.* Ch. Vi., vii. Have an elegiac tone, unlike the other chapters.

THE BOOK OF MICAH: CHAPTER BY CHAPTER

Reigns of Jotham, Ahaz and Hezekiah, kings of Judah.	1	Testimony against Samaria and Jerusalem.
	2	Judgments for oppression and injustice, Announcement of the coming up of the breaker.
And Pekah and Hoshea, two last kings of Israel.	3	Accusations against the rulers of Israel. And against false prophets. Zion and Jerusalem to be ploughed as a field, and lie in heaps.
Messiah.	4	Messiah's kingdom and glory.
	5	Messiah's birthplace: Bethlehem Ephratah. Assyria to be waste. Destruction of idolatry.
On sacrifices.	6	God's controversy with Israel. Reminded of redemption from Egypt, and escape from the enmity of Balaam. God not pleased with sacrifices. God requires mercy and justice.
	7	The scantiness of grape gleanings symbolic of the small number of the godly. "I will look unto the LORD." Confusion of the nations.

NAHUM

Prediction of the downfall of Assyria.

THE ESSENTIAL SUMMARY OF NAHUM

Nahum's name means "Consolation". The circumstances of his life are unknown except that he was a native of Elkosh, which was probably a village in Galilee. Opinions are divided about exactly when Nahum prophesied. The best interpreters adopt Jerome's position that he foretold the destruction of Nineveh in the time of Hezekiah, after the war of Sennacherib in Egypt, mentioned by Berosus. Nahum speaks of the taking of No-Amon, of the haughtiness of Rabshakeh, and of the defeat of Sennacherib as things that were past. He implies that the tribe of Judah was still in their own country, and that they celebrated their festivals there. He notices also the captivity and dispersion of the ten tribes. The subject of his prophesy is, in accordance with the superscription, "the burden of Nineveh," the destruction of which he predicts.

COMMENTARY ON THE BOOK OF NAHUM

Nahum was probably a native of Elkosh in Galilee (*cf.* Capernaum, the village of Nahum); a late Christian tradition refers to Alkush near Mosul, the ancient Nineveh. The prophecy is altogether against Nineveh. Starting, as all the prophets do, from a conception of Jehovah, a God of vengeance to His enemies but long suffering (i. 2, 3), the prophet presents a theophany of this God for the purpose of executing judgment once for all on the oppressor of His people and delivering them (3–15). Ch. ii., a more particular picture of the same subject, containing brilliant sketches of the city's fall—the besiegers (ii. 3, 4), the besieged, the capture, and dispersion of the inhabitants (5–10), with a taunting proverb over the harrying of the ancient den of lions (11–13). Ch. iii., the same theme under other figures, as that of a harlot and enchantress intoxicating the nations with the cup of her sorceries, *i.e.* her political influences and mercantile enterprises. The harlot shall be stripped and exposed in the eyes of all whom she enchanted (iii. 1–7). She shall share the fate of No-Amon, and all her traders shall flee from her, as the locusts strip off their shards and fly away (8–19). The prophecy has great literary brilliancy, with strong patriotic feeling (i. 13; ii. 1), but more rarely enters the deeper moral sphere 19; i. 2, 3). Its composition lies between two ascertained points, the fall of Nineveh (606), and that of No-Amon or Thebes in Upper Egypt, taken by Assurbanipal about 660. The prophets do not usually pursue abstract themes; their revelations, though going beyond immediate movements, are usually suggested by them. The occasion of the prophecy may have been some recent aggression of Assyria, or more probably some powerful coalition against Nineveh, either that before which it actually fell or some earlier one, which prompted the prophet to express his certainty of the city's doom (ii. 1; iii. 12).

THE BOOK OF NAHUM: CHAPTER BY CHAPTER

Reign of Hezekiah.	1	Majestic description of God's goodness to His people and destruction of His enemies.
Nineveh.	2	Taking of Nineveh described.
	3	Utter destruction of Nineveh.

HABAKKUK

A prediction of the doom of the Chaldeans.

THE ESSENTIAL SUMMARY OF HABAKKUK

Habakkuk may have delivered his prophecy in around the twelfth or thirteenth year of the reign of Josiah (B.C. 630, 629). He foretells the doom of the Chaldeans. This is followed by a series of denunciations by the nations who had suffered from their oppression. The strophical arrangement of these "woes" is a remarkable feature of this prophecy. The book concludes with the magnificent psalm in chapter iii.

COMMENTARY ON THE BOOK OF HABAKKUK

Habakkuk, of whom nothing is known, prophesied in Judah during the last years of the Kingdom. The book has two parts: ch. i., ii. the prophecy, and ch. iii. a lyrical hymn. This remarkable writing looks more like a passage of the Wisdom literature rather than of Prophecy, being occupied almost entirely with the moral problem of evil and oppression, whether in Israel or in the world, under the eyes of the just and almighty God. 1. The prophet complains that his outcries against the evil, the injustice and lawlessness in Judah remain unheard by Jehovah, who calmly beholds it (i. 1–4). 2. He receives the reply that the LORD is raising up that bitter and hasty nation the Chaldeans to chastise the wrongdoers (5–11). 3. The answer aggravates the evil, making it as wide as mankind while before confined to Israel. The character of the Chaldeans fills the prophet's mind, and the moral problem is only enveloped in deeper darkness (12–17). 4. Baffled and exhausted the prophet betakes himself to his watchtower to await the answer of the LORD. It comes in the shape of a moral distinction: "his soul is not upright in him; but, the righteous shall live in his faithfulness"). The distinction carries in it its final verification in events, though this may not come at once (ii. 1–5). 5. It is, however, certain; and the downfall of the Chaldeans is celebrated in a hymn of triumph, so instinct with moral feeling that not only men (6–8), but inanimate things (v. 11) are endowed with a conscience that rises against the selfishness and barbarous inhumanity of the conqueror (6–20). The moral breadth of the prophet is comparable only to some parts of Job (vii. 1 *seq.*; ix. 24; ch. xxi., xxiv.), while his faith in the necessary triumph of the religion of Jehovah in contrast with idolatry has risen up to be a principle based on reflection (ii. 14, 20), as in the last chapters of Isaiah. The brilliant hymn, ch. iii., is a lyrical expression of the same conceptions. Though fashioned on older models (Deut. xxxiii.; Judg. v.; *cf.* Ps. lxviii.), the hymn is a powerful delineation of the manifestation of Jehovah to judge the earth and deliver His people.

THE BOOK OF HABAKKUK: CHAPTER BY CHAPTER

Reigns of Manesseh or Jehoiakim supposed.	1	Prophecy of the destruction of the Jews by the Chaldeans.
	2	Judgments on the Chaldeans. The "glory of the LORD" to fill the earth. Testimony against dumb idols.
Habakkuk's prayer.	3	Prayer of Habakkuk.

ZEPHANIAH

**A prediction of the overthrow of Judah for its idolatry and
wickedness.**

THE ESSENTIAL SUMMARY OF ZEPHANIAH

Zephaniah prophesied in the days of Josiah, the good king
of Judah (about 630 B.C.). Although the period of Josiah's
reign was a time of spiritual revival, the words of this
prophet show that this movement towards God was far from
universal. A remnant of the people still bowed down to Baal,
even in the immediate neighbourhood of Jerusalem.

Zephaniah's prophecy contains two oracles in three chapters
directed against idolaters in Judah, against surrounding regions
and against wicked rulers, priests and prophets. It closes with
cheering promises of Gospel blessings.

COMMENTARY ON THE BOOK OF ZEPHANIAH

Zephaniah, whose ancestry is carried back four degrees
to a Hizkiah, supposed by some to be King Hezekiah,
prophesied in the time of Josiah (639–608). The book is a
sort of prophetic compend, speaking first of universal judgment,
ch. i.—iii. 8, and then of universal salvation in the knowledge of
Jehovah, ch. iii. 9–20. This judgment or "Day of the LORD" is the
pouring out of His wrath on all created things (i. 1–3); in particular on men, on Judah (i. 4—ii. 3), then on all the nations (ii. 4–15).

234

It falls on Judah for her idolatries (i. 4–7), on the royal house for their foreign affectations and violence (8, 9), on the merchant classes (10, 11), on all ungodly and indifferent, who say, the LORD will not do good or do evil—the Day of the LORD shall be on all, a day of blood and darkness (12–18). Let men turn that they may be hid in this terrible day (ii. 1–3). It falls too on the nations round about, the Philistines on the west, Moab and Ammon on the east, Cush on the south, and Assyria on the north (ii. 4–15). Ch. iii. 1–8 repeats the threat of universal judgment more compendiously. Then follows the promise that the knowledge of the LORD shall be given to all nations (iii. 9); Jerusalem shall no more be proud, but humble (iii. 11, 12; Ezek. xvi. 63), her captives shall be restored, and the LORD her King shall rule for ever in the midst of her (iii. 10–20).

The prophecy dates before the fall of Nineveh, 606 (ii. 13); ch. i. 4 "remnant of Baal" is hardly evidence for time after Josiah's reformation (621), nor i. 5, iii. 4 for time before it. The great conception of the prophecy is "the Day of the LORD," the time of the LORD's final interposition to judge evil and introduce His universal kingdom. This "day" was a general conception of the prophets, but the presentiment that it was near was awakened in two ways: 1, by the moral condition of men, Israel or the world. Many times this seemed so corrupt or violent that the feeling could not be repressed that the Judge must speedily intervene (Is. ii. 12). Or 2, by great convulsions (Is. xiii. 6) or calamities (Joel i. 15; ii. 1) desolating the earth at the time. Jehovah was visibly present in these disasters; He was so near that men felt He was about to reveal Himself in His fullness in that great and terrible day. There seems a reference to some visible instrument in God's hand when the prophet speaks of the LORD's guests, bidden to His sacrifice (i. 7),—possibly the Scythians, who broke into western Asia at about this time. The expressions, "I am, and there is none else," ii. 15, echoes Isaiah xlvii. 8; and "proudly exulting ones," iii. 11, again Isaiah xiii. 3.

THE BOOK OF ZEPHANIAH: CHAPTER BY CHAPTER

About the reign of Josiah.	1	God's judgments on idolatrous Judah predicted.
The just LORD.	2	Predicted judgments on Philistia, Moab, Ammon, Ethiopia and Assyria.
	3	Rebukes to Jerusalem. "The remnant of Israel." "A name and a praise among all the earth."

HAGGAI

Prophecies concerning the rebuilding of the Temple.

THE ESSENTIAL SUMMARY OF HAGGAI

Haggai is the first of the minor prophets who prophesied after the Captivity. History and tradition are both silent on the subject of his tribe and parentage. It is likely however that he was one of the exiles who returned with Zerubbabel and Jehusa. He began to prophecy around 520 B.C. and the aim of his prophesying was to encourage his countrymen to begin again the building of the Temple, which had been so long interrupted. In this he was successful, the Median king Darius having granted a decree for this purpose. The exceeding glory of the second Temple was, as he had foretold, that Christ, "the desire of all nations came to it," and made the place of his feet glorious.

COMMENTARY ON THE BOOK OF HAGGAI

Haggai prophesied in the second year of Darius Hystaspes (520, i. 1). His short book, which reflects the depressed condition of the small community of the Restoration, naturally occupied with the care of providing for their own subsistence more than with zeal for the public service of their God, contains four brief oracles. 1. Ch. i., complaint of the people's absorption in their own material interests to the neglect of God's house; a picture of their abject condition, due to their religious indifference; and an exhortation to put their hand forthwith to the work of raising the temple. The exhortation had the effect desired (i. 14, 15). 2. ii. 1–9, an oracle designed to comfort those who had seen the former house and could not but consider the present one pitiful and mean in comparison (*cf.* the touching narrative of Ezra iii. 11–13). A glory shall belong to the present house to which the former never attained, for the great "shaking" of the Day of the LORD is near, and all nations shall come to it dedicating their "desirable (precious) things," their silver and gold to the LORD (ii. 7–9; *cf.* Is. lx. 5), and His glory shall fill it (Is. lx. 13). Possibly Haggai himself may have remembered the former house. 3. Ch. ii. 10–19, a parable: Does holy flesh sanctify that which it touches? No, but the touch of the unclean pollutes all about it. So the secular spirit of the people has hitherto brought a curse on all their labor and increase; but from henceforth the LORD will bless them. 4. Ch. ii. 20–23, a dim outlook into the future with presentiments of vast changes in the world at the hand of the LORD, when the kingdoms of the nations shall decay and crumble before the kingdom of the LORD (Dan. ii. 44), but the descendant of the house of David shall be near to the LORD as a seal.

THE BOOK OF HAGGAI: CHAPTER BY CHAPTER

Jews return to Jerusalem, with Ezra.	1	Israel incited to rebuild the Temple.
	2	The glory of Messiah's presence predicted. Convulsion of nations before Messiah's advent; addressed to Zerubbabel, Messiah's type.

ZECHARIAH

Prophecies relating to the rebuilding of the Temple and the Messiah.

The Essential Summary of Zechariah

Zechariah was the son of Berechiah and a grandson of Iddo the priest. (Ezra calls him the son of Iddo.) He was a priest as well as a prophet, and succeeded his grandfather in the sacred office. He returned from Babylon with Zerubbabel and began to prophesy while still young, around two months after Haggai. The two prophets, with united zeal, encouraged the people to resume the work of rebuilding the Temple.

Zechariah's prophecies concerning the Messiah are more specific than those of most other prophets and many of them are couched in symbols. The book opens with a brief introduction, after which six chapters relate a series of visions setting forth the fitness of the time for the promised restoration of Israel, the destruction of the enemies of God's people, the conversion of the heathen, the coming of the Messiah, the branch, the outpouring and blessed influences of the Holy Spirit, and the importance and safety of faithfully adhering to the service of their covenant God. Chapter vii. relates to commemorative observances. Chapters ix.–xi. predict the prosperity of Judah during the times of the Maccabees, together with the fate of Persia and other adjacent kingdoms. The remaining three chapters describe the future destiny of the Jews, the siege of Jerusalem; the triumphs of Messiah, and the glories of the last day, when "Holiness to the LORD" shall be inscribed on all things.

In what may be called the peculiarities of his prophecy, Zechariah approaches nearly to Ezekiel and Daniel. Like them, he delights in visions; like them, he uses symbols and allegories, rather than the bold figures and metaphors which lend so much force and beauty to the writings of the earlier prophets. Like them, he beholds angels ministering before Jehovah, and fulfilling his behests on the earth. He is the only one of the prophets who speaks of Satan. That some of these peculiarities are owing to his Chaldean education can hardly be doubted.

Zechariah's vision.

COMMENTARY ON THE BOOK OF ZECHARIAH

Zechariah, son of Berechiah, son of Iddo (Neh. xii. 4, 16), a contemporary of Haggai (Ezra v. 1; vi. 14), prophesied from 2nd to 4th year of Darius I. (520–518). The book has two great divisions: ch. i.–viii., a series of visions sketching the future of the people of God, and ch. ix.–xiv., prophecies of an obscure kind, belonging to a different situation. Two things characterize the visions: first, the prophetic revelation, formerly a thing internal to the prophet's mind, is here made external, and analysed into two elements,—visions, and an interpreting angel who explains them. Secondly, so Jehovah Himself is externally manifested in the Angel of the LORD, and His power and efficiency in His operations are personified in the shape of horsemen and the like.

The Visions: i. 1–6, introduction: warning to hear and repent, by the example of the fathers, who refused to hear, and were overtaken by God's judgments, justly as they acknowledged. 1 Vision, i. 7–17, riders on horses of various colors, which go over all the earth to report on the state of the nations in the interests of Jerusalem. Meaning: the LORD is jealous for Jerusalem, and wrath with the nations at ease; He returns to Zion, where His house shall be built, and His city peopled. 2 Vision, i. 18–21, four horns— all the agencies that have scattered Israel; and four craftsmen— the divine agencies that shall counteract and destroy them. 3 Vision, ch. ii., a man with a measuring line to measure Jerusalem. The city shall be immeasurable and overflow with people; the LORD shall be a wall of fire around her, and many nations shall be joined to her in that day. 4 Vision, ch. iii., Joshua, the high priest, in filthy garments, standing before the angel of the LORD, with Satan at his right hand to accuse him (cf. Job i. 6–11). Satan is rebuked; the LORD who has chosen Jerusalem has plucked the brand from the burning. The beautiful vision might be a reflection of the feeling of the people, their abject condition awakening a sense of their sin and the fear that the LORD had not returned to them in truth. They are comforted with the assurance that His favor and forgiveness are with them, dispensed through the ministries among them; these ministries are but types of a more perfect one, when through the Branch (Messiah, Jer. xxiii. 5; xxxiii. 15) the LORD will remove the iniquity of the land in one day. 5 Vision, ch. iv., a lampstand surmounted by a bowl of oil, which feeds by tubes the seven burning lamps of the lampstand, two olive trees on either side supplying the bowl with oil. The lamps might represent the light shed by the people or that shed among them. The oil is the symbol of the Spirit, through whom, and not by might or power, all Israel's work and destiny shall be accomplished. This Spirit is dispensed through the two anointed ones ("sons of oil"), representing the priestly and royal rule (Joshua and Zerubbabel). 6 Vision, v. 1–4, a symbol of the curse that shall light on sin in the land. 7 Vision, v. 5–11, symbol of the removing of the sin of the people to Shinar, the land of their foes (Lev. xvi. 21). 8 Vision, vi. 1–8, horsemen, also called "winds" (Rev. vii. 1), going to all quarters of the earth—symbols of agencies by which God shall subdue the nations, foes of His people. Ch. vi. 9–15, symbolical action to teach that the Branch (Messiah), who shall truly build the Temple of the LORD, shall be a Crowned Priest. Ch. vii., viii., reply to a question about fasting: the LORD is indifferent whether men fast or eat; He desires that they execute judgment and show mercy (vii. 8–10). The fasts shall be turned into festivals of joy (viii. 19). Ch. i.–viii. are of profoundly spiritual meaning.

Ch. ix.—xi. 1. An invasion from the North sweeps over Damascus, Tyre and the Philistines; the last are incorporated in Israel (ix. 1–7). Zion is saved; her King comes to her, righteous and victorious, meek and Prince of Peace (8–10). Her captives are restored, and Judah and Ephraim, miraculously strengthened of God, are victorious over the Greeks; and shall no more seek to diviners, but to the LORD (ix. 11—x. 2). 2. A similar theme. Good shepherds displace the evil ones; Judah miraculously strengthened, with Ephraim fully restored, shall humble the pride of Assyria and Egypt (x. 3–12). 3. Invasion of Lebanon and the Jordan-land (xi. 1–3). The prophet is commissioned to feed the flock destined for slaughter (4–8); renounces the thankless task (9–14); the flock falls into the hands of an evil shepherd (15–17). Ch. xii.—xiv. 1. Final war of the nations against Jerusalem, and their defeat (xii. 1–9). 2. The Spirit poured out on Jerusalem, and a fountain opened for sin and uncleanness (xii. 10—xiii. 6). 3. Ch. xiv. appears a duplicate of xii., with the difference that Jerusalem falls for a time into the hands of the nations before the LORD appears for her salvation. These prophecies are enigmatic and of uncertain date. To some writers, ch. ix.—xi. appear of date anterior to the fall of Samaria, because of reference to Ephraim (ix. 10–15; x. 7; xi. 14), to diviners and teraphim (x. 2), Assyria (x. 10), a king of Gaza (ix. 5), and to the Messiah (ix. 9; *cf.* Is. lxii. 11); while ch. xii.—xiv., though posterior to the death of Josiah (referred to xii. 11), must be pre-exilic, because of reference to idols and false prophets (xiii. 2–6). Others consider ch. ix.—xiv. the work of one writer, living not long after Alexander, because of reference to the Greeks (ix. 13), and the exile (ix. 11; x. 6, 9, 10); the prominence of the priesthood (xii. 13), and the final war of the nations against Jerusalem, which reflects Ezek. xxxviii., xxxix. "Assyria," "Egypt," &c. would be ancient names used for Syria and the kingdom of the Ptolemies.

THE BOOK OF ZECHARIAH: CHAPTER BY CHAPTER

Contemporary with Haggai.	1	Visions of the:
		  Red horses and myrtle trees;
		  Four horns and four carpenters;

Visions.	2	Measuring line;
The Branches.	3	Joshua and Satan; God's servant, the BRANCH, both a priest and a king.
	4	Golden candlestick and olive trees.
	5	Flying roll, Ephah, lead, woman, and women with wings.
	6	Chariots and horses. Joshua crowned: a type of the BRANCH, both a priest and a king.
	7	Inquiries on fasting. Exhortations to reformation.
	8	Encouragements to rebuild Jerusalem.
"Thy King cometh."	9	Threatenings to the heathen nations: Syria, Tyre and Philistia. Promises of the coming of the Messiah, with peace and prosperity.
	10	Promises of Israel's restoration.
Beauty and Bands.	11	Lamentations over the fallen great. The staves of Beauty and Bands cut asunder.
	12	Jerusalem a cup of trembling, and a burdensome stone to her enemies. The spirit of grace and supplication to be poured out on Jerusalem.
Fountain opened.	13	The fountain opened for sin, and for uncleanness. The Shepherd smitten, and the sheep scattered.
	14	The second coming of the Messiah. The glory of the Last Days. The Feast of the Tabernacles. HOLINESS UNTO THE LORD.

MALACHI

**Prophecies relating to the calling of the Gentiles
and the coming of Christ.**

THE ESSENTIAL SUMMARY OF MALACHI

Malachi (that is, the angel or messenger of Jehovah) is the last, and is therefore called "the seal" of the prophets, and his prophecies constitute the closing book of the Canon. Of his personal history nothing is known. He is believed to have been contemporary with Nehemiah, and it is most likely that he delivered his prophecies after the second return of Nehemiah from Persia (Neh., xiii. 6). From the striking parallelism between the state of things indicated in Malachi's prophecies and that actually existing on Nehemiah's return from the court of Artaxerxes, it is on all accounts highly probable that the efforts of the secular governor were on this occasion seconded by the Preaching of "Jehovah's Messenger," and that Malachi occupied the same position with regard to the reformation under Nehemiah, Which Isaiah held in the time of Hezekiab, and Jeremiah in that of Josiah. The last chapter of canonical Jewish history is the key to the last chapter of its prophecy.

The whole prophecy naturally divides itself into three sections, in the first of which Jehovah is represented as the loving Father and Ruler of his people (chaps. i. 2,—ii. 9); in the second, as the supreme God and Father of all (chap. ii. 10—16); and in the third, as their righteous and final Judge (chap. ii, i7—end),

COMMENTARY ON THE BOOK OF MALACHI

It is not certain whether Malachi ("my messenger," iii. 1, or contraction of Malachiah, "messenger of the LORD") be a proper name or a title of honor given to an anonymous prophet. The exact date of the prophecy is also uncertain. The Temple has been completed (i. 10), the ritual though neglected is in operation; but the condition of the people remains depressed, leading to murmuring against God (ii. 17). The practices criticized: mixed marriages and cruel divorces (ii. 10 *seq.*), with neglect of the tithes (iii. 8), are those reproved by Nehemiah (xiii. 23; xiii. 10). They may, however, have prevailed for long, and the reference to the governor (i. 8; cf. Neh. v. 14) suggests that he was a foreigner at the time. The prophecy may belong to the second half of the fifth century. There are two parts: i. 1—ii. 9, and ii. 10—iv. 6 (iii. 24 in Heb.), the first directed more to the priesthood, and the second more to the practices and mind of the people. 1. The introduction (i. 1–5) recalls to mind the love of the LORD to the people, illustrated in the histories of Israel and Esau. The latter had been made a desolation, while

Malachi, the last of the prophets.

245

Israel had been restored and would be blessed. 2. Ungratefulness of Israel and dishonor they do to Him who is their "father" and "master" in neglecting His service and bringing the blemished and the blind to His table. It were better that the doors of the temple were closed! (6–14). 3. Such evils are due to the secularity of the priesthood. How unlike is the degenerate Levi of today to the ideal Levi of former times (ii. 1–9).

The second part has two main points: 1. The mixed marriages and repudiation of native wives (ii. 10–16). Have not all children of Israel one God for father? Did not one God create them a people? (Is. xliii. 1, &c.). Why should they mix with the heathen, and cruelly wrong their wives of the daughters of Israel? The instance of Abraham is of another kind (ii. 15). 2. The people's murmuring over their lot, complain that God makes no discrimination in His rule between the good and the wicked, and impatient desire for His coming (ii. 17–iv. 6). Answer: The LORD's coming is nigh. He will send His messenger to prepare His way (Elijah, iv. 5; *cf.* Is. xi. 3); the LORD will come to His temple, and the angel of the covenant whom they desire (the angel of the covenant differs from the LORD only in this that He is the LORD in visible manifestation, Zech. i. 11; iii. 1). Who shall abide His coming? For He shall sit as one refining silver (ii. 17—iii. 6; cf. iii. 13–18; iv. 1–3). Even now their wretchedness is not due to any moral slackness on the part of God, but to their own hereditary evil. They rob God of that due to Him. Let them return unto the LORD, and He will return unto them! (iii. 7–12).

THE BOOK OF MALACHI: CHAPTER BY CHAPTER

After the Temple was rebuilt.	1	Severe reproof of unfaithful Israel. The Gentiles to be brought in.
	2	Charges against priests and people.
	3	Messiah and his forerunner promised. God's book of remembrance.
God's Jewels. Messiah's forerunner.	4	The day of fiery trial. The rising of the Sun of righteousness. Messiah's forerunner predicted under the character of Elijah.

The Apocrypha

Heliodorus, II Maccabees verses 23–27.

THE APOCRYPHA

A collection of writings not recognized as belonging to the Canon
of Scripture but nevertheless included in the Latin Vulgate and in
the Greek Septuagint.

THE ESSENTIAL BACKGROUND TO THE APOCRYPHA

The primary meaning of Apocrypha, "hidden, secret,"
seems, toward the close of the second century, to have
been associated with the signification "spurious," and
ultimately to have settled down into the latter. The conjectural
explanation giyen in the translation of the English Bible, "because
they were wont to be read, not openly and in common, but as it
were in secret and apart," is, as regards some of the books now
bearing the name, at variance with fact. The testimonies of the
Fathers harmonize with the belief that the use of the word, as
applied to special books, originated in the claim, common to
nearly all the sects that participated in the Gnostic character, to a
secret, esoteric knowledge, deposited in books which were made
known only to the initiated. The books of our own Apocrypha
bear witness both to the feeling and the way in which it worked.
Books in the existing Apocrypha bear the names of Solomon,
Daniel, Jeremiah, Ezra. These books represent the period of transition and decay which followed on the return from Babylon,
when the prophets who were then the teachers of the people
had passed away, and the age of scribes succeeded. Uncertain as
may be the dates of individual books; few, if any, can be thrown
further back than the commencement of the third century B.C.
The latest, the Second Book of Esdras, is probably not later than
30 B.C., 2 Esdras vii. 28, being a subsequent interpolation. The

alterations of the Jewish character, the different phases which Judaism presented in Palestine and Alexandria, the good and the evil which were called forth by contact with idolatry in Egypt, and by the struggle against it in Syria, all these present themselves to the reader of the Apocrypha with greater or lesser distinctness.

THE FIRST BOOK OF ESDRAS

Esdras is the Greek form of the Hebrew Ezra, The first and second books of Esdras are called in the Vulgate, and in all the earlier editions of the English Bible, the third and fourth books. In the Vulgate, 1 Esdras means the canonical book of Ezra, and 2 Esdras means Nehemiah. The original manuscript of the first book-of Esdras of the Apocrypha is lost. The book is evidently a compilation from 2 Chronicles, Ezra, and Nehemiah. Chapters iii., iv., and v. to verse 6, are the only original portions of the book. The design of the writer is evidently to introduce and give scriptural sanction to the legend about Zerubbabel, and to explain the obscure passages of Ezra; in the last attempt he has failed signally.

THE SECOND BOOK OF ESDRAS

This book was originally called "The Apocalypse of Ezra." The original manuscript, which was written in Greek, is lost. The common Latin text, which is followed in the English version, contains two important interpolations (chapters i.-ii., xv.-xvi.), which are not found in the Arabic or Ethiopian versions, and are separated from the genuine Apocalypse in the best Latin manuscripts. Both of these passages are evidently of Christian origin. The original Apocalypse (chapters iii.-xiv.) consists of a series of angelic revelations and visions, in which Ezra is instructed in some of the great mysteries of the moral world, and assured of the final triumph of the righteous.

The Book of Tobit

The Book of Tobit contains an agreeably written Jewish work of fiction, its action taking place in Assyria, whither Tobit (a Jew) had been carried as a captive by Shalmaneser. However, it must have been written considerably later than the Babylonian captivity, and cannot be regarded as a true history.

The story is briefly as follows: Tobit is a Jew of the tribe of Naphtali, living in Nineveh, a pious God-fearing man and very strict in the observance of the Jewish law. Trouble comes upon him, and he loses his eyesight. He sends his son Tobias to fetch 10 talents of silver, which he had left in the hands of his kinsman Gabael who dwelt at Rages in Media. Tobias takes a travelling companion with him, who is in reality the angel Raphael. On the way they stop at Ecbatana and lodge at the house of one Raguel, whose daughter Sara has through the evil spirit Asmodeus been seven times deprived of husbands on the night of wedlock. Tobias on the ground of kinship claims her in marriage; and her parents grant consent. By magical means, with which Raphael had supplied him, he is enabled to expel the demon Asmodeus. During the marriage festivities the angel journeys to Rages and obtains the money from Gabael. Tobias and his wife then return to Nineveh; and by further application of magical means Tobias is enabled to restore his father's sight. Raphael having revealed his true nature disappears. Tobit breaks forth into a song of thanksgiving. He and his family end their days in prosperity.

In modern times the moral excellence of the book has been rated highly. It is a beautiful and complete picture of the domestic life of the Jews after the return.

The Book of Judith

The Book of Judith purports to describe a romantic event in the history of the Jews. Nebuchadnezzar has sent his general Holofernes to punish the Jews for rebellion. The march of the Assyrian army upon Jerusalem is stayed by the resistance of a city called Betulia. Holofernes lays siege to Betulia, which is reduced to great extremities. Judith, one of the inhabitants, a rich and beautiful widow, obtains permission to leave the city with one attendant and repair to the camp of the Assyrians. There she is able by her beauty to excite the favor of Holofernes; and, seizing her opportunity, she drugs him with wine, cuts off his head, and returns with it to her city. The Jews, exultant at the sight, rush out and massacre the panic-stricken Assyrians. Judith ends her days the object of her country's affection and regard for her courage and holiness.

Judith beheads Holofernes.

THE REST OF THE BOOK OF ESTHER

This book consists of chapters which were added to the Canonical Book of Esther by some writer of a later date. These Apocryphal additions contain (1) the dream of Mordecai (ch. x., xi.); (2) the conspiracy of the eunuchs Gabatha and Tharra against the king (ch. xii.); (3) the letter of Artaxerxes for the destruction of the Jews (ch. xiii. 1–7); (4) the prayer of Mordecai in their behalf (ch. xiii. 8–18); (5) the prayer of Esther for herself and her people (ch. xiv.); (6) the queen's petition to the king (ch. xv.); (7) the king's letter revoking his former edict, and commanding that the 13th day of Adar should be celebrated as a festival (ch. xvi:). These chapters merely expand in greater detail the narrative of the Canonical Book.

THE BOOK OF THE WISDOM OF SOLOMON

This is one of the most remarkable extant specimens of Jewish Wisdom literature. From internal evidence it seems most reasonable to believe that the book was composed at Alexandria, sometime before the time of Philo, about B.C. 120–80. It is an imitation of the Proverbs of Solomon.

THE BOOK OF ECCLESIASTICUS, OR THE WISDOM OF SIRACH

The Wisdom of Jesus, the Son of Sirach, or Ecclesiasticus, is the full title, of this book in the English Bible. The former is the title given it in the Septuagint, and the latter that of the Vulgate, the naive indicating that the book was publicly used in the services of the early Church. We know nothing of its author, but his Palestinian origin is supported by internal evidences. It is an important monument of the religious state of the Jews at the time of its composition: As an expression of Palestinian theology it stands alone. It marks the growth of that anxious legalism which was conspicuous in the sayings of the later doctors. Life is already imprisoned in rules; religion is degenerating into ritualism; knowledge has taken refuge in schools.

THE BOOK OF BARUCH

This book is remarkable as the only one in the Apocrypha which is formed on the model of the Prophets; and though it is wanting in originality, it presents a vivid reflection of the ancient prophetic fire. The assumed author is evidently the companion of Jeremiah, but the details of the book are inconsistent with the assumption. It exhibits not only historical inaccuracies, but also evident traces of a later date than the beginning of the captivity. The date of its composition is probably about the time of the war of liberation (B.C. 160), or somewhat earlier.

THE SONG OF THE THREE HOLY CHILDREN

This is a spurious addition to Daniel, and appears in the Greek versions of that book in chapter iii. The Song in the Greek Bible follows upon Dan. iii. 23, and is followed by Dan. iii. 24. It purports to be the Song sung by Shadrach, Meshach and Abed-Nego (Ananias, Azarias and Misael of verse 66) in the midst of the burning fiery furnace (vv. 29–68), but it is preceded by the prayer of Azarias (vv. 3–22) and a description of their preservation in the flames which consumed the Chaldean servants (vv. 23–27). There is no proof that this fragment ever existed in Hebrew, and it was never acknowledged by the Jews as a part of the genuine book.

THE HISTORY OF SUSANNA

This story describes how Daniel as a young man procured the vindication of Susanna from a shameful charge, and the condemnation of the two elders who had borne false witness against her. It is probably an example of a large class of anecdotes which popular tradition associated with the names of bygone heroes.

BEL AND THE DRAGON

In this fragment we have two more anecdotes related of Daniel. In the first, Daniel discovers to the king Cyrus the frauds practised by the priests of Bel in connexion with the pretended banquets of that idol. In the second he bursts the sacred dragon that was worshipped at Babylon; and having been on that account cast for six days by the Babylonians into the lions' den, he is not touched by the lions. The prophet Habakkuk is transported from Judea by the angel of the LORD to fetch him food; and on the seventh day the king releases Daniel and puts to death his enemies.

THE PRAYER OF MANASSES

There is very little reason for giving this title to the penitential prayer called after the name of the King of Judah. Except the statement that the speaker is "bowed down with many iron bands" there is no ground for the traditional identification which is, in all probability, the guess of some ingenious copyist. The prayer itself is for the most part built up of sentences and phrases taken from the Canonical Scriptures.

THE FIRST BOOK OF MACCABEES

This book contains a history of the patriotic struggle, from the first resistance of Mattathias to the settled sovereignty and death of Simon, a period of thirty-three years, B.C. 168–135. The great marks of trustworthiness are everywhere conspicuous. Victory, and failure, and despondency are, on the whole, chronicled with the same candor. There is no attempt to bring into open display the working of Providence. The testimony of antiquity leaves no doubt but that the book was written first in Hebrew. Its whole structure points to Palestine as the place of its composition. There is, however, considerable doubt as to its date; perhaps we may place it between B.C. I 20–100.

THE SECOND BOOK OF MACCABEES

The history of the Second Book of Maccabees begins earlier than that of the first book, and closes with the victory of Judas Maccabeus over Nicanor. It thus embraces a period of twenty years. It is less trustworthy than the first book.

In the second book the groundwork of facts is true, but the dress in which the facts are presented is due, in part at least, to the narrator. The latter half of the book (chapters viii.-xv.) is to be regarded, not as a connected and complete history, but as a series of special incident's. from the life of Judas, illustrating the Providential interference of God on behalf of His people, true in substance, but embellished in form.

THE OTHER BOOKS OF MACCABEES

There are two other books of the Maccabees, entitled the Third and the Fourth, not included in the English Apocrypha. The Third Book of Maccabees contains the history of events which preceded the great Maccabean struggle. The Fourth Book of Maccabees contains a rhetorical narrative of the martyrdom of Eleazar and of the "Maccabean family," following, in the main, the same outline as Second Maccabees.

Judas Maccabeus assembling his warriors.

The New Testament

No room at the inn ...

THE GOSPELS

The life, death and resurrection of Jesus Christ our LORD.

THE ESSENTIAL STORY OF THE GOSPELS

THE BIRTH OF JESUS CHRIST

God chose Mary, a virgin betrothed to a carpenter in Nazareth, to bear his son. When the archangel Gabriel appeared to her and announced this astounding news, Mary went to share it with her kinswoman, Elizabeth, who was married to a priest called Zacharias. Elizabeth too was with child and would give birth to John the Baptist.

It was at the time Mary's son was due, that the Romans decreed a census of the land they ruled, and for this every citizen was directed to return to their own native town to be counted. So Joseph and Mary set off for Bethlehem, but when they arrived they found accommodation difficult to find, for the town was swollen with people returning from the countryside to register. The inns being full, the family were forced to accept the only lodging available, in a stable, where a manger stood in for a crib.

Far to the east, wise men had been told of a new King of the Jews, to whom they should pay obeisance. A star would guide them to him, and when they arrived in Judaea, news of their arrival sped through the streets of Jerusalem, reaching the ears of the king. Herod was instantly suspicious, recognizing the potential threat to his throne, and called the three visitors to his presence, where he interrogated them, then sent them on their way with instructions to report back when they had found the child. And the celestial messenger duly led the wise men to the stable.

The wise men did not report back to Herod, however. Warned in a dream of the consequences of such an action, they quietly departed to their lands in the east, leaving an infuriated Herod unable to locate what he saw as a potential usurper. His reaction was infamous. He decreed that all children in the Bethlehem area under two years of age be slaughtered. This massacre of the innocents was foreseen by God, of course, who sent a message to Joseph in a dream, that he should take his wife and the child to Egypt until it was safe. So they slipped out of Bethlehem by night and made the journey beyond Sinai, and there, in the land of the Pharaohs, the infant Jesus was weaned.

Upon the death of King Herod, Judaea was split into three, and the threat of a usurping King of the Jews was forgotten. An angel told Joseph that they could return, and they made their way home to Nazareth.

John the Baptist

Jesus grew up living the life of a normal boy of his time but showing also a precocious knowledge of scripture. As childhood gave way to youthful manhood, he began working in his father's workshop, learning the trade of carpentry. In later life, he would be spoken of as the carpenter from Nazareth.

Meanwhile his kinsman, John, was abroad in the country, gathering large crowds to his meetings at which he preached the word of God and told the people that they should make themselves ready for the Messiah, whose arrival was imminent. Those who accepted his message he baptized, a symbolic cleansing of their lives, in the River Jordan.

Now grown to full adulthood, Jesus was ready to embark upon his momentous ministry. He sought out John by the banks of the Jordan, where he was baptized. His mission on earth was about to begin, but not before he spent a soul-searching forty days and nights in the dry, stony wilderness, in total solitude. During this time the devil tempted him to misuse his divine powers, but each time Jesus sent him away.

The Ministry of Jesus

Much of Jesus' ministry – his teaching and healing work – was to be spent in the northern province of Galilee, especially about the shores of the Sea of Galilee. Here he encountered men who would become the first of his followers, or disciples – Andrew and his brother Simon Peter, James and John (sons of Zebedee), all fishermen; and Philip and Nathanael. The first to recognize him was Andrew, a follower of John the Baptist, for John was now directing his followers to Jesus, whom he named "the Lamb of God."

Jesus' first miracle was at Cana, not far from Nazareth, where he was born. With his mother and several of his followers, he had been invited to a wedding there, and as the festivities wore on the wine ran out. Mary was worried and came to Jesus: and reluctantly he told the servants to fill six stone water jars with water, then to serve the guests from these. When they did so, the water had turned into wine, so impressing the bridegroom that he complimented the host on saving the best for last.

However, Jesus' teaching work had not yet begun, and with his new companions he went south to Jerusalem for the feast of the Passover. When he entered the Temple there he beheld a sordid scene not in keeping with the high religious purpose of the building, for there were moneychangers and traders everywhere, selling cattle, sheep, and doves. Fashioning a whip from some cords, he overturned the counting tables and chased them out, crying, "Make not my Father's house a house of merchandise!" (*John 2: 16*) This caused a stir in the city, and many were intrigued, including a priest named Nicodemus, a Pharisee. One night, he came to Jesus to find out more, and Jesus told him that, even at his age, he must be 'born again'. A member of the Sanhedrin, Nicodemus was to become a believer in Jesus and to lend Joseph of Arimathea help after the crucifixion.

Returning to Galilee via Samaria, Jesus and his companions one day stopped by Jacob's Well, at Sychar, and the disciples went to find food. When a local woman approached the well, Jesus asked her for water, and they fell into conversation. He was able to tell her something of her past, which so impressed her that she realized he was a prophet and told her friends. The returning disciples were astonished at the conversation, for the Jews and the Samaritans maintained a long-held mutual antagonism. And indeed, on another visit, Jesus found himself without a welcome there.

When they got to Cana, a royal officer sought him out, a measure perhaps of his spreading reputation. His son, he said, was in Capernaum and dying; could Jesus save him? Jesus told him that when he went home he would find the child healed, and the officer set off. On the road he encountered his servants bringing the good news that the boy was better; and the officer discovered that he had recovered at the exact moment Jesus had spoken to him.

At Nazareth, Jesus entered the local tabernacle on the Sabbath and read from the book of Isaiah: "The Spirit of the LORD is upon me, because he hath anointed me to preach the gospel to the poor; he hath sent me to heal the brokenhearted, to preach deliverance to the captives, and recovering of sight to the blind, to set at liberty them that are bruised, to preach the acceptable year of the LORD" (*Luke 4:18–19*) and told them that the scripture was now fulfilled. The priests were astonished, and outraged when Jesus implied their own shortcomings – "Physician, heal thyself" – and that because of their disbelief the gospel would be offered to non-Jews. But, Jesus said, "No prophet is accepted in his own country" (*Luke 4:24*), and they ran him out of town.

But his fame among the ordinary folk was beginning to draw crowds. At Capernaum, on the northern coast of the Sea of Galilee, Jesus addressed the people on shore from Simon Peter's boat. When he had finished speaking, he heard Peter and Andrew complaining about their lack of success with the fish, so he guided them to a particular place and told them to cast their nets. Such was the prodigious catch that Andrew and Peter called to their partners, James and John, for help in landing the fish. Later, ashore, Jesus turned to Andrew and Peter and said: "Come ye after me, and I will make you to become fishers of men." At once they laid down their nets and were soon joined by James and John.

Most potent in spreading the fame of Jesus were the miraculous healings he performed, visible and impressive proof of his powers. At the synagogue in Capernaum, he cast unclean spirits from a man; he cured Peter's mother-in-law of a fever; he cured a paralytic; and a leper. Wherever he stayed, word spread of this sensational healer, and the sick came or were brought to him, such that it began to impede his progress.

Meanwhile John the Baptist, continuing his work, had publicly criticized the ruler of Galilee, the tetrarch Herod, for setting aside his wife in order to marry Herodias, the wife of his half-brother, which was contrary to the Law of Moses. For this he had been cast into prison but not executed – he had become a familiar and popular figure in the countryside.

It was about this time that Jesus recruited another disciple, Matthew. He was a "publican," a tax-collector, a profession despised throughout the ages. When Jesus dined with Matthew and other tax-collectors (whom the priests regarded as sinners), the Pharisees were scandalized that one who purported to be a man of God should keep such company. As for Matthew, taking up Jesus' call was a courageous step, for as a relatively wealthy man he would lose everything.

When Jesus went to Jerusalem again for the next Passover, he visited a place called the Pool of Bethesda, where the sick and disabled came because the waters were said to have restoring properties. There he treated a man who had been crippled for years and had nobody to help him into the healing waters – "Rise, take up thy bed, and walk." (*John 5:12*) But that day was the Sabbath, which the priests alleged he had broken. Several other such accusations were made after the disciples were seen eating ears of corn in a field on the Sabbath; and when Jesus healed a man's withered hand on the Sabbath. To these petty restrictions imposed by officious priests, Jesus replied, "I come in my Father's name and ye receive me not ... The Sabbath was made for man, and not man for the Sabbath: therefore the Son of Man is LORD also of the Sabbath." (*Mark 2:27–28*) Was it lawful on the Sabbath to do good or to do evil; to save life or to destroy it? The priests now conspired to destroy him, for they could not succeed in arguing with him. Seeing this, Jesus took his disciples back north to continue healing and teaching.

One day Jesus ascended a mountain to spend the night in prayer, and at daybreak he called and ordained twelve disciples whom he would send forth to preach, heal sickness, and cast out devils. He then came down to the lower slopes, where a multitude of people had gathered to witness healing and to hear him speak. There followed one of his most significant lessons, which is now known as the Sermon on the Mount. In this he set out his fundamental message in a wide-ranging discourse that all could understand, emphasizing the moral and spiritual aspects of the Law, the love of God, and how people should behave to one another.

God's blessing, he told them, would be manifested to those who lived their lives free from selfishness and greed. In nine simple sayings, which have become known as the Beatitudes, he set out the basic essentials of good living.

He went on to discuss the Law and the testimony of the Prophets, consistently stressing their authority, but interpreting them in a practical and easily comprehensible manner. He warned against the hypocrisy of superficial piety ostentatiously displayed in prayer, fasting, and giving to charity but without spiritual substance. Purity of the heart would receive its own reward; happiness lay not in material things but was available to those who put their trust in God.

He explained a number of specific issues to which all could relate as examples of how the Law should be applied. Looking at a woman lustfully, he said, was already committing adultery in one's heart; divorce was acceptable only in cases of marital unfaithfulness; and where oaths were concerned, one should let "yes" and "no" be absolute. Concerning retaliation, he replaced the old "eye for an eye" with "turn the other cheek," and instead of hating them, love your enemies and pray for those who persecute you. Fasting and giving to the poor should not be done in an ostentatious way; nor should one be hasty to judge others, "lest ye be judged yourself." And he warned against false prophets.

When he had finished this momentous address, he came farther down the hillside among the people, curing a leper, and the crowd gradually dispersed, their heads full of this new and inspiring teaching.

Jesus continued traveling through the cities and villages, preaching and performing miraculous cures, but still the priests rejected him and now sought a sign from him. On one occasion the crowd was so dense that his mother and the disciples could not get near him; when they were pointed out to him, Jesus said, "Who is my mother? And who are my brethren?" And he stretched forth his hand toward his disciples, and said, "Behold my mother and my brethren! For whosoever shall do the will of my Father which is in heaven, the same is my brother, and sister, and mother. (*Matthew 12:48–50*)

Jesus continued using parables to teach, placing questions of spiritual and moral behavior in real-life situations that all could understand.

John the Baptist, in prison, had become puzzled by what must have been conflicting reports brought to him by his friends to his prison cell. Jesus sent him messages of reassurance that he was indeed who John thought he was.

One evening, after speaking before crowds by the shore of the Sea of Galilee, he took ship with his disciples for the other shore. As they crossed, a great storm blew up, imperiling the boat as Jesus slept in the stern. The disciples, in fear for their lives at the severity of the weather, woke him and he reassured them: "Why are ye fearful, O ye of little faith?" Then he told the wind and sea to be still, and the waters became calm again.

By now Jesus was attracting large crowds, and he saw that he could not speak to them all himself – "The harvest truly is plenteous, but the laborers are few" – so he sent out his disciples in pairs, empowered to cure disease and cast out devils, preaching that the Kingdom of Heaven was at hand. But he warned them: "Behold, I send you forth as sheep in the midst of wolves: be ye therefore wise as serpents and harmless as doves. But beware ... He that receiveth you receiveth me ..." (*Matthew 10:1,40*)

Meanwhile John the Baptist languished in Herod's prison. The king's wife, Herodias, was determined to have him killed and manipulated Herod with her degenerate daughter Salome. John was beheaded and his body buried by his followers, who hastened to tell Jesus.

When the disciples returned, Jesus took them out to a quiet place to rest, near Bethsaida, but news of their presence attracted attention, and soon a great crowd had gathered. So Jesus spoke and healed, but as the day progressed on the disciples began to worry that in this wilderness there was nothing for the people to eat. All they could bring to hand was a boy who had five barley loaves and two small fish. So Jesus blessed the food and told the multitude to sit in groups on the grass, and from those loaves and fish the whole crowd of 5,000 were miraculously fed, with twelve basketfuls left over. Some of the people were so excited by this that thy tried to take hold of him and proclaim him King, but Jesus and his followers made a quick departure.

That evening the disciples took ship and the wind again rose, so that the rowers found themselves making little progress. Suddenly they were struck with fear as they saw a figure coming up beside them, then realized that it was Jesus, walking upon the water. They cried out, and Peter asked Jesus if he too could walk on the sea. But after a few steps, his confidence failed and he began to sink until Jesus – "O thou of little faith, wherefore didst thou doubt?" – helped him back into the boat and the wind ceased. When they made land at Gennesaret, a host of people came to meet them, bringing their sick to be healed.

At Capernaum, Jesus expounded upon the miracle of the loaves and fishes in allegorical language: "I am that bread of life." But many could not understand and took his words about sacrificing his flesh and blood for their eternal life literally. Many turned away. But a short time later he repeated the miraculous feeding of a crowd, this time of some 4,000, with just seven loaves and a few small fish.

Despite these big crowds, many had stopped following him, while the priests still refused to accept him and demanded a sign, which exasperated him. But his disciples remained firm. Jesus questioned them about how the people saw him. Some, they said, thought he was John the Baptist; others Elias, or Jeremiah or another of the prophets of old risen again. But, he asked them: who did they think he was? It was Peter who spoke up: "Thou art the Christ, the Son of the living God." Jesus blessed him and told him that he was Peter (which means "rock") and that upon this rock would he build his Church; and he should have the keys to the Kingdom of Heaven.

Jesus now broke the news to his disciples that he was destined to go to Jerusalem, suffer and be rejected by the priests, be killed and rise again on the third day. Surely not, responded Peter, but Jesus rebuked him. (*Matthew 16:22–28*)

A week later Jesus took Peter, James and John up a mountainside to pray by night, and there they witnessed his Transfiguration

– his face and body shining in glory as a dazzling bright light, while he spoke with two figures about his death. These were Moses and Elias (Elijah), come to give him strength. Then a bright cloud enveloped them all and a voice spoke to them: "This is my beloved son, in whom I am well pleased: hear ye him." The vision cleared and Jesus told them they must say nothing of what they had seen until after he had risen from the dead.

One day the question arose as to whether Jesus should pay the Temple tax, or tribute, which was at that time set at two drachmas per head. Jesus replied obliquely but told Peter that to avoid offending the priests they should pay. He told him to cast a line in the sea and open the mouth of the first fish he caught: he did, and found there a four-drachma coin, enough to pay for both their taxes.

In Judaea, Jesus heard that there were threats to his life, so he returned to Galilee and appointed seventy of his followers to go out, again in pairs, to the cities and villages he could not himself visit. Shortly after, he ventured to Jerusalem for the Feast of Tabernacles, independently of the disciples, and took the possibly risky step of speaking in the Temple. But he was not arrested. When the priests' officers approached him, he convinced them and they went back to the priests empty-handed. When the Pharisees reacted angrily, Nicodemus (both a priest and a secret follower of Jesus) told them that they must not find a man guilty before they had judged him.

While Jesus was in Jerusalem, a woman was brought to the Temple accused of adultery. According to the Mosaic Law, she should be stoned to death – which Jesus invited them to do: "He that is without sin, let him first cast a stone at her." Abashed, they left, and Jesus asked her who had accused her. No one, she replied. "Neither do I condemn thee," said Jesus, "go, and sin no more."

More discourse and debate with the hostile priests followed, ending almost in violence, for they would not understand who he was. Jesus then returned to Galilee to receive the seventy disciples he had sent out, and they greeted him with joy at their evident success, heartening Jesus himself.

Again he received criticism for curing people on the Sabbath – first a woman who for some eighteen years had suffered such an ailment in her back that she was bent nearly double; Jesus straightened her, then cured a case of dropsy. He spoke of humility – a man invited to a wedding should sit in the lowest place so that the host might bring him to sit higher up – "For whosoever exalteth himself shall be abased; and he that humbleth himself shall be exalted."

Poorly received in Samaria, Jesus entered a village and encountered ten lepers who approached him for help. So he cleansed them and all went away joyous except one, who turned back and thanked Jesus. "Arise, go thy way," replied Jesus," thy faith hath made thee whole."

It was in Bethany, a short distance east of Jerusalem, that Jesus made a special friendship with two sisters, Mary and Martha, and their brother Lazarus. One day, Martha was busy about the house and complained to Jesus that her sister left her to do the work while she sat at Jesus' feet. "Martha, Martha," he replied, "thou art careful and troubled about many things: But one thing is needful: and Mary hath chosen that good part, which shall not be taken away from her." (*Luke 10:38–42*)

Finding a man blind from birth, the disciples asked Jesus whether the sin lay in the man or his parents that he had been born thus. Neither, replied Jesus, anointing the eyes of the blind man and sending him to the Pool of Siloam, to wash. Wiping off the clay, he opened his eyes and could see for the first time. Word of this miracle spread, and it perplexed the Pharisees, who could neither understand nor accept it and threw the man out of the Temple. Jesus told them that he was the "good shepherd: the good shepherd giveth his life for the sheep." His sheep, he said, knew him. But they, the priests, did not believe, for they were not his sheep. Angered, they sought to harm him, but he escaped beyond the Jordan, where John had baptized him.

A message now arrived from Jesus' friends in Bethany – Lazarus was desperately ill. Martha came to meet him and told him Lazarus had been dead these four days: but this Jesus already knew. If he had been there, he would not have died, said Martha; though she knew he would rise again at the last day. But Jesus said, "I am the resurrection and the life: he that believeth in me, though he were dead, yet shall he live: and whosoever liveth and believeth in me shall never die." Mary joined them, in tears, and

Jesus asked them to lead him to the tomb. He cried out, "Lazarus, come forth," and the brother appeared, still wrapped in the grave clothes, but alive. This miraculous raising of the dead had serious consequences, for it made sensational news that reached the ears of the High Priest in Jerusalem. The threat the priests perceived from a man credited with such a miracle (especially after previous reports of his miracles) was confronting them, and they determined that they should find a way to put him to death.

And once more Jesus told his disciples about his sufferings to come, but once again they were unable fully to appreciate the importance of what he was saying and what would transpire in the coming days.

Passion Week

Jesus had declared his intention of celebrating the Passover in Jerusalem but chose not to attempt finding a place to stay in the city, which would be crowded with the faithful. Instead he stayed with his friends Martha, Mary, and Lazarus at Bethany, no more than a two-mile walk from Jerusalem. Jesus and the disciples arrived there on the Friday, six days before the Passover, and that night they dined at the house of Simon the leper. While they were eating, Mary went out and fetched an alabaster box containing fragrant ointment, with which she anointed Jesus' head and feet, wiping his feet with her hair. But some of the disciples, led by Judas, were indignant at such apparent waste of a very precious fragrance: a more fitting action would have been to sell the ointment and donate the proceeds to the poor. Jesus rebuked them: the poor, he said, "are always with you, and you may do good to them"; but he would not always be there.

On the Sunday, Jesus and the disciples set out for Jerusalem. His presence at Bethany had already attracted great public attention, for his fame as a teacher and healer had spread far and wide, especially after the raising of Lazarus. As they drew near to the city, the crowds came out to welcome him, and Jesus sent two of his companions to a nearby village to find a donkey and a colt, so that when he entered the city gates he fulfilled Zechariah's centuries-old prophecy.

The crowds thronged about him as he rode the donkey, lining the route and crying "Hosannah, Blessed is the King of Israel that cometh in the name of the LORD" and throwing down their cloaks and palm-tree branches in his path. (But, as he rode in triumph through the noisy multitude, Jesus wept for Jerusalem, knowing the disaster that would befall this city in the years to come.)

While the entry to Jerusalem was joyous and passionate, it further increased the concern of the priests. Jerusalem was tense: relations between the people and the Roman garrison were still very uneasy following outbreaks of rioting not long before. They feared that this young prophet could stir up more unrest leading to bloodshed. At the Temple, his actions did little to calm their apprehension: overturning the tables of the moneychangers and vendors of sacrificial birds, he accused the traders of desecrating the Temple – "You have made it a den of robbers!"

After spending much of the day receiving the sick and the lame who came to be healed, Jesus returned to Bethany for the night and came back into Jerusalem next day. In the Temple, the priests and scribes questioned him closely; among them were some who already believed in him but would not admit it in public. The more outspoken questioned his authority, and he replied with parables, effectively questioning their own authority and contrasting their lack of belief in him with the belief of the people. The priests, he implied, were not worthy of their responsibilities as guardians of the faith.

The Pharisees then attempted to snare him with their questions. Was it lawful to give tribute to the Roman emperor? The implication of a negative answer would be tantamount to treason: but Jesus simply asked them to produce a coin. Whose image was on it? Caesar's, they replied. Then, said Jesus, render to Caesar the things which are Caesar's and to God the things that are God's. Another question was about the Resurrection: if a man had been married several times in his lifetime, which of his women would be his wife when they rose from the dead? Again Jesus replied simply: that God was the God of the living, not of the dead.

One of the Pharisees was a lawyer. He asked Jesus which was the greatest Commandment. The first and the second, Jesus replied; which silenced the priests. Then Jesus spoke to all the crowd. The teachers of the Law and Pharisees sat in Moses' seat, he said; while they told the people what to do, they did not practice what they preached. They were hypocrites, snakes, a brood of vipers.

As he left the Temple, Jesus pointed to the building and forecast its destruction. It would be the end of an age, he told his disciples, and gave them an apocalyptic vision of an ending that could come at any time. Therefore, he said, keep watch, because you do not know the day or the hour. He spoke in parables – of the wise and foolish virgins, of the two sons, the ten talents, and the tenants – in explanation. On the Last Day, he said, God would divide the nations and the people as sheep from goats, sending them to eternal life or to everlasting punishment.

To his disciples Jesus again foretold his betrayal and crucifixion. Meanwhile, Caiaphas, the High Priest, was gathering the chief priests, scribes, and elders to discuss what they should do about Jesus. They could not kill him on the feast day, but Judas Iscariot, one of Jesus' disciples, now made the way for them. They struck a shameful bargain – for thirty pieces of silver, Judas would betray him.

On Wednesday night, Jesus did not return to Bethany but slept on the Mount of Olives, outside the city walls to the east. Next day was the feast of the unleavened bread, and the disciples came to him to ask where they would eat for Passover. So he sent Peter and John to a certain house in the city, where an upper room would be made ready. Assembled there that evening, Jesus and his twelve disciples sat down to what has become known as the Last Supper.

When they had eaten, Jesus rose, took a towel, filled a basin with water and began to wash the astonished disciples' feet. It was Peter who objected first: surely this was not right, that his master should wash his servants' feet? Jesus completed his task then told them the significance of what he had done. "The servant is not greater than his LORD; neither is he that is sent greater than he that sent him. If ye know these things, happy are ye if ye do them." (*John 13:16–17*)

As they went on talking, Jesus again shocked them by telling them that one of their number, sitting at this very table, would betray him. They were horrified. Peter whispered to know whom he meant, and Jesus replied by offering a sop to Judas, who soon rose from the table and went out. Much troubled, the remaining disciples sought to know what was about to happen, and he told them that he was going where they could not follow. Peter pleaded that he would follow even to death and would gladly lay down his life for Jesus. But Jesus told him that before cockcrow he would deny Jesus three times. In vain, Peter protested. Now the perplexed disciples clamored to know what would happen when he left them, and in a lengthy discourse he sought to comfort and reassure them.

Then he led them out into the night, beyond the city walls and across the valley of the Kidron (Cedron), to the Garden of Gethsemane on the western slopes of the Mount of Olives, where they had often gone before. There, leaving all but Peter and John behind, he went a little way off to pray, asking the two disciples to keep watch. Alone, he prayed that God would relent: "if it be possible, and all things are possible unto thee, take away this cup from me..." After a while he returned to find Peter and John fast asleep; waking them, he gently chided them – "the spirit is willing, but the flesh is weak" – then returned to his prayers. A second time he came back to find them asleep, and prayed again. This time an angel came to him, to give him strength, and he prayed earnestly. At last he returned to the slumbering disciples, and they rejoined the others.

Soon the tranquillity of the hillside grove was broken by the sound of voices and a tumult of men armed with swords and staves, their way lit by torches and lanterns. It was a band of the priests' men, with many followers, come to arrest Jesus. They asked for him by name, and he identified himself; whereupon Judas kissed him, the agreed signal that this was indeed the man they sought. As they went to seize him, Peter drew his sword and struck out, severing the right ear of Malchus, the High Priest's own servant. Jesus told him to put up his sword – did he not realize, Jesus admonished him, that if he prayed to God he could muster twelve legions of angels to protect himself? But how then would the scriptures be fulfilled? And he touched Malchus' ear, healing it. The disciples fled, leaving the officers of the priests to bind Jesus and lead him back into the city.

Jesus was taken first to Annas, father-in-law of the High Priest, then to Caiaphas himself, who had assembled the Sanhedrin, a council of the chief priests, elders, and scribes. Here, in the middle of the night, they sought to arraign Jesus and condemn him to death. They began questioning him, one of the officers hitting him, but they could neither intimidate him nor force a confession of guilt. Then they produced a stream of false witnesses, but these contradicted each other in many details. At last Caiaphas ran out of patience and took the floor himself, asking Jesus directly if he were indeed Christ, the Son of God. Jesus' answer angered the priest, and the assembly erupted in vehement outrage, spitting at the prisoner, blindfolding him and hitting him.

All this was witnessed by Peter, who had followed from a distance and managed to gain entry to the assembly hall. There he was recognized by a maid as one of Jesus' disciples, but he denied it. The same thing happened again, and finally he was spotted by a kinsman of Malchus, whose ear he had cleaved in Gethsemane. For a third time, Peter denied having anything to do with Jesus; and as he spoke these words the cock crowed. Looking up, he saw Jesus looking back at him as they led him away.

Later they brought Jesus before a full meeting of the Sanhedrin, which attempted to question him further and then condemned him. But a death sentence could only be carried out by the Romans, not by the Jews. So Jesus was taken before Pontius Pilate, Governor of Jerusalem. The overriding concern of this senior Roman officer was for the maintenance of law and order; he had already had to contend with too many riots and bloodshed in this city. So his approach was circumspect: to execute Jesus or spare him might equally stir up passions that could get out of control. Pilate questioned Jesus and could find no fault in him. But the crowd of priests insisted that Jesus had been going about fomenting trouble, inciting the people to rebel from Galilee to Jerusalem. At the mention of Galilee, Pilate saw a potential escape from his dilemma, for justice in the north of the province was the responsibility of Herod, Tetrarch of Galilee.

For his part, Herod, in Jerusalem for the Passover, was interested to meet Jesus, of whom he had heard much and hoped to see a miracle. But Herod's interrogation achieved nothing, for Jesus would not answer despite the continual mockery and accusations hurled at him by the priestly mob. Bored, Herod sent him back to Pilate, this time wrapped in a costly robe to show his contempt for the man called "the King of the Jews."

A weary Pilate told the priests that a death sentence was excessive; he would punish him and let him go. It was customary at the time of the Passover for the Romans to free a prisoner at the choice of the people, so Pilate offered this option to the crowd. They would have none of it and instead chose another prisoner, an infamous bandit named Barabbas, with much blood on his hands. Pilate was in a difficult position; his instinct to release Jesus reinforced by a message from his wife, who had seen in a dream that Jesus was indeed a just man.

But the crowd were insistent and would not quieten until they had their way, shouting "Crucify him!" Pilate saw there was no choice. Symbolically, he washed his hands, released Barabbas and sent Jesus for punishment. The soldiers were merciless in scourging him, and in mocking him as "King of the Jews" they set a crown of thorns upon his head and jeered as they bowed before him. Bloodied and with the plaited crown still upon his head, Jesus was once more brought before the mob. "Behold the man!" announced Pilate; but they grew ever louder in their calls for execution, now crying out that this was a rebel against Rome. At the judgment seat, called Gabbatha, Pilate delivered Jesus to be crucified that day.

While this was happening, the wretched Judas saw the evil he had set in motion and regretted his treachery. He returned to the Temple and threw down the thirty pieces of silver, crying out that he had betrayed an innocent man. The priests were unmoved: they had what they wanted. And Judas slunk away to hang himself.

Five days earlier, Jesus had entered Jerusalem in triumph, his way strewn with branches in joyous welcome. Now he left the city in a dreadful procession, dragging a heavy wooden cross through streets lined by a jeering mob. It was a long, slow journey, made with two criminals also condemned to crucifixion. Exhausted by the beating and scourging of the night and morning, Jesus collapsed more than once under the great weight of the cross, until eventually the soldiers dragged a man from the crowd, named Simon from Cyrene, and forced him to bear it.

At the hill of Golgotha, Jesus was stripped, laid on the cross and nailed to it by his hands and feet. They offered him wine mixed with gall, but he would not drink, and then the three crosses were erected, Jesus between the two criminals. On his cross they had nailed a board, at Pilate's command, inscribed in Aramaic, Greek, and Roman: "This is the King of the Jews" (despite the objections of the priests). As was the custom, the soldiers divided his garments and cast lots for his coat. Bystanders, joined by the priests, jeered and mocked Jesus – if he were indeed the king of the Jews, they said, why did he not save himself? One of his fellows in crucifixion joined in – could he not save all three? But the other man, a thief, rebuked him. We deserve our punishment for our deeds, he said; but this man has done nothing.

The hours of agony continued, an unnatural darkness fell, and Jesus cried out to God. When he gave up the ghost, the earth shook, rocks cracked asunder and the veil in the Temple dividing the sanctuary was torn apart. Graves opened and the spirits of the dead were seen floating in the city. Awestruck, the centurion on Golgotha proclaimed, "Truly this was the Son of God."

Crucifixion could often take days to kill a man, but it was forbidden to let the bodies of executed men hang there after sunset on the Sabbath, which was the following day. So, to hasten the death of the victims, the soldiers went to break their legs. But when they came to Jesus they perceived that he was already dead; instead one of them pierced Jesus' side.

Joseph, a wealthy man from Arimathaea, and a secret follower of Jesus, had meanwhile obtained permission from Pilate to take possession of Jesus' body. Now, with another secret follower, the Pharisee Nicodemus, he had the body anointed with oils and perfumes, and then wrapped in a linen shroud. They made their way to a nearby rock-hewn sepulcher, which Joseph had prepared, and within, watched by Mary and Mary Magdalene, they placed the body, sealing the tomb with a great stone door.

The Resurrection

On the Sabbath, the priests set a watch upon the tomb, fearing that the body of Jesus might be carried away and pretense made of his having risen from the dead. They were joined there at sunrise on the following day by Mary Magdalene and Mary, the mother of James, bringing oils to anoint the body again. As they approached, the earth shook and an angel descended, rolling back the stone door. The guards fled, and the women cautiously entered the tomb. There sat an angel clad all in white. Jesus, he told them, had risen from the dead; they should go quickly and tell the disciples.

They returned soon with Peter and John, who examined the empty sepulcher. All that remained were the linen wrappings of the body. When the two disciples departed to tell the others, Mary Magdalene remained, in tears, outside the tomb, overwhelmed by grief. She was the first to see the risen Jesus, whom she first mistook for the gardener. But when she told the disciples, they did not believe her.

Emmaus was a village not far from Jerusalem, and later that day two of Jesus' followers were walking, discussing the amazing events they had witnessed, when they were joined by another man. When he fell in with them, Jesus was not recognized; nor during their walk, as he discussed and explained the scriptures to them. Only when they invited him to dine with them and he broke and blessed the bread did they realize who this was; and in a moment Jesus vanished. The two hastened to Jerusalem to tell the disciples what they had seen and heard.

That evening ten of the disciples assembled discretely, behind closed doors, not knowing whether the priests might continue their persecution. Suddenly in their midst stood Jesus, terrifying them and showing them his pierced hands, feet, and side so that they were sure it was truly their master. When they told all this to Thomas, the missing disciple, that night, he doubted their account and was only persuaded eight days later when Jesus appeared and invited him to touch his wounds.

The third time Jesus appeared to them was in Galilee, where several of them were fishing on the Sea of Tiberias. They had worked through the night but had nothing to show for their efforts. In the morning, they beheld a figure on the shore, who directed them to where the fish were in abundance. They recognized him and came ashore with a goodly catch, then dined with him.

The final meeting of the disciples with Jesus was in Jerusalem. He led them out to Bethany, telling them that they must go forth and preach and assuring them of the divine support that would strengthen their endeavors. Then they saw him no more: he blessed them and ascended to heaven, and the disciples returned to the city, joyful and full of hope in the expectation for what they would do.

THE FOUR GOSPELS

The books of the New Testament fall into two main divisions: those that contain the Gospel, i.e. the life and words of Jesus Christ, and those that contain the history and writings of the earliest leaders of the Church.

Characteristics of the Gospels

The Gospel is contained in four books, two called after apostles, two after companions of the apostles. The same Person is brought before us, in the main the same story is told, four times over. But there is no mere repetition, for each writer sees the life he is describing from his own point of view, and no two of them were writing for the same class of readers. Thus St. Matthew's interest lay in the past, and he wrote to show his own countrymen, the Jews, how the life of Jesus had fulfilled all that was written in the Law and the Prophets concerning the Christ. St. Mark lives in the present. He writes for Romans and gives them a living picture of a living man. St. Luke looks forward to the day when all flesh shall see the salvation of God, and writing in the first instance for his own countrymen, the Greeks, brings before them one who was fitted to be the Savior of all nations in every age. St. John, writing long after the other three for the instruction of the Christian Church, gazes on the eternal mysteries which had been brought to light by the Incarnation of the Word.

Corresponding to these differences between the writers of the Gospels and between the classes of readers to which they were originally addressed, there is a difference between the features in the character of the LORD which stand out most prominently in each. Thus the first three help us to see in Jesus the perfect Son of man, St. John shows us the same Jesus as the perfect Son of God.

Again, St. Matthew brings before us the King and the Judge of Israel. The characteristics of his portrait are authority and tenderness. St. Mark brings before us the Prophet, the Man of God mighty in word and deed. Energy and humility are the characteristics of his portrait. St. Luke, whose Gospel ends, as it begins, in the Temple, brings before us our great High Priest, instant in prayer to God and of perfect sympathy with men. St. John's Gospel reveals the glory of the only-begotten of the Father in a life of absolute obedience.

Growth of the Written Gospels

The facts on which the apostles laid most stress in the earliest public teaching were the death and resurrection of the LORD. But we learn from Acts i. 22 that it was regarded as essential that an apostle should have personal knowledge of the life and teaching of Jesus during the whole period between the Baptism of St. John and the Ascension: and it is this period which was embraced in the earliest form of the written Gospel. St. Mark traces "the beginning of the gospel of Jesus Christ" from the advent of the Baptist; and we may well believe that, had the close of his book been preserved to us, it would have carried on the narrative beyond the Resurrection. But it soon became necessary to prefix to this some account of the Nativity, and other events connected with it: and such accounts we have in the Gospels of St. Matthew and St. Luke. The outline of the Gospel story was now complete. It remained for St. John to supply important details which were omitted by the Synoptists, to throw new light on the progress of the revelation of Christ's Person, and generally to present His life and teaching in a theological aspect to meet the growing needs of the Church. It is not easy to determine whether, or to what extent, the writers of the different gospels were independent of each other. An examination of passages found in St. Mark in common with St. Matthew, and in some cases with St. Luke, gives the impression that in very many instances St. Mark presents us with the earliest form of the narrative; and we may feel confident that in these instances the words which St. Mark gives us lay before the other Synoptists, each of whom has modified them from his own standpoint, sometimes by compressing the story and sometimes by adding further detail from other sources of his own. Similarly, when certain passages common to St. Matthew and St. Luke are compared, another early basis seems to come into view. Whether these early bases lay before the evangelists as written documents, or only as an oral tradition the words of which had gradually become fixed through constant repetition, is open to question. But the terseness of the narratives and the general absence of comments such as would naturally fall from a teacher's lips, point rather in the direction of a written record.

THE GOSPEL OF ST. MATTHEW

The first of the four Gospels demonstrates how the life and ministry of Jesus was foretold by the prophets.

COMMENTARY ON THE GOSPEL OF ST. MATTHEW

The genealogy brings before us in outline the whole past history of Israel. The closing words of the Gospel point onward to the end of the world, but the main subject of the book is the life of our LORD from His Birth at Bethlehem to His appearance in Galilee after His Resurrection. It may be divided into four parts:— I. The first 16 chapters) forms an introduction to the ministry, emphasizing the relation of the Nativity to history and prophecy (i., ii.), and narrating as its immediate preparation the work of the Baptist, and the Temptation (iii.—iv. 11). It closes with the removal from Nazareth to Capernaum. II. The second (iv. 17–xvi. 20) describes the ministry in Galilee, working out in six stages the history of the growth of faith in the Messiahship of Jesus of Nazareth, culminating in St. Peter's confession (xvi. 16), the central point of the whole Gospel.

1. The first stage (iv. 17–25) describes the call of the earliest disciples and the rousing of popular attention. 2. The second (v.—vii.), in the Sermon on the Mount brings under one view the main points of the new teaching. In it Jesus claims to perfect what Moses had begun, and on His own authority declares the laws of the Kingdom of Heaven. 3. The third (viii.—xi. 1) describes ten mighty

works by which the powers of the Kingdom were revealed, and tells of the selection and the commissioning of the twelve. 4. The fourth (xi. 2–xii.) shews our LORD's attitude to those who questioned His claims. The doubt of the Baptist and the answer to it lead up to a stern rebuke of the towns of Galilee and to one more tender invitation (xi. 2–30); then come three great controversies with the Pharisees with respect to the Sabbath (xii. 1–21), the source of His authority over evil spirits (22–37), and the

Choosing the Twelve.

demand for a sign from Heaven (38–45). The section closes with a declaration of the true ground of spiritual kinship (46–50). 5. The fifth (xiii.) contains seven parables in which our LORD revealed the secrets of the Kingdom to those who could hear, and closes with His rejection at Nazareth. 6. The sixth (xiv.—xvi. 20) begins with the story of the death of the Baptist (xiv. 1–12). Then follows the feeding of the 5000 and other miracles (13–36), rousing the enthusiasm of the people, which is checked by the return from Jerusalem of the Pharisees, who openly challenge Jesus on a question of tradition (xv. 1–20). Then follows a journey northwards outside the limits of the Holy Land (21–39), a return to the lake and a fresh conflict (xvi. 1–12), after which He again retires northwards, and the Galilean ministry is crowned by the confession of His Messiahship by St. Peter (13–20).

III. The third division (xvi. xxv.) leads up to the public assertion of Messiahship. Throughout it our thoughts are turned towards Jerusalem; the events of humiliation and of triumph that are to happen there are the main subject of the teaching. The journey to claim the Messiahship openly at the capital is the main subject of the narrative. It contains three parts: 1. The first (xvi. 21–xx. 16) consists of scenes on the road to Jerusalem, beginning with the first prophecy of the Passion which followed immediately on the great confession at Cesarea Philippi (21–28), and the Transfiguration so closely connected with both (xvii. 1-21). Then comes a scene at Capernaum (22–xviii. 35) containing 'a second prophecy of the Passion, the miracle of the tribute money, and a series of teachings on humility, discipline, and forgiveness, for the guidance of the leaders of the Church. It is closed by a scene in Peraea, (xix. 1–xx. 16) which includes teaching on marriage, and reveals the conditions of spiritual blessing in answer to the questions 'What shall I do?' 'What shall we have?'

2. The second (xx. 17–xxiii.), after a third prophecy of the Passion and a second lesson to the disciples on humility (xx. 17-28), contains the triumphal entry into Jerusalem (29–xxi. 11), the cleansing of the Temple and the controversy to which that act gave rise (12–xxii. 46), and a solemn denunciation of the Pharisees (xxiii.).

3. In the third (xxiv., xxv.) the LORD instructs His disciples concerning the judgment which was coming on the rebellious city and on all the nations of the earth.

IV. The last division (xxvi.–xxviii.) contains the story of the Death and of the Resurrection, bringing out especially the national guilt in the Crucifixion and the national evasion of the evidence for the Resurrection. The closing scene takes us back to Galilee. The closing words declare that the King has received a worldwide dominion, and that the promise of Emmanuel is fulfilled for His servants to the end of time.

THE GOSPEL OF ST. MATTHEW: CHAPTER BY CHAPTER

Christ's genealogy.	1	Genealogy of Christ in His reputed father's line. The miraculous conception. His name – JESUS, for He shall save.

Christ's birth.	2	Birth of Christ. The wise men from the East. Herod's subtlety. Joseph's dream, and escape into Egypt. Herod's murder of the infants. Death of Herod. Joseph's return, and sojourn at Nazareth.
Preaching of the Baptist.	3	Preaching of John the Baptist. His baptism of Christ.
Temptation. Ministry.	4	Christ tempted by the devil. Christ leaves Nazareth for Capernaum. Calls Peter, Andrew, James and John. Exercises His ministry. Works miracles.
Sermon on the Mount.	5	Sermon on the Mount: • The Beatitudes. • The law magnified. • On adultery. • On oaths. • Peace and meekness. • Against hypocrisy.
The LORD's prayer	6	• The LORD's prayer. • On covetousness. • On anxious care.
    Building on the rock.	7	• On rash judgment. • On earnestness and constancy in prayer. • The strait gate. • Cautions against false prophets. • Parable of the wise and foolish builders.
Miracles of healing. Tempest. Swine.	8	The leper cleansed. Centurion's servant healed. Peter's wife's mother cured. The scribe and Christ. The tempest stilled. Devils cast out of the possessed into swine.
Paralytic cured. Jairus's daughter.	9	The palsied man cured. Matthew called. Christ eats with publicans and sinners. Defends His disciples for not fasting. The touch of His garment. Jairus's daughter raised. Sight given to the blind. Speech given to the dumb, from whom He casts out a devil.

Miraculous cures.	10	The twelve commissioned, and endowed with miraculous power.
	11	Jesus bears testimony to John. He upbraids Chorazin, Bethsaida and Capernaum. He invites the heavy-laden.
	12	The disciples pluck corn on the Sabbath. Christ cures the withered hand. Christ cures also the possessed man, who was blind and dumb. Sin against the Holy Ghost. Sign of the prophet Jonas.
Parables.	13	Parables of the: Sower; • Tares; • Mustard-seed; • Leaven; • Hid treasure; • Merchantman; • Net cast into the sea; • Householder.
5000 fed.	14	John the Baptist killed. Five thousand miraculously fed. Christ walks on the sea. The hem of His garment touched.
"Doing good".	15	Traditions of the elders. The woman of Canaan. "Many" healed. Four thousand miraculously fed.
	16	A sign from heaven asked. Peter's confession of Christ. On taking up the cross.
The Transfiguration.	17	The Transfiguration. Epileptic cured. The tribute miracle.
Lost sheep.	18	Diciples' ambition. A lesson on little children. Cutting off right hand &c. Parable of lost sheep. Parable of unmerciful servant.
	19	Matrimony and divorce. The young ruler.

Two blind men.	20	Parable of the husbandman. Christ predicts his sufferings. (See also xvii, 22, 23.) Zebedee's sons. (See also xviii, 1.) Two blind men. (See also ix, 27.)
The fruitless fig-tree.	21	Christ's entry into Jerusalem. (Mark xi.; Luke xix. 29.) The fig-tree withered. (Mark ix, 13). Christ perplexes the chief priests. Parable of the husbandmen and vineyard.
Parables.	22	Parable of the marriage feast. On paying tribute to Caesar. On the resurrection and marriage. The lawyer's question answered. Christ's question on the 110th Psalm. Humility taught.
	23	Eight woes against the scribes and Pharisees.
	24	Christ foretells the destruction of Jerusalem; and also the end of the age.
Ten virgins. **The judgment.**	25	Parable of the ten virgins. Parable of the talents. The sheep and the goats.
Judas. **Gethsemane.** **Peter's denial.**	26	Conspiracy against Christ. Woman and the alabaster box of ointment. Judas sells his Master. LORD's Supper instituted. Peter's cowardice foretold. Christ's agony in the garden. Judas betrays Christ. False witnesses accuse Him. Peter denies Christ.
Pilate. **Crucifixion.** **Burial.**	27	Christ delivered to Pontius Pilate. Judas repents and hangs himself. Christ arraigned before Pilate. Pilate delivers Christ up to the Jews. Christ mocked, smitten, &c. Christ crucified. Joseph of Arimathea begs Christ's body and buries it. The watch at the grave.
Resurrection.	28	Resurrection of Christ. Excuse made by the Jews. Christ commissions the eleven.

THE GOSPEL OF ST. MARK

A brief history of the life of Christ, supplying some incidents omitted by St. Matthew.

COMMENTARY ON THE GOSPEL OF ST. MARK

The Gospel of St. Mark, as tradition and internal evidence agree in assuring us, contains reminiscences of St. Peter's preaching. It begins with a twofold reference to prophecy introducing a short notice of the work of the Baptist (i. 1–8). Then Jesus Himself appears, and is baptized with water and the Spirit; and in the power of the Spirit meets the tempter (9–13). Then come the opening of the Galilean ministry (14–39), the first preaching (14, 15), the call of the first disciples (16–20), and a full account of one day's work in Capernaum (21–39).

So far we have had popular excitement but no opposition. The next section (i. 40—iii. 6) defines our LORD's relation to the Pharisees, showing His loyalty to Moses even in touching a leper (40–45) and the ground of His authority to forgive sins (ii. 112), and again, the disregard of traditional notions of propriety (13–22) and of traditional rules of Sabbath observance (23 iii. 6), which brought upon Him the deadly opposition of the religious leaders.

The next section (iii. 7—vi. 6) defines our LORD's relation to the people. It shows how true disciples were sifted out from the crowd, and describes the appointment and training of the twelve from their selection to their first independent commission. It begins with the appointment of the twelve 7–19). Then

Jesus declares the source of His authority over evil spirits, and the ground of spiritual kinship (20–35). He illustrates in parables the conditions for the reception of truth (iv. 1–20), responsibility for the spread of it (21–25), and its own inherent power of growth (26–32). The section closes with three examples of His work among the people and of their attitude towards Him, first among the Gerasenes (iv. 35—v. 20), next on the way to, and within, the house of Jairus (v. 21–43), and lastly at Nazareth (vi. 1–6).

From this point until the final crisis at Jerusalem (vi. 6—x. 31), the narrative illustrates stages in the training of the twelve. The section begins with an account of their first practical experience of the work (6–13) and with the example of the end of a prophet in Israel (14–29). On their return they share with their Master in one of His most wonderful works (30–44), and learn that He is watching over them even from afar (45–52). The controversy with the Pharisees touching purification (vii. 1–23), and the work which He did for aliens on alien land (24—viii. 10), taught them that no kind of meat and no race of men was unclean in the sight of God. Then, after a rebuke for their dulness (11–21) and a miracle which is remarkable as being the one instance of a gradual cure, and which in consequence supplies a natural illustration of the slow development of their spiritual sight (22–26), their faith is brought to the test of open confession (27–30) and disciplined by the prophecy of the coming Passion (31—ix. 1); then follows the Transfiguration (2–13), giving 'a surer hold on the prophetic word,' and the cure of the demoniac boy (14–29), illustrating the conditions of success in mighty works.

The rest of the section (ix. 30—x. 31) records the teaching on the way to Jerusalem. First (ix. 30–50) at Capernaum He teaches the twelve to be humble and tolerant and self-disciplined. Then in Penea (x. 1–31) He explains the doctrine of marriage to the Pharisees and to His own followers (1–12). By blessing the little children, and by His answers to the young ruler and to Peter, He teaches that a childlike heart and detachment from worldly things are conditions of entrance into the Kingdom.

The crisis at Jerusalem (x. 32—xiii.) turns on the question of authority. The character of the authority is made clear in the answer to the sons of Zebedee (x. 32–45). Then publicly accepting the title of the Son of David, first from Bartimaeus and then from the multitude, He enters Jerusalem to claim His true position (x. 46—xi. 11). He exercises the authority so claimed in a miracle of judgment and in the cleansing of the Temple (12–26). His claim is challenged and justified (27—xii. 12), and tested by cunning questions (13–37), after which He takes leave of the people with a parting warning against their leaders (38–40) and a gracious recognition of 'a very humble act of devotion (41–44). Chapter xiii. contains His last teachings for His disciples, on the signs of His return.

The story of the Passion is contained in chapters xiv. and xv. The Gospel breaks off abruptly in the middle of the story of the Resurrection (xvi. 8). A later hand has added a short compendium of the appearances after the Resurrection, apparently drawn for the most part from the other Gospels.

The empty tomb (from the "longer" ending of St. Mark's Gospel).

THE GOSPEL OF ST. MARK: CHAPTER BY CHAPTER

The beginning of Christ's ministry.	1	Gospel of the Son of God. John the Baptist. Christ baptized. Christ's temptation. Christ's ministry. Disciples first called. Unclean spirit cast out. Simon's wife's mother and others cured. A leper cleansed.
	2	Sick of the palsy cured. Levi [Matthew] called. Children of the bride-chamber not fasting. Disciples pluck ears of corn on the Sabbath.
The Twelve.	3	Withered hand cured. Many healed. The twelve commissioned and qualified. Christ charged with receiving aid from Beelzebub. Sin against the Holy Ghost.
Parables.	4	Parable of the sower. Candle and bushel. Seed growing up insensibly. Grain of mustard seed. The tempest calmed.
Miracles.	5	Demoniac cured. Herd of swine. Issue of blood cured. Jairus's daughter raised.
	6	Twelve disciples sent out, two and two. They work miracles. John the Baptist beheaded. Feeding the five thousand. Christ walks on the sea.
Deaf cured.	7	What defiles a man. "The dogs eat the crumbs." Deaf cured – "Ephphatha!"
The blind man at Bethsaida.	8	Four thousand miraculously fed. Caution against the leaven of the Pharisees. Blind man cured at Bethsaida. Peter – "Thou art the Christ!" Christ foretells His death and resurrection. Peter rebuked.

The Transfiguration.	9	The Transfiguration. Deaf and dumb spirit cast out. Christ's death and resurrection again foretold. Disciples taught humility. One casting out devils in Christ's name. Cup of water given in Christ's name. Offending Christ's little ones. "Where their worm dieth not."
"Forbid them not."	10	Abuse of divorces. Christ "much displeased." He blesses children. The wealthy ruler. Christ a third time depicts His sufferings and death. Ambition of Zebedee's sons. Blind Bartimaeus.
"Hosanna!" Fruitless fig-tree.	11	Christ's entrance into Jerusalem. The fig-tree withered. Money-changers driven out of the temple.
The widow's mite.	12	Parable of the husbandmen and vineyard. On paying tribute to Caesar. On the resurrection and marriage. The first and second commandments. The widow and the two mites.
"Watch!"	13	Christ foretells the destruction of the temple. "I say unto you, Watch!" The alabaster box of ointment.
Betrayal.	14	Christ's last Passover. Christ betrayed and arraigned. Peter denies Christ.
Crucifixion. Burial.	15	Christ before Pilate. Barabbas released. Christ insulted. Christ crucified. Centurion's saying at the crucifixion. Joseph of Arimathea buries Christ.
Christ's reappearance.	16	The women at the sepulchre Christ's reappearance. The disciples' commission.

THE GOSPEL OF ST. LUKE

The history of the life of Christ, with especial reference to His most important acts and discourses.

COMMENTARY ON THE GOSPEL OF ST. LUKE

In his Preface (i. 1–4) St. Luke pleads the example of many predecessors for the attempt he is about to make and promises on the ground of careful investigation an orderly and accurate account of the traditions of the Gospel narrative received from eyewitnesses.

He then begins with an account of the Birth, Infancy, and Boyhood, of John the Baptist and of the Savior (i., ii.), bringing into prominence throughout the action of the Holy Spirit, the work of women, the adoration of the poor, and the anticipation of a coming deliverer. He sketches next the ministry of the Baptist (iii. 1–20), noting its place in the history of the world, and the lessons it contains for Gentile as well as for Jew. Then the account of the Savior's ministry begins (iii. 21). He comes forward as one of the chosen people to John's baptism. After the baptism the Spirit descends upon Him, and the voice of the Father claims Him as His Son. He is now of full age, a true son, as the genealogy shows, of Adam, the son of God. Led by the Spirit into the wilderness He meets and foils the devil (iv. 1–13) and returns in the power of the Spirit to commence His work in Galilee (14, 15). At His old home the largeness of His mission is made the ground of His rejection (16–30). At Capernaum, after a day of healing, He has to leave those who would try to keep His works of power to themselves (31–44).

At this point, clearly out of strict chronological sequence, St. Luke introduces his account of the call of the first four disciples (v. 1–11) after a miraculous draught of fishes. Then follow, in close connexion as in the first two Gospels, the healing of the leper (12–16) and of the paralytic (17–26), the call of the publican and the feast at his house (27–39), and two conflicts with the Pharisees touching the Sabbath (vi. 1–11); a group well fitted to illustrate characteristic aspects of the work He had come to do.

The settled opposition of the Pharisees creates the necessity for a new organization. So He chooses twelve apostles to be more directly associated with Him in His work (12–19). The ministry under these new conditions opens with a sermon (20–49), in great part identical with the Sermon on the Mount recorded by St. Matthew; unfolding a new conception of happiness and duty, and laying down the privileges and conditions of discipleship. Then He shows the power of His word by healing a centurion's servant, and calling back the widow's son to life (vii. 1–17).

Then in answer to the Baptist He leaves His work to be its own witness (vii. 18–23), and warns the people that none but the children of wisdom can understand her ways (24–35). An example of His meaning is supplied by the scene in the house of Simon the Pharisee (36–50), where He vindicates His prophetic character by reading the hearts of men, and the sinful woman is saved by her faith in Him.

Turning now to those who are willing to listen, He utters and expounds the parable of the sower, and declares the true ground of kinship with Himself (viii. 1–21). Then a group of four mighty works—the stilling of the storm, and the cure of the demoniac, followed by the healing of the issue and the raising of Jairus's daughter—reveals here, as in the first two Gospels, His power to control the natural and spiritual forces of the universe, and to restore health and even life itself in answer to the faith of men (22–56).

After these lessons the Twelve are sent out on their first independent commission (ix. 1–6), and on their return take part in the feeding of the five thousand (10–17). St. Luke then passes on at once to the scene in which their faith is brought to the test of open confession, and they are first told of the coming Passion (18–27). Then follows the Transfiguration (28–36) and the healing of the demoniac boy at the foot of the Mount (37–42). Then, in view of the work which they will have to do after He has gone, He calls on His chosen to pay heed to His teaching (43–45), to be humble one towards another (46–48), sympathetic towards all workers in the same cause (49, 50), and patient even under provocation (51–56). His face is now set towards Jerusalem, and He has need of more fellow-workers. So St. Luke brings before us three typical applicants for discipleship (ix. 57–62), and then describes the mission of the Seventy, with its strange blending of sadness and joy (x. 1–24). It was a last appeal to the cities and villages of Palestine, and its rejection would seal their doom; at the same time it was in itself an evidence that the work had not been in vain—the Father had revealed His secret unto babes.

Then come the parable of the Good Samaritan (25–37) and the story of Martha and Mary (38–42), revealing the double aspect of the disciple's duty, in active benevolence towards every fellow-creature and in patient hearkening to the Master's word, and crowned by a lesson in prayer (xi. 1–13). At this point our thoughts are turned from the disciples to the people at large. The appeal made to them had hitherto met with merely passive resistance. Men heard, and refused to repent or to obey. Henceforward He meets active opposition by warnings of coming judgment. The first stage in controversy deals with the evidence for the Savior's mission. In connexion with His power over evil spirits and the people's demand for a sign from heaven, He declares that His work is its own evidence, but bids them beware lest the good He is doing should prove the occasion of a worse evil (xi. 14–26); and by examples taken from Gentile lands in less favored generations He warns them to be faithful to the light that they still possess, lest it should be taken away (29–36).

The next stage contains a deliberate attack on the religious leaders of the people, showing how the Pharisees, by fixing their attention on outward rather than inward purity, had lost all sense of proportion in duty, and while making an idol of popularity had become a source of pollution instead of purification for the people (xi. 37–44), and how the lawyers, having lost all sympathy with the people, were on the point of crowning the guilt of their fathers, and were barring the gate which they had been commissioned to open (45–52). From the leaders He turns to the people, and warns them first against the hypocrisy which springs from fear of men and forgetfulness of God (xii. 1–12); then against a false estimate of the value of riches (13–21), and against anxiety about the supply of earthly needs (22–34), bidding His disciples rather lay up heavenly treasure in expectation of His coming (35–40), using and not abusing the powers entrusted to them (41–48), and not flinching even under fiery trial (49–53). Turning back to the multitude, He closes with an earnest appeal for timely repentance (54–59). The warning with which this chapter closes is carried on into the next. Lessons drawn from incidents of the time are enforced by a parable declaring that the last year of grace has begun (xiii. 1–9). The opposition of a ruler of the synagogue to a miracle on the Sabbath illustrates once more the contrast between the rival claimants for the leadership of the people (10–17). Two parables picture the universality of the Kingdom (18–21), and the people are warned that the privileges they have enjoyed will not of themselves prevent their exclusion from it (22–30). And then, in answer to the Pharisees, the LORD prophesies the consummation of the guilt and the doom of Jerusalem (31–35).

In the next section (xiv.—xvii. 10) the contrast between the Savior and the Pharisees is still further developed, and the Gospel is offered freely to the outcast. It begins with yet another cure worked on the Sabbath in the presence of the Pharisees (xiv. 1–6). Then in conversation at a feast He brings out the laws of courtesy among guests and of true hospitality (7–14), and hints that these laws apply to the heavenly banquet by a parable (15–24) which foretells the exclusion of the self-satisfied, and the admission of the needy. The offer of salvation is thus thrown open to all. But they are warned to count the cost of discipleship before closing with it (25–35). Even so it proved attractive to the most degraded (xv. 1, 2), and the Savior, in the parables of the Lost Sheep, the Lost Coin, and the Lost Son, entreats the Pharisees to share with Him the joy of this return of the lost (3–32). Then turning to His disciples, He warns them in the parable of the Steward of their responsibility to God for the powers entrusted to them, and bids them win eternal friendship by their use of their earthly possessions (xvi. 1–13). As this teaching only moved the Pharisees to sneer, He denounces their self-righteousness and their misunderstanding of the Law (14–18). Then in the parable of the Rich Man and Lazarus He illustrates the spiritual dangers arising from earthly possessions (19–31). The section closes with lessons to the disciples on the duty of avoiding offences (xvii. 1, 2), and of untiring forgiveness, on the power of faith, and on the impossibility of merit (3–10).

In the last stage of the journey to Jerusalem, after blessing the faith of the grateful Samaritan leper (11–19), Jesus develops the doctrine of the Kingdom (xvii. 20—xix. 48). He shows first how, when, and where the Kingdom is to be expected (xvii. 20–37); then the need of importunate prayer for its manifestation (xviii. 1–8), hinting that the coldness of the Church was the real cause of the delay, and showing, by the parable of the Pharisee and the Publican, the condition of an acceptable approach to God (9–14). At this point St. Luke comes back to the regular current of the Synoptic narrative, which he left in ix. 51; and by a group of narratives containing the blessing of the children, the answer to the rich young ruler, and Peter's question, 'What shall we have?' he teaches, as do St. Matthew and St. Mark, that a childlike heart is a condition of entrance to the Kingdom (15–17), and that clinging to wealth excludes from, while sacrifice opens, the gate to eternal life (18–30). Then he adds to the prophecy of the Passion (31–34) and to the healing of the blind man already connected with Jericho (35–43), the repentance of Zacchaeus (xix. 1–10) and the parable of the Pounds by which Jesus tried to teach His disciples not to expect the Kingdom till His return (11–27). Then he describes the entry into Jerusalem (28–48), catching an echo of the angels' song in the Hosannas of the crowd, and recording the tears which the sight of the doomed city drew from its King even in the moment of His triumph. His description of the trial by cunning questions follows, with one omission, the same lines as that in St. Mark. First the authority of Jesus is challenged by the rulers; in His reply He makes them confess their incompetence to judge any teacher's credentials (xx. 1–8) and lays bare the grounds of their opposition to His Father's messengers (9–18). Then He solves the difficult question of the lawfulness of paying tribute to Caesar (19–26), and meets the doubts of the Sadducees touching the Resurrection (27–40) and after a counter question, by which He sought to lead them back to the Scriptures for a full prophetic description of the Person of the Messiah (41–44), He takes leave of the people with a warning against the ostentation of the scribes (45–47) and a gracious recognition of the poor widow's sacrifice (xxi. 1–4). His last public utterance described the signs which should precede, the distress which should accompany, and the redemption which should follow the fall of Jerusalem (5–28), closing with an exhortation to sober watchfulness (29–36).

The narrative of the Passion and Resurrection (xxii.–xxiv.) begins with an account of the preparations of the enemy (xxii. 1–6), followed by the Last Supper, and the Lord's last teachings, promises, and warnings, to His disciples (7–38). Then after His prayer (39–46), He is arrested as if He were a dangerous malefactor (47–53), denied by His chief apostle (54–62), insulted by the high priest's servants (63–65), condemned by the Sanhedrin (66–71), and at last, in spite of an acquittal both by Pilate and by Herod (xxiii. 1–12), is sentenced to be crucified (13–25). The story of the Cross begins with a warning to the daughters of Jerusalem (26–31); then from the Cross itself He made intercession for the transgressors and accepted the robber's penitence,

Jesus tried before Pilate.

and refusing to save Himself, committed His Spirit into His Father's hands (32–49).

We then read how He was laid in the grave by Joseph of Arimathea as the Sabbath drew on (50–56), and how faithful women came at dawn on the third day and found the grave empty, and heard from angels that He was alive (xxiv. 1–12). Then He Himself appears to two sorrowing disciples (13–32), and to the assembled brethren (33–49), calming their excitement (36–39), assuring them of the reality of His resurrection body (40–43), explaining to them the prophecies of His sufferings, and bidding them proclaim to all nations the forgiveness He had won for them, as soon as they had received the promised Spirit (44–49). The Gospel closes with the Ascension (50–53).

THE GOSPEL OF ST. LUKE: CHAPTER BY CHAPTER

Zacharias.	1	The angel Gabriel appears to Zacharias. Birth of John the Baptist foretold. Zacharias struck speechless.
The Virgin's hymn.		The angel Gabriel appears to the Virgin Mary. Mary visits Elisabeth. The Virgin's hymn, "My soul doth magnify the LORD." Circumcision of John the Baptist. Zacharias's prophecy.
Christ's birth.	2	Birth of Christ. Angel's message to the shepherds. Shepherds go to Bethlehem. Circumcision of Christ.
Simeon. Anna.		Simeon's song and prophecy. Anna, the prophetess. Jesus among the doctors.
John the Baptist. Genealogy.	3	Preaching of John the Baptist. Christ's genealogy traced on the mother's side, he being called son of Heli, Mary's father.
Temptation.	4	Temptation of Christ. Address at Nazareth on "The Spirit of the LORD is upon me." Cure of Simon Peter's wife's mother. Demons cast out.

Miraculous draught.	5	Miraculous draught of fishes. A leper cured. Christ heals the palsied man. Levi [Matthew] called. Parables of old garment and old bottles.
The Twelve.	6	Plucking corn on the Sabbath. Christ chooses twelve apostles. Christ heals diseases. Christ's Sermon on the Plain. The beatitudes. Blessed are the poor – the hungry – the hated. Woe to the rich – the full – &c. "Love your enemies." The beam and the mote. The tree and its fruit. Wise and foolish builders.
The widow of Nain. **Parable of creditor and debtors.**	7	Centurion and sick servant. Widow of Nain. John's message to Christ. Woman anointing Christ's feet. Parable of creditor and two debtors.
	8	Account of Mary Magdalene. Parable of the sower. The tempest stilled. The demoniac healed. The hem of His garment. Ruler's daughter raised.
	9	Christ commissions His twelve disciples. Herod's alarm. Five thousand fed. The Transfiguration. Epileptic cured. False zeal of James and John reproved. Certain man that would follow Christ.
The Good Samaritan.	10	Seventy disciples sent forth. Christ rejoices in spirit. The Samaritan "neighbor." Martha and Mary.
The LORD's prayer.	11	The LORD's prayer. Parable of the importunate friend. Strong man armed. Sign of Jonas. Six woes declared.

The rich fool.	12	Fear not killers of the body. God and the sparrows. On confessing Christ. The rich fool. Cautions against anxiety. The "girded." Good and wicked servants. Dissensions occasioned by the gospel. Agreeing with an adversary.
The barren fig-tree.	13	Galileans. The tower in Siloam. Repentance. Parable of barren fig tree. Parable of mustard seed. The strait gate. Lamentation over Jerusalem.
Parables.	14	Christ cures a man having the dropsy. On healing on the Sabbath. The uppermost seat. Parable of the great supper. Building a tower / kings going to war (counting the cost). Salt and savour.
	15	Parable of lost sheep. Parable of lost coin. Parable of prodigal son.
	16	Parable of the unjust steward. Two masters: God and Mammon. Parable of rich man and Lazarus.
Ten lepers.	17	Trespasses of a brother. Parable of servant returning from field. Ten lepers cured. Coming of the Son of man.
	18	Parable of the unjust judge. The Pharisee and the publican. Christ receives little children. The rich ruler. Blind man cured.
Zacchaeus. **At Jerusalem.**	19	Zacchaeus. Parable of the ten pounds. Christ's entry into Jerusalem. Christ cleanses the temple.

THE GOSPEL OF ST. LUKE

	20	The chief priests and scribes seek to kill Him. Parable of the vineyard. On paying tribute to Caesar. Christ refutes the Sadducees on the resurection. Christ's questions on Psalm 110. Warnings against the Scribes. The widow and the two mites.
	21	Christ foretells the destruction of Jerusalem The coming of the Son of Man.
The Lord's Supper. **Judas.**	22	Passover and Lord's Supper. Warning to Simon Peter. Christ's agony. Judas betrays Christ. High priest's servant maimed and cured. Peter denies Christ. Christ arraigned.
Pilate. **Crucifixion.** **Burial.**	23	Christ accused before Pilate. Pilate chastises Christ. Pilate and Herod are friends.* Barabbas released. Christ crucified. Two other malefactors. Three of the utterances on the cross. Inscription on the cross in three languages. Conversion of a malefactor.* Miraculous darkness. The centurion's exclamation. Joseph of Arimathea buries Christ. Women prepare spices for embalming the body of Christ.
Resurrection. **Ascension.**	24	Resurrection of Christ. The women at the sepulcher. Disciples going to Emmaüs. Christ appears to the apostles. Christ's ascension and blessing. Disciples worship in the Temple after the ascension.*

Mentioned by Luke only.

THE GOSPEL OF ST. JOHN

**The life of Christ, giving important discourses not
related by the other evangelists.**

COMMENTARY ON THE GOSPEL OF ST. JOHN

The object of this Gospel is to produce faith, and life through faith, in Jesus as the Christ, the Son of God (xx. 31). It begins with a description of Him who is to be the subject throughout—the Word (i. 1–18), who in the beginning was with God, the source of life in all creation and of light in each man, who had become flesh, and as God Only-begotten had made the Father known. This manifestation was attested by the Baptist and by chosen witnesses who had seen its glory and felt its power. The Baptist disclaims for himself any office but that of a herald (19–28), and points to Jesus as the Lamb of God, anointed with the Spirit with which He will baptize the world (29–34).

The next day the experience of the chosen witnesses begins. Spending time and sharing conversation with Him reveals His insight into, and His power over, the hearts of men (35–51). Returning home with six companions, He works His first sign at a marriage feast (ii. 1–11). The first stage of His revelation is now complete. He has shown Himself to His friends as the Light of men and the Life of creation.

His first public act is the cleansing of the Temple. The act recalls to the disciples a feature in the Messianic portrait, but it only raises the question of authority in the minds of the Jews, who are told that they are powerless to destroy the outward symbol of

God's presence among men (13–22). The people did not remain as coldly critical as their leaders. But Jesus refused to trust Himself to their undisciplined enthusiasm (23—25). And the reason for this reserve is brought out in the conversation with Nicodemus (iii. 1–15). Nicodemus accepts Jesus as a teacher sent from God, and comes to Him for an exposition of His doctrine, expecting to understand it clearly, as soon as it is put before him. He learns that this is impossible. No one can see or enter the kingdom of God without the new birth to which both John and Jesus testified. Nor can one who has not himself come from heaven reveal its secrets. Still the Son of Man has come from heaven. And believers shall find life in Him when He has been crucified. For the gift of life was the object of His mission and not judgment, though judgment was inseparably connected with His coming (16–21). With this the account of the first stage in the public ministry closes. It contains a call in act and teaching to repentance and faith as the conditions of entrance into His kingdom.

Next comes the account of a brief ministry of baptism on the part of Jesus's disciples in Judea, leading to an answer given by John to his disciples explaining his own relation to Jesus (22–30), and to a declaration (31–36) of the source and character of the teaching of the Son of God, and of the consequence of disobeying Him.

Returing to Galilee, Jesus passes through Samaria, and in conversation with a Samaritan woman by Jacob's well (iv. 1–26) lays claim to the power of bestowing on man a gift of living water. Then after awaking in her the consciousness of His prophetic power, He declares the advent of a revelation of God as Father which shall set worship free from local limitations and so render obsolete the distinction between Samaritan and Jew. Then He explains to His disciples the sustaining power of obedience to the Father's will (27–38) and the law of the spiritual harvest-field which, transcending the limitations of time, unites the sowers and reapers of every age in a common joy. Meanwhile the woman's report brings out her townsfolk to hear for themselves, and to confess their faith in the Savior of the world (39–42). Leaving Samaria, Jesus establishes Himself in Galilee (43–45), and a second sign (46–54) crowns a faith that was independent of sight. Though Galilee thus becomes the regular scene of His ministry,

He did not neglect Jerusalem. The healing of a paralysed man there (v. 1-9) led to an important public statement of what He claimed to be and do. A charge of Sabbath-breaking arose out of the cure. Jesus met the charge by pleading His Father's example (10-17). The claim to divine Sonship involved in this plea led to a second charge (18), which Jesus met by disclaiming any power independent of His Father, while He repeated and expanded the claim to include the power of raising the dead and of judgment, declaring that His voice had a quickening power for those who heard it, and that His judgment, based on His obedience, was just (19-30). He then summarizes the evidence in support of His claim—the witness of the Baptist, of the works given Him by His Father, and of the Scripture—and shows why His self-abnegation was unintelligible to them (31-47).

The next scene brings us back to Galilee and contains two signs: the feeding of the five thousand (vi. 1-14) and the walking on the water (15-21). The first of these led to a long public discussion; the second was kept secret from the multitude. Jesus begins the discussion of the first sign with an appeal to men to come to Him for the satisfaction of their highest needs. To attain this they must surrender themselves in faith to Him. Such surrender requires evidence in support of His claim. This is supplied by the nature of the gift that God had given to the world in Him, the true manna, the bread of life. It requires also an action of their own will—they must come. This also is the Father's gift (22-40). Murmuring against this teaching is met by a further exposition of the Father's working in the hearts of men (41-46) and of the gift of His own Flesh for the life of the world (47-51). Cavils against the possibility of such a gift are met by as statement of the necessity and of the effect of participating in it (52-59). This teaching caused a secession even of disciples, and led to Simon Peter's confession and to the declaration of the presence of a traitor in the twelve (60-71).

These two chapters contain a complete statement of our LORD's public teaching about His own nature and the work that He came to do for men, and about the conditions and the necessity of faith in Him.

The next six chapters contain the controversy with the Jews at Jerusalem. Jesus, who has hitherto revealed Himself chiefly as the source and stay of the Life of men, reveals Himself now as their true Light. The revelation begins at a Feast of Tabernacles (vii.—x. 21). Jesus, having refused to go up publicly to the Feast (vii. 1-9), appears suddenly when it is at its height, and finds a division of opinion among the people about Him (10-13). He declares first (14-24) that knowledge of the source of His teaching would come through obedience to it, and not through murderous attacks upon Him for a supposed violation of the Law of Moses; that they did not know as yet His true origin (25-31); and that ere long He would return whence He came and be out of their reach (32-36). Then (37-52) He promises to believers refreshment and the power to refresh. This teaching rekindles the controversy about Him in the crowd, and questionings arise even in the Sanhedrin. His next claim is to be the Light of the world: (viii. 12-20), because He alone knows whence He came and has the Father with Him in judgment and in testimony. He then points out the way to truth and freedom (21-59). Only by faith in Him could they find deliverance from their sins (21-23). But they must wait for proof of the truth of His claim till by their own act He had been raised on high (24-30). Meanwhile, abiding in His word would bring a freedom from slavery which none but the Son could give (31-36) and which they needed, for, as their conduct showed, they were true sons neither of Abraham nor of God, but of the devil (37-47). This teaching seemed to them like the raving of a demoniac (48), but it is reasserted—He is the Son and honors His Father, and His word has promise of immortality: He knows the Father and is 'before Abraham was born' (49-59). Then (ix. 1-7), after teaching His disciples to spend their time in helping and not in judging their brothers, Jesus works a sign to illustrate His claim to be the Light of the world. The sign attracts the attention of the Pharisees (8-12). The fact being undeniable, they try to browbeat the man who had been cured into an admission that the author of his cure was a sinner. Failing in this, they excommunicate him (13-34). Jesus seeks him out, reveals Himself to him, and passes sentence on the Jews for their conduct (35-41). Then working out the contrast between true leadership and false, He shows that the true shepherd enters by the door and is recognised by the porter and by His sheep (x. 1-6). In contrast with thieves who aim only at self-aggrandizement or at wanton destruction, He claims to be the door through which the sheep pass to find rest and food (7–10). In contrast with hirelings He claims to be the Good Shepherd who knows His sheep and will lay down His life for them, that He may unite them into one and prove worthy of His Father's love (11–18). This teaching brings out once more the divisions of the people and the old charge of possession (19–21).

At the Feast of the Dedication He is once more pressed to declare Himself, and replies that He has already declared Himself in word and deed, but that only His sheep understand Him and are safe in His, that is, His Father's keeping (22–31). This claim to divine power is called blasphemy. But Jesus supports it by reference to the titles conferred on the judges of Israel in the Old Testament, and by the works which His Father wrought through Him (32–39), and then He retires beyond Jordan (40–42). The death of a friend calls Jesus out of His retirement even at the risk of His life (xi. 1–16). He first reveals Himself to Martha as the Resurrection and the Life, and then goes with her and with her sister weeping to the tomb (17–38) and calls Lazarus back from the grave (39–44). This is the last sign before His own Resurrection, and it brings the conflict with the Jewish authorities to a head. The Pharisees combine with the chief priests in decreeing His death as the only way of saving the nation (45–53). Jesus meanwhile waits at Ephraim until it is time to go up to the Passover (54–57). Six days before the feast He returns to Bethany, and is anointed as for His burial by Mary, the sister of Lazarus, though Judas protests against the waste (xii. 1–11). The next day He enters Jerusalem in triumph (12–19). The request of certain Greeks to see Him leads to His last public teaching on the fruitfulness and necessity of sacrifice, by suggesting the thought of the harvest which the Gentile world would yield (20–26). The shadows of His coming Passion then gather round His soul, and He prays aloud for the glory of His Father's Name. A Voice from heaven answers Him, and then He proclaims the judgment of the world, the casting out of its prince and the drawing of all men to Himself through the Cross (27–33). These words suggest a difficulty. Can the Lamp of the Anointed be put out? It is met by a solemn warning. Men may shut out the light from themselves (34–41). So the public ministry closes with a last declaration of the consequences of faith and unbelief (42–50).

The teaching contained in chapters xiii.—xvii. was addressed to disciples, to prepare them for the new relation with Himself which His death would introduce; to teach them the work which they would have to do for Him after He had left the world, and the power of prayer in His Name; and to make them long for the coming of the Paraclete who would unite them to their Lord and make them strong to work for Him. It begins with the cleansing of the company, first by a symbolic washing (xiii. 1–20), and then by the dismissal of the traitor (21–30). Being now left alone with the faithful, He gives them the new commandment to keep for His sake, and after His example (31–35). He warns Peter that the strength in which he was trusting would that night prove weakness (36–38). He then explains the purpose of the coming separation, and tells them that they know the way to follow Him (xiv. 1–4); for He is the Way to the Father (5–7), who has already been revealed in the Son (8–14). Then coming back to His commandments, He consecrates them as means by which His disciples can show their love to Him and receive the gift of the Spirit, marking their distinction from the world, and completing their illumination (15–26). Meanwhile He gives them His peace, and bids them rejoice with Him in His return home (27–31). At this point the company seem to have left the upper room and to have gone together for a last visit to the Temple courts. There, under the figure of the vine, the consecrated symbol of God's chosen people, He explains to His disciples the fruitfulness which His Father expected from the branches, and the method by which it might be secured (xv. 1–10). He then reminds them of His own claim on them for fruitfulness (11–16), and bids them love one another, bearing the world's hatred as He had borne it (17–25), and sharing with the Spirit in witnessing for Him before men (26, 27). The world's enmity might mean even death, but the Advocate would plead their cause against the world (xvi. 1–11), and would lead them into all the truth (12–15). Even the separation from Himself was only for a time, and the pain of it would prove fruitful in abiding joy and prevailing prayer (16–24). His last words promise yet closer communion in the time to come, both with the Father and the Son (25–28). The self-confident expression of faith with which these words are greeted calls out a renewed warning of coming failure, but the warning fades away into an assurance of ultimate and perfected victory in Him (29–33). Turning now from conversation with men, He pleads with His Father for the restoration of His eternal glory (xvii. 1–5). Then He pleads for those who have believed in Him, that the Father would keep them in unity (6–11), taking up the work which He Himself must now relinquish (12, 13), and that He would sanctify them in the truth for which they would be His accredited representatives in the world (14–19). Then the horizon of the prayer extends till it includes all whom their labors would gather out of the world (20–24). It ends with an adoring acknowledgment of the Name which the world knew not, but which the Son had made known and would make known to men till the Father's love had found a resting-place in their hearts (25, 26).

Leaving the Temple courts, the little band cross the Kidron to Gethsemane. There Jesus surrenders Himself to the soldiers who come, led by Judas, to arrest Him (xviii. 1–11). The only stage in the trial before the Jews recorded by St. John is the preliminary examination before Annas (12–27). When Jesus is brought before Pilate, he refuses to condemn Him at Jewish dictation, and draws from Him a description of the kingdom which He claims. He then offers the people a chance of delivering their king, but they choose Barabbas (28–40). After this Jesus is scourged at Pilate's orders, and mocked by the soldiers. The Jewish rulers however will be satisfied with nothing less than crucifixion in expiation of the blasphemy of His claim to be the Son of God. This new charge leads to a fresh examination of the prisoner, by which the judge is taught the source of his own authority. He dares not however face a charge of disloyalty to the emperor, so he prostitutes justice to the threats of those who disclaim any king but Caesar (xix. 1–16). The sentence is pronounced, and the King is crucified under His royal title, in spite of the protests of the Jews (17–22).

At the foot of the cross the soldiers fulfil prophecy by their division of the prisoner's raiment (23, 24); and Jesus commits His mother to the keeping of the disciple whom He loved (25–27). This done, after one more utterance perfecting the Scripture, He pronounces His work finished and gives up the ghost (28–30). The necessity for haste caused by the approach of the Sabbath leads to the piercing of His side (31–37), and to burial in the rich man's tomb (38–42). Early on the first day of the week Mary Magdalene finds the tomb empty, and brings the news to Peter and John (xx. 1, 2). They verify the fact for themselves, and one of them understands its meaning (3–10). Mary stays by the tomb, and the LORD Himself appears to her and sends her with a message to His brethren (11–18). That same night He appears to the disciples and gives them a commission to the world (19–23). A week later, He appears to them once more, and after drawing from the doubter a most explicit confession of faith in His divinity, He pronounces a blessing on those who had believed without seeing (26–29), and the Evangelist records it as his purpose in writing his Gospel to produce such faith (30, 31). The last chapter records a third appearance to a group of disciples on the lake, accompanied by a miraculous draught of fishes and a mysterious breakfast on the shore (xxi. 1–14). After the meal, Simon Peter receives a special commission to shepherd his Master's flock, in recognition of his real, and now no longer self-reliant, affection (15–17). Then he is taught what to expect in his old age, but no direct answer is given to his question touching St. John (18–23). The Gospel is closed with an attestation of the truth of the author (24), added apparently when the work was done, by the members of the little group of early disciples at whose instigation, according to an early tradition, St. John composed his record.

THE GOSPEL OF ST. JOHN: CHAPTER BY CHAPTER

The Word.	1	Christ the Word – the Life – the Light. John, Christ's witness. Christ rejected by "his own." The Word made flesh. John the Baptist's testimony.
The Lamb of God.		Christ the Lamb of God. Andrew and Simon, Philip and Nathanael called.
Christ's first miracle.	2	Marriage in Cana. Water turned into wine. Christ scourges profaners of the Temple. He predicts His resurrection.

Nicodemus. "**Lifted up.**"	3	Christ and Nicodemus. Regeneration. Brazen serpent and anti-type. Light and darkness. John baptizes at AEnon. John's witness to Jesus.
	4	The woman of Samaria. Christ heals a nobleman's son.
	5	Paralysed man healed at the pool of Bethseda. Christ's testimony from His Father: from his forerunner; His works; and the Scriptures.
"**It is I.**"	6	Christ feeds five thousand (Matt. xiv.; Mark vi.; Luke ix.) Christ walks on water. His discourse from the manna. Himself the Bread of Life. Many disciples leave Christ. Peter confesses Christ.
	7	Christ goes to the Feast of the Tabernacles. Christ charged with having a devil. Christ's address on the last great day of the Feast. Officers afraid of taking Christ. Nicodemus speaks for Christ.
The Light.	8	Woman taken in adultery. Christ the Light of the world. Jews' boasted descent from Abraham.
	9	Christ cures a man born blind. The Pharisees cavil.
The Good Shepherd.	10	Christ the Door. Christ the Good Shepherd. Christ's discourse on His sheep.
	11	Lazarus raised from the dead. The Jews seek to kill Jesus.
Entry into Jerusalem.	12	Mary of Bethany anoints Jesus's feet. Judas Iscariot reproves her. Christ's entry into Jerusalem. He foretells His death. He treats of unbelief.
Washing the disciples' feet.	13	Christ washes His disciples' feet. Judas's base design. The new commandment. Peter's confidence.

The Comforter.	14	Christ our forerunner – the many mansions. Christ promises the Comforter. Christ's legacy of peace.
The True Vine.	15	Christ the True Vine. Love and hate.
"Ask."	16	Office of the Holy Spirit. "A little while." Encouragement to "ask."
Christ's prayer.	17	Christ's prayer – • For Himself. • For His apostles. • For believers in general.
Christ betrayed. **Christ denied.**	18	Judas betrays Christ. Peter cuts off the ear of Malchus. Christ before Caiaphas. Peter denies Christ. Christ before Pilate.
Crucifixion **Burial of Christ's body.**	19	Jesus scourged and mocked. Jesus delivered for crucifixion. Regard had by Joseph of Arimathea and Nicodemus for the body of Jesus.
The Resurrection.	20	Christ's resurrection. He appears to Mary Magdalene. He appears to the apostles. Incredulity of Thomas.
Charge to Peter.	21	Christ appears at the Sea of Tiberias. Miraculous draught of fishes. Christ's charge to Peter.

THE ACTS OF THE APOSTLES

The history of the labors of the apostles, and of the foundation of the Christian Church.

THE ESSENTIAL STORY OF ACTS

Following Jesus' Ascension, it fell to the eleven remaining apostles to carry on his work and to spread the word of the Kingdom of Heaven and the way of the LORD. They held a meeting with more than a hundred other followers and decided upon a replacement for Judas in order to bring their number back up to twelve (symbolic of the twelve tribes). They cast lots and the choice fell upon a long-time believer, Matthias, who had been one of the seventy disciples Jesus sent out during his ministry.

Fifty days after the feast of the Passover, the Jews celebrated the feast of Pentecost, or Festival of Weeks. When the apostles and followers assembled, a great wind blew through the room they were in, and tongues of flame descended upon the heads of the twelve. The Holy Ghost had entered them, empowering them to heal, teach the way of the LORD – and at the same time the curse of Babel was reversed, for all who heard them speak, no matter their native tongue, could understand them. Peter addressed those present, telling them that Jesus, the Messiah, had risen from the dead; and that day alone some 3,000 people were converted.

The apostles began healing and preaching just as Jesus had done, but teaching also the Resurrection. One of the first to be healed was a crippled beggar, a familiar face at the Temple gate, whom Peter healed. Arising, he went into the Temple, where all who knew him were filled with wonder.

Now there was not just one man performing miracles but twelve. And they were not only teaching the Resurrection but openly blaming the Sanhedrin for the death of Jesus. The priests reacted by persecuting them, starting with Peter and John, who spent a night in jail before appearing before Annas, Caiaphas, and the Sanhedrin. They were threatened and released this time, but it was not long before the apostles were again imprisoned. This time, at dead of night, an angel descended and opened the locked doors, freeing them – next morning the priests beheld the apostles at work as usual, at Solomon's Porch, and were astounded. Brought before the council yet again, they were sentenced to be scourged and released with more warnings – this after an intervention by the law teacher Gamaliel. His argument was simple: if this were a movement springing from human origins, it would surely fail; if not, they were fighting God himself.

And so the apostles continued their work, news of their activities bringing in the sick and lame from far and wide. This active, empowered fellowship of believers shared their possessions and pooled their resources, supported also by donations made by the faithful. Many sold property and gave the proceeds to the community. One such was Joseph, a Levite, whom the apostles named Barnabas. By contrast, a couple named Ananias and Sapphira sold land and gave only half of the received moneys pretending it was the whole amount; this met with stern condemnation by Peter, who called it deception and lying to the LORD. Both husband and wife fell down dead, which sent a frisson of fear through the Church.

One of the believers elected as a deacon, or administrator, was Stephen, who was destined to become the first Christian martyr. Arrested for blasphemy, and condemned by the testimony of false witnesses, he made a strong speech to the Sanhedrin – to no avail. Their fury boiled over: they dragged him outside, stoned him to death and embarked with much greater ferocity in persecuting the followers of Jesus. The Greek speakers among the faithful were particularly singled out, so they scattered to the countryside, leaving the nucleus of the apostles in Jerusalem.

Samaria was Philip's destination, and here he found a receptive audience. Indeed, the enthusiasm of those who heard him led Philip to call Peter and John, who also met with great success, baptizing and dispensing the Holy Spirit. Among those who came to them was a magician of much repute named Simon, who was baptized and then offered Peter money if he would grant him the Holy Spirit. "May your money perish with you!" retorted Peter – the gift of God could not be bought. Meanwhile Philip directed his attention toward Gaza, and on the road encountered an Ethiopian eunuch, treasurer of the Queen of Cush, who had been to Jerusalem to worship. The traveler was reading from the Book of Isaiah, and he asked Philip to explain it. They fell into conversation which ended in the Ethiopian being baptized.

Foremost among the persecutors in Jerusalem was a man called Saul. Born in Tarsus of a well-to-do family, he was a Benjamite Pharisee who brought the enthusiasm of a zealous bigot to his work. After hunting out the followers of the Way of the LORD in Jerusalem – he was there at the stoning of Stephen – he obtained letters of introduction to the synagogues of Damascus and departed for that city intending to put new vigor into the persecutions there. On the road to Damascus, he experienced one of the most momentous conversions in history – a great flash of light blinded him, and as he lay terrified in the road Jesus spoke to him. He would later change his name to Paul and become one of the two greatest proponents of the new faith and would make the way of the LORD an international movement.

First, Paul was led to Damascus, and one of the disciples, directed to him by God, healed his eyes. For some days Paul remained there and confounded the priests by beginning to preach the very faith he had come to condemn. Soon the priests conspired to kill him, but Paul escaped over the city walls and made his way back to Jerusalem, where he made contact with the apostles. Naturally, they were extremely wary of this former enemy, but Barnabas spoke up for him, and they began to believe in his conversion. His presence in Jerusalem, and the story of his incredible change of attitude soon reached the authorities, and the brethren got him out of Jerusalem to Caesarea, where he took ship for his home city. In time, however, the fury of persecution in Jerusalem gradually diminished, affording the disciples more freedom to spread the word.

Peter, meanwhile, experienced a vision that was just as momentous in its consequences as Paul's conversion. He had been active along the coast of the Mediterranean: at Lydda, he healed a paralytic; and at Joppa he even raised from the dead one of the female disciples there, Tabitha (or Dorcas). Then on the way to Caesarea, where he had been summoned by a Roman centurion, he had a strange vision, which took him some while to interpret. He realized eventually that God was telling him that everyone could be welcomed into the way of the LORD, Gentiles and the uncircumcised as well as Jews. They must not call any man clean or unclean – baptism must be available to all. The centurion, already a believer, was baptized together with his friends and family, the first non-Jewish converts. When Peter returned to Jerusalem he faced criticism from his fellow apostles, but he told them of his vision and its evident meaning. It was controversial, but the apostles accepted this; among the wider following, there was more circumspection.

After the period of relative peace, a new wave of persecution began, led by Herod Agrippa I (grandson of Herod the Great), who began making arrests, including James, brother of John, whom he put to the sword. Seeing that this pleased the priests, he seized Peter just before the Passover and threw him into prison, where he was chained and heavily guarded. But the angel of the LORD came to his rescue by night, waking him and leading him from the building, as if in a dream, past the jailers. When he turned up at the house of Mary, mother of John, the apostles gathered there were astonished to see him. Shortly afterwards, Herod Agrippa died.

Meanwhile Antioch, an important city in northern Syria, had become the focus of the faith in that area, having attracted a number of followers fleeing the earlier persecutions in Jerusalem. A strong community of believers grew there, and Barnabas was sent from Jerusalem to meet them. He then brought Paul from Tarsus to preach; and it was from this city that they would begin their missionary journeys.

Cyprus was their first destination, where they converted the Roman Proconsul, Sergius Paulus, despite the opposition of his attendant, Bar-Jesus, or Elymas, whom Paul blinded; and then Asia Minor, where in Pamphylia their reception was mixed. At Pisidian Antioch and Iconium, they met opposition from the Jews – but not from the Gentiles, whom they embraced. They withdrew to Lystra, but here they were mistaken for gods and then the local Jews had them stoned, leaving Paul for dead outside the city walls. Via Derbe, they returned to Antioch in Syria.

Over the following years the implications of Peter's great vision and the activities of Paul and Barnabas became a source of discontent among some of the faithful. Was Christianity (a term first used for the new faith in Antioch) to be for the Jews alone or for the uncircumcised Gentiles too? A delegation from Jerusalem came to Antioch, and a sharp debate ensued, with the result that Paul and Barnabas led a party to Jerusalem to settle the matter – all of their future work depended upon the resolution of this question. At a meeting that marked a turning point in the movement, the fundamentalist Jewish Christians insisted that Gentiles accepting the way of the Lord must be circumcised, while Peter spoke of his vision and Paul and Barnabas told them of their successes among the Gentiles of the north. After much debate, a potential, damaging schism in the movement was averted: two of the faithful, Silas and Judas Barsabas, were sent to Antioch with a letter asking simply that the Gentiles accommodate Jewish Christians by respecting their food laws. There was no mention of circumcision. Now all was clear, and the task of taking the message to the Gentiles could proceed in earnest.

Paul set off on his second missionary journey, taking with him Timotheus (Timothy) and Silas. They traveled through Phrygia and Galatia in Asia Minor and then crossed the Hellespont to the continent of Europe. At Philippi, an important city in Macedonia, Paul established a community of believers but, as so often, encountered resistance too. Trouble was sparked by a slave-girl employed as a fortune-teller, who recognized Paul and Silas as servants of God. When she persisted in following them and calling out, Paul turned and cast out the devil within her, but now her psychic abilities were no longer of value to her owner. A riot resulted, and the apostles were imprisoned, this time chained to heavy blocks of wood. That night an earthquake shook the city, the doors of the jail flew open, and their chains were loosened. When the jailer discovered that they had not taken the opportunity to escape, he threw himself at their feet and was baptized. Shortly after, the authorities released Paul and Silas, but Paul upbraided them for so treating a citizen of Rome, whom they had no right to imprison.

From Philippi, the apostles traveled along the great Roman road, the Egnatian Way, to Thessalonica, and then went south to Athens, where they engaged in debate with scholars of the Epicurean and Stoic schools of philosophy. At Corinth they made an extended stop, but after a while ran into trouble again and were seized. However, the local Roman Governor, Gallio, refused to become involved and emptied the court when the local authorities attempted to bring them to trial.

They returned to Asia Minor and at Ephesus encountered an Alexandrian named Apollos, one of a number who had been baptized by John the Baptist. They now baptized them in the name of Jesus Christ. They also came across a number of sorcerers attempting to effect healings, so they instructed them in the way of the LORD, and the sorcerers publicly burned their magic books.

Via Caesarea, Paul returned to Jerusalem but was soon back in Antioch planning his next mission. This took him back to Ephesus, where his success had caused a backlash. Ephesus was the site of one of the Seven Wonders of the World, the temple to Artemis, long since destroyed but still the focus for worshippers. The silversmiths there saw their trade in statuettes of the goddess threatened by the new religion, and a certain Demetrius raised a riot in protest during which the apostles were jostled but escaped. Their route lay toward Macedonia again. Paul was now revisiting established Christian communities, encouraging them and helping to keep them in touch with the expanding movement. At many meetings, he preached, sometimes at great length. On one occasion, he spoke for so long that a young man named Eutychus fell asleep tumbling from a window; the fall was thought to have killed him, but Paul revived him.

They crossed over to Macedonia again and made the circuit to Corinth, then back to Philippi, along the coast of Asia Minor, and back to Tyre and Jerusalem. During these long travels, they faced the usual hazards of non-believers, bigots, and Jews, but Paul reinvigorated the Christian communities everywhere with his formidable courage and passion. During these travels, he wrote letters (epistles) to various communities putting in writing many of the ideas and thoughts he must have imparted verbally at his many meetings, and these have become fundamental sources of Christian theology and philosophy.

His reception in Jerusalem was warm, but serious trouble lay ahead, as predicted by a prophet named Agabus in Caesarea, where he stayed for a few days with Philip. Paul was not deterred.

While he was away it had been put about that he was teaching that Jews living among the Gentiles should not have their children circumcised, thus contradicting the Mosaic Law. Sure enough, his enemies saw him in the Temple and seized hold of him, leading to uproar in the city. His fate was not sealed, however: as a Roman citizen, he was not flogged, and the Roman commander, Claudius Lysia, became cautious. Next day Claudius sent him before the Sanhedrin, where he stood, defiant, and told them that he was a Pharisee. This upset the priests completely, for Paul preached Resurrection and believed in angels and spirits – as did the Sadducees, but not the Pharisees. In the chaos that followed, the Romans took him away for his own safety, and after a plot to kill him was betrayed they moved him by night to imprisonment in Caesarea.

Here the provincial Governor, Felix, found himself under pressure from the High Priest, who brought a lawyer called Tertullus to bring charges of troublemaking. Felix had heard about this new religion and talked privately with Paul, effectively keeping the priests at bay, but no conclusion was reached, and Paul waited in jail for some two years. Then Felix was replaced by a new Governor, Porcius Festus, which induced the priests and Jewish leaders to try again to bring him to trial. This time Paul, as a Roman citizen, lodged his right to appeal to the Emperor in Rome.

A few days later the Tetrarch, Herod Agrippa II, paid a courtesy visit to Porcius in Caesarea, and they spoke about the Christian prisoner. Herod Agrippa decided that he would see Paul himself, and the result – after Paul told him the story of his conversion – was that the King could find no fault in him. However, his judgment to let Paul go free was complicated by the fact of his appeal to Caesar, and it was finally decided to send him to Rome.

The long journey across the Mediterranean was made in three stages, first to Myra, on the coast of Asia Minor, where they went aboard a large Alexandrian ship bound for Rome. The weather was bad, however, and after a difficult journey past Cyprus and Crete, they were shipwrecked on Malta (Melita), and forced to wait out the winter there.

Paul's relationship with his guards seems to have been relaxed, and indeed they stayed with Publius, the Governor of the island. When the Governor's father fell sick of dysentery, Paul cured him, and many other sick people were brought to him for healing. The final stage of the journey took them to Puteoli, where they were met by friends who accompanied them along the Appian Way to Rome.

Paul on the Appian Way.

There is no mention in the Bible of an audience with the Emperor, but Paul was held under house arrest for some two years, during which he spoke to local Jews and preached the message of the way of the LORD.

The Bible tells us nothing about the ultimate fate of the apostles. All but John probably died violently, as martyrs. The traditional story is of Paul's execution by beheading in Rome, where Peter, after undocumented travels also met his fate, according to tradition crucified upside-down, having told his captors that he was unworthy to die in the same manner as Jesus. These executions probably took place about ad 64/65, following the great fire in Rome, when the Emperor Nero used the Christian community as a scapegoat. John, the last of the fellowship that had received the Holy Spirit in 33, lived longest, dying probably about the end of the first century.

COMMENTARY ON THE BOOK OF ACTS

This book, as its opening words imply, is the ' Second Part' of the Gospel according to St. Luke, completing the account given in that work of the things which Jesus began to do and teach between His Incarnation and His Ascension by an account of His administration of His Kingdom through the Spirit from His Throne in Heaven.

The unity of authorship throughout the book is sustained by strong linguistic evidence; and the author claims to have been an eyewitness of some of the events that he narrates. Thus it will be noticed that he marks his own accession to St. Paul's company at Troas (xvi. 10), and drops the use of the first person when St. Paul leaves Philippi (xvii. 1). About seven years later the narrative once more brings St. Paul to Philippi. The author rejoins him and goes with him to Jerusalem (xx. 16—xxi. 17). We have no hint of his movements during the two years of St. Paul's imprisonment at Caesarea. But he embarks with St. Paul for Rome, and is still at his side when he enters the Imperial city (xxvii. 1—xxviii. 15).

Analysis

The simplest outline of the book is supplied by our LORD's words in i. 8, "Ye shall be my witnesses both in Jerusalem (i.–v.), and in all Judaea and Samaria (vi.–ix. 31), and unto the uttermost part of the earth" (ix. 32–xxviii.).

I. The witness in Jerusalem begins, after a prelude containing the story of the Ascension (i. 1-14) and of the election of Matthias (15-26), on the day of Pentecost, with the fulfilment of the promise of the Father in the outpouring of the Spirit (ii. 1-13) and with Peter's explanation of the meaning of the sign (14-36), followed by the gathering and training of the first band of converts (37-47). We are then shown how on two critical occasions the Sanhedrin deliberately refused to accept the apostolic witness. The first occasion arose out of the arrest of Peter and John for preaching in the Temple after the healing of the paralysed man (iii. 1–iv. 4), and issued in a threat on the part of the rulers (5-22), answered by increased earnestness in prayer and work on the part of the Church (23-31), even though the leaven of hypocrisy which appeared in Ananias and Sapphira threatened her purity and called for a startling judgment to cast it out (32–v. 11). The second occasion arose out of the development of popular enthusiasm (12-16) and issued in a formal condemnation of the apostolic doctrine (17-42).

II. The witness in all Judaea and Samaria (vi.–ix. 31) is recorded in three stages, after the account of the appointment of the seven deacons (vi. 1-7). The first gives the occasion of the dispersion in the account of the martyrdom of Stephen (vi. 8–viii. 3). The second contains the work of Philip (viii. 4-40), including the evangelization of Samaria, where his work is supplemented by Peter and John (14-25), and the baptism of the Ethiopian eunuch (26-40). The third describes the conversion and the early preaching of Saul of Tarsus at Damascus and in Jerusalem (ix. 1-31).

III. The account of the spread of the witness to the end of the world falls into three subdivisions. The first (ix. 32–xi. 26) contains the opening of the door for the world-wide extension of the Gospel by the baptism of Cornelius (x. 1–xi. 18), and the establishment of the Church in Antioch (xi. 19-26). The second (xi. 27–xv. 35) describes the activity of the Church of Antioch through its accredited representatives Barnabas and Saul, including (a) the alms sent by their hands to Jerusalem at the time of the famine and Herod's persecution (xi. 27—xii.); (b) the solemn commission given them to evangelize, which issued in the establishment of Churches in Cyprus, at Antioch in Pisidia, at Iconium, at Lystra, and at Derbe (iii., xiv.); and (c) the successful protest which they raised against the claim put forward by some members of the Church of Jerusalem to impose circumcision on all converts from heathenism (xv. 1-35). The third (xv. 36—xxviii.) contains in two stages an account of the independent missionary activity of Paul, the first culminating in the establishment of the Church in Ephesus (xix. 20); the second in two years' undisturbed preaching at Rome (xxviii. 30, 31). In the first of these we read how Paul, after his separation from Barnabas (xv. 36—xvi. 5), was led on step by step to Macedonia, where in face of bitter opposition he preached with great success (xvi. 6—xvii. 15) before passing on to Athens (xvii. 16-34) and to Corinth (xviii. 1-17). Leaving Corinth after nearly two years he revisits Jerusalem and Antioch (xviii. 18-23) and finally settles clown for three years' work at Ephesus (xviii. 24—xix. 20). The preaching at Rome was in like manner the goal of a long course of providential leadings (xix. 21—xxviii. 30). His stay at Ephesus was closed abruptly by a riot (21-41); he passed thence through Macedonia to Corinth, and then pressed on to Jerusalem in spite of constant warnings of the danger that awaited him, only pausing at Miletus to bid farewell to the elders of the Ephesian Church (xx. 1—xxi. 16). After arriving at Jerusalem he had hardly time to greet the Church (xxi. 17-36) before he was seized by a Jewish mob, and was called upon to defend himself before the people (xxi. 37—xxii. 29) and before the Sanhedrin (xxii. 30—xxiii. 10). Then, after escaping from a plot against his life (11-35), he defended himself before Felix (xxiv.), before Festus (xxv. 1-12), and before Agrippa (xxv. 13—xxvi.); and finally, after an eventful voyage, was carried a prisoner to Rome (xxvii. 1—xxviii. 16). On his arrival he makes a solemn appeal to his fellow-countrymen and then turns to work among the Gentiles.

THE BOOK OF ACTS: CHAPTER BY CHAPTER

Ascension of Christ.	1	Christ shows Himself to His disciples forty days. Directs them to wait at Jerusalem for the promise of the Spirit. Christ's ascension. Disciples return to Jerusalem from Mount Olivet. Assemble in an upper room. Peter proposes to choose another apostle. Account of the end of Judas. Matthias chosen by lot.
Pentecost. **Peter's first sermon.**	2	Pentecost. The gift of tongues. Peter's first sermon. Three thousand souls converted. Wonders and signs wrought.
Lame man healed.	3	Peter and John at the Temple. Lame man cured at the gate Beautiful. Peter preaches and exhorts to repentance and faith in Christ.
Peter's second sermon. **Prayer of the Church.**	4	Peter and John imprisoned. Five thousand converted by Peter's sermon in Solomon's porch. Peter and John brought before the Sanhedrin. Speech of Peter. The rulers dismiss the apostles, and command them to preach no more. Prayer of the Church for the apostles assembled with them. Union and liberality of the Christians. Generosity of Barnabas.
Ananias and Sapphira. **Gamaliel.**	5	Deaths of Ananias and Sapphira. Miraculous cures. The apostles imprisoned. And angel releases them. They teach in the Temple. They are brought before the Council. Peter's defense. Gamaliel's prudent speech. Theudas; Judas of Galilee; impostors. The apostles beaten and dismissed.
	6	Seven deacons chosen. Stephen falsely accused.

Stephen's death.	7	Stephen's defiance, including a history of the patriarchs, of Moses and of the Israelites. Stephen stoned to death.
Saul persecutes. **Philip and the eunuch.**	8	Saul's persecution of the Church. Simon the sorcerer would purchase the Holy Ghost. Peter's severe rebuke of Simon. Gospel preached in Samaria. Ethiopian eunuch baptized by Philip.
Saul's conversion. **Saul preaches Christ.**	9	Saul's miraculous conversion on his way to Damascus. Vision of Ananias. He restores Saul to sight. He baptizes Saul. Saul preaches Christ in the synagogues of Damascus. He escapes a plot by being let down over the city wall in a basket. Alarm of the disciples on his joining them at Jerusalem. Paul again in peril of his life. Prosperity of the churches. At Lydda, Peter cures Aeneas of the palsy. He restores Tabitha (Dorcas), a benevolent woman, to life.
Cornelius. **Peter's vision.**	10	Vision of Cornelius the centurion at Caesarea, a devout Jewish proselyte. Peter's vision of the descending sheet and the clean and unclean creatures. Three messengers from Cornelius wait on Peter at Joppa. Peter and certain brethren visit Cornelius at Caesarea. Peter's sermon in the house of Cornelius.
Scattering.	11	Peter vindicates his conduct in visiting the Gentiles. The apostles, scattered after the martyrdom of Stephen, preach at Phenice, Cyprus and Antioch. Barnabas visits Antioch, and there witnesses the grace of God. Agabus predicts a dearth. The disciples send relief to Jerusalem.

Herod kills James. **Peter's release.**	12	Herod kills James and imprisons Peter. Peter released by an angel. He goes to the house of Mary, the mother of John Mark, where there was a meeting for prayer. Rhoda's joy on seeing Peter. Herod, enraged at his escape, kills the keepers.
Herod's death.		Herod's presumption, and awful end.
Barnabas & Saul (Paul).	13	Barnabas and Saul sent to the Gentiles. Saul also called Paul. Sergius Paulus, the deputy of Cyprus, wishes to hear Paul and Barnabas.
Elymas the sorcerer.		Bar-jesus, or Elymas, opposes the gospel. He is smitten with blindness. The deputy believes. Paul preaches at Antioch, in Pisidia.
	14	Paul and Barnabas persecuted at Iconium. They flee to preach at Lystra and Derbe. Paul cures the cripple at Lystra.
A cripple cured.		The people and the priest of Jupiter take Paul and Barnabas for gods. Jews from Antioch and Iconium persuade the people to stone the apostles.
Return to Antioch.	15	Paul and Barnabas return to Antioch in Syria. Dispute respecting circumcision. The question referred to Jerusalem. Peter's address. Barnabas and Paul testify to the work among the Gentiles. James endorses Paul's view.
Decision of the council.		The council send their determination by letters to the churches. Paul and Barnabas return to Antioch. They purpose to visit the scenes of their labors. Barnabas wishes to take Mark, which Paul disapproves; and they separate. Barnabas and Mark sail to Cyprus.
Paul and Silas.		Paul takes Silas, and visits Syria and Cilicia.

Lydia converted. **A demon cast out.** **Jailer converted.**	16	Paul takes Timothy with him from Lystra. Paul's vision, at Troas, of the man of Macedonia. Lydia, of Thyatira, converted at Philippi. Paul casts out a demon from a damsel. Paul and Silas scourged and imprisoned. Conversion of the jailer and his house. Paul and Silas set at liberty.
Thessalonica. **Berea.** **Paul at Athens.**	17	Paul preaches at Thessalonica. Jason's house assaulted. Commendation of the Bereans. Paul at Athens. He preaches at Mars' Hill (Areopagus). Quotes Greek poets (Aratus and Cleanthus). Dionysis, Damaris, and others converted.
At Corinth. **At Ephesus.**	18	Paul visits Aquila and Priscilla at Corinth. Paul preaches at Corinth. Crispus, the chief ruler of the synagogue, believes with his house. Others also believe. Paul stays a year and six months. Paul taken before Gallio, deputy of Achaia, who dismisses him. Sosthenes, a chief ruler of the synagogue, beaten. Paul's vow; or it might be Aquila's vow. Paul at Ephesus.
Apollos.	18	Apollos "mighty in the Scriptures" at Ephesus. Aquila and Priscilla instruct him.
Sceva's seven sons. **Uproar about great Diana.**	19	Paul baptizes certain disciples. Sceva's seven sons wounded by the man with an evil spirit. Ephesians burn their books of magic. Demetrius, the silversmith, complains against the apostles. Uproar at Ephesus: "Great is Diana." Town clerk's advice.
Eutychus raised.	20	Paul goes to Macedonia and remains three months. Paul preaches at Troas. Eutychus falls from a loft while Paul is preaching, but is restored to life. Paul's address and farewell to the elders of Ephesus.

	21	Paul lands at Tyre on his journey towards Jerusalem.
		Certain disciples try to dissuade him from going to Jerusalem.
		Paul visits Philip the evangelist at Caesarea.
		Philip's four daughters prophesy.
Agabus.		The prophet Agabus predicts Paul's imprisonment at Jerusalem.
		Paul's resolution to accomplish his purpose.
Paul in the Temple.		He is prevailed upon to submit to certain Jewish customs, to remove prejudices.
		The Jews beat Paul.
		He is rescued by the chief captain, but bound in chains.
Paul's account of his conversion.	22	Paul, from the castle stairs, relates in Hebrew his conversion.
		The Jews raise another tumult.
		The chief captain orders Paul to be scourged.
		Paul pleads his citizenship as a Roman and escapes the scourge.
	23	Paul pleads his cause before the Council.
Ananias.		Ananias, the high priest, commands him to be smitten on the mouth.
		Paul's indignant prediction.
		Paul pleads his connection with the Pharisees, and divides them and the Sadducees.
		The chief captain orders an escort to guard Paul to the castle.
		God encourages Paul.
		Conspiracy of forty to take Paul's life.
		Paul's nephew reveals it to the chief caption.
Paul sent to Caesarea.		The chief captain sends Paul in the night, well guarded, to Caesarea.
		The letter of Claudius Lysias to Felix the governor.
	24	Subtle pleading of Tertullus against Paul.
		Paul's able reply.
		He is remanded.
Paul before Felix.		Felix and Drusilla hear more from Paul.
Felix trembles.		While Paul reasons, Felix trembles.
		After two years, Porcius Festus succeeds Felix, who leaves Paul bound.

	25	The Jews scheme to bring back Paul to Jerusalem, and to kill him.
		Festus defeats the scheme, resolving to see him at Caesarea.
		Paul appeals to Caesar.
		Agrippa and Berenice visit Festus.
Paul before Agrippa.		Paul brought up to be examined before them.
	26	Paul relates his life and conversion.
		Effect on Agrippa.
	27	Paul sails towards Rome.
		He is fourteen days and nights in a tempest.
		Comforted by an angel.
Paul shipwrecked.		Shipwrecked; and crew and passengers saved.
		The prisoners saved from being put to death by the interposition of the centurion.
At Melita.	28	Paul on the island of Melita (Malta).
		Kindness of the inhabitants.
		Paul shakes a viper from his hand.
		He cure the father of Publius (the chief man) of a fever and flux.
Various cures.		He cures others also.
Leaves Melita.		Quits the island after three months.
		Lands at Syracuse.
		Is met by the brethren at Appii Forum and the Three Taverns.
At Rome.		Paul allowed a private residence at Rome, guarded by a soldier.
		He vindicates himself to the Jews.
		Preaches for two years in his own hired house.
		Suffers no interruption , during that time, in his labors.

THE EPISTLES OF ST. PAUL

The letters of St. Paul, mainly to young churches.

St. Paul's Ministry, dating from his Conversion, lasted about thirty years. All his extant letters belong to the last half of this period, and may be divided into four groups, separated from one another by a marked interval of time and to a certain extent by peculiarities of language and of doctrine.

First Group: 1 and 2 Thessalonians

These two letters were written from Corinth during St. Paul's first visit to Europe. Thessalonica was the most important city in Macedonia, politically and commercially. It was a seaport, and it commanded by land all the traffic which went Romewards by the Via Egnatia. It contained also a large colony of Jews. The community to which the letters were addressed was in its infancy. Very few months can have elapsed since St. Paul's first appearance among them (Acts xvii. 1), and he had been driven from the town before he had had time to consolidate his work. Still at least one enduring result had been secured. His heart had been knit into one with theirs, and he found the trial of absence hard to bear. Once and again (1 Thess. ii. 18) he had made plans to return to them, but in vain. Still, he had been able to send Timothy to cheer them, and to bring him word how they fared.

The First Epistle is the outcome of his thankfulness on Timothy's return, and the Second followed some time later.

The special aspect of doctrine prominent in these two epistles illustrates the first stage of the apostolic preaching, as it is brought before us in the Acts. We see there (xvii. 16–34) that St. Paul began his work in a heathen city by a call to repentance, in

328

the name of the living God, and in preparation for the coming of Christ in judgment on the world. We find him here, in his letters to a newly constituted Church, recalling constantly thought of the Presence of God (1 Thess. i. 3, 9, [ii. 19], iii. 9, [13]), and drawing lessons of warning and comfort and hope from the certainty of the appearing of the Judge and Savior. His doctrine had been misunderstood, and some had disregarded his commands, but his authority in the Church was unchallenged. The enemies of the Gospel are as yet outside the fold.

Second Group: 1, 2 Corinthians, Galatians, Romans

All the Epistles in this group were written between Easter 57 and Easter 58 – 1 Corinthians towards the end of St. Paul's three years in Ephesus; 2 Corinthians and probably Galatians during his journey through Macedonia, and Romans from Corinth.

St. Paul's first visit to Corinth had lasted nearly two years. Corinth was the centre of all that was left of purely Greek life, and it was the meeting-place of many nationalities because the main current of the trade between Asia and Western Europe passed through its harbours. St. Paul's converts came mainly from among the Greeks, men gifted by race with a keen sense of the joys of physical existence, with a passion for individual freedom, and a genius for rhetoric and dialectics; but trained in the midst of the grossest moral corruption, undisciplined and self-conceited.

Sometime before the first of these letters was written he paid them a second visit (2 Cor. xii. 14, xiii. 1) to check some rising disorder (2 Cor. ii. 1, xiii. 2), and wrote them a letter, now lost (1 Cor. v. 9). They had also been visited by Apollos (Acts xviii. 27), perhaps by St. Peter (1 Cor. i. 12), and by some Jewish Christians who brought with them letters of commendation from Jerusalem, and claimed allegiance as personal disciples of Christ (1 Cor. i. 12; 2 Cor. iii. 1, v. 16, xi. 23).

The Epistles of this group illustrate a second stage in the apostolic teaching. The readers to whom they were addressed were men who had passed through the excitement of their first awakening, and had begun to feel the need of guidance in shaping their lives in accordance with the will of God. They are written to point such men to the cross of Christ as the true secret of abiding peace through the emancipation and renewing of the will, and to guard them against being drawn away from the true freedom of obedience to the law of the Spirit by a specious slavery to the carnal ordinances of the Mosaic law. It is at first sight strange that such truths should be presented in a garb so fiercely controversial; but humanly speaking it was inevitable. The old order could not yield place to the new without a struggle. Looked at from the outside the simple gospel of the grace of God had nothing to recommend it. It might easily pass for a purely visionary system, which no one but a madman could invent or entertain. None but those who surrendered themselves to it could form a conception of its inherent truthfulness and power. On the other hand the upholders of a strict conformity to the Jewish law could appeal to the sanction of an undoubtedly divine appointment, approved by the example of generations of faithful Israelites, sanctioned by the practice of the original apostles, nay even consecrated afresh by the submission of the LORD Himself. Surely the weapons of the Spirit had need to be mighty if they were to prevail against a fortress so strongly entrenched as this.

Third Group: Philippians, Colossians, Ephesians, Philemon

An interval of four or five years, spent by St. Paul "almost entirely in captivity", separates the Epistles of the third group from the Epistles of the second. They were all written from Rome.

The Epistle to the Philippians is the most nearly related in language and doctrine to the Epistle to the Romans. Before it was written, St. Paul had been at Rome long enough to feel that Christianity was making real progress among the soldiers of the Pretorian guard (i. 13).

The remaining Epistles of this group, the Epistles to the Colossians and Ephesians, And the Epistle to Philemon, were clearly written at the same time. Onesimus, who was the bearer of the Epistle to Philemon, is commended to the care of the Church of Colossae (iv. 9); Tychicus is the bearer both of the Epistle to the Colossians (iv. 7, 8) and of the Epistle to the Ephesians (vi. 21). It is characteristic of St. Paul that the little letter to Philemon should take its place side by side with these two great dogmatic Epistles. His contemplation of the deepest truths finds its natural fruit in the fulfilment of the homeliest duties.

The characteristic doctrine of the first group, as we have seen, is the Second Advent; that of the second is the Cross and the Resurrection. The characteristic doctrine of the third group is the Ascension and the present sovereignty of Jesus Christ over the world and over His Church. This is seen to involve an eternal dignity. The ascent corresponds to a previous descent (Eph. iv. 9), and carries with it the motive power of a complete consecration for all whose eyes are opened to realize the true grandeur of their position as risen and ascended with their LORD.

The Epistles belong to a period of quiet settled life in communities that were at least beginning to be consolidated. Problems of thought began to press for solution as well as problems of action. The gospel is shown to be the guide to a true philosophy, as well as to possess the power to produce right conduct, and to satisfy the social as well as the individual needs of men.

Fourth Group: The Pastoral Epistles, Titus and Timothy

The fourth group of St. Paul's Epistles belongs to the period which elapsed between the last mention of him in the Acts and his martyrdom at Rome. Our knowledge of his movements during this period depends entirely on these Epistles, except that an early tradition declares that he fulfilled the intention expressed in Rom. xv. 28 and visited Spain. Assuming that these letters are genuine, it is clear that he must have been set free from his first Roman imprisonment, and have spent at least some part of his time in revisiting his old friends in Greece and Asia Minor. To this interval of freedom we must assign the Epistle to Titus and the First Epistle to Timothy.

The Pastoral Epistles are occupied mainly with questions relating to the internal discipline and organization of the Christian body, and with the ideal of the Pastoral Office. The development and training of the life of godliness have taken the place of instruction in the faith. At the same time it is striking to notice the earnest reiteration with which St. Paul in these Epistles emphasizes the universality of God's saving purpose (1 Tim. ii. 4, iv. 10; Tit. ii. 11, iii. 4), and the bounty which shines out in every part of His creation (1 Tim. iv. 4, vi. 13, 17).

THE EPISTLE TO THE ROMANS

A treatise by St. Paul on the doctrine of justification by Christ.

COMMENTARY ON ROMANS

This Epistle was written from Corinth towards the end of the stay recorded in Acts xx. 3. St. Paul was at the moment contemplating a visit to Jerusalem fraught with imminent peril to himself (Rom. xv. 31). He hoped, if he escaped with his life, to visit Rome. This letter was meant in part to prepare the Church there to receive him when he came. It was meant also as a permanent record of the doctrinal results which St. Paul felt that he had attained as the fruit of the fierce conflict with Judaizing Christians through which he had just passed. For this purpose the Church that was slowly gathering – as the result of isolated and casual efforts in the capital of the world – was both by its position and its constitution an eminently suitable correspondent.

In the salutation (i. 1–7) St. Paul declares his commission to preach the Gospel of the fulfilment of God's promises in His Son to all the Gentiles, and so to the Romans. He then thanks God for their faith, and expresses his longing to visit them (8–13) and preach to them the Gospel of the Righteousness of God (14–17).

This Gospel met the crying need of the whole world, for God's wrath against sin was only too evident (18–32). He had revealed Himself in Creation, but men had refused to acknowledge Him (18–23). So He had left them to be the prey of unnatural lusts

(24–27), and to their own perverted judgment of right and wrong (28–32). Some indeed blind their eyes to their own relation to this wrath by assuming a position as the judges (ii. 1–16) or the teachers (ii. 17—iii. 8) of others; but God requires obedience, not censoriousness (ii. 1–11), trying each man with absolute fairness by the light he has received (12–16), and setting no store on the possession of the Law and Circumcision unless the heart is in correspondence with them (17–29). The Jew indeed was privileged above other men in being intrusted with the Oracles of God (1, 2). But God's faithfulness did not depend on his (3, 4). And God's wrath may righteously rest upon the nation for its repudiation of the trust, even though that very repudiation brings out God's truthfulness into clearer relief (5–8).

Is it then better to be a Gentile than to incur the additional responsibility of the possession of a trust? By no means. But Jews as well as Gentiles are, on the evidence of their own Scriptures, under the dominion of Sin (9–18). And Law reveals, it cannot break the chains of Sin (19, 20). So Jew stands on the same level as Gentile in his need of the revelation of the righteousness of God and of the redemption that is in Christ Jesus (21–26). He cannot claim to possess it in his own right on the ground of his own conformity to his law, nor to exclude Gentiles from it for their lack of circumcision. It is the gift of the One God to all men who by faith lay hold of it and thereby lay the foundation for true obedience to the Law (27–31).

Of this Righteousness by Faith, Abraham is the great example (iv.). He did not earn it by his faith any more than the Psalmist earned his forgiveness by turning from his sin (1–8). Nor did Circumcision give, it only sealed to him, his claim to possession of it (9, 10). So even the uncircumcised ranked as his children if they shared his faith, and even the circumcised might be shut out if they lacked it (11, 12). For through it only, and not through the possession of a Law, could they hope to inherit the promise (13–15). Otherwise some of that universal seed would be shut out from the blessing in spite of the promise, by accepting which Abraham had shown his Faith, and found Righteousness (16–22). Following his example, we too find Righteousness in accepting the assurance of divine aid given us in the Death and Resurrection of Our LORD (23–25).

Having this Righteousness, let us bring forth the fruits of it—Peace to God-ward, and Joy even in persecution (v. 1-5). Peace, because the death of Christ declares God's love even for sinners; and Joy, because the life of Christ is a pledge of abundant deliverance to all who accept the reconciliation He has wrought (6-11).

Do you ask how one man's work can be available for another? Look at the parallel presented by the heredity of sin. Just as a single man gave Sin an entrance into the world and Death a throne, even so—only much more abundantly—from one man grace and life overflow to all his brethren. The parallel is in fact exact. As one man's fall brings condemnation and entails a sinful nature, so one man's obedience brings acquittal and enrighteousment, for all men. This result is not due to the Law. Law is merely parenthetical and negative. It aggravates transgression. Free forgiveness dethroned Sin, and now reigns through Righteousness in place of Death (12-21).

But is sin tolerable because forgiveness is free? Nay, the sacrament of forgiveness is the pledge of death to sin as well as of life in the Risen LORD (vi. 1-4). Nothing but our own death to sin can set us free from sin, and we can accept even this living death in the hope that is set before us (5-11). We can spurn Sin's claim to dominion over the servants of a God who is now revealed not as Taskmaster but as Father (12-14). But we must beware of presuming on the tenderness of this new relation. Revolt against the habitual obedience involved in it is a return to the old slavery for the old wage. You may call the new relation a slavery if you like. But the Owner is God—His commands righteousness—His aim sanctification—and the goal, as the starting-point, is a free gift of eternal life (15-23).

Take a fresh illustration from the power of death to dissolve the marriage-bond (vii. 1-3). Our death in Christ has broken the bond by which, while we were in the flesh, we were wedded to the Law, and His resurrection has united us afresh to God (4-6). The fruit of our old union was sinful lust (though the Law itself is not Sin but the revealer of Sin), for it gave Sin an occasion for exciting lust in me and so destroying the life I once had (7-12). And so the very excellence of the Law revealed the hideousness of Sin and the misery of slavery to it (13-16). It opened my eyes to the presence within me of a terrible power other than myself enslaving my will (17–20), and forced me to cry aloud for a deliverer, conscious, in spite of my devotion to the Law, of my own impotence, left to myself, to obey it (21–25).

This fearful slavery is past for all who are in Christ Jesus. God, by the mission and the sacrifice of His Son, has succeeded, where the Law failed, both in condemning Sin and in securing full obedience to the Law from all who accept the new principle of life. The old principle—the flesh—is hopelessly alienated from God. But the possession of the new principle—the Spirit of Christ—is the distinguishing mark of the Christian, and it carries with it the promise of new life, even for the mortal body (viii. 1–11).

Surrender to this Spirit taking effect in the resolute mortification of corrupt habits is Life, because it brings with it the consciousness of son-ship and a share in the inheritance (12–17). The perfecting of our redemption will bring with it the deliverance for which the whole creation groans. The hope of it brings patience (18–25). And we have yet another companion in our groanings—the Spirit—who gives expression to our voiceless longings; and so we know that God is on our side. He has begun a work which can only end in glory, and He will carry it out to the end (26–30). With God on our side pledged to our deliverance by the sacrifice of His Own Son we fear no condemnation. No created thing can shut us out from the Son so revealed (31–39).

In this triumphant strain St. Paul brings the exposition of his gospel to a close. His tone changes suddenly at the opening of the next section (ix.–xi.). He is face to face with the bitter fact of the failure of his kinsmen to accept their own Messiah (ix. 1–5). This failure, real as it is, is not a failure on the part of God. He had from the first made it clear that 'the Seed' comprised a selection only out of all the natural descendants of Abraham (6–13). Nor can His selection, though it depends solely on His own will, be charged with injustice. His chief characteristic is Mercy (14–18). Man cannot indeed challenge God's absolute sovereignty over His creatures (19–21), but he can see even now longsuffering and mercy in His exercise of it in the call of the Gentiles into covenant, and in the salvation according to prophecy of the 'Remnant of Israel' (22–29). Still the bitter fact remains that the mass of Israel fails, where Gentiles succeed, in grasping the offered righteousness (30–33), because, in spite of their zeal for God (x. 1–4), they refuse to recognize His perfected work (5–15) and so turn a deaf ear to His messengers (16–21). Still God has not rejected His People. He has preserved a Remnant for Himself, while the curse falls on the rebellious (xi. 1–10). And even their fall is not final (11, 12).

At this point St. Paul turns directly to the Gentiles and draws a warning for them from this failure of men who had been in covenant with God. They had less ground to expect lenient treatment than 'the natural branches' if they proved faithless (13–24). At the same time, the thought of the kindness that embraced even wild olive shoots suggests a hope, which at last bursts out into clear expression, that when Israel's present rejection has borne its full fruit in the conversion of the Gentiles, God's promise shall be fulfilled in all its breadth, and His all-embracing mercy be finally revealed (25–36).

In the next section (xii.—xv. 13) St. Paul sets himself to work out the true principles of Christian conduct (xii. and xiii.), and to apply them to the solution of a special difficulty (xiv.—xv. 13). He first lays his foundation deep in the revelation that he has just given of the mercies of God (xii. 1, 2). Then he calls upon each Christian to use his gift for the good of the whole body, avoiding pride and the spirit of revenge (3–21). As a member of a State he is bound to recognize God as the source of all civil authority (xiii. 1–7), and to fulfil all civil obligations by love (8–10), living in the light and so being kept from deeds of darkness (11–14). In matters indifferent in themselves, such as the sanctity to be ascribed to particular kinds of diet or to particular seasons, each man must judge for himself and leave his brother to God (xiv. 1–12), only taking care not to hurt his brother's conscience or his own (13–23), following Christ in bearing the infirmities of the feeble-minded (xv. 1–6), and in an all-inclusive charity (7–13).

The rest of the Epistle is taken up with purely personal matter. St. Paul explains once more (14–21) his relation to them as Apostle of the Gentiles. He tells them of his plan to visit them on his way to Spain, after he has taken the contribution of the Greek Churches to Jerusalem (22–29), asking earnestly for their prayers for his safety, as though he knew even then the dangers that were likely to befall him, and for the success of his mission (30–33).

He commends Phoebe, the bearer of the letter (xvi. 1, 2), and sends greeting by name to various kinsfolk and friends (3–16). Before he closes he adds a short but earnest warning against false teachers, whose appearance among them there was reason to dread (17–20). After the Grace and a few more salutations (21–23) the whole Epistle closes with yet another noble doxology for the revelation of the eternal counsels which God had vouchsafed (25–27).

THE EPISTLE TO THE ROMANS: CHAPTER BY CHAPTER

Paul the Apostle.	1	Paul states his call to the Apostleship. Glories in the gospel Describes the iniquities of the heathen.
	2	The self-righteous and wicked Jews condemned.
Justification by faith.	3	Superior advantages of the Jews. Jew and Gentile under sin. Justification, not by the works of the law, but by faith.
	4	Abraham thus accounted righteous; and so the pattern of all believers.
	5	Happy consequences of justification. Sin and death by Adam – righteousness and life by Christ.
	6	Believers forbidden to live in sin.
	7	Believers redeemed from the bondage of the law. The law of use to show us sin. Contrast between the flesh and the spirit.
No condemnation.	8	No condemnation to believers. Carnal mind and spiritual mind contrasted. Believers children of God by adoption. Their support under trials. The triumph of faith.

Gentiles called.	9	Paul's love and anxiety for his brethren the Jews. Promises fulfilled in Abraham's spiritual seed. Vindication of God's sovereign grace. Calling of the Gentiles. Failure of the Jews to attain to righteousness.
	10	Paul laments the obstinate rejection of Christ by the Jews. Shows that the Gospel is adapted alike for Jew and Gentile. The means provided for embracing the Gospel.
"All Israel shall be saved."	11	The rejection of the Jews neither total nor perpetual. Illustrations from the first fruits and grafts.
	12	Self-dedication to God. Exhortations to moral virtue.
Duties of Christians.	13	Duties we owe to magistrates. Obedience to the moral law. Avoidance of the works of darkness.
	14	Forbearance with weak brethren.
	15	Same subject. Intended journey to Jerusalem to relieve the saints with contributions from Macedonia and Achaia. Request for prayers of the Christian brethren.
	16	Paul commends Phoebe to the Romans. Numerous salutations. Cautions against divisions.

THE FIRST EPISTLE TO THE CORINTHIANS

A letter from St. Paul to the Corinthians, correcting errors into which they had fallen.

COMMENTARY ON I CORINTHIANS

The immediate occasion of this letter was the departure of Timothy on a mission which was meant to extend to Corinth (1 Cor. iv. 17, xvi. 10; Acts xis. 22), the arrival of visitors from Corinth bringing news (1 Cor. i. 11, xvi. 17), and a letter from the Corinthian Church asking for St. Paul's advice on various matters (1 Cor. vii. 1, 25, viii. 1, xi. 2). It takes up one after another the different topics suggested by the news or the letter, and derives such unity as it possesses from the unity of the correspondents and not from logical connexion between its successive themes.

The Epistle opens with a salutation (i. 1–3) reminding them of their union with fellow-worshippers throughout the world in consecration to a common LORD, and a thanksgiving (4–9) for their faith in the past, for God's gifts of utterance and knowledge to them in the present, and for His faithfulness as a sure ground of hope for them in the future.

St. Paul then grapples at once with the twin spirits of partisanship and insubordination that threatened the unity of the Church and his authority among them (i. 10—iv. 21). He first lays bare the evil, and brings it face to face with the absolute claims

339

of Christ (i. 10–17). Then, because the evil sprang from forgetting how teachers and learners were related to one another and to God, he reminds them that the story of the Cross owed nothing of its power in their hearts to his eloquence (18–25), to philosophic culture or to earthly position (26–31).

It seemed impotent and foolish to the world, but through it the Spirit revealed God's power to their faith (ii. 1–5) and God's wisdom (6–16) to those who had eyes to see it. But the Corinthians were still carnal, if not babes (1–4). Their partisanship proved them blind to the truth (5–17) that no teacher is more than an instrument in God's hands (5–9), set to his own task and rewarded for his own toil, but working with his fellows on one building (10–15), which it is woe for any man to destroy (16, 17). He has thus shown them that the power of the message (i. 18–31), insight into its depths (ii.), and its fruitfulness (iii. 1–17), come entirely from God. Let them not look for light to their own wit or to their teachers'. They are Christ's (18–23), and their teachers too are His, out of reach of their criticism, and accountable to Him alone (iv. 1–5). Did they still take pride in partisanship? The lot of God's apostles was abject humiliation (6–13). Did they resent the sting of this rebuke? They must bear with a father's pleading (14–17), and, if need be, submit to his scourge (18–21).

The subject of the next section (v.—vii.) is chastity. In it St. Paul deals first with a grievous scandal, and then with questions concerning marriage raised by the Corinthian letter. He first passes judgment on the offender, and on them for their toleration of him (v. 1–8), explaining, by the way the duty of the Church to exercise discipline over the members of her own body (9–13), and suggesting the establishment of Church courts for the settlement of the disputes, which to their shame still arose between believers (vi. 1–11). The obligation to chastity rests on the redemption and consecration of the body (12–20). There is no doubt a beauty in the celibate ideal, but those that have not a special gift of continency had far better marry (vii. 1–9). The marriage bond must not be broken. When separation is inevitable, the way of reconciliation must not be closed by a fresh marriage. This is the LORD's express command (10, 11). Further difficulties St. Paul meets on his own authority. In cases where only the husband or the wife had accepted Christianity, he recommends the Christian neither to seek nor to refuse separation (12–16), on the general principle that a Christian should stay in that state in which God's call had found him or her (17–24). On the same principle, virgins in the present crisis had better not marry (28–31). The anxieties of wedded life hinder service (32–36). Still marriage is not forbidden (36–38). In like manner a widow may marry again, but she had better not (39, 40). The next section (viii.–xi.) treats of 'meats offered to idols' and of the order of Christian worship. St. Paul first justifies the doctrinal position of the 'stronger brethren.' It should matter nothing to a healthy conscience whether or not a piece of meat had formed part of a sacrificial victim (viii. 1–6). But the force of association was too strong for many. And what Christian could assert his freedom at the risk of leading a brother into sin (7–13)?

ix.–x. 13 contains an episode on Christian self-denial. The practice is illustrated by reference to St. Paul's refusal of maintenance at the hands of the Corinthian Church. He, if any one (ix. 1, 2), might claim support from them (3–14). But for his own satisfaction he forbore (15–18). On principle he met each man on his own ground, for the Gospel's sake (19–23). And self-denial was a regular part of his Christian training (24–27). This leads him to enforce the necessity for watchful self-discipline by warnings drawn from the history of Israel in the wilderness (x. 1–13). So he returns to the subject of idolatry, giving the reason why they must by all means keep clear of it. The statue of the god and the meat of the victim might be innocent in themselves, yet they were sacraments of demoniacal communion (14–22). So in practice they must be careful neither to confound liberty with license (23, 24), nor care with scrupulosity (25–30). God's glory and man's good supply a sure guide to conduct in every case (31–33).

In treating of public worship (xi. 2–34) he first enforces the rule that women should not appear unveiled in the assembly (2–16). Then he rebukes the partisanship and the disorder that disgraced even their sacred feasts (17–22), reminding them of the story of the institution of the Eucharist, and its direct relation to the death of the LORD and to their hopes of His return (23–27), and bidding them take heed to God's protest against the irreverence which would treat the Sacrament of their corporate Unity as an occasion for emphasizing divisions (28–34).

The next section (xii.–xiv.) expounds the relative importance, and regulates the use, of the gifts that accompanied the outpouring of the Spirit in the earliest days of the Church. The Corinthians needed a test of inspiration. The earliest creed supplied it (xii. 1–3). Genuine spiritual gifts were diverse, but one Spirit gave each his portion for the good of all (4–11), and the variety was necessary to the completeness of the body. So the weak must not envy the strong (12–20), nor the strong despise the weak (21–27). The Church had need of every kind, and each might aspire after the best (28–31). But aspiration without love is ambition and destructive of the unity of the body, so he reminds them that all gifts are worthless without love (xiii. 1–3), sketches love in action (4–7), and shows that love in contrast with intellectual endowments is by nature eternal (8–13). Then coming back to 'the gifts' (xiv.) he brings out the claims of prophecy to the first place in their esteem in contrast with the more popular 'speaking with tongues,' on the ground that 'prophecy' was directly edifying to the congregation, while an ecstatic utterance in a tongue was useless without an interpreter (1–19), and that a tongue would repel, while prophecy would convert an unbeliever (20–25).

Then follow regulations for the use of these gifts in public (26–33), and the silence of women in the church (34–36), concluding with a strong assertion of the authority at the back of these regulations (37–40). In ch. xv. St. Paul argues with the opponents of the doctrine of the resurrection of the dead. He begins by an appeal to history (1–11). His preaching and their faith had rested from the first on the historical fact of a resurrection (12–34). To one who believed the apostles, and was conscious of the working in his own heart of the powers of the age to come, this one instance was enough to show that the resurrection of the dead was neither impossible (12–15) nor 'contrary to experience' (16–19). In fact the resurrection of all men was as directly involved in Christ's resurrection as their death had been in Adam's fall. It would only be worked out stage by stage, but at last God should be all in all (23–28). Meanwhile, in this hope men seek baptism for the dead, endure a living martyrdom, and nerve themselves to moral effort (29–34).

Passing now from the fact to the manner of the resurrection (35–58), he first points out that the life in each seed passes through death into a new body (35–38), then that appropriate bodies are found even now for very different kinds of life on earth and in heaven (39–41), and then, in the light of these analogies, declares that the life of a man passes into a new and glorious embodiment even through the corruption of the grave (42–44). Our present bodies are made, as Adam's was, out of earthly materials to be the organs of our earthly life. Bodies fit to be the organs of our risen life must be made, as the last Adam's is, out of heavenly materials (44–49). Earthly frames are out of place in the new order, so whether with or without death they must be transformed, that mortality may be swallowed up in life, and death and sin be vanquished by the grace of God. In this hope we can work (50–58).

The letter closes (xvi.) with directions about the collection for the Christian poor at Jerusalem (1–4), an account of St. Paul's plans (5–9), Timothy's (10, 11), Apollos' (12), final exhortations (13–18) and salutation (19–24).

I Corinthians: Chapter by Chapter

	1	Salutation. Exhortation to union. Preaching of the cross.
Preaching the Gospel.	2	Gospel preaching, the highest wisdom, and attested by the Spirit.
Paul and Apollos.	3	Strifes about preachers condemned. The building of God's Church.
	4	Ministers God's stewards. Sufferings of the apostles.
	5	The incestuous person.
Going to law.	6	Censures for going to law. Christians temples of the Holy Spirit.
Marriage.	7	Of marriage and its duties.
	8	Of eating meat offered to idols.
	9	Privileges of an apostle. Support of ministers.

The Lord's Supper.	10	Israel typical of the Christian Church. Temptation. The Lord's Supper.
	11	Women prophesying. Institution of the Lord's Supper.
Spiritual gifts.	12	Spiritual gifts. Christian sympathy.
Love.	13	The excellence of charity [ἀγάπη, love].
	14	Extraordinary gifts.
The resurrection.	15	The resurrection.
	16	Collecting for the poor saints. Exhortations to watchfulness, love, &c.

A library of epistles.

THE SECOND EPISTLE TO THE CORINTHIANS

**St. Paul confirms his disciples in their faith and
vindicates his own character.**

COMMENTARY ON II CORINTHIANS

Shortly after writing the first letter St. Paul was driven from
Ephesus by a riot (Acts xix.). After staying but a short time
in Troas his deep anxiety to learn what reception his letter
had met with hurries him on into Macedonia, and there at last
Titus meets him (vii. 6). The news on the main point was altogether good. His messenger had been well received (vii. 13), the
Church had eagerly cleared herself of all complicity in the great
offence (vii. 7–11), and had excommunicated the offender 5–11).
So the strain is relaxed and the Apostle's heart overflows with
thanksgiving. But a root of evil still remained among them, and
even while he gives thanks he warns them of dangers (vi. 14) and
of punishment in store for the impenitent on his arrival (xiii. 2).
But this is not all. He had gained his point; but to do it he had
had to strain the bond that united him to his converts almost
to bursting, and he felt that a personal coolness had sprung up
between them (vii. 2, xii. 15) which his unscrupulous opponents
had been turning to their own account. So, though almost at
their doors, he cannot come to them till he has poured out his
whole heart toward them, telling them all his hopes and fears,

and with tremendous irony picking up, for a contest in boasting, the gauntlet which his calumniators had thrown down.

After the salutation (i. 1, 2) the Epistle opens with a thanksgiving for the consolation which attends Christian suffering (3–7) arising out of his own experience in the terrible crisis through which he had just passed in Ephesus, and of the confidence in God's protection which that crisis had been sent to deepen (8–11), a confidence grounded on a conscience void of offence towards God and towards them (12–14). He had indeed disappointed them of the double visit he had led them to expect. But he had not acted out of mere fickleness; as the herald of God's faithfulness to His promises he could not so trifle with his word (15–22). His change of plan came, as his letter had done, out of his desire to spare them a second painful interview (23—ii. 4). The chief offender had suffered enough now; it would be well to forgive him (5–11). Returning from this digression he describes his journey northwards to Troas and the restlessness which hurried him on, in spite of promising openings for work, into Macedonia to meet Titus (12, 13). And then he breaks off once more into thanksgiving to God for leading His ministers in triumph in Christ, and for the power for life or for death of the word faithfully spoken as in His sight (14–17).

These words form the starting-point of a long digression on the characteristics of the Christian ministry (iii. 1—vi. 10), as exemplified by the true apostles. Their converts are their credentials (iii. 1–3) written on their hearts by the Spirit of God, open for all the world to read. Awful as is the responsibility of the work, God gives strength to fulfil it. Its true function is to impart life (4–6). The glory that invests it transcends that which shone on the face of Moses (7–11) and needs no veil to hide its fading. Its ministers never leave the presence of the LORD, and reflect with increasing power the glory on which they gaze (12–18). The veil that hides the glory from some lies on their own blinded hearts, and not on the message delivered in all honesty by men entirely devoted to the service of the LORD (iv. 1–6). In themselves they are but mortal men, dying continually after the pattern of Jesus. But the fear of death could not silence men who believed in the God who had raised Jesus (7–15) and who had already given them an earnest in the Spirit of an eternal vesture, which would satisfy all their present yearnings (16—v. 5), making them long to be at home with their LORD, and watchful from moment to moment to be pleasing to Him, before whom they must one day give an account of the use made of their bodies (6-10). The secret of their devotion lies in the love of Christ which they are commissioned to proclaim (11-15). The reconciliation which they minister comes from God. Its home is in Christ (16-19). In His name they plead the fact of the atonement (20, 21), and witness to the reality of the power of present deliverance (vi. 1, 2), proving by their demeanour in all the circumstances of their ministry that their commission comes from God (3-10).

Coming back from this digression to face the actual dangers that threatened the Corinthian Church, Paul pleads with them for a return of perfect confidence (11-13) and for resolute consecration in view of the dangers of pollution from intercourse with the heathen world (14—vii. 1). But the most pressing danger is of estrangement from him, and so he turns to plead with them by his intense affection for them and his confidence in them (2-4). This confidence had been signally justified by the news brought by Titus, which had caused him joy even though it told of their sorrow. For that sorrow had been according to God, and gave proof of real zeal for the Apostle (5-12), justifying his confidence, and inspiring affection in the heart of Titus (13-16).

From this record of the past he passes to subjects connected with his approaching visit; first to the collection for the poor saints at Jerusalem, which it was important that he should find completed on his arrival (viii., ix.). He tells them first of the noble example set by Macedonia (viii. 1-7) and pleads with them by the example of Christ (8, 9), illustrating the limits of generosity from the account of the gathering of the manna (10-15). He introduces his commissioners to them (16-24) and explains the necessity for their visit, to prevent any chance of the failure of his boasting on their behalf (ix. 1-5), concluding with an exposition of the law, and the source, and the fruits of liberality (6-15). This was a difficult subject to handle, because St. Paul was more anxious about the spirit than the amount of the collection. The next subject was even more delicate. A violent personal attack had been made on him by certain rival teachers. He begins by pleading with them not to drive him to take strong measures (x. 1, 2). He has the power (3-6). His authority is undeniably derived from the LORD Himself, and he is prepared to be as strong in act as in his written word (7-11). In contrast with rivals who puffed themselves, and were acting out of their proper sphere, the bounds of his jurisdiction certainly included them, and the LORD gave him his credentials (12-18). His anxiety for them betrayed him into folly. O that they would be as patient with him as with the false doctrine of his rivals. His claims were at least as great as theirs (xi. 1-6). No doubt he had refused to let them support him (7-11). Let his rivals show their sincerity by following his example. A pretended zeal for righteousness was no sign that they were not ministers of Satan (12-15). At this point ' the folly' that he had tried to restrain bursts out. If others boast, so will he. They will bear with him (16-20). He can match his rivals in their claims to Jewish distinctions. He can leave them far behind in the long roll of the sufferings which marked him as a minister of Christ (21-33). He had had his visions, but he would speak rather of his thorn, and what the LORD had told him about that (xii. 1-9). From that they could learn the secret of this extraordinary boasting (10). Coming back once more to them, and the approaching visit, he apologizes for this outburst, begging their pardon for refusing support from them for himself (11-13). He will not change his method (14, 15). Neither directly nor by others has he made a profit out of them (16-18). This is no apology. It is only an effort to save himself the humiliation of having to put the unrepentant to shame (19-21). Let them be warned in time. If driven to it he will use the power of the Risen Christ (xiii. 1-4). But their repentance would be far better than any opportunity for the demonstration of his power (5-10).

The Epistle closes with a few parting exhortations to love and peace, ending with the Grace (11-14).

II CORINTHIANS: CHAPTER BY CHAPTER

Divine comfort.	1	Encouragement under troubles. Paul's affection for the Corinthians.
	2	Treatment of a penitent. Success of Paul's ministry.
Law and Gospel.	3	Ministry of the law and the gospel contrasted.
	4	Paul's comfort in his afflictions, and . prospects of future glory.
The Judgment seat. Reconciliation.	5	Paul's hope of immortale glory. A future judgment a motive for fidelity. Constraining power of the love of Christ. The "new creature." Doctrine of reconciliation.
	6	Exhortation to receive the gospel. A faithful and laborious ministry. Christians and idolaters must not be united.
Purity.	7	Exhortation to purity. Godly sorrow.
	8	Liberality of the Macedonian churches.
Christian liberality.	9	Christian liberality enforced.
	10	The Apostle's weapons not carnal. Apostolic authority. Paul's bodily presence weak. His unwillingness to boast.
	11	Paul's zeal and disinterestedness. His labors and sufferings.
Paul's visions.	12	Paul's visions and revelations.
Self-examination.	13	Stubborn offenders threatened. Self-examination enforced. Exhortation to Christian harmony.

THE EPISTLE TO THE GALATIANS

St. Paul maintains that we are justified by faith and not by rites.

COMMENTARY ON THE EPISTLE TO THE GALATIANS

Galatia was evangelized (Acts xvi. 6) by St. Paul *c.* 51 A.D., and revisited (Acts xviii. 23) *c.* 54 A.D. The warmhearted Celts gave him an enthusiastic welcome on his first appearance among them (Gal. iv. 15). But even before his second visit signs of serious moral danger had begun to show themselves (Gal. v. 21). This letter (c. 57 A.D.) is wrung out of St. Paul by the news of a wholesale defection from the truth of the Gospel in favor of a return to the bondage of the Jewish Law. The Epistle was probably written after 2 Corinthians and before the Epistle to the Romans, perhaps from Macedonia.

After a salutation which helps to prepare us for what is coming by an emphatic statement of the Apostle's authority, and of the redemption wrought by Jesus Christ (i. 1–5), St. Paul indignantly rebukes the Galatians for the lightness with which they had parted with the gospel he had delivered to them (6–9). Then, as the attack on his teaching was bound up with an attack on his authority, he proves, step by step, his independence of the original apostles in his gospel (10–12) by the historical fact of his life as a persecutor (13, 14), his conversion (15–17), and his first short visit to Jerusalem (18–24), telling them how he had resisted the pressure which would have forced circumcision on Titus (ii. 1–5) and how his special sphere of work among the Gentiles had received cordial recognition (6–10), and, lastly, how he had been forced to rebuke even St. Peter for his time-serving at Antioch (11–14). In giving the grounds for this rebuke he passes from the defence of himself to his theology. Jewish Christians had acknowledged their inability to work out their own salvation through the Law. They had taken their stand as sinners by the side of the Gentiles that they might be justified by faith in Christ (15, 16). This step must not be retracted (17, 18). The New Life did not, could not, come from the Law, else Christ had died for no purpose (19–21).

He then turns directly to the Galatians and argues out the whole theological position with them. He appeals to the memory of their own conversion. They had not earned their new life, nor the gifts by which it had been accompanied, by legal obedience; they had grasped them by faith, as Abraham had done (iii. 1–6). The true child of Abraham is known by his faith (7–9). Those who take their stand on legal obedience are subject to the curse of the Law for their failures. The redemption from that curse in Christ brings the blessing of Abraham within reach of the Gentiles (10–14). The Law had no power to affect the conditions of the promise already made to Abraham and his seed (15–18). Its object was to make men feel the slavery of sin and so prepare them for the fulfilment of the promise (19–22). This transitory function has been abolished by the appearance of Christ (23–25). Jew and Gentile alike are now sons of God in Christ (26–29). God has Himself declared our minority at an end (iv. 1–5), giving us the Spirit of His Son (6, 7). Such is the position from which the Galatians are in danger of falling back (8–11). So the Apostle pleads with them by the memory of all that they had been to each other to remain true to him and his gospel (12–20), and gives them yet another illustration of the superiority of the Gospel to the Law drawn from the allegory latent in the story of the two sons of Abraham (21–31).

Passing now from argument to command he tells them plainly that they were forfeiting Christ by going back to the Law (v. 1–6) in deference to false guides (7–12). Let them beware however of supposing that they were set free by the Gospel to please themselves. The love of the Gospel was the fulfilment of the Law. Surrender to the Spirit brought with it freedom not only from the dominion of the Law but also from the lusts of the flesh (13–26). Sympathy must be the mark of the Christian in all his relations (vi. 1–6). We reap according to our sowing (7–10). Then, taking the pen into his own hand, he adds in a postscript yet one more warning against their deceivers (11–13); one more declaration of the power of the Cross (14–16); one more personal appeal (17); and then closes with the Grace.

GALATIANS: CHAPTER BY CHAPTER

A divine commission.	1	Reproof for being attracted by error. Paul's commission to preach the Gospel.
	2	Paul's visit to Jerusalem. His reproof to Peter for temporizing. Justification by faith. The life of faith.
Justification by faith.	3	Reproof for instability. Justification by faith. The law a guide to Christ.
Adoption. **Hagar and Sarah.**	4	The adoption of sons. If a son, then an heir of God. The weak and beggarly elements. Allegory of Hagar and Sarah.
	5	Christian liberty enforced. Brotherly love commended. Fruits of the flesh and Spirit.
	6	Tenderness towards offenders. Christian liberality enforced. Glorying in the Cross. "A new creature."

THE EPISTLE TO THE EPHESIANS

A treatise by St. Paul on the power of divine grace.

COMMENTARY ON THE EPISTLE TO THE EPHESIANS

The thoughts which had been stirred by the danger in Colossae had clearly an importance for a much wider and more influential circle than could be touched even if the Colossians were diligently to circulate their own Epistle among their neighbours in the little Phrygian valley of the Lycus both in Laodicea and Hierapolis. And further, there were some elements in the conception of the place which the Church, by virtue of her organic connexion with the Christ, occupies in relation to the whole counsel of God, that could not be fully developed in the stir and stress of controversy. Accordingly St. Paul sends by the same messenger a second letter, in which he expounds in detail the work which the Church has been elected to perform in the world and the relation in which the various members stand one to another in the unity of the one body. These thoughts were no doubt not entirely new to St. Paul, but they must have matured and deepened as he watched from its centre at Rome the practical working of a world-embracing empire, and gave thanks for the success of his mission to Jerusalem in averting the threatened breach between Jewish and Gentile Christians.

The letter was not, according to the true text (Eph. i. 1, R.V. marg.), addressed exclusively to any particular Church. It seems to have been, like the First Epistle of St. Peter and the Revelation, in some sort a circular letter, carried round by its bearer from church to church in Asia Minor. For instance, it is probable that this is the letter which the Colossians are to expect from Laodicea (Col. iv. 16). In any case the Church at Ephesus must have been the most important of the Churches to which it was sent, and the centre from which copies of it would be most freely circulated; and so it may not unnaturally have been regarded as in a special sense addressed to that Church. But it seems difficult to imagine that if St. Paul had been in any sense concentrating his attention on them his work should show no trace of the peculiar intimacy that existed between them (Acts xx. 17 ff.). And this at least is certain, that none of St. Paul's Epistles reads so little like a private letter and so much like a theological treatise.

After the salutation (i. 1, 2) the Epistle begins with a solemn ascription of blessing to God for the blessings bestowed on His chosen in Christ (3-7), especially in opening their eyes to see the goal of His eternal purpose (8-10) and in gathering Jew and Gentile into a present share in His inheritance (11-14). Then, still standing as it were at the head of his people, with his face turned towards God, he pours out his thanksgiving for their faith, and prays that their eyes may be opened to the full grandeur of their true position (15-18) and to the power which had been operative in the enthronement of their Head (19-23), and in their own deliverance from the death of sin (ii. 1-4) to a new life of active obedience to the will of God (5-10).

After this he turns to his readers and, in what we may call the first section of the Epistle proper (ii. 11—iii. 21), pleads with them to bear in mind these facts of their true position (11-22), first reminding them of the gulf which had in times past shut them off both from their fellow men and from God (11, 12); then showing them how this gulf had been bridged by the Incarnation and the Passion (13-15), the Resurrection and the Ascension of Christ Jesus (16-18), and finally working out under the figure of a spiritual temple their present living union with their brothers and with God (19-22). His exhortation is on the point of culminating in intercession when he pauses for a moment to explain to them the special relation in which he stood both to them and to this grand new revelation which God had granted to their age and generation as a step towards the working out of His eternal purpose (iii. 1–12). This delay is due to a fear lest the fact of his imprisonment might prove a stumbling-block in the way of their faith in his gospel. This once removed (13), he can turn once more to the Father and pray Him to strengthen them to enter into and be transfigured by this revelation of His love (14–19). The section closes with a doxology (20, 21).

In the second section of the Epistle (iv. 1–vi. 9), St. Paul works out in detail the practical consequences of the truths developed in the first. The first claim which the recognition of our unity makes upon us is for humility and meekness (iv. 1–6). But while each is thus bound to keep himself in check for the sake of the rest, each has his own gift to contribute towards the perfect development of the whole organism (7–16). In order to fulfil these claims each man is called upon to break decisively with his evil past (17–19), and to put on the new man (20–24). He then illustrates what is meant by this general direction in certain definite points of character and conduct (25–v. 5), and enforces the necessity for Christian consistency by the thought of the power of the Christian example (6–14). Christians must therefore be watchful and zealous in the evil days, sensible and sober even in the midst of spiritual joy (15–21). In fulfilling the natural relationships of a home they must bear in mind the divine source of all authority; so the husband will find a perfect pattern of devotion, and the wife of submission, in the interchange of surrender and obedience between Christ and His Church (22–33). Children will learn the secret of obedience and parents the secret of discipline in the LORD (vi. 1–4); servants will render a perfect service and masters learn to respect their subordinates in the constant recognition of His presence (5–9).

The last section of the Epistle contains a description of the armor which is provided in Christ for the Christian for the great spiritual battle which he is called upon to fight in carrying on his Master's work in the world (10–20). A few words commending the bearer of the letter follow (21, 22), and then the Epistle closes with a blessing and the Grace (23, 24).

EPHESIANS: CHAPTER BY CHAPTER

"Chosen in Him."	1	Election and adoption by grace. The mystery of God's will. Paul's prayer for the Ephesians.
"He is our peace."	2	The quickening power of grace. Christ our reconciliation. Christ the church's foundation.
	3	Paul's honor in being called to preach the gospel to the Gentiles. Further prayer for the Ephesians.
Unity.	4	Exhortations to unity. The gift of the apostles, &c., for edifying the Church. Exhortations to moral virtues.
	5	Practical godliness. Duties of husbands and wives.
Whole armor of God.	6	Duties of children, servants and masters. The Christian's armor.

THE EPISTLE TO THE PHILIPPIANS

St. Paul sets forth the beauty of Christian kindness.

COMMENTARY ON THE EPISTLE TO THE PHILIPPIANS

Philippi was a Roman military colony commanding the great high road between Europe and Asia, and endowed by Augustus with special privileges of citizenship. The Church there was the earliest founded by St. Paul in Europe (Acts xvi. 11–40). His first visit terminated abruptly, and it seems probable that St. Luke was left behind to take charge of the infant community. St. Paul himself, however, was not forgotten; the Church, though poor (2 Cor. viii. 2), was generous and grateful, and found occasion to send him supplies, not only while he remained in their neighborhood, but after he had moved on to Corinth (Phil. iv. 15, 16). He passed through Philippi six years later (Acts xx. 2) on his way from Ephesus to Corinth, and again on his return (Acts xx. 6) from Corinth to Jerusalem. And when the news of his removal to Rome reached Philippi they sent one of their number, Epaphroditus (25), to minister to him in their name.

The strain of work in the capital proved too severe, and Epaphroditus had to be invalided home (26–30). And this is the letter that St. Paul sent by his hand to his affectionate friends. Its main purpose is to express his gratitude and affection, and to cheer them up under the disappointment of his own protracted

357

imprisonment, and of the failure of their effort to help him. At the same time he uses the opportunity to warn them against false teaching, and to exhort them to unity, to humility, and to a vigorous striving after holiness.

The Epistle opens, after the salutation (i. 1, 2), with a joyful thanksgiving (3–8) based on the sacrifices they had made for the spread of the gospel, and on his own assurance of their ultimate perfecting, leading to a prayer on their behalf (9–11) for more love in growing light and developed fruitfulness. Then addressing himself directly to them, he takes each of the darkest facts of the situation and makes it minister to joy (12–30): his own imprisonment (12, 13), the increased activity of his rivals (14–20), the danger in which he stood (21–26), and the trials through which in any case they must pass before he could see them again (27–30). Passing from an exhortation to unity in the face of these inevitable trials he appeals to them with the whole weight of his own personal affection to overcome party spirit in the humility taught by the perfect example of Jesus Christ (ii. 1–11). Then in view of God's presence within them (12–18) he exhorts them to perseverance in Christian effort that they may prove worthy children, a blessing to the world and a glory to himself.

At this point St. Paul leaves doctrine and exhortation to tell them of his plans. He hopes to send Timothy to bring back news of them, as soon as the issue of the trial is clear (19–24). Meanwhile their own messenger Epaphroditus is returning home. He has fallen ill in doing noble work (25–30).

The letter seems now on the point of closing (iii. 1), but the sense of the danger to which they might be exposed from false teachers forces from him an explicit statement of the truths which they denied. So he warns the Philippians, almost fiercely, against giving up the spiritual circumcision for the carnal (2–4). He points out the worthlessness of legal (5–7), and the ceaseless effort after holiness which sprang from laying hold of evangelical righteousness (8–16); and in stern contrast with those whose sense-bound imaginations could not rise to the thought of anything but a material purification, he reminds them that a Christian's citizenship is even now in heaven, and that the transfiguration of the body is included in his hope (17–21). Passing from controversy, he adds a few brief counsels for a peaceful life

(iv. 1–9). Then after a grateful acknowledgment of their liberality (10–18) and a prayer for them, culminating in a doxology (19, 20), the Epistle closes with parting salutations (21, 22) and the Grace (23).

PHILIPPIANS: CHAPTER BY CHAPTER

"Making request with joy."	1	The apostle's thankfulness and prayer for the Philippians. The gospel furthered by his bonds. He rejoices in the diffusion of the gospel by others.
"The mind of Christ."	2	He exhorts to a consistent conversation. Exhortations to humility and kindness. Christ set forth as a pattern. Working out salvation. Holding forth the word of life. Recommendation of Epaphroditus.
"Beware of dogs."	3	Warnings against teachers of circumcision. His former zeal as a Pharisee. His estimation of the worth of Christ. His pursuit after Christian perfection. "We look for the Savior."
"Stand fast."	4	"Stand fast in the LORD!" "Rejoice always!" Whatsoever things are true … honest … just … pure … lovely … of good report … think on these things. How to be abased, and how to abound.

THE EPISTLE TO THE COLOSSIANS

**St. Paul warns his disciples against errors,
and exhorts to certain duties.**

COMMENTARY ON THE EPISTLE TO THE COLOSSIANS

The Epistle to the Colossians was the result of a visit from Epaphras, the evangelist of the Church in Colossae (7, 8). From him St. Paul had learnt the faith, and the dangers which threatened the faith, of a community with which he was personally unacquainted (ii. 1). The difficulty was a subtle one. It sprang from a deep consciousness of sin and from an earnest effort to attain moral purification by mechanical means, the careful observance of external ordinances (ii. 16) and ascetic restrictions (ii. 20), coupled with special devotion to a host of angelic mediators. This new danger, though in some respects the exact opposite of the danger which had proved so serious in Galatia, sprang, as that had done, out of Jewish influence. Its attractiveness was due not only to the satisfaction which it offered to the craving after sanctification, but also to the apparent completeness of the scheme of the universe with which it was connected and the show it made of deep speculation and practical wisdom. To meet the danger St. Paul is driven to bring forth, out of the treasure-house of Christ, stores of wisdom and knowledge hitherto almost unsuspected. Christ is in His own Person the one principle of the unity of the universe, and the principle of evil cannot be directly identified with anything that He has made. When the members of the Church learn to recognise their present union with their risen and ascended Head they possess the secret of perfect sanctification.

In the thanksgiving which, as usual, directly follows the opening salutation (i. 1, 2), St. Paul lays stress first on the inherent fruitfulness of the gospel message (3–6); then he tells them how he came to be interested in them (7, 8), and how he prayed for their growth in the knowledge of God's will so that their lives might be worthy, fruitful, strong, and full of gratitude to the Father for transferring them to the kingdom of His Son (9–14), who is His own Image, the Author and the Goal of all creation (15, 16), pre-eminent not only in the old order but in the new (17, 18), because the Father willed that He should be the abiding home of all divine perfection and the reconciliation of the universe (19, 20), with a power which had already begun its work in them (21, 22), and which required from them nothing but faithful adherence to the hope of the one world-embracing gospel (23). St. Paul was the appointed recipient and guardian of this new revelation of the universality of the gospel; so he passes naturally from this mention of it to explain his own relation to it in suffering for it, in working it out into all its consequences, and in striving to bring it home to the heart and mind of every man (24–29). And so they could understand how it was that he took a prayerful interest even in those who like themselves had never seen him (ii. 1–5).

After this introduction he is able, without seeming to intrude, to plead for and to enforce a fundamental truth, which some of their own teachers were forgetting, that the secret of holiness is to be found, not in cunningly-devised external regulations, but in union with Christ in all the glory of His true nature, and in the realization of our share in the fruits of His death and resurrection (6–19). The consequence of this for us is that we are free from all mechanical restrictions (20–23), and called even now to live with Christ in God (iii. 1–4). In the light of this revelation of our true state we can work out our own salvation by doing to death every evil inclination (5–8) and clothing ourselves in our divine ideal (9–11), especially cherishing all qualities that tend to union with our brethren (12–14), in constant remembrance of the peace and the power of Christ both in public worship and in every act of daily life (15–17).

Leaving the general exposition of Christian duty he describes the special duties of wives and husbands (18–19), children and parents (20, 21), slaves and masters (22—iv. 1); and then he calls on all Christians for prayerfulness and prudence in their relations with the heathen world outside (2–6). The letter ends with a commendation of its bearers (7–9); greetings from his companions to the Colossians (10–14); a special message from himself to the Laodiceans (15–17); and the Grace (18).

COLOSSIANS: CHAPTER BY CHAPTER

"God's dear Son."	1	Paul gives thanks for the faith and love of the Colossians. He prays for their growth in grace. Glory of Christ as the Son of God – LORD – Creator – and Head of the Church. The mystery of God.
	2	Exhortations to constancy. Cautions against vain philosophy. "You hath He quickened." Abolition of the ritual law.
"Risen with Christ."	3	"Risen with Christ." Mortification of corruptions. Mutual duties of believers. Relative duties. Masters and servants.
	4	Exhortation to prayers. Grace of speech. Paul's fellow-laborers.

THE FIRST EPISTLE TO THE THESSALONIANS

**St. Paul exhorts his disciples to continue in the
faith and in holy conversation.**

COMMENTARY ON I THESSALONIANS

After the salutation (i. 1), St. Paul begins this Epistle with thanksgiving (2–10) for the certainty of the Thessalonians' election, and for the effect produced on others by the example of their conversion. He recalls (ii. 1–12) the memories of his stay among them, reminding them, perhaps in self-defence against Jewish slanders, of the courage and sincerity, the tenderness and self-devotion, with which he had exhorted them to walk worthily of the GOD who was calling them to His Kingdom. This thought gives rise to a fresh thanksgiving (13–16) for the power of God's Word in their hearts, and for the persecutions in which they were sharing with the Churches in Judea, and with God's messengers in every age.

Then coming back to his own personal relations with them 17–iii. 13), he tells them of the pain (ii. 17–20) which separation from them had caused him, of his object (iii. 1–5) in sending Timothy on his late visit, of his gratitude to God (6–8) for their constancy, and of his prayers (9, 10) for another sight of them. The section closes with a solemn prayer (11–13) for his own restoration to them, and for their sanctification. Personal meetings being for the present denied, written admonitions and instructions (iv., v.)

must take their place. So he exhorts them to growth in grace (iv. 1, 2) by personal chastity (3–8), love of the brethren (9, 10), and unobtrusive diligence (10–12). He instructs them in the true relation of the doctrine of the Second Advent (iv. 13—v. 11) to the consolation of the bereaved (iv. 13–18), and to the warning (v. 1–6) and edification (7–11) of survivors.

Paul adds in conclusion short, far-reaching exhortations (12–24) to the laity (12, 13), the clergy (14, 15), and to the whole Church (16–22), culminating in a prayer and a promise (23, 24). Salutations, instructions, and the Grace (25–28) bring the letter to a close.

I Thessalonians: Chapter by Chapter

"Work of faith; labor of love."	1	Commendations of the faith and love of the Thessalonians. The happy influence of their example.
	2	The apostle's faithful, sincere, tender, and disinterested labors. The opposition of the Jews.
"Our glory and joy."	3	Paul's care to the Thessalonians.
	4	Exhortations to holiness. Christ's second coming.
	5	Christ's coming a motive to vigilance. Esteem for those who labor in the Lord. Precepts for Christian conduct.

THE SECOND EPISTLE TO THE THESSALONIANS

**St. Paul corrects an error concerning the speedy
coming of Christ a second time.**

COMMENTARY ON II THESSALONIANS

In the interval that separated the Second Epistle from the First,
the Church suffered severely from persecution (i. 4), and the
prospect of an immediate return of the LORD fostered an
unhealthy excitement (ii. 2) and seemed to countenance improvi-
dent idleness (iii. 6). Traditions of the Apostle's teaching, his 'first
letter', or at least a letter purporting to be his (iii. 17, cf. ii. 2), had
been used to fan the excitement.

After the salutation (i. 1, 2), he gives thanks (3–10) for their
steadfastness under persecution, and for the certainty of righteous retribution in the day of the LORD. Thanksgiving then passes
into prayer (11, 12) for their perfecting. In the main body of the
letter (ii. 1–12) he restates the doctrine of the day of the LORD,
to guard against misrepresentation and to allay their excitement
(1, 2). Before that day could come the revelation of evil must be
perfected (3, 4), and the existing check on that revelation must be
removed (5–7). When it did come it would bring with it a decisive
manifestation of the judgment which was already at work (8–12).
The thought of judgment leads once more to thanksgiving for
God's favor towards them (13, 14), to an appeal to them to stand
firm (15), and to a prayer (16, 17) for their consolation. The Epistle

concludes (iii.) with a request for their intercessions (iii. 1, 2), a declaration of faith in, and a prayer to the LORD of the hearts of men (3–5), and finally with an emphatic assertion of the duty (6–16) of subordination and of work. Verses 17 and 18 contain the Apostle's signature, the Grace.

II THESSALONIANS: CHAPTER BY CHAPTER

	1	Further commendations of the faith and love of the Thessalonians. The *Apocalupsis*.
Mystery of Iniquity.	2	The great apostasy. Destruction of the Man of Sin ("That Wicked"). Thanksgiving for the salvation of the Thessalonians.
"Stand fast."		Exhortations to stand fast.
	3	Paul asks for prayer that the "word of the LORD" may have free course. Exhortation to "patient waiting." "Be not weary in well-doing."

THE FIRST EPISTLE TO TIMOTHY

St. Paul was a mentor to Timothy who he regarded as a spiritual son.

COMMENTARY ON I TIMOTHY

In the course of these later journeyings, St. Paul must also at some time or other have reached Ephesus, and on his departure have felt it necessary to leave Timothy behind him to check the growth of certain unprofitable forms of speculation. He did not anticipate a long absence from the city (iii. 14). Still, as a delay might occur, he writes to him, perhaps from Macedonia (i. 3), to give him counsel and encouragement in the fulfilment of his duty. The special tendency he was required to check was due certainly in part, and perhaps altogether, to Jewish influence. Traces of it were to be found even in Crete (Tit. i. 14, iii. 9). It may perhaps be simply a later stage of the same error which St. Paul had combated in the germ at Colossae. It contained two elements; one purely fanciful, busied with 'endless genealogies' and 'old-wives' fables'; the other pretentiously practical, even while it wasted all its strength in the effort to define the minutest details of legal obligation (1 Tim. i. 7, vi. 4, 20; 2 Tim. ii. 14; Tit. i. 14). There was nothing solid or healthy in such stuff, and if it led to any neglect of the simplest moral obligations it was fraught with serious danger to the faith.

This was the danger immediately pressing (i. 3). There was a more serious danger looming in the future. Men would soon be found to brand as evil various parts even of God's own creation (iv. 1-5), and Timothy's bias towards asceticism (iv. 8, v. 23) might give this false doctrine a spurious attractiveness.

After greeting his 'true son' (i. 1, 2), St. Paul reminds him of his commission to keep in check the frivolous speculations and foolish legalism of some teachers (3-11) who endangered the simple truth of the grace of God which was illustrated so clearly by St. Paul's own experience (12-17); and exhorts him to watchfulness by the memory of his ordination and by two warning examples of failure (18-20).

After this introduction he begins by giving special directions (ii., iii.) for the ordering of public worship and for the character and conduct of ministers. He exhorts the Church to pray for every member of the human race in the light of the universal purpose of God and the all-inclusive ransom (ii. 1-7). He bids women be modest in dress, and silent in the public teaching of the congregation (8-15). He details the special qualities required of those who fill official positions in the Church (iii. 1-13), and shows The peculiar sacredness which belongs to each congregation as a Pillar in the spiritual Temple of the Truth (11-16).

In the next section (iv.) St. Paul warns Timothy of the approach of a dangerous form of false teaching (1-5), and bids him meet the danger in himself and others by spiritual rather than bodily discipline (6-10), and by special, attention to his own growth and teaching (11-16). Then follows a section (v.—vi. 2) containing a series of hints to guide him in his relations with the old and young of both sexes (v. 1, 2), with special reference to widows (3-16), to elders (17-20), to the administration of discipline (21-25), and to the relation of Christian slaves to their masters, heathen or Christian (vi. 1, 2).

The last section of the Epistle (3-21) contains a description of the dangers to which believers, and especially teachers, were exposed from the love of money (3-10); an earnest exhortation to Timothy to keep clear of this and other dangers, based on the great facts of the Christian faith and hope (11-16); a message to the rich (17-19); then yet one more appeal to Timothy (20, 21) and the Grace.

I Timothy: Chapter by Chapter

The law.	1	"Unto mine own son in the faith." Right use and end of the law. Paul a pattern of divine mercy. Hymeneus and Alexander apostates.
	2	Prayers to be made for all men. Female dress.
Bishops and Deacons. **The Church.**	3	Qualifications of bishops and deacons. Conduct of their wives. The pillar and ground of the truth.
Apostasy.	4	The apostasy. Duties of the gospel minister.
	5	Directions respecting widows. The "elders" to be cared for.
	6	Duties of servants. On contentment and covetousness. Solemn charge to Timothy.

THE SECOND EPISTLE TO TIMOTHY

St. Paul writes again to Timothy, from prison in Rome.

COMMENTARY ON II TIMOTHY

The circumstances under which this Epistle was composed confer on it a peculiar pathos, and stamp the mark of heroic grandeur on its indomitable trust. It was written from Rome after the first stage of a new trial (iv. 16). St. Paul was in serious danger, and some even of his trusted friends had deserted him (iv. 10). In the bitterness of his isolation he longs for the presence of his `darling son' (i. 2) and writes to bid him come at once and bring Mark with him (iv. 11). This is his immediate object in writing, but the contents of his letter are mainly determined by another consideration. As he writes the sword of the executioner is hanging over his head, and the blow may fall at any moment. So he takes this opportunity, which may so well be his last, to give full expression to all the affectionate solicitude of his loving heart for one who had been for many years his faithful companion. Words written under such conditions, especially if they were sealed with the blood of the writer, must have had a peculiar power to nerve one who was still young for the work he had to do, and who perhaps was constitutionally disinclined to stand alone, to take up and wear the mantle that was now falling from the shoulders of his aged, deserted, and yet still triumphant, master.

After greeting his beloved child (i. 1, 2), he gives thanks for the memory of his faith inherited, like St. Paul's, from his forefathers (3–5); bids him stir up his gift and bear witness bravely (6–11); and tells him the secret of faithful guardianship (12–14). Then after a short notice of desertions, and of the loyalty of Onesiphorus (15–18), he appeals to Timothy to be diligent in teaching 1, 2), in self-discipline (3–7), in enforcing the full Christian creed for which he himself was suffering (8–13). He calls on him to keep strictly to what is solid and profitable in teaching, as in the presence of God (14–19), and since He can find a use for any vessel in His House if only it be clean (20, 21), he bids him aim at purity of heart, avoiding contentions that he might win souls (22–26). He then tells him of dangers ahead (iii. 1–9) from false teachers who will win temporary success. He reminds him of the sufferings that they had shared in early days (10–13), and bids him be faithful to the lessons of his childhood, the Scriptures that were given to fit God's people for their work (14–17). Then with the utmost solemnity he adjures him to be diligent in proclaiming his message, even though truth should be less popular than fiction (iv. 1–5), and all the more because his own work is done (6–8).

The letter closes with an urgent summons to Timothy to come to Rome, giving him various commissions to fulfil by the way (9–13), warning him against an enemy, and announcing the issue of the first stage of his trial (14–18). The last verses (19–22) contain messages to and from various friends, and the Grace.

II Timothy: Chapter by Chapter

Early advantages.	1	Timothy's early advantages. Paul exhorts him not to be ashamed of the gospel. Life and immortality brought to light. Desertion of Phygelius and Hermogenes. Kindness of Onesiphorus.
Duties of a minister.	2	The good soldier of Jesus Christ. Timothy to avoid false teachers, such as Hymeneus and Philetus. Character of "the servant of the LORD."
The last days.	3	The perilous times of the last days. Timothy's early knowledge of the Scriptures.
Salutations.	4	Another solemn charge to Timothy. "I have fought a good fight!" Timothy to join Paul at Rome. Salutations from Christian brethren at Rome.

THE EPISTLE TO TITUS

**St. Paul encourages Titus in the performance
of his ministerial duties.**

COMMENTARY ON THE EPISTLE TO TITUS

At some time during his travels, St. Paul must have visited Crete with Titus in his company. Seeing the dangers to which the faith was exposed in the island from the lack of organization in the Church there, and being unable to stay long enough himself to do all that was required, he had left Titus behind 'to remedy defects and appoint presbyters in the several cities' (i. 5). St. Paul, however, had no intention of setting Titus to work there permanently, and suitable messengers being to be had (iii. 13), he sent this letter by them partly to give his 'true son' some hints for his guidance in the difficult task that had been laid upon him, and partly to bid him come to Nicopolis as soon as Artemas or Tychicus came to relieve him (iii. 12).

After a salutation, expanded to contain a full description of the faith which it was St. Paul's glory to serve (i. 1–4), he reminds Titus of his commission to ordain elders (5–9) and to correct refractory members in the Cretan Church (10–16). He then describes the character which he should aim at producing in the various members of his flock, whether freemen (ii. 1–8) or slaves (9, 10), remembering the educational value of the gospel message (11–14). In fulfilling his own office he must be firm (15), insisting on submission to authority, and meekness (iii. 1, 2); teaching meekness by the memory of our natural state, apart from the new life of the gospel (3–7), and deriving firmness from confidence in his message as a matter for practical application to life, and not for quibbling subtilty or self-willed speculation (8–11).

The Epistle closes with a brief notice of the Apostle's plans, parting injunctions, greetings, and the Grace (12–15).

TITUS: CHAPTER BY CHAPTER

Work in Crete.	1	Qualifications for Christian elders or overseers. Character of false teachers.
	2	Exhortations to be given to the aged, to the young, and to servants. Practical influences of the gospel.
The grace of God.	3	Submission to authorities. Good works enforced. Treatment of heretics. Salutations.

THE EPISTLE TO PHILEMON

St. Paul urges a converted friend to be merciful to a runaway slave.

COMMENTARY ON THE EPISTLE TO PHILEMON

Onesimus, a runaway slave, had been won for Christ in Rome, and was now returning to Colossae, to the duty he had left. St. Paul sends this letter with him to his old master, who chanced to be also one of St. Paul's spiritual children.

After the salutation (1–3), St. Paul gives thanks for the good fruits of Philemon's faith (4–7), and then pleads with all the power of his personal influence for Onesimus, who had run away from his master to find a new master in Christ, and was now coming back to his duty (8–20). He then holds out the prospect of a visit from himself (21, 22), and adds a few greetings from his friends (23, 24) before he closes with the Grace (25).

PHILEMON: SIGNIFICANT VERSES

His love and faith.	v.1	Paul's love to Philemon.
	v.7	Philemon's love to the saints.
	v.9	Paul the aged.
	v.10	Onesimus converted.
The runaway slave.	v.12	Sent back to Philemon by Paul, having run away from his service.
	v.14	Paul's intercession on behalf of Onesimus.

THE EPISTLE TO THE HEBREWS

**This letter, to a congregation of Jewish Christians, maintains
that Christ is the substance of ceremonial law.**

THE ESSENTIAL SUMMARY OF HEBREWS

There are some similarities between the opening verses of
the Gospel of St. John and the beginning of this Epistle. In
both writings, God is at once brought prominently before
us. And both St. John and the writer of the Epistle to the Hebrews
magnify the LORD Jesus Christ and emphasize His divinity.
Indeed, the entire purport of the Epistle, as the entire scope of
the Gospel of John appears to be, is to affirm and demonstrate
the Divinity of Christ.

The second chapter speaks of the "signs, wonders, miracles,
and gifts of the Holy Ghost," in evidence of the great salvation. The third chapter argues that Christ Jesus, "the Apostle
and High Priest of our profession," is counted worthy of more
glory than Moses. The fourth chapter cautions those addressed
to fear lest they should "come short" of the rest spoken of. The
fifth and seventh chapters deal with the Melchizedec priesthood, and show that Abraham is inferior to Melchizedec, and
consequently to Jesus: who, "because He continueth ever, hath
an unchangeable priesthood." The sixth chapter, like the fourth,
warns against apostasy in most solemn words, which cannot be
explained away. The eighth and ninth chapters contrast the old

and the new covenants or testaments; of all, gathering as it were into a nutshell the argument as to the High Prieshood of Christ, which – through chapters 3, 4, 5, 6, and 7 – "Of the things which we have spoken this is the sum." The tenth chapter deals with "sacrifice and offering" under the law, and goes on to tell of the "new and living way"; and encourages those addressed to "draw near with a true heart." The eleventh chapter is the muster roll of the men of faith. The twelfth and thirteenth are mainly taken up with exhortations growing out of what has preceded.

COMMENTARY ON THE EPISTLE TO THE HEBREWS

The title of this Epistle suggests that it was written to the Christian Jews in Palestine. The contents confirm the accuracy of the title. The persons addressed are of Jewish birth feeling the fascination of their national creed and the ritual in which it was embodied. They have long been Christians, having received the Gospel from its first witnesses (ii. 3). But the first generation of their leaders has passed away (xiii. 7), and under the influence of renewed persecution at the hands of their own countrymen, coupled with disappointment because the LORD has not yet come, they are in danger of renouncing their faith in Jesus and returning to Judaism. These conditions would naturally arise in Palestine, *e.g.* after the martyrdom of James the Just in A.D. 62.

The author of the Epistle has withheld his name, and neither the voice of tradition nor of criticism enables us to fill up the blank left by his silence. The phraseology of the Epistle, no less than its elaborate symmetry and polished rhetoric, distinguishes it from the Epistles of St. Paul. It was written in the company of some Italian Christians (xiii. 24), but there is no certain indication of the place of its composition. It begins without any formal salutation.

Analysis
God has in our day crowned all His former utterances by speaking to us in a Son who is higher than the angels; for they, as the references to them in the Psalms prove, are subordinate

377

beings attending on the heirs of salvation, and bidden to do homage to the Firstborn; while He is clothed with divine prerogatives and is called to a throne at His Father's right hand (i. 1–14). This utterance then demands stricter attention from us, who have heard it, than even the utterance made through angels on Sinai (ii. 1–4). For the whole universe is by divine decree subjected not to angels but to man, and the glorification of Jesus is the visible first stage in the working out of that subjection (5–9), even His Passion finding a place in the development as the means of our deliverance from the fear of death and of His own perfecting for His present function as the High Priest of His brethren (10–18). Consider then carefully the position of Jesus as our High Priest. He is the Son set over the household of God in which Moses was but a servant (iii. 1–6). We as members of His household shall do well to take warning from the history of Israel in the wilderness, lest we miss our entrance into rest, as they did, through unbelief (7—iv. 2). For the promised rest is still before us (3–11), and we live under the eye of an all-seeing Judge (12, 13). So let us cling to our creed and boldly claim the help which our High Priest is able and willing to give (14–16). For both of the qualifications for a high-priesthood among men—sympathy arising out of personal experience of human weakness (v. 1–3), and divine appointment (4)—are found in the Risen Christ, as appears from the words of God in the Psalms, and from the record of the Agony in the Garden (5–10). The more special characteristics of His High-Priesthood belong to an advanced stage in Christian education, for which you ought by this time to be more ready than you are (11–14). Still let us leave the rudiments and press on (vi. 1–3), for though God's blessings misused issue in a curse (4–8), we have confidence on your behalf, only we would that hope were as active among you in appropriating your inheritance, as love is in your ministry to your brethren (9–12). You have in the oath of God to Abraham a most solid ground for clinging to the hope which like an anchor links you to your unseen champion (13–20), the High Priest after the order of Melchisedek. What, then, are the characteristics of this High-Priesthood? It is royal, and it is abiding (vii. 1–3); it is superior to the Levitical (4–10), for that is in itself transitory (11–14), belonging to an imperfect dispensation (15–22), and composed of constantly shifting elements (23–25), while this is free from all imperfection of sin or infirmity; it is the eternal office of the divine Son (26–28). It is exercised in heaven in the archetypal tabernacle (viii. 1–5), and is based on the nobler, that is, the new covenant, of which Jeremiah spoke (6–13). The ordinances and the instruments of worship under the first covenant belonged entirely to this world. The Tabernacle and its furniture were material (ix. 1–5); the very arrangement of the Tabernacle declared the imperfection of the revelation, and the sacrifices and ordinances themselves were powerless to effect any but a material cleansing (6–10). Christ, on the other hand, by the blood of His sacrifice can cleanse the conscience itself (11–14). The new covenant is established in His death (15–17), even as the old was ratified, and all that belonged to it cleansed, with the blood of victims (18–22). The scene of His work is the actual presence of God, and His sacrifice needs no repetition (23– 28). The impotence of the former sacrifices is revealed by the fact of their repetition (x. 1–4) and by the substitution of spiritual obedience for them in the Psalmist's prophecy (5–10). Christ's sacrifice, however, is single (11–14), and perfectly effectual (15–18). In the strength of it let us draw nigh to God ourselves and stir up one another to faithfulness (19–25); for our responsibility grows with our privileges (26–31); and you have shown some capacity for endurance (32–34); you will not surely lose heart, with the deliverance promised to faith almost in sight (35–39). Faith has been the mark of the saints in every age (xi. 1, 2). Abel's sacrifice, Enoch's walk with God, Noah's obedience, Abraham's wanderings, and the birth of Isaac, all show the working of faith (3–12) and their longing for a heavenly country (13–16). By faith Abraham offered Isaac, and the patriarchs blessed their children, and Moses was preserved, and the people redeemed from Egypt, and established in Palestine (17–31). In short, God's heroes in every age have been heroes of Faith (32–38), even though they had to wait for us for their perfecting (39, 40).

With their example before you, and with your eyes fixed on the Cross of Jesus, you cannot faint (xii. 1–3). As sons, you must expect to be chastened by your Father (4–13). Only guard against evil in yourselves (14–17). For the Christian Sion is at once more blessed and more awful than Sinai (18–24); and the final shaking of both heaven and earth is at hand (25–29). So do not despise simple duties (xiii. 1–6). Imitate your first teachers (7–9). Beware of being drawn away by strange teaching from union with Jesus in His sacrifice (10–16); submit to your present leaders (17). Pray for us (18, 19); and may God bless you (20, 21).

A few brief notes of news and greeting bring the letter to an end (22–25).

THE EPISTLE TO THE HEBREWS: CHAPTER BY CHAPTER

"Heir of all things."	1	"God hath spoken by His Son." The Son of God contrasted with angels.
	2	Danger of neglecting Christ's salvation. He was humbled only to be exalted.
	3	Christ's superiority to Moses. Caution against an evil heart of unbelief.
	4	Jesus secures a better rest than Joshua. Caution against drawing back. Encouragement to press on, since Christ has previously entered.
Priesthood of Christ.	5	Christ our High Priest. His priesthood after the order of Melchizedec.
	6	Awful nature of apostasy. God's fidelity to His oath and promise.
	7	Superiority of Christ's priesthood, after the order of Melchizedec.
	8	Christ, mediator of a new and better covenant.
Tabernacle and its ordinances.	9	The tabernacle and its ordinances. Christ's sacrifice superseded all others.
"Let us draw near."	10	The sacrifices under the law were but typical. Encouragement to approach God through the Christian High Priest. Cautions against apostasy.
Faith.	11	Definition of faith. Examples of faith.

The Cloud of Witnesses.	12	Perseverance enforced from the cloud of witnesses, and example of Christ. Beneficial effects of Divine chastisement. Esau's reckless contempt of his birthright. Contrast between Mount Sinai and Mount Sion.
Law and Gospel.		The Law superseded by the Gospel.
Christian duties.	13	Exhortations as to: • Brotherly love. • Hospitality. • Sympathy. • Marriage. • Contentment. • Praise. • Submission to pastoral authority. • Stability. • Courage. • Benevolence. Prayer and benediction.

THE EPISTLE OF ST. JAMES

A treatise on the efficacy of faith united with good works.

THE ESSENTIAL SUMMARY OF JAMES

The general opinion is that the leader of the Church in Jerusalem was St. James, known as the 'Brother of the LORD'. Tradition holds that he is also the author of this Epistle. The Epistle is addressed to the "twelve tribes of the dispersion" – probably to Jewish Christians over a large extent of country, including many from the Ten Tribes. It is a practical Epistle and strongly enforces holiness of life and work, exhorting readers to be "doers of the word, and not hearers only." It speaks of "pure and undefiled religion" as something that can be seen and recognized, and protests against the "respect of persons" and the invidious distinction of classes. While the Epistle to the Hebrews speaks of faith, James argues that our actions are the visible and tangible evidence of faith. He gives earnest cautions concerning ruling the tongue. He protests against strife and contention, and throughout he brings God into the earthly scene as the One his readers are called to serve, the One who will set them right. Twice in the last chapter he speaks of the "coming of the LORD".

COMMENTARY ON THE EPISTLE OF JAMES

This Epistle is addressed to the faithful Israelites scattered throughout the world, who are regarded as symbolically representing the whole nation. It was written, as the imagery employed in it shows, from Jerusalem, or at least from Palestine.

The author, who writes as a Christian (i. 1) to Christians (ii. 1), describes himself simply as James. There can be no reasonable doubt that tradition is right in identifying him with 'the brother of the Lord' who occupies so prominent a position in the Church at Jerusalem after the death of James, the son of Zebedee (Acts xii. 17; Gal. ii. 9). The brethren of the Lord, according to the common tradition in Palestine in the second century, were really what we should call half-brothers, children of Joseph by an earlier marriage. They were not (Acts i. 14) of the original Twelve, but James, by virtue of his official position, clearly ranks as an apostle (Gal. i. 19). He seems to have remained to the end of his life a strict observer of the Mosaic law, and to have been regarded with veneration even by his unbelieving countrymen. Trained as he must have been among those who were looking for the redemption of Jerusalem (Luke ii. 38), three truths would naturally lie at the root of his religious life. First he would learn to believe in one God, Creator of heaven and earth, who had made man in His own image (i. 18, 23, iii. 9, iv. 5). Then he would learn of the favor which God had in time past shown to His people, poor and weak though they might seem to men (ii. 5). Thirdly he would learn to look forward to a coming day of judgment and deliverance (v. 3, 7, 8). His faith in our Lord Jesus Christ (ii. 1), in whom the glory that marked God's presence with His people had found permanent embodiment, who had shared as Messiah the lot of the poor, and who was Himself the Judge standing before the door (v. 9), deepened, defined, but did not disturb this simple Jewish faith. He seems to have had little interest in theological speculation. At any rate the object of his letter is to enforce in the spirit, and often in the language, of the Lord, with the earnestness and fire of a prophet of the olden time, the moral and practical consequences of his creed.

It does not seem to have been called forth by any special crisis. The difficulties it deals with are just those which would be sure to assail Jewish-Christian circles as soon as the faith in the Messiahship of Jesus had begun to crystallize into a dogma. They are just the national besetting sins reappearing in a slightly altered form. At the same time, it is hard not to suppose that he is aiming directly in ii. 20–24 at some Jewish-Christian misinterpretation of St. Paul's language in Rom. iii. 24. In that case the Epistle must have been written not long before his death. It would naturally be disseminated by means of the crowds who gathered at Jerusalem at feast times (Acts ii. 5 *ff.*).

According to the account in Josephus, with which the account in Hegesippus is not necessarily inconsistent, St. James fell a victim to the intrigues of Annas the high priest between the death of Festus and the coming of Albinus (A.D. 62).

James begins his Epistle (i. 1) with the regular Greek form of salutation (V. Acts xv. 23, xxiii. 26). He then passes at once to illustrate the power of the truth to transfigure our common estimate of things to be desired or shunned, and so to regulate our attitude towards them (2–18). He shows how trials may minister to joy (2–4), how a felt need may become a link uniting us to God (5–8), and how the absence or the presence of this world's goods may alike afford ground for exultation (9–11). Trial, for all its potency of blessing (12), has a darker side—it may pass into temptation; but this is not owing to God's willing, but to man's lusting (14, 15). So he comes to the expression of the fundamental truth which underlies the whole paragraph, the flawless and unchanging of Him to whose pure will we owe our being (16–18). He then passes to consider the special developments in character and conduct which will follow naturally from faith in such a Creator (19–27). These are: an ear open to receive His Word (19–21); a will steadily set on embodying the revealed purpose of His creation (22–25); then, as the true ritual of outward devotion, watchful self-restraint and active charity (26, 27).

He then proceeds to warn his readers against various dangers to which as Jews they were naturally predisposed (ii. 1—iv. 12). They were tempted, in flagrant contradiction to their faith in Jesus Christ, to pay court to a man simply on the ground of his outward possessions (ii. 1–4), in spite of the preference which God had shown for the poor (5), and in spite of the violence and impenitence of the rich (6, 7). The consideration of this subtle form of mammon-worship leads him to explain how we may test the rightness of our actions (8–13) and the vitality of our faith (14–26). He shows first that the royal law of love is the one test of right conduct (8). Anything which, however slightly, violates

"For what is your life?"

that law is actual transgression (9) and brings absolute guilt (10, 11). So we must bear in mind the conditions of our enfranchisement, and forgive as we would be forgiven (12, 13). Then he shows that faith without corresponding action is profitless, whether it be regarded as the expression of a generous sentiment (14–17) or as the intellectual apprehension of a truth (18, 19), and illustrates from scriptural examples the power of obedience such as Abraham's to perfect the development of faith, which God recognizes and blesses even in its germ (20–24), and the necessity of acting, as Rahab alone of the Canaanites had done, on a true conviction if we are to enjoy the fruits of it (25, 26). He then passes to the second danger (iii.). Each was inclined to regard himself as qualified to teach others, or at least as justified in wrangling fiercely with them in defense of what he held to be the truth. St. James checks the first of these tendencies by a simple statement of our natural incapacity to control our own tongues (1–12). He checks the second by contrasting the bitter and factious spirit of a boasted orthodoxy with the sweet reasonableness and genuine devotion of true wisdom both in its source and in its fruits (13–18).

From this he proceeds to a third danger to which the presence of such contentions among them pointed. They were the outward signs of an inward discord (iv. 1). Unregulated desires were making them the source of confusion round about them (2), turning even their prayers into sin (3). Their hearts were given to the world (4), and in spite of the threats (5) and the promises (6) of Scripture, they were in proud rebellion against God. Their one hope lay in a penitent humbling of themselves before God (7–10), leaving their neighbors to settle, each on his own account, with his own conscience before God (11, 12).

James's Epistle is now drawing to a close, and his thoughts are full of the approaching Advent; but he does not introduce it in its complete Christian form at once. He begins with the obvious uncertainty of human life and uses the thought in that shape to rouse such as needed rousing from confidence in their own forethought. Then he turns to those were inclined to trust in their riches (v. 1–6). He points to forces already at work to destroy their hoarded treasure, and reminds them that the power of these possessions over their possessors would not perish with them (1–3), and then, in the language of the Old Testament prophets, denounces their injustice, their crass forgetfulness, and their violence against God's servants (4–6). Then turning directly to the faithful, he exhorts them to endure to the end, patiently, firmly, silently, in the certain hope of the now imminent Advent of their LORD and Judge (7–9), after the example of the prophets and in the light of Job's experience (10, 11). He warns them with special seriousness against the use of oaths in conversation. Their yea would be yea in the realized presence of their Judge (12). In sure trust in His present and ready help let them pray for one another and confess their sins one to another, especially in seasons of suffering (13–16), remembering the power of prayer revealed by the life of Elijah (17, 18), and the blessedness of being the instrument of converting even a single soul (19, 20).

THE EPISTLE OF JAMES: CHAPTER BY CHAPTER

Trial of faith.	1	The twelve tribes addressed. "The dispersion." Firmness under trials. Hearers and doers of the word. Pure and undefiled religion.
Respect of persons.	2	Invidious distinction of persons forbidden. The poor of this world, rich in faith. On keeping "the whole law." On helping brethren and sisters in need. Faith without works is dead.
The tongue.	3	Government of the tongue. The wisdom from above.
Warnings.	4	Against – Strife and contention. Worldly association. Pride. Evil speaking. Presumption.
The prayer of faith.	5	Against oppressors of the poor. Exhortation to patience. Prayer, and its power.

THE FIRST EPISTLE OF ST. PETER

A Church leader advises his flock about Godly behavior.

THE ESSENTIAL SUMMARY OF I PETER

This Epistle is addressed to the "strangers of the dispersion" – in this respect resembling the Epistle of St. James but to those in a more limited area. The Apostle Peter speaks to Christians in Pontus, Galatia, Cappadocia, Asia Minor and Bythynia.

St. Peter tells his readers that they are being built up into a "Royal Priesthood", and exhorts them to live godly lives, in love and harmony with each other.

COMMENTARY ON I PETER

The First Epistle of St. Peter was written to the Christians belonging to the different provinces of what is now called Asia Minor. It was written from "Babylon" (v. 13), that is, apparently, Rome, and may be dated shortly after the outbreak of the Neronian persecution A.D. 64, if we may assume that this persecution, which began in the capital, spread, or seemed likely to spread, rapidly to the provinces. In any case St. Peter, who had received a special commission to strengthen men who were in danger of being terrified into a denial of their LORD (Luke xxii.

32), writes this letter to help scattered communities to bear a fiery trial that was coming upon them.

His salutation (i. 1, 2) reminds them of the rock on which their election rested, of the means through which it took effect upon them, and the goal to which it led. Then rising at once above all earthly anxieties, he blesses God (3–12) for the new life which the resurrection of Jesus Christ had brought with it, a life strong in the assurance of present protection, and bright with the hope of the salvation which had aroused the earnest inquiry of those prophets who in old times had seen the vision of the Messianic sufferings on the road to glory (10–12).

Roused by this hope, Christian men must strive earnestly after holiness (13–21), filled with holy fear by the thought of the impartial and unswerving justice of their Judge, the costly ransom that had been paid to set men free from sin, and the power of the resurrection to quicken faith and hope in God. Obedience to God will find expression in fervent love to man through the power of the new life brought by the gospel message (22–25) and fed by living contact with the Corner-stone (ii. 1–6), in touch with whom each stone would grow into its place in the Building which is at once priesthood, sacrifice, and shrine. For the same Stone (7–10) that trips up the disobedient confers on believers all the privileges of the Israel of God.

In respect to particular duties (ii. 11—iv. 11), he exhorts Christians, remembering the importance of their good name for the conversion of the heathen world, to keep the flesh in subjection (11, 12) and to render loyal obedience to all constituted authority (13–17). Slaves, especially, are called upon to bear even undeserved punishment patiently (18–25), and as their lot is the meanest and hardest of all, he brings out the most precious treasure in his store for their help, giving them at once the pattern and the motive for the patience required of them, by recalling the sufferings which Christ had borne without murmuring for their sake. He bids wives (iii. 1–6) win their husbands to the faith by their obedience and by the simplicity of their life and demeanor. He bids husbands (7) pay honor to weakness, and calls on all Christians (8–12) for the graces necessary to attain the promised blessing. Persecution (13–17) faced in this spirit has no terrors, but the prospect of it calls for watchfulness lest the force of their witness should be marred by arrogance or moral laxity. When it comes (18–22) there is strength to endure in the thought of the sufferings of Christ and of the fruit which they had borne for Him, opening a new sphere to His working, even before His ascension to His throne in heaven.

The thought of these same sufferings, and of the mystical union of the believer with them, forms the ground of a renewed appeal to the mortification of the flesh (iv. 1–6), which is supported also by the thought of the judgment to come on the dead no less than on the living. The section closes (7–11) with an exhortation to each man, in view of the end, to exercise his special gift for the good of all, and the glory of Jesus Christ.

Coming back from the questionings which the approaching persecution would be sure to raise in their minds, he reminds them that a share in the Messianic sufferings (12–19) was an earnest of glory and a token of the brooding of the Spirit over them, and so a ground for thanksgiving, though not for presumption or moral carelessness.

This thought brings him back once more to practical exhortations (v. 1–6). He calls on elder and younger to recognize their duties one towards another, safeguarding both authority and obedience with humility. By humble submission to the divine discipline (7–11) they might find freedom from all anxiety, in calm reliance on divine aid.

The concluding salutations (12–14) contain an exhortation to enter on and stand fast in this true grace of God.

I Peter: Chapter by Chapter

	1	The "dispersion" addressed.
		"Blessed be the God and Father."
		God's abundant mercy.
		Salvation by Christ, the subject of prophecy.
"Be ye holy."		Exhortation to diligence and holiness enforced by the motives drawn from the character of God, and the price of redemption.

390

Growth in grace.	2	Exhortation to growth in grace. Believers living stones of the Church, and Christ the chief corner-stone. "Ye are a chosen generation." Peter "beseeches" to godly life. A word to servants.
Duties of Christians. "Spirits in prison."	3	Duties of Christian wives and husbands. Suffering for righteousness sake. Christ preaching to the spirits in prison.
	4	Call to newness of life. Exhortations to prayer, love, hospitality, &c. Encouragement under reproach for Christ.
	5	Elders exhorted to feed the flock of God. The younger exhorted to safety. Sobriety and vigilance enforced.

THE SECOND EPISTLE OF ST. PETER

**Exhortations to a Christian life, with various
warnings and predictions.**

THE ESSENTIAL SUMMARY OF II PETER

There is some doubt as to whether this Epistle was indeed (like I Peter) written by the Apostle himself. It would certainly appear to have been written some time later. The writer warns his readers against false teachers of the faith, and encourages them as they wait for the LORD. Their time is not the same as God's time, and they must not lose heart but wait steadfastly for the Day of Judgment, remaining vigilant and growing in grace.

There are many close resemblances between this second Epistle of Peter and the Epistle of Jude.

COMMENTARY ON II PETER

Both in point of language and of attestation this Epistle presents difficulties which are as yet far from being completely solved. It is written apparently to the same Churches as the first (iii. 1). The salutation, however, contains no names—it only hints more definitely than before that the readers directly intended are Gentiles by birth. It is written in the near prospect of death (i. 14), and aims at guarding against a form of Antinomianism similar to that which St. Jude combats in his Epistle, and at rekindling hope in the promised appearing of the LORD. It must have been written after the Epistle of St. Jude, the language of which it adopts and adapts freely all through.

The prayer in which, as usual, the salutation culminates expands without a formal break into a declaration of the grace already bestowed on believers, and an exhortation to them to respond to it by a steady growth in hope of the yet more abundant blessings in store (i. 1–11). This exhortation springs, as he goes on to tell them, from his conviction that his own departure, which according to the LORD's express declaration (John xxi. 18 ff.) was to precede the Advent, was now close at hand, and from his desire that these truths should not be forgotten when he was gone (12–15). For the faith that he had preached had been the outcome of his own experience (16), notably on the Mount of Transfiguration (17, 18), an experience which had strengthened his hold (19), as he bids them strengthen theirs, on 'the prophetic word' (Matt. xvi. 28), with this one caution, that they must not expect to understand prophetic scriptures in their own unaided strength, apart, that is, from the Spirit under whose inspiration they had in the first instance been delivered (20, 21). This thought of the need of a present inspiration leads him to the consideration of the danger to which they would be exposed from the presence in their midst of a counterfeit inspiration (ii.). The characteristic note of this dangerous teaching would be the denial of Christ's claim on His redeemed (ii. 1). However great the success of its exponents they are doomed (2, 3). For God has already, even in the act of delivering His servants from destruction, given proof of the severity of His judgment on the sinful (4–9), especially such filthy blasphemous brute beasts as these who, not content with their own licentiousness, set nets, as Balaam had done, to catch others (10–16). Such teachers are utterly worthless, and their boasted freedom sheer slavery to corruption, the more degrading because it is a return to a degradation once left (17–22).

Coming back from the prophetic picture to the immediate present, he exhorts his readers to remain faithful to themselves, to the commandment they have received (iii. 1, 2), and to his warning against such as would try to cover their own disobedience by scoffing at the long delay in the appearing of their Judge (3–7). He reminds them that God has a different standard of time from men, and that He is not dilatory, though He is reluctant to punish (8, 9). Still His day will come with startling suddenness (10), and the faithful are called to live in constant expectation of it, and of the new heaven and new earth to which it will open the way by its fiery destruction of the old (11–13). This expectation would help to keep them pure. Only they must guard against misinterpretations of St. Paul's Epistles (14–16). The sum of the whole matter is briefly this—Guard against lawless guides, and see that you grow in grace (17, 18).

II PETER: CHAPTER BY CHAPTER

Precious promises.	1	Design of the "precious promises". To faith add virtue, knowledge, temperance, patience, godliness. Diligence in making the calling and election sure. Putting off the tabernacle. Christianity not cunningly devised fables.
False teachers.	2	False teachers described. "The angels that sinned." Cautions against falling away.
"The last days."	3	In the last days – scoffers. Destruction of the old world by water. Destruction of this world by fire. Difficulties on Paul's writings. Exhortation to steadfastness and growth in grace.

THE EPISTLES OF ST. JOHN

**Three short Epistles from a revered Elder of the Church
emphasizing the importance of love.**

THE ESSENTIAL SUMMARY OF THE EPISTLES OF ST. JOHN

None of these Epistles contains any direct statement of the name of its author. In the first he claims to write in the name of the original witnesses of the gospel history (i. 1–4), but gives no further description of himself. In the second (1) and third (1) he calls himself simply the Elder. There can be no doubt, however, from their identity in strongly marked peculiarities of thought and expression, that all three are rightly ascribed to one and the same author, the evangelist of the fourth Gospel.

The first Epistle presupposes a knowledge of the facts recorded in St. John's Gospel, and was probably written after it. It contains the practical application of the truths revealed in the life of the Incarnate Word to the life of men, together with warnings against the dangers which beset a true faith in the Incarnation even before the end of the first century, both from teachers who claimed an authority independent of His in the revelation of truth or the determination of duty, and from teachers who shrank from the acknowledgment of a real manifestation of the Godhead in human flesh. The second Epistle is closely connected with the first in the character of the false teaching which it finds occasion to condemn (v. 7; cf. 1 John iv. 2). The 'elect lady' addressed in it is nameless, unless indeed these words are to be read as a proper name, 'Eclecta Cyria.' Neither the second nor the third Epistle contains definite indications of the date of its composition, nor have we any further information in regard to the persons or incidents referred to in them.

COMMENTARY ON THE FIRST EPISTLE OF JOHN

The Epistle begins, as the Gospel had done, with a careful description of its subject (i. 1–4). Writing as the last surviving representative of the apostolic band, the writer sums up their experience and declares the secret of their evangelistic zeal. They had received through their own senses the revelation of a life which in itself is above sense. It had existed before they became conscious of it. It continued to exist after it had passed out of their sight (1, 2). It had introduced them to a living fellowship which left them unsatisfied so long as it remained unshared (3, 4). So the apostles were the bearers of a message to men which was to issue in fellowship with God. The next section (i. 5—ii. 6) contains a declaration of the message, and of the conditions of fellowship. The message is summed up in a revelation of the character of God. God is light (5). The condition of fellowship is likeness to God (6, 7). In spite of the obstacle presented by our present sinfulness (8, 9) and our past sins (10), the Father has made provision in His Son to enable us to satisfy this condition (ii. 1, 2). We may know that we are satisfying it, if we are keeping His commandments (3–5) and walking in the footsteps of His Son (5, 6).

This condition may seem too elementary, too indefinite, or too exacting. So in the next section (7–17) St. John explains that the condition is not a new one, though it is seen in growing light (7, 8), that it affects the most definite earthly relationships (9–11), and that it is already satisfied in the members of the Church by the power of the Father's name (12–14). Only they must be watchful lest the attractions of the world should make them unmindful of His love (15–17). The attractions of the world could only be safely met in the power of a revelation of the Godhead in flesh which would completely satisfy the cravings which had found expression in every form of idolatry. So we pass from thoughts which spring directly from the doctrine of the Father (e.g. i. 2, 3, 9, ii. 1, 12, 15) to the consideration of different aspects of the doctrine of the Son (ii. 18 —iii. 24). For it was the office of the Christ to reveal the invisible God (St. John xiv. 6 *ff*.). And the most searching trial in life springs from the need for discriminating between rival claimants to that office. St. John's readers had been forewarned of this trial and had already had experience of it (18, 19). But they were endowed with the power of discrimination (20, 21), and their faith in Jesus as the Christ supplied them with a ready test by which to unmask pretenders (22, 23), at the same time that it opened the door into the promised life (24, 25). Abiding in Him they had a pledge of growing illumination (26, 27), and would show the outward sign of their new birth (28, 29).

So we pass to the next section (iii. 1–12). The work of the Son does not stop with the revelation of the Father. He was manifested to impart to us out of His own Sonship the nature and the name of sons. This portion of His work is in one sense complete already. We are sons here and now (1). In another sense the hope of perfected sonship is our motive in that self-purification (2, 3) which it was the object of His life on earth to make possible, by casting out the spirit of lawlessness (4–6) and so undoing the devil's work (7, 8). This object is not achieved till the seed of His sonship bears fruit in us in unwavering obedience to God (9, 10) and love to our brethren (11, 12). For His work is not merely to reveal the nature and confer a right to the name, it is definitely to impart the life (13–24) of sonship. This life finds expression in active love in us (13–15), after the pattern and in surrender to the claim of His love for us as revealed in His death (16–18). So we are reminded of the true place of the cross in relation to His work. It is from it that the new life of love in us springs, and so in it we have the secret of abiding peace in spite of sin (19, 20), and of prevailing intercession when we are living in the obedience, that is, the faith and the love, of sons (21–24). The work of the Son in us and for us culminates in mutual indwelling, and it becomes a reality to us by the operation of His Spirit (24).

So we pass from the consideration of the work of the Son who reveals the Father, to the consideration of the work of the Spirit (iv.—v. 12) who is sent in the Name of the Son (*cf.* St. John xiv. 26, xvi. 12–15), and whose characteristic office among men is therefore witness to the Incarnation. By this He provides a test of Truth both in teachers and hearers of the word (iv. 1–6). In this lies the inspiration (7–10), on this rests the obligation, of love among men (11–16). For God, being Love, has in the Incarnation perfected the manifestation of His love for us, that we might love Him without fear (17, 18) and our brethren for His sake (19–21).

Each separate element in this supreme revelation has a power of its own (v. 1–12). Faith in the Messiahship, faith that is in Jesus as the perfect revelation of the Father, brings the gift of divine sonship, and with the sonship love for the newly-found brethren, in obedience to the Father (1–3). Faith in the Divine Sonship, faith, that is, in Jesus as endowed with all His Father's authority over men, brings with it an assurance of victory over the world in the memory of His baptism and of His triumph through death, to both of which the sacraments and the Spirit bear living, harmonious, and sufficient evidence (4–9). The surrender in faith of the whole of a man's being to the Divine Son is life (10–12). With this declaration the message that the letter has to convey is complete. Its object has been just this, to rouse men to the consciousness of the life that is in them (13). Nothing remains but to point to prayer as the characteristic expression of this life (14–17) and to sum up the ultimate certainties in a Christian man's conviction (18–21).

I John: Chapter by Chapter

"The Word of Life."	1	Divinity and humanity of Christ, "the Word of Life." Fellowship with the Father and the Son. Walking in the light.
Christ our Advocate. Christian love.	2	Christ the Advocate with the Father. The propitiation for our sins. His commandments to be kept. Christians must love each other. Reasons for not loving the world. Many antichrists.

Sons of God.	3	The sons of God. "When He shall appear. Children of God contrasted with Children of the devil. This is the message, that we should love one another.
"God is love." Christian evidences.	4	Trying the spirits. God's love to us a motive to love our brethren. Evidences of being children of God. Whomsoever believeth – is born of God.
Witness of the Spirit.	5	On overcoming the world. "He that believeth hath the witness in himself." Confidence in prayer. "A sin unto death." No habitual sin in a Christian. Idols to be avoided.

COMMENTARY ON THE SECOND EPISTLE OF JOHN

For the truth's sake, the Elder and all who know the truth love the 'elect lady' and have good hope for the time to come (1–3). He writes, rejoicing in his experience of her children, to exhort her to encourage mutual love in simple obedience to the old commandment, and to turn a deaf ear, even to refuse all hospitality, to the advanced teachers who claim to have outgrown the doctrine of a Christ coming in the flesh (4–11). He has more to say, but he had rather speak than write (12, 13).

II JOHN: SIGNIFICANT VERSES

"The elect lady."	1	A Christian lady and her children commended.
	4	Walking in truth.
Warnings.	7	Warning against deceivers and antichrists.
	10	On bidding "God speed."

COMMENTARY ON THE THIRD EPISTLE OF JOHN

The Elder praises Gaius for the good report which some of his guests have brought of his truth (1–4) and of his hospitality (5–8). He then sternly condemns the contumacy of Diotrephes (9, 10), and after commending Demetrius, the carrier of the letter, he closes, in the hope of an early meeting, with various salutations (11–14).

III JOHN: SIGNIFICANT VERSES

Gaius.	1	Gaius commended for piety and hospitality.
A contrast.	9	Diotrephes and Demetrius contrasted.

THE EPISTLE OF ST. JUDE

An Epistle warning of false teachers and exhorting believers to hold steadfast to their faith and not be discouraged.

THE ESSENTIAL SUMMARY OF THE EPISTLE OF ST. JUDE

The writer of this Epistle considered that he would be readily identified as the "brother of James." Then the brother was, no doubt, someone of importance in the Church. In all probability he was that James who was the presiding Elder at Jerusalem, and who wrote the Epistle bearing his name. The resemblances to the Second Epistle of St. Peter are frequent and striking.

COMMENTARY ON THE EPISTLE OF JUDE

The author of this Epistle is Jude, brother of James, and therefore one of the brethren of the LORD (17). There is nothing in the salutation to help us to identify the readers for whom this Epistle was intended. It is clear, however, from the rest of the letter, that they were well known to St. Jude. They had at one time been pupils of apostles (18), but now that by death or absence they had lost apostolic guidance, they were in serious danger from the presence among them of men who, while railing ostentatiously against the objects of pagan superstition, gave themselves up to all the licentiousness of pagan worship, declaring themselves, owing to their special illumination, to be

401

above all law, and practising the vilest immorality under cover of some hideous perversion of the doctrine of the grace of God. St. Jude writes to rouse his "beloved" to a sense of their danger and at the same time to help them to meet it calmly, because they had been taught to expect it, and because, while doing what they could to help their brethren through it, they were safe in God's keeping.

After the salutation (1, 2), in which he reminds his readers of God's love and the protection of Jesus Christ, he proceeds at once to tell them that his desire to write to them had been transformed into an overmastering necessity by the appearance of certain ungodly persons among them who had perverted the doctrine of the grace of God (3, 4). The news had made him long to remind them of God's judgments on idolatrous Israel in the wilderness, on the rebellious angels, and on the Sodomites, whose example these men did not scruple to follow (5-7). Each feature in their degradation showed that these apostates at least had need of each of these warnings. Witness their filthy licentiousness, their rejection of all sovereignty over them, beginning with their LORD's, and their irreverent railing at the spiritual powers, in whose idolatrous feasts, as the one thing that they thoroughly understood, they did not scruple to share. In fact they had fallen into the old pitfalls—Cain's, who had grudged God's acceptance of his brother; Balaam's, who had prostituted his office for gain; and Korah's, who had risen in proud rebellion against God's appointed minister (8-11). Their true character was revealed by their fruits (12, 13). The judgment of such impiety, as the book of Enoch testified, was sure (14, 15). They were self-condemned. They pleased themselves while they murmured against God, and they swallowed their big words against idols whenever it was worthwhile (16). Let the faithful then recall the apostolic warnings against such men and keep guard over themselves (17-21), while doing all that could be done to save their brethren (22, 23).

The Epistle closes with a doxology (24, 25), which brings once more before them the sufficiency of the protection on which they could rely, even when they were forbidden to rely on anything of their own.

THE EPISTLE OF JUDE: SIGNIFICANT VERSES

Warnings.	2	The common salvation.
	3	"Earnestly contend for the faith."
	6	The angels which fell.
	7	Sodom and Gomorrah. Examples of divine vengeance.
Michael.	9	Michael's contention with the devil.
Enoch's prophecy.	14	Enoch's prophecy.
	20	Duty of believers.
	25	Christ "the only wise God."

THE REVELATION OF ST. JOHN THE DIVINE

The future of the Church foretold.

THE ESSENTIAL SUMMARY OF REVELATION

The book belongs, in its character, to the prophetical writings, and stands in intimate relations to the prophecies of the Old Testament, and more especially with the writings of the later prophets, as Ezekiel, Zechariah, and particularly Daniel, inasmuch as it is almost entirely symbolical. It consists of a series of visions witnessed by the new elderly St. John "in the Spirit" at Patmos.

It is an expanded illustration of the first great promise, "the seed of the woman shall bruise the head of the serpent." Its figures and symbols are august and impressive. It is full of prophetic grandeur, and awful in its hieroglyphics and mystic symbol; seven seals opened, seven trumpets sounded, seven vials poured out; mighty antagonists and hostile powers full of malignity against Christianity, and for a season oppressing it, but at length defeated and annihilated; the darkened heaven, tempestuous sea, and convulsed earth fighting against them, while the issue of the long combat is the universal reign of peace and truth and righteousness—the whole scene being relieved at intervals by a choral burst of praise to God the Creator, and Christ the Redeemer and Governor.

Thus its general scope is intelligible to all readers, or it could not yield either hope or comfort. It is also full of Christ. It exhibits

His glory as Redeemer and Governor, and describes that deep and universal homage and praise which the "Lamb that was slain" is forever receiving before the throne.

Many attempts have been made to explain this book. The interval between the apostolic age and that of Constantine has been called the Chiliastic period of Apocalyptic interpretation. The visions of St. John were chiefly regarded as representations of general Christian truths, scarcely yet embodied in actual facts, for the most part to be exemplified or, fulfilled in the reign of Antichrist, the coming of Christ, the Millennium, and the Day of Judgment. Immediately after the triumph of Constantine, the Christians, emancipated from persecution and oppression, and dominant and prosperous in their turn, began to lose their vivid expectation of our LORD's speedy advent, and their spiritual conception of His kingdom, and to look upon the temporal supremacy of Christianity as a fulfilment of the promised reign of Christ on earth. The Roman Empire, become Christian, was regarded no longer as a subject of 'prophetic denunciation, but as the scene of a millennial development. This view, however, was soon, met by the figurative interpretation of the Millennium as the reign of Christ in the hearts of all true believers. As the barbarous and heretical invaders of the falling empire appeared, they were regarded .by the suffering Christians as fulfilling the "woes" denounced in Revelation.

Modern interpreters are generally divided into three great divisions:

1. The Historical or continuous expositors, in whose opinion the Revelation is a progressive history of the fortunes of the Christian Church from the first century to the end of time.
2. The Praeterist expositors, who are of opinion that the Revelation has been almost, or altogether, fulfilled in the time that has passed since it was written; that it refers principally to the triumph of Christianity over Judaism and Paganism, signaled by the downfall of Jerusalem and of Rome.
3. The Futurist expositors, whose views show a strong reaction against some of the extravagances of the two preceding schools. They believe that the whole book, excepting perhaps the first three chapters, refers principally, if not exclusively,

to events which are yet to come. Bishop Newton wisely says: "To explain this book perfectly is not the work of one man, or of one age; probably it never will be clearly understood till it is all fulfilled."

Each of these three schemes is open to objection. Against the Futurist it is argued, that it is not consistent with the repeated declarations of a speedy fulfilment at the beginning and end of the book itself (see chaps. i. 3; xxii. 6, 7, 12, 20). Christians, to whom it was originally addressed, would have derived no comfort from it, had its fulfilment been altogether deferred for so many centuries. The rigidly literal interpretation of Babylon, the Jewish tribes, and other symbols, which generally forms a part of Futurist schemes, presents peculiar difficulties. Against the Praeterist expositors, it is urged that prophecies fulfilled ought to be rendered so perspicuous to the general sense of the Church as to supply an argument against infidelity; that the destruction of Jerusalem, having occurred twenty-five years previously, could not occupy a large space in prophecy; that the supposed predictions of the downfall of Jerusalem and of Nero appear from the context to refer to one event, but are by this scheme separated; and, moreover, placed in a wrong order; that the measuring of the temple and the altar; and the death of the two witnesses (chap. xi.) cannot be explained consistently with the context. Against the Historical scheme, it is urged that its advocates differ very widely among themselves; that they assume, without any authority, that the 1260 days are so many years; that several of its applications—e. g., of the symbol of the ten-horned beast to the Popes, and the sixth seal to the conversion of Constantine—are inconsistent with the context; that attempts by some of this school to predict future events by the help of the Revelation have ended in ridiculous failures.

In conclusion, it may be stated that two methods have been proposed by which the student of the Revelation may escape the incongruities and fallacies of the different interpretations, whilst he may derive edification from whatever truth they contain. It has been suggested that the book may be regarded as a prophetic poem, dealing in general and unspecific descriptions; much of which may be set down as poetical imagery, mere embellishment.

But such a view would be difficult to reconcile with the belief that the book is an inspired prophecy. Another suggestion is made, or rather revived, by Dr Arnold, his sermons *On the Interpretation of Prophecy*: that we should bear in mind that predictions have a lower historical sense; as well as a higher spiritual sense; that there may be more than one typical, imperfect, historical fulfilment of a prophecy, in each of which the higher spiritual fulfilment is shadowed forth more or less distinctly. The recognition of this would pave the way for the acceptance in a modified sense of many of the interpretations of the Historical school, and would not exclude the most valuable portions of other schools.

The Apocalypse, despite its figurative presentation, throws light upon the whole mass of the doctrine of our faith. The doctrines of the Trinity of God, and of the relation of God to Christ, are here unmistakably raised above all Monophysitism, Arianism, and inner-Trinitary subordination. The Creation here appears, in the reflex light of the new Paradise, as the original plan of a world of eternal spirit-life. The human race is represented by a selection of elect ones, of whom Christ is the absolute centre, glory and support. How fully, furthermore, are the fundamental traits of Redemption, Reconciliation and Salvation portrayed in contrast to the gloomy night side of human life and perdition! Dark as are many parts of the Apocalypse and difficult of interpretation, the Book as a whole, is radiant with the promise to God's people of a final and complete victory in their conflict with the kingdom of Satan. Though long delayed, as we mortals reckon time, it shall come at last with a brightness above the sun, and the earth shall be lighted from pole to pole with its glory. Then comes the end of time, and God shall stand upon the mountains of his absolute eternity and Christ at his right hand radiant in his mediatorial glory, and from beneath the throne shall flow forth the waters of life to make glad all the paradise of the redeemed.

COMMENTARY ON THE REVELATION OF ST. JOHN

The Revelation or, to call the book by its Greek name, the Apocalypse of St. John, was sent in the first instance (i. 4) to seven Churches in Asia Minor. The voice of tradition is practically unanimous in identifying the author, who calls himself simply John, with the son of Zebedee, the evangelist of the fourth Gospel. There is a serious difference of opinion as to the date of its production. The common opinion is based almost entirely on a statement by Ireneus (v. xxx. 1–3), who was a pupil of the personal disciples of St. John, to the effect that 'it' (i.e. apparently 'the Revelation') 'was seen almost in his own time, at the end of the reign of Domitian' (96 A.D.). There are various traces, however, of a different tradition, notably in Epiphanius (*Haer.* XLI. 12), which connects St. John's exile to Patmos, and by implication the writing of the Revelation, with the persecution of Nero (64–68). This earlier date seems imperatively demanded by internal evidence. The difference in style for instance between the Revelation and the Gospel requires a substantial difference in date of composition if we are to maintain, as we have otherwise strong grounds for maintaining, the unity of their authorship. Again, the book itself, according to the simplest explanation of its own symbolism, claims to be written (xvii. 10) at latest under Galba or Vespasian (A.D. 68, 69). But the strongest argument of all lies in the fact that a book which has seemed to so many, when interpreted on the hypothesis of the later date, a dark and all but hopeless enigma, becomes, when once the earlier date is accepted, what it was clearly meant to be, a luminous and most inspiriting revelation. In 68, 69 A.D. Jerusalem was already invested by the Roman legions. The tremendous crisis was now close at hand which, according to our LORD's express prediction, was to mark His return in judgment on the guilty nation (cf. Matt. xxiv., xxv.). In spite of His warning (Matt. xxiv. 23–27), men might fail to recognize Him when He came, because He did not manifest Himself in a visible form. They might think, especially if they were still in heart bound to the outward aids to worship afforded by Judaism, that the Fall of Jerusalem was a sign that God had finally withdrawn from, and not that He had at last wedded Himself to, the creatures He had made. They needed clear words to help them to understand that 'state of salvation,' that 'new heaven and new earth wherein dwelleth righteousness,' which His coming was to induce.

It will be noticed that on this interpretation the primary application of the words of this prophecy is to events that lay in the immediate future at the time that it was delivered. And this is certainly what the language of the book itself most naturally suggests (*e.g.* i. 1, 3, xxii. 6, 20). Nor is there anything in the book necessarily inconsistent with this interpretation. 'Babylon,' that is, the old Jerusalem, fell, and vengeance for the righteous blood (Matt. xxiii. 35) that she had shed was exacted from her in 70 A.D. The triumph of Christianity over the Roman Imperial system (xix. 19–21) was not indeed outwardly perfected for two or three centuries, but the martyrs in the Neronian persecution had already won the victory in the first, and in some respects the fiercest and most deadly, of all the engagements in the long campaign. There is only one short section (xx. 7–10) which seems expressly to contemplate a far distant crisis in the history of the world. The value of the book for us will lie therefore primarily in the help which it can give us towards understanding a certain definite series of historical events in the past. If we read these events in the light which this book casts upon them, we shall learn to understand the principles, and in some degree the methods, of the judgment which Christ comes to execute on the world in every age. If we study the picture that St. John gives us of the new Jerusalem which he saw descending out of heaven from God in his own age, we shall understand, and understanding shall, according to the most sure promise of the Book itself (i. 3, xxii. 7), enter upon the enjoyment of 'the full hope of His calling, the riches of the glory of His inheritance in the saints' (Eph. i. 18).

Analysis

The opening verses (1. 1–3) tell us that the object of the book is to reveal Jesus Christ, and that this revelation was given by Him from God through His angel to John for the guidance of His servants in an approaching crisis. Then John sends greeting in his own name (4, 5) to the seven churches from the eternal God, from the 'Seven Spirits,' and from Jesus Christ crucified, risen and ascended. This greeting passes into a doxology for the love of the Redeemer (5, 6), and to a prophecy of the approaching advent (7). After this introduction, the main subject of the book is opened by a solemn declaration of the Name of God, from whom the whole prophecy comes (8). Then John explains the circumstances under which he had received his commission to write

(9–20). During his exile in Patmos he had seen a vision of the Son of Man in the midst of seven lamps, holding seven stars in his hand (9–16). He fell as dead at the sight, but Jesus raised him, bade him record his vision, and then sent a message to each of the seven Churches symbolized by the lamps and the stars (17–20).

1. As invisibly present among His people, He rebukes the Church in Ephesus for the cooling of her first love, and promises, to 'those who overcome the special temptations to which they are exposed, food from the tree of life (ii. 1–7).

2. As conqueror of death, He exhorts the Church in Smyrna to firmness under an approaching persecution, and promises the victor deliverance from the second death, i.e. the lake of fire (xx. 14), which would destroy the wicked, as the cities of the plain had been destroyed in old time (8–11).

3. As the wielder of the sword, He warns the Church in Pergamum of the presence of Nicolaitans among them, promising, as to men who proved superior to the temptations which had assailed Israel in the wilderness, hidden manna, and the white stone of a pure initiation (12–17).

4. As God's vicegerent over Israel, He pronounces judgment on the woman Jezebel, and promises the faithful in Thyatira a share in His own dominion over the Gentiles, and the morning star (18–29).

5. As the source and guardian of spiritual life, He warns the Church in Sardis of the approach of spiritual death, but promises that those who keep themselves free from pollution shall not be expunged from the roll of the true Israelites (iii. 1–6).

6. As the true steward over the household of God, He declares the right of the Church in Philadelphia to membership in God's family, in spite of Jewish opposition, promising them, as a reward for their endurance, protection through the coming persecution, and a place in the fabric of the spiritual temple which is shortly to be revealed (7–13).

7. As the fulfilment of the promises of God, and the beginning of His new creation, He rebukes the Church in Laodicea for her indifference and her self-satisfaction. He warns her to expect chastisement, and invites her to admit Him as her guest, and promises the victor a share in His own throne (14–22).

The first stage in the revelation of Jesus Christ is now complete. He is seen to be the present and living judge and protector of all Christian communities. The second stage opens with a vision in heaven: a throne, and One sitting on the throne, surrounded by four-and-twenty elders, representing the Church of both dispensations, and by four living creatures, representing the material universe, engaged in perpetual worship of the Source of all creation (iv.). Then a sealed book, and He who alone could open it, under the figure of a slaughtered Lamb (v. 1–7), who receives the praise of the living creatures and of the elders for the redemption He has wrought (8–10), and the praise of the angels in recognition of His inherent dignity (11, 12), and then, in union with Him that sits upon the Throne, the adoration of each member of the whole creation (13, 14). Then, one by one, He opens the seven seals. After each of the first four, one of the living creatures says 'Come,' and a rider on horseback goes out to execute judgment on the world. These represent Wars of conquest (vi. 1, 2), Civil war (3, 4), the heartlessness of Trade (5, 6), and Pestilence (7, 8). The opening of the fifth seal is followed by a cry for vengeance from the slaughtered saints whose blood has been poured on the heavenly altar, and they are bidden to wait till the tale of the victims of persecution is

Opening of the Seventh Seal

411

complete (9–11). When the sixth seal is opened, a convulsion shakes the heaven and the earth, the powers in heaven that men have worshiped fall from their spheres, and earthly potentates cower before the wrath of the Lamb (12–17). This seal represents the judgment on the Gentile world which, as the LORD had foretold (Matt. xxiv. 29), precedes the judgment on Jerusalem. Before the seventh seal is opened, there is a pause for preparation. The four winds, which seem to represent hordes of Barbarian invaders (xx. 8), are kept in check until the members of the true Israel are marked out for deliverance in the coming judgment by the seal of the living God (vii. 1–3). St. John first hears the number of the sealed, which is symbolically complete (4–8), and then catches sight of the multitude, gathered from every nation to which that perfect number corresponds, and hears them sing Hosanna for their deliverance, to God and to the Lamb, and all the hosts of heaven join them in their praise (9–12). One of the elders declares the conditions of membership in that multitude, and the blessedness of it (13–17). The opening of the seventh seal is followed by silence in heaven (viii. 1). Then the seven angels of the Presence receive seven trumpets (2), and, as a prelude to their work, another angel offers the prayers of the saints before God, and then, filling the censer with fire from the altar, casts it to the earth (3–6).

The first four trumpets are followed by judgments affecting the four divisions (xiv. 7) of the material creation, dry land (7), sea (8, 9), springs of waters (10, 11), the heavenly bodies (12). A flying eagle then marks the difference between these four trumpets and the next three (13). After the fifth trumpet, a star falls from heaven (ix. 1), marking the quenching of the light which the chosen nation had been commissioned to give out to the world. The consequence of this apostasy is seen in the opening of the pit, and in the issuing therefrom of a locust swarm that has power over all except those who are protected by the seal of God (2–12). The sixth trumpet is followed by the loosing of a vast host of horsemen, yet more terrible and deadly than the locusts, from the banks of the Euphrates, the spiritual boundary between Jerusalem and Babylon (13–19). In spite of these judgments, men still cleave to their idols and their sins (20, 21). The pause before the seventh trumpet is marked by the descent of a strong angel with a little book open in his hand (x. 1). He cries aloud, and seven thunders, whose voices St. John is forbidden to record, echo his cry (2–4). Then the angel solemnly declares that in the days of the seventh angel the revelation made to the prophets of old shall be perfected (5–7), and St. John is bidden to take and eat the little book, in token that, in spite of this declaration, there is still work left for him to do (8–11). Then he is bidden to measure the Sanctuary, which represents the sound core of the nation, and to leave the rest to its fate at the hand of the Gentiles, and to the final pleading in sackcloth of the two divine witnesses (xi. 1–3). These witnesses are the two national institutions of prophethood and priesthood which, even in their degradation, bore witness for God in the nation and in the world. Their witness, however, in its present form is not destined to endure. They fall, as national institutions, with the fall of their nation, and by the same foe (7, 8; *cf.* xvii. 16). But in themselves they are immortal; and even while men are exulting in the relief brought by the cessation of their witness, they rise again with their bodies, and ascend in the sight of their enemies to the throne of their risen and ascended LORD in heaven, becoming independent of their former national embodiment in the universal Church (9–12). The moment of the measuring is marked by an earthquake and a partial ruin which issues in a momentary conversion (13, 14). The seventh angel then sounds, and the walls of the spiritual Jericho fall flat. But for the present, all that we are called upon to contemplate is the revelation of the eternal and universal kingdom, which is brought into clear light by the collapse of that which was local and transitory (15), and to listen to the thanksgiving of the elders for the judgment which has avenged the slaughtered saints (16–18). Then the heavenly temple opens, the ark of God's covenant is seen secure in the innermost shrine (19), and the second stage in the revelation of Jesus Christ is over. The judgment on Jerusalem will make it clear that all the divine prerogatives of Israel have reached their goal, and have found an eternal embodiment in Him.

In one sense the book is complete at this point. It has no fresh facts to bring before us. Still, the same series of facts may be looked at from a fresh point of view, and be found pregnant with a fresh revelation. They have been sketched out so as to enable us to trace the process of the preservation of all that was imperishable in the old system. They may be sketched also, so as to show

413

how all in it that could not stand the fire was burnt up. With this object, a fresh start is made, and a fresh series of symbols (yet *cf.* xi. 7, xiv. 1) is brought before us. The ancient Israel, the bride of Jehovah, appears in a form which is the visible embodiment of Joseph's dream (Gen. xxxvii. 9), and at the moment of the fulfilment of the great end of her being (xii. 1, 2) Israel's foe, the mighty, proud, devouring, world-spirit, appears in the form of a red dragon, the exact antithesis of the Lamb, waiting to devour the woman's Son at His birth (3, 4). The Son is born, and raised to His predestined Throne in spite of the dragon (5), and the woman waits in the wilderness (6) while the witnesses are prophesying in sackcloth (xi. 3). Meanwhile the ascension of the Son is the signal for the casting forth of the dragon from heaven (7-9). The accuser of His Brethren cannot stand before their Advocate, and those who ascend with Him are beyond the reach of their foe (10-12). Israel, however, even the faithful Israel, so far as it is still on earth, is not altogether out of the reach of the dragon, though she is kept safe from his attacks by the protection of the strong Roman sense of justice (13, 14), and by the friendship of 'the earth' (15, 16). The dragon then seeks an alliance in 'the sea' (17-xiii. 1). Out of the sea rises a monster, in many respects a visible counterpart of himself, and with him the dragon shares his kingdom (xiii. 2). This monster, as we shall be told more distinctly later on (xvii. 7-11), represents the material organization of the Roman empire which, as it recovered from what seemed its death-blow in the death of Nero, might well seem invincible, and deceive with its blasphemous pretensions all but the elect (3-8). Nevertheless a righteous recompense was in store for it, in the assurance of which the saints could suffer and be strong (9, 10). Even as it was, the first monster was powerless without the assistance of a second that comes up 'out of the earth,' representing the spiritual organization of the empire and the established worship of the city and the emperor (11). The work of this second monster, the false prophet (xvi. 13), is to enforce the worship of the first monster (12), and by copying the signs of true prophets to induce men to make and worship its image (13-15). And finally, that nothing may be wanting to complete the diabolic travesty of the heavenly court, he compels all who would traffic in his kingdom to enrol themselves as the soldiers and servants of the monster, by receiving his mark—his name or some equivalent—on hand or brow (16–18).

This array of material forces seems overwhelming. It is not; the Lamb is the true king in the material as in the spiritual realm. And the next vision shows Him to us in His capital (Ps. ii. 6), surrounded by His troops that had been sealed to His service and had learnt His song, because they had been redeemed by His blood (cf. v. 9) to be the first-fruits of humanity, consecrated pure and without blemish to God (xiv. 1–5). Then three angels appear one after another with messages to the world: the first with the eternal gospel of the fear of God (6, 7), the second with tidings of the judgment on 'Babylon' (8), the third with a warning of a similar judgment in store for the worshipers of the monster (9–11). This last message may call for resistance even unto blood, and the Judgment when it comes will mark the commencement of the reign of the Saints (xix. 20, xx. 4); so a heavenly voice declares the blessedness of those that die in the LORD (12, 13). This vision is followed by a representation in outline of the Judgment which it proclaimed. First the Judge is seen on a cloud holding a sickle (14). Then at the voice of an angel He reaps His harvest-field (15, 16). Then a second angel appears (17), and, at the bidding of a third angel, reaps the vine of the earth, and casts the grapes into the winepress of the wrath of God (18–20).

All the fresh symbolism is now before us, together with a sketch in outline of the approaching Judgment. We are now ready to trace the working of it out in detail in the vision of the angels with the seven bowls or vials (xv. 1). The vision opens with a hymn of praise, sung by those who had triumphed over the deceits of the false prophet, for God's judgment on their oppressors (2–4). Then the seven angels appear out of the Temple vested as priests, and receive their bowls, i.e. basins such as those used in the Temple worship to catch the blood of the slaughtered victims, from one of the living creatures (5–8), and they are bidden to pour them out on the earth (xvi. 1). The emptying of the first four bowls is followed, as the first four trumpets had been, by judgments on the four parts of the physical creation, the dry land (2), the sea (3), the springs of waters (4–7), the sun (8, 9). The fifth bowl is emptied on the monster's throne, and his kingdom is thrown into a darkness which may well symbolize the confusion which followed on the suicide of Nero (10, 11). The sixth (*cf.* ix. 14) dries up the Euphrates (12), and, there being now no boundary between the sacred and profane, the Trinity of evil is allowed to gather all the forces of the earth to meet God in the mount of 'Megiddo' (13–16). After the seventh bowl, the judgments are declared to be finished (17), all earthly confederacies and earthly potentates fall to the ground or disappear, and 'Babylon' is judged (18–21). The meaning and the process of this judgment are explained in the next two chapters. First we are shown 'Babylon,' the apostate Jerusalem, under the figure of a woman that has cast of her allegiance to her true LORD, and entered into alliance with earthly powers, which she degrades by her apostasy (xvii. 1, 2). She appears first in all her glory, riding on a scarlet monster, drunk with the blood of the saints (3–6). Then the symbolism of the monster is explained. It represents the Roman empire, marvellous in power, but doomed to pass away (7, 8). The monster's seven heads are the seven emperors. The woman is seated on them, for the prosperity of Jerusalem rested on the favor of Caesar. Of the seven emperors, five, from Augustus to Nero, had already fallen; one, Vespasian, is, and one, Titus, is not yet come to the throne (9, 10). The monster itself, *i.e.* the imperial organization consolidated by these seven successive heads, has a life of its own, though it is doomed (11). Its ten horns represent the tributary princes or, perhaps, the governors of the provinces, that are willing to unite with it in. the war against the Lamb (12–14). Before this can be, however, the horns and the monster turn and rend the woman who had been once endowed with sovereignty — the Roman legions utterly destroy Jerusalem (16–18). Then we learn what is thought of this destruction in heaven. First a bright angel declares the fact (xviii. 1–3); then a voice calls God's people to come out of her and to leave her to her doom, the Jewish Christians are bidden to regard themselves no longer as Jews (4–8), and then the same voice records the mourning of the princes (9, 10), the merchants (11–16), and the sailors (17–19) over her desolation, while heaven and her victims exult because justice has overtaken her (20). Then a mighty angel shows by a sign that her desolation is final (21–24), and the heavenly host sing Hallelujah (xix. 1–3). The elders and the living creatures take up their song, and a voice from the throne echoes it (4, 5). Here again a great crisis in the revelation is over. But the whole judgment has not yet been fully declared, nor its fruits made known. The Christ has yet to vindicate His sovereignty against the blasphemous pretensions of Rome. He is not yet wedded to His Queen. So the heavenly hymn rises yet again; but this time it is to herald the Bridal of the Lamb (6–8), and a prophetic voice declares the blessedness of His invited guests (9, 10). The feast itself is not yet. There is stern work to do first. Heaven opens, and the Lamb appears as a warrior, mounted, armed, and crowned, surrounded by His soldiers, and bearing the names of 'Word of God,' and 'King of kings and LORD of LORDS' (11–16). The monster gathers his forces for the battle and is overcome—the Church is stronger than the empire—and it is cast, together with the false prophet, into the lake of fire (17–21).

Two out of the three arch-foes are now overcome. Only the Dragon remains, the purely spiritual foe, who had used the powers of Rome to gratify his ancient hatred against God. And he, too, meets his match. As the apostate Israel had set him free (ix. 1, 11), so the faithful Church would master, chain, and cast him back into the abyss for 1000 years (xx. 1–3). During his confinement the saints are seen in their true position as reigning over the earth with a sovereignty over which death has no power (4–6). But he must be yet more decisively overthrown. So he would be let loose once more to gather his forces against the city of God in order that his new host might be destroyed and he himself cast with his old allies into the lake of fire (7–10). Meanwhile the great white throne is already set up, and the Lamb sits on it in judgment on the old world, judging the dead so that all, even those who had not known Him after the flesh (*cf.* Matt. xxv. 34), might, if they were worthy, share the reign of His saints (*cf.* v. 6), and casting the unworthy, with the two great terrors of the heathen world—death, and the shadow world beyond it—into the lake of fire (11–15). And now the light breaks in upon a new world, a new heaven, the Father's home, and a new earth from which the power that isolated His children from one another has disappeared, and on which the new Jerusalem can rest—the outward symbol of God's abiding presence among men, and a pledge from Him of the removal of the primeval curse on death and toil (xxi. 1–4). This vision is confirmed by the words of Him that sitteth on the throne, 'the Beginning and the End,' who offers the new life to all who thirst for it, and the new inherit-ance to all who have the courage to enter in and take possession (5-7). For the fearful and the foul there is nothing but the fire (8). When this voice ceases, one of the same angels that had revealed the foulness of the apostate Jerusalem is appointed to reveal the beauty of the faithful Bride (9; *cf.* xvii. 1), and St. John sees the new Jerusalem glowing with the light of God's presence in the midst of her, protected by a mighty wall and by angel guard-ians, yet open towards every quarter, and combining apostles and patriarchs in one compact structure (10-14). The form of the city is a perfect cube, like the form of the Holy of Holies (15-17). Every variety of precious stone found a place in the foundations; the gates were pearl and the pavement gold (18-21). God Himself and the Lamb supplied the place of shrine and light and lamp (22, 23). Her influence spread far beyond herself; heathen nations felt the blessing of her light; and earthly monarchs brought her their choicest offerings. None but the unclean found her portals shut (24-27). Through her streets flowed the Water of life; and the Tree of life, now at last open to all, grew on either bank, bearing all the year its various fruit, and even with its leaves healing the nations. And there, through all the ages, shall be the throne of God and the Lamb, and His consecrated servants shall serve Him, illuminated by His presence and sharing in His throne (xxii. 1-5). Now at last the revelation of Jesus Christ is complete. He has shown Himself to us as the living LORD and Judge of His Churches, as the Deliverer and Avenger of His Saints, LORD of all the kings of the earth, and Judge of quick and dead; and now we see Him eternally one with the Father on His throne in the New Jerusalem.

The book ends with a solemn declaration of the divine source of the revelation, though it come through human channels (6-9), and with a command to make it known (10, 11), in view of the nearness of the advent described and the blessedness of the reward (12-15). Then Jesus Himself adds His authorization, and the Spirit and the Bride pray for the coming (16, 17). Then John adds a solemn declaration of the necessity of faithful dealing with the words of the communication (18, 19). Jesus once more asserts the truth of the proclamation, and John prays for its fulfil-ment (20). The book closes with the Grace (21).

Revelation: Chapter by Chapter

First vision: of "things that are." **The seven churches.**	1	Purpose of the Revelation. Salutation to the seven churches. Second coming of Christ. Christ Alpha and Omega. St. John in Patmos. Seven golden candlesticks. Seven churches in Asia: Ephesus, Smyrna, Pergamos, Thyatira, Sardis, Philadelphia, Laodicea. Vision of Christ in glory and majesty.
Ephesus.	2	Epistle to the church of EPHESUS. *Commendations for:* • Labor; • Patience; • Discipline; • Hating the doctrine of the Nicolaitanes [a licentious sect.] *Censure for:* • Decline in love. *Exhortation to:* • Remember; • Repent; • Do the first works. *Promise of:* • The Tree of Life for him that overcometh.
Smyrna.		Epistle to the church of SMYRNA. *Commendations for:* • Enduring tribulation; • Being rich in grace. *Censure on:* • Some hypocrites. *Exhortation to:* • Be faithful unto death! *Promise of:* • A crown of life; • Preservation from the second death.
Pergamos.		Epistle to the church of PERGAMOS. *Commendations for:* • Constancy, even when Antipas was martyred. *Censure for:* • Great laxity in discipline. • Holding the doctrine of the Nicolaitanes.

	2	*Exhortation to:* • Repent *Promise of:* • The hidden manna; • A white stone; • A new name.
Thyatira.		Epistle to the church of THYATIRA. *Commendations for:* • Charity; • Faith; • Patience. *Censure for:* • Tolerating some impure person or party called Jezebel. *Exhortation to:* • "Hold fast." *Promise of:* • Power over the nations. • The morning star.
Sardis.	3	Epistle to the church of SARDIS. *Commendations for:* • A few, for purity. *Censure for:* • Having only a name to live. *Exhortation to:* • Watch; • Strengthen; • Remember; • Hold fast; • Repent. *Promise of:* • White raiment for him that overcometh. • Name in the Book of Life; • To be confessed before the Father.
Philadelphia. **No blame.**		Epistle to the church of PHILADELPHIA. *Commendations for:* • Constancy; • Courage in confessing Christ. *Censure for:* • NONE [The only Church without censure.] *Exhortation to:* • Hold fast. *Promise of:* • "I will keep thee from the hour of temptation." • To be a pillar in God's temple. • To be inscribed with the name of God.

Laodicea. **No praises.**		Epistle to the church of LAODICEA. *Commendations for:* • NONE [The only Church without some commendation.] *Censure for:* • Lukewarmness; • Pride; • Ignorance to self. *Exhortation to:* • Obtain true riches; • Be clothed in white; • Seek the anointing of the eyes. *Promise of:* • A seat on Christ's throne to him that overcometh.
The Second vision: **of "things which** **shall be."**	4	A throne in heaven. The four and twenty elders. The four living creatures full of eyes. Honors paid to Him that sat on the throne.
	5	The book sealed with seven seals. The Lamb who alone could open it. The elders worship the Lamb.

Opening of the
seven seals.
	6	FIRST SEAL: –
		    White horse ridden by a conqueror.
		SECOND SEAL: –
		    Red horse and destruction.
		THIRD SEAL: –
		    Black horse and rider with balances.
		FOURTH SEAL: –
		    Pale horse and rider death.
		FIFTH SEAL: –
		    Souls of the slain under the altar.
		SIXTH SEAL: –
		    Great earthquake, with darkened sun, &c.

	7	The four angels hold back the four winds. The tribes of Israel sealed.

Sounding of the
seven trumpets.
	8	SEVENTH SEAL: –
		    Silence in heaven.
		    Seven angels with seven trumpets.
		    Angel with a golden censer.
		FIRST TRUMPET: –
		    Hail and fire follow.
		SECOND TRUMPET: –
		    A great mountain; burning and cast into the sea.

	8	THIRD TRUMPET: – A great star (Wormwood) fell on rivers and waters. FOURTH TRUMPET: – Sun, moon and stars smitten. Angel, flying in the midst of heaven, pronounces "Woes" on the earth.
First woe. **Second woe.**	9	FIFTH TRUMPET: – A star falls from heaven. The bottomless pit opened. The plague of locust scorpions. SIXTH TRUMPET: – Four angels loosed from the river Euphrates.
	10	Vision of an angel, clothed with a cloud, a rainbow on his head, &c. He has a little book in his hand. He swears that time (delay) shall be no longer. John, by command, eats the little book.
Two witnesses. **Third woe.** **A wonder in heaven.**	11	The temple measured. The two witnesses prophesy. The witnesses are slain, but lie unburied. A great earthquake destroys the tenth part of the Great City. SEVENTH TRUMPET: – Voices in heaven saying, "The kingdoms of this world are become," &c. The four and twenty elders fall down and worship.
A red Dragon.	12	A woman clothed with the sun. A great red Dragon, with seven heads, ten horns and seven crowns. The woman flees into the wilderness. The Dragon makes war with her seed.
Seven-headed beast. **Two-horned beast.** **"666".**	13	A beast with seven heads, ten horns and ten crowns; and upon his heads names of blasphemy. Another beast with two horns like a lamb. His number: six hundred, threescore and six.
The Lamb. **Fall of Babylon.**	14	The Lamb on Mount Zion with a hundred and forty four thousand, redeemed from the earth. Angel proclaims the everlasting gospel. The fall of Babylon. "Blessed are the dead which die in the LORD." Son of Man with golden crown and sickle. Winepress of the wrath of God.

	15	Seven angels with the seven last plagues. Sea of glass and fire. Song of Moses and the Lamb. Seven golden vials full of wrath.
Seven vials poured out. **"Armageddon."**	16	First Vial poured out upon the earth: a grievous sore fell on the worshippers of the Beast. Second Vial poured out upon the sea: which became as blood, and every living thing therein died. Third Vial poured out on the rivers and fountains, which became blood. Fourth Vial poured out on the sun: and men were scorched and blasphemed. Fifth Vial poured out upon the throne of the Beast: and his kingdom became full of darkness and pain. Sixth Vial poured out upon the Euphrates: the waters of which dried up, to prepare a way for the kings of the East. "Blessed is he that watcheth." Three unclean spirits, like frogs. Battle of Armageddon. Seventh Vial poured out into the air: a great voice from the throne proclaimed, "It is done!" Tremendous earthquake, destruction of cities and great storm of hail.
"Mystery, Babylon."	17	The judgment of the great whore. Her apparel described. On her forehead written, "Mystery, Babylon the Great, the Mother of Harlots and Abominations of the Earth." "Drunk with the blood of the saints." Carried by the Beast with seven heads and ten horns. The seven heads and ten horns explained.
"Babylon is fallen."	18	Proclamation of the fall of Babylon. The kings and merchants weep and mourn. Heaven called upon to rejoice.
"Alleluia." **"A lake of fire."**	19	Ascription of praise to God: "Alleluia." Marriage of the Lamb. The "Faithful and True" riding on a white horse. "King of Kings and Lord of Lords." Supper of the great God. The Beast and the False Prophet cast into the lake of fire.

First resurrection. **General resurrection.**	20	Angel with key of bottomless pit. The Dragon chained 1000 years. The First Resurrection. Destruction of Gog and Magog. General resurrection and judgment. "The Book of Life."
New heaven and a new earth.	21	"A new heaven and a new earth." "The holy city, new Jerusalem."
	22	The River of Life, and Tree of Life. Those admitted into, and those shut out of, the celestial city. Threatenings for those who add to or diminish from "The words of this prophecy." "Surely I come quickly." Amen.